John B. Chrisman
Philadelphia.
Pa

Aug 1. A.D. 1854.

Painted by J. Fox — E. A. Jewett & Co. Engravers Buff'lo

J. B. Finley

SKETCHES

OF

WESTERN METHODISM:

Biographical, Historical, and Miscellaneous.

ILLUSTRATIVE OF PIONEER LIFE.

BY

REV. JAMES B. FINLEY.

EDITED BY

W. P. STRICKLAND, D. D.

Cincinnati:
PRINTED AT THE METHODIST BOOK CONCERN,
FOR THE AUTHOR.

R. P. THOMPSON, PRINTER.
1854.

PREFACE.

Our book explains itself, so far as the object we had in view in getting it up is concerned. To supply a desideratum in the history of western Methodism, at least, so far as taking the incipient steps in that work is concerned, has prompted our endeavors. We have been at a great deal of labor in furnishing our readers with memorials of the past, connected with the lives of our early itinerant preachers, and collateral incidents in the history of the west, and we hope our labor has not been in vain.

Our readers will here find, as they turn over these pages, much, we trust, that is interesting and valuable in reference to olden time; and while they shall trace the life and labors of the pioneer Methodist preachers, in planting the standard of the cross in these western wilds before many of them were born, we hope they may be induced to engage with like zeal and devotion, to sustain the interests of the Church, and hand down to posterity, unimpaired and unadulterated, what our fathers have so nobly contended for in the well-fought field of itinerant life.

The noble examples furnished in these sketches, of untiring labor and self-sacrificing devotion of those who cheerfully gave up all for Christ and the advancement of his cause, should stir up every impulse of our nature to emulate their virtues and strive to imitate their truly-heroic deeds. We would that our materials had been more ample for the work we had undertaken, that the sketches we have given of the pioneers might have been more satisfactory. Much had already perished, and the waves of oblivion were rapidly washing out the few traces that remained; but we have gathered up what we could, and have presented them in a form, not only sufficiently reliable for all purposes of reference for the future historian, but, we flatter ourselves, sufficiently attractive to render the book one of interest to all.

Should our life be spared, we intend to prosecute this work still further; and as the materials will prove more abundant as we advance to the preachers of the present day, we hope to give increasing interest to our memorials of western Methodism. We have already promises from brethren in various conferences, spread over what was, in the days of our fathers, the Western conference, to warrant the expectation that a full and reliable history of our Church, and the many interesting incidents connected with its rise and progress in the great valley of the west, can be gathered up, that will prove a source of instruction and deep, powerful interest in rousing to higher activity, in promoting the advancement of the Redeemer's kingdom.

J. B. FINLEY.

Cincinnati, May 1, 1854.

CONTENTS.

CHAPTER I.

INTRODUCTION OF METHODISM INTO THE WEST.

CHAPTER II.

AUTOBIOGRAPHY OF REV. WILLIAM BURKE.

CHAPTER III.

AUTOBIOGRAPHY CONTINUED.

CHAPTER IV.

MICHAEL ELLIS.

CHAPTER V.

ORIGIN AND PROGRESS OF METHODISM IN CINCINNATI.

CHAPTER VI.

FRANCIS POYTHRESS.

CHAPTER VII.

BARNABAS M'HENRY.

CHAPTER VIII.

THOMAS SCOTT.

CHAPTER IX.

JOHN KOBLER.

CHAPTER X.

BENJAMIN LAKIN.

CHAPTER XI.

JOHN SALE.

CHAPTER XVI.

JAMES AXLEY.

CHAPTER XVII.

JOSEPH OGLESBY.

CHAPTER XVIII.

WILLIAM BEAUCHAMP.

CHAPTER XIX.

GOVERNOR TIFFIN.

CHAPTER XX.

JOHN A. GRENADE.

CHAPTER XXI.

WESTERN METHODIST BOOK CONCERN.

CHAPTER XXII.

JOHN COLLINS.

CHAPTER XXIII.

NATHAN EMERY.

CHAPTER XXX.

MARCUS LINDSEY.

CHAPTER XXXI.

THE DUTCHMAN'S EXPERIENCE.

CHAPTER XXXII.

JOHN STRANGE.

CHAPTER XXXIII.

WILLIAM P. FINLEY.

CHAPTER XXXIV.

RUSSEL BIGELOW.

CHAPTER XXXV.

HENRY B. BASCOM.

CHAPTER XL.

THE INTREPID MISSIONARY.

CHAPTER XLI.

THOMAS DRUMMOND.

CHAPTER XLII.

INDIAN CAMP MEETING.

CHAPTER XLIII.

CONVERSION OF AN INSPECTOR-GENERAL.

CHAPTER XLIV.

PIONEER WOMEN.

CHAPTER XLV.

RHON-YAN-NESS.

SKETCHES

OF

WESTERN METHODISM.

CHAPTER I.

INTRODUCTION OF METHODISM INTO THE WEST.

MANY years ago, during the Revolutionary struggle, and before the bloody scenes of Lexington or Bunker Hill were enacted; before these states were declared independent, and before there was a President in the chair of the Union; when all the western country was a waste, howling wilderness, untenanted except by the savage who roamed over its broad prairies, or through its dense forests, or sped his light canoe over the surface of its mighty rivers, the pioneer Methodist preacher might have been seen urging his way along the war-path of the Indian, the trail of the hunter, or the blazed track of the backwoodsman, seeking the lost sheep of the house of Israel in these far-off, distant wilds. Before the sun of civilization shone upon these mountains or in these vales, or over these prairies, or on these rivers, the herald of the cross, with his messages of mercy, was seen wending his way to the desolate haunts of savage man. To pursue such in their godlike journey and labors of benevolence, will be the object of our work. History may record the deeds and achievements of mighty warriors of olden time, effected by the sword: be it ours to follow the Christian pilgrim warrior over the fields of his labor, and toil, and sacrifice, and recount the victories achieved by the cross.

The history of Methodism in the western country is, to a great extent, an unwritten history. With the exception of a few biographies and historical sketches, and a few detached and scattered fragments, gleaned from time to time by historical societies, from the pioneers who yet linger among us, but little has been made a matter of permanent record. A thousand hallowed associations start up in the mind at the mention of venerable names whose voices, as embassadors of Jesus, waked the echoes of these dense and extended forests fifty years ago. What mind is not thrilled and delighted with the adventures and incidents of pioneer life in the wilds of the west? When we hear them we seem to be listening to the tales of fiction wrought out from a fervid imagination, designed only to please for the while, and then to pass away and leave the mind to the contemplation of life's sober realities; but instead of being the fanciful, overwrought productions of that wonderfully inventive faculty, they are graphic descriptions of a real life, in which the simple narration of truth becomes more strange than the most glowing fiction.

But what, we ask, were the privation and heroic deeds of daring of the pioneer backwoodsman, leveling the forest, or roaming the woods in search of game, when compared with the toils, hardships, and privations of the pioneer preacher of the Gospel? If the lives of the one are an example to their descendants of an energy and an enterprise which danger and the greatest difficulties could not intimidate or destroy, the self-sacrificing devotion of the other, urged on by a spirit of benevolence as boundless as the wants and woes of humanity, has left to the Church and the world an example of heroism abounding in every thing morally sublime. Their heroic deeds, in bringing to the cabins of the sturdy pioneer, as well as the wigwams of the savage, the blessings and benefits of religion, will be treasured up in memory, if not recorded upon the page of history, and will live as long as one is found to recount them to the generations yet to come. The names of Ellis, Tiffin, M'Henry, and Burke; of M'Cormick, Scott, Kobler, Lakin, Gatch, Sale, Collins, Parker, Axley, and a host of others who planted Methodism in the west, will ever have a place in our memory, and be handed down to future generations as those whose arduous and abundant labors have produced what we so richly enjoy; and though no splendid monuments of brass, or marble, or even rude, simple stones may tell where their ashes rest, yet in the faithful urn of a thousand hearts their memories shall live forever fresh, and the fair fame which they achieved on the well-fought field will be better than the precious ointment which loses its fragrance and departs with the dead. In the language of one, "It is a homage due to departed worth, whenever it rises to such a hight as to render its possessor an object of general attention, to endeavor to rescue it from oblivion, that, when it is removed from the observation of men, it may still live in their memory, and transmit through the shades of the sepulcher some reflection, however faint, of its living luster. By enlarging the cloud of witnesses with which we are encompassed, it is calculated to give a fresh impulse to the desire of imitation; and even the despair of reaching it is not without its use, by checking the levity and correcting the pride and presumption of the human heart." A few of these early pioneers yet linger among us; but every year their number grows less, and with their departure perishes to a great extent the history of early Methodism. They came here when all was a wilderness; when the "Queen of the

West"—where we now live to sketch their history—and its sister cities, consisted of a few block-houses, to protect them from the savages, and a few rude hamlets. They have seen the mighty west grow up around them, with its towns, and cities, and teeming population; and their lives are identified with its very history. While they yet remain we will sit by them and listen to their eventful history, gathering instruction from the past, and hope and encouragement for the future, that we may thereby grow wiser and better.

As autobiographies are more interesting and satisfactory than any sketches, however graphically or faithfully written, we shall avail ourselves of such, whenever we can obtain them; and where this is impossible, we shall leave no means untried to obtain the most reliable information from living cotemporaries. If our object were simply to make a book, we need not travel beyond the precincts of our own library or personal knowledge—the latter of which alone would furnish us materials of a historical and biographical character sufficient to fill volumes.

We shall begin with the oldest pioneer preacher now living in the west, an octogenarian, bending with the weight of years, but yet engaged in active life, and enjoying a green old age, with health and faculties alike unimpaired by the ravages of time. We shall introduce him to our readers, and he shall speak for himself; not, however, with that tongue which, in the days of his prime, possessed an eloquence and a power that few could rival and none surpass; but with the pen, the silent pen, which he yet wields almost as vigorously as in the days of his youth. The venerable Burke, bending beneath the weight of more than "threescore years and ten"—the first Secretary of an annual conference in America—shall tell you, in his own quaint but nervous style, the history of his life and times.

The very presence of this venerable man, who entered the ministry within a year or two of the time when Washington ascended the chair of state—upward of sixty-four years ago—not only brings around us the heroes and patriots of the Revolution, but the very fathers of Methodism, and we seem to talk with Asbury, and Coke, and M'Kendree; Watters, Gatch, Everett, and Vasey, and a host of other cotemporaries, who have long since passed away. This history will connect us with the first Methodist missionaries to America; will take us back to the days of Embury, and Webb, and Pillmore, and Boardman; when the only home of Methodism was a rigging-loft, in an obsure quarter of New York city, and a small, despised band constituted all of a Church that was destined to spread over this vast continent, from the lakes to the everglades of Florida, and from Maine to Oregon and California. It will record, in part, the history of a society which, in a period of eighty-six years—within two years of the age of our venerable friend and father—has increased from a little company of ten or twelve to upward of a million, and which has more ministers, more churches, and more persons attending its ministry, than any other denomination in the world. We shall, in his autobiography, see him when but a mere youth, the foremost of a pioneer band, encountering the perils of the wilderness, which he crossed eleven times during the Indian war, braving its dangers, and submitting to its hardships and privations with a zeal and devotion worthy of the high and holy calling in which he was engaged, and which would damp the ardor and check the zeal of many of the aspirants of the present day. But we must not anticipate, and shall introduce our readers at once to the narrative.

CHAPTER II.

AUTOBIOGRAPHY OF REV. WILLIAM BURKE.

I WAS born in Loudon county, state of Virginia, on the 13th day of January, in the year of our Lord one thousand seven hundred and seventy. My ancestors by my father were from Ireland, and settled in St. Marys, Maryland, about the commencement of the settling of that colony. My grandmother on my mother's side was born in Wales, brought up in London, emigrated to America about 1750, and settled in Fairfax county, Virginia, in the neighborhood of Mount Vernon; was an inmate of the family of General Washington, and married a gentleman by the name of Compton, and settled in a place called Clifton's Neck, in sight of Mount Vernon. My grandfather died before my recollection, and left two sons and three daughters, all of whom married and settled in Fairfax county. They all became wealthy, and lived to a good old age. My grandmother lived to the advanced age of one hundred and ten, and died a member of the Church of England. My grandfather on my father's side had two children by his first wife, who also lived in Fairfax county. After the death of my grandmother he moved to Albemarle county, where he had, by a second wife, several children; and while engaged in opening a farm, in the early settlement of that country, was killed by the falling of a tree. With that branch of the family I had no acquaintance. However, in 1810 I became acquainted with some branches of the family who were settled in Cumberland county, Kentucky, and who had lost the original name, and wrote their name Burks. They were settled on the Cumberland river, at a town called Burksville.

My father, after his marriage to Rhoda Compton, moved to Loudon county, at that time a frontier county, and was engaged with Washington in what was termed Braddock's war. My father, John Burke, had three sons and one daughter, John, Mary, Anson, and William. John and Mary died when young. My brother Anson is now living in Williamson county, Tenn., at the advanced age of eighty-six. He had four sons and one daughter, all living around him, except William Wesley, who came to Cincinnati, Ohio, and died here in 1849. My father, at the commencement of the Revolution, took the side of liberty, and was among the first who enrolled his name under Colonel Leven Powell, as a minute man, and was in that service one year at Hampton, Virginia, and again at Yorktown, at the taking of Cornwallis, where he suffered every thing but death. During the summer of 1775, while my father was at Hampton, the first Methodist preacher visited Loudon county; namely, Joseph Everett. My mother went some considerable distance to hear him, in hopes to meet with some intelligence from my father. I have no recollection of hearing any more of the Methodists till 1780, when Philip Cox commenced preaching at Bacon Fort old church, the parish in which my father then lived, and in which I was baptized. There being no parson at that time, the Methodists were allowed to preach in the church. I was then ten years old, and can recollect many circumstances that transpired during that year. It was the fashion at that day for the ladies to wear enormous high rolls on the head, and a report had been in circulation for some time that a calf had been born near Alexandria with one of those rolls on its head. P. Cox gave out that the next time he came round, in four weeks, he would show them a wonder. The whole country was in expectation that he would exhibit the calf, and a great concourse of people assembled. The preacher arrived, but instead of the calf he commenced by giving out his text: "And there appeared a great wonder in heaven, a woman clothed with the sun," etc. This gained the attention of the multitude: and from that time Methodism took root in that section of country.

In 1781 Francis Poythress and Michael Ellis were stationed on the circuit; and in the winter of 1781 and 1782, under the preaching of Mr. Ellis, I was strangely and deeply affected; but it wore off by degrees; for at that time I was going to school, where we had but little of religion taught. My father and mother joined the society at Royell's, Bacon Fort old church, in the early part of 1780. Nothing very special occurred that waked up my attention till the summer of 1784, when it was given out that Thomas Vasey, one of the newly-ordained preachers, was to preach in Leesburg. He preached in the court-house to a very large concourse of people; and numbers who had been in the habit of hearing the Methodists preach, were astonished to hear him perform the morning service as laid down in the Methodist prayer-book. The practice and the book have long since been laid aside. The means of education were very limited in those days, and in that part of the country; consequently, I was limited to what was then called an English education, all of which I completed in the years 1785 and 1786.

In the spring of 1787 my father determined to remove to the state of Georgia. We accordingly set out early in the spring. The preceding year had been very unfavorable for crops in the south; and having arrived in North Carolina, not far from Guilford court-house, we fell into a neighborhood of Virginians, from Fairfax county, and with whom my father and mother had been acquainted, and they persuaded us to spend the summer with them. We did so, with the intention of going to Georgia the next spring; but my father being pleased with the country, determined to settle himself in North Carolina, and accordingly purchased a tract of land in one mile of the high ford, Haw river. In the neighborhood I formed new associations, became very profligate and vain, and entered fully into all the amusements of the day. My dear mother was very pious, and I was her darling boy. The course I was then pursuing gave her much pain and affliction. She used every means in her power to dissuade me from it, and used to pray for me day and night. In the latter part of the year 1790 I was awakened under the preaching of Isaac Lowe. In the fall of that year the society established a weekly prayer meeting, and I was a constant attendant, and had formed the resolution never to stop short of obtaining experimental religion.

The practice then among the Methodists was to call upon all the seekers of religion to pray in public at the prayer meeting. I was called upon, and took up my cross, and continued to pray at every prayer meeting. In the month of February, 1791, after the preacher concluded, he opened the door to receive members. I went forward alone and gave my name, and there was great joy manifested at the return of so great a prodigal, and I was the first-fruits of a great revival. In the month of March I attended a quarterly meeting at Smith's meeting-house, on Guilford circuit. On Saturday and Saturday night I was in great distress, and slept but little. On Sunday morning early I betook myself to the woods and wandered about and prayed earnestly for deliverance. At nine o'clock the love-feast began. I can not recollect much that was done. I fell senseless to the floor, and the first I can recollect I was on my feet giving glory to God in loudest strains, to the astonishment of many.

After my ecstasy was over, and I came to reflect, my load of sin was gone. I felt no more condemnation, but could not say that I was born again. In this situation I remained for eight days; and on the next Sunday evening, after having returned from meeting, I betook myself to the woods, and at the root of a large whiteoak-tree, while engaged in prayer, God gave me the witness of the Spirit, and from that moment I went on my way rejoicing. We continued our prayer meeting with increasing interest, and very soon one and another would get converted, and our meetings would sometimes continue all night. The class-leader, who in those days would open and conduct the prayer meeting, put me forward to open the meetings, and I commenced after prayer to give an exhortation. The heavenly flame spread through the neighborhood, and the neighboring classes caught the holy fire, and in a short time hundreds attended our night meetings. I have often walked five and six miles to a night meeting, and spent the whole night, while the mourners were down in the house and all over the yard, crying mightily to God for mercy. That year George M'Kinney, a son of thunder, was sent to Guilford circuit, who entered fully into the work, and great numbers were added to the Church. In the month of June of this year, I made my first attempt at preaching from a text. The words were, "Let the wicked forsake his way, and the unrighteous man his thoughts; and let him return to the Lord, who will have mercy upon him, and to our God, who will abundantly pardon." I had great liberty, and found favor in the eyes of the people. I continued to exercise my gift in exhortation and preaching whenever opportunity presented. In the month of August I attended a quarterly meeting at the Hawfield, New Hope circuit, at the Tartemele. There was a great collection of people on Sunday. Thomas Ware was elder; but

Thomas Bowen was at the quarterly meeting on a tour south, and preached the first sermon on Sunday; and at the close of the sermon they set me up to exhort. I had a voice like thunder, and it seemed as though there was a fire in my bones. The dry bones began to tremble, and sinners began to leave the house; the fire was too warm for them. Upon the whole, we had a good time. Many in that quarter had never seen the like before. Brother Isaac Lowe was then traveling on New Hope circuit. He was a married man, and his family lived in the neighborhood of my father's, and we returned in company home. In the fall, at the beginning of October, brother Lowe insisted that I should accompany him round New Hope circuit. Accordingly, I arranged my business so as to make the tour of six weeks. We went on together, preaching time about, till he was taken sick and returned home, and left me to complete the round. I did so, and then returned home, where I found him recovered from his illness. One of the preachers had left Guilford circuit and gone home. I was requested to take his place. I did so, and traveled that winter on that circuit. On one of my rounds I fell in with Thomas Anderson, the presiding elder. He inquired if I had any permit to exhort or preach. I told him I had not, and before we parted he gave me a license, which was the only license I ever had, till my name was on the minutes of the annual conference. The annual conference for that year was at M'Knight's, on the Yadkin river, on the second of April. There was no formal application made by me to travel, and no vacancy offering, I returned home, and had thoughts of settling myself for life, and began to make preparations for building a house and opening a farm; but my mind was not at rest. During the summer and fall I used to preach three, four, and five times a week, and ride forty and fifty miles. The conference for this year was held at Green Hills, at which conference I was admitted on trial, and appointed to West New River circuit, on the head waters of the Kanawha river, in the state of Virginia. On my way to my appointment I stopped at home a few days, and having furnished myself with several suits of clothes, I started all alone for the west, crossed the Blue Ridge at the Flower Gap, entered the circuit at brother Forbes's, on what was called the Glades, lying between the Blue Ridge and New river. This was about the first of February, 1792. This was a four weeks' circuit, and between four and five hundred miles round. It extended in length from the three forks of New river, over the Alleghany Mountains, on the waters of Roanoke; and from north to south from Walker's creek to the Glades, near the Blue Ridge. The country is very mountainous, high and cold; and in Montgomery, Wythe, and Grayson counties it is too cold to produce Indian corn with any degree of certainty. Rye was produced in great abundance.

The first preachers that visited that country was in the year 1783. It was then called the Holston country. The head waters of the South Fork of the Holston extended as far east as Wythe and the borders of Grayson counties, extending west as far as the Three Islands. In this tract of country the first preachers began their operations. They were Jeremiah Lambert, Henry Willis, Mark Whitaker, Mark More, and Reuben Ellis, the elder. The district included Salisbury and Yadkin circuits, in North Carolina, and Holston in the west. In 1787 the Holston circuit was divided into two circuits, Holston and Nolachucky, and Philip Bruce appointed elder. Two new preachers were sent—Jeremiah Masten and Thomas Ware—in 1788. Two new circuits were made out of the old ones this year; the Holston circuit, embracing all the settlements on the East and North Forks of

Holston, and all the settlements on the Clinch river, including the counties of Washington and Russell, in Virginia, and Blount county, in the Western territory. French Broad included all the settlements west and south of the main Holston to the frontiers bordering on the Cherokee nation. West New river was this year made a circuit, and Greenbriar added, which was composed of the new settlements on Greenbriar river, and part of the head waters of the James river; Edward Morris elder.

In 1789 John Tunel was presiding elder and Bottetourt circuit added. In 1790 two districts were formed; one was composed of West New River, Russell, Holston, and Green circuits—Charles Hardy presiding elder. This year John M'Gee and John West were on Green circuit; John West is still living in the bounds of the Pittsburg conference. Bottetourt, Greenbriar, and Kanawha circuits—Jeremiah Able presiding elder. This year the Little Kanawha circuit was formed, and Jacob Lurton was the preacher in charge. In 1793 he was on Salt River circuit, Kentucky, and married a Miss Tooley, on Bear Grass, Jefferson county, and located, and for many years lived on Floyd's Fork of Salt river. He was an original genius, and a useful preacher. In 1791 Mark Whitaker was presiding elder, and Charles Hardy and John West were on the West New River circuit. Charles Hardy located this year, and the latter part of the year I succeeded him. John West remained with me on the circuit till the Holston conference, on the 15th of May, 1792. Nothing material transpired while on this circuit. The state of religion was at a low ebb in all the circuits. Most of the preachers had not been much in the work for several years, and Discipline had been much neglected. Mr. Asbury, on his return from the Kentucky conference, met the conference at Huffaker's, Rich Valley of Holston, on the 15th April, 1792. Hope Hull, who had accompanied him from Georgia, and Wilson Lee, who was now returning from Kentucky, and accompanying the Bishop on to the east, were with him. Both preached at this conference with great success. General William Russell, who had married the widow of General Campbell, and sister of Patrick Henry, who had embraced religion, together with his amiable lady, and who lived at the salt-works, on the North Fork of Holston, attended this conference and accommodated a number of the preachers. Upon the whole, we had a good time for those days. Stephen Brooks, from the Kentucky conference, was appointed to Green circuit, in charge, and I was appointed with him, and Barnabas M'Henry, who came also with the Bishop from Kentucky, was the presiding elder. We had an entire set of new preachers for the whole district—Salathiel Weeks and James Ward on the Holston circuit, both from Virginia; David Haggard, Daniel Lockett, and Jeremiah Norman, from North Carolina. Brother Norman was on Russell, and brothers Haggard and Lockett on West New River. The presiding elder and all the preachers entered into a covenant to attend strictly to the Discipline. When brother Brooks and myself arrived at our charge, which was in a few days after the conference rose, we mutually agreed to enforce the rules of the society; and by midsummer we had the satisfaction of seeing a gracious work in many places on the circuit.

A very peculiar circumstance took place some time in July. On Nolachucky there was a rich and thickly-settled neighborhood, which afterward went by the name of Earnest's neighborhood. There was but one Methodist in the neighborhood, the wife of Felix Earnest, who attended preaching when she could, being about five or six miles distant from the appointment. Felix was a very wicked man. Being one day at a distillery, and partially intoxicated, the Spirit of God arrested him. He immediately went home, and inquired of his wife if she knew of any Methodist meeting any where on that day. It happened to be the day that brother Brooks preached, in the adjoining neighborhood, and he immediately put off for the meeting. He arrived there after meeting had begun, and stood in the door, with his shirt-collar open, and his face red, and the tears streaming down his cheeks. He invited brother Brooks to bring preaching into the neighborhood. He did so, and in two weeks I came round and preached to a good congregation. The word of God had free course, and was glorified. The whole family of the Earnests was brought into the Church, with many others, and by the first of September we had a large society formed. I left the circuit in September, but the work continued. In a short time they built a meeting-house; and in the spring of 1795 the Western conference had their annual sitting at the meeting-house, and Felix was a local preacher. Our second quarterly meeting was in the beginning of August, at the Pine Chapel, south of the French Broad river, and below the mouth of Little Pigeon river. It was a good time. It was given up by all that it was the best love-feast that they had ever seen. On my next round, which was in September, the Cherokee war was just breaking out. After I crossed the French Broad and Little rivers, and arrived at the extreme point of the settlement, I found the inhabitants in a state of alarm on account of the war. I preached that day, and at night the whole neighborhood collected, bringing intelligence that the Indians were in the settlement. In the morning I started for my next appointment, on the south bank of Little river, having a guard of two brothers, who piloted me through the woods part of the way; but becoming alarmed for the safety of their families, left me to make the best of my way. I arrived a little before noon, but found it would be impossible to collect a congregation. The people were moving in and concentrating at a certain point, for the purpose of fortifying, and by night we were the frontier house. After dark the lights were all put out, and each one sat down with his gun on his lap. One of the company started about nine o'clock to go where the Indians were collected for fortifying; but soon returned, and said the Indians were plenty in the neighborhood.

I immediately determined to make my journey to the next preaching-place, which was about ten miles, and I was obliged to travel under cover of the night; but I had one difficulty to encounter, having nothing but a small path, and the river to cross, and an island to reach in the river. The night was dark, and the timber very thick on the island, and I could not prevail on any of them to leave the house or give me any assistance; however, I put my trust in God and set off. After having passed the first part of the river I alighted from my horse, and undertook to keep the path on foot. I succeeded beyond my expectation, reached the shore at the proper point, and proceeded without meeting with any difficulty. About two o'clock I arrived at the house, where my appointment was for that day, proceeded to the door, and sought admittance, but found no inmates. I knew there were cabins on the opposite side of a marsh, and I commenced hallooing as loud as I could. I soon brought some of them out, who wished to know who I was, and what I wanted. They suspected that the Indians wished to decoy them, and were preparing to give me a warm reception of powder and lead, when the lady, at whose house we preached, came out and knew my voice. They then came over and conducted me to the place where the whole neighborhood was collected, and the next day I recrossed the French Broad river, which placed me beyond the reach of danger. I passed up through the circuit, leaving the frontier appointments on the south side of the river, which were Pine Chapel, Little and Big Pigeon. The first intelligence I had from that quarter was, that all the inhabitants in the neighborhood of the Pine Chapel were massacred in one night by the Indians.

The first General conference in the United States met late in the fall of this year. The presiding elder and S. Weeks, from the Holston circuit, both left for the General conference; and the presiding elder moved me from Green circuit and put me in charge of the Holston, and sent brother J. Ward to fill my place. Brother Ward had but moderate talents, but was a devoted and good man; and through his instrumentality good was done on the Holston circuit. In the neighborhood of the Salt-Works a number had been added to the Church. Among the number was the heiress, Miss Sally Campbell, daughter of General Campbell, who distinguished himself at the battle of King's Mountain. Her mother, Mrs. Russell, had, for some time, been a member of the Church, and was among the most excellent ones of the earth. Late in the fall of this year General Russell and family made a visit to the eastern part of Virginia, among their old friends and relations. The General was taken sick and died. His daughter, Chloe Russell, had just married a circuit preacher by the name of Hubbard Saunders. During their visit Miss Sarah Campbell was married to Francis Preston, Esq., of Virginia, whose son is now senator in Congress from South Carolina. The surviving part of the family did not return during my stay on the circuit. We had some good times on our field of labor, at Baker's, near the Three Islands, and at Acuff's. I remained on the circuit till Christmas, when, by the direction of the presiding elder, brother Norman and myself changed, and I was on Clinch circuit. This was a frontier circuit, the whole north side of it being exposed to the savages. On this circuit I first began to eat bear-meat, and buffalo tongues. I entered this circuit with a determination, by the help of God, to have a revival of religion, and in some degree succeeded. It was a three weeks' circuit, and I was alone, without even a local preacher to help me. Through the winter we had a considerable revival at Elk Garden, head of Clinch river, at Bickley's Station, and at several other preaching-places. On the last Saturday and Sunday in March, 1793, we held our quarterly meeting at Bickley's Station. We had a good time. During the past year we had many conflicts, a new country Indian warfare going on all the winter on our southern borders. The preachers had received about enough quarterage to keep soul and body together. On Monday morning, after the quarterly meeting, I started for the annual conference, which met on the third day of April. We met Bishop Asbury and William Spencer, from the Virginia conference, and Henry Hill, from North Carolina. The conference business concluded on Saturday; Sunday was taken up in preaching; and on Monday morning we started for Kentucky. Several of our friends volunteered to guide us through the wilderness. Francis Asbury, Barnabas M'Henry, Henry Hill, James Ward, and William Burke were all the preachers. These, together with some who met us at Bean's Station, on Holston, made our company up to sixteen. We were all pretty well armed except the Bishop. It was about one hundred and thirty miles through the wilderness, with but one house in Powell's Valley, where we staid the first night. Next morning, by sunrise, we crossed Cumberland Mountain, and entered into the bosom of the wilderness.

I will here introduce a plan that Mr. Asbury suggested

before we left the settlements. It was to make a rope long enough to tie to the trees all around the camp when we stopped at night, except a small passage for us to retreat, should the Indians surprise us; the rope to be so fixed as to strike the Indians below the knee, in which case they would fall forward, and we would retreat into the dark and pour in a fire upon them from our rifles. We accordingly prepared ourselves with the rope, and placed it on our pack-horse. We had to pack on the horses we rode corn sufficient to feed them for three days, and our own provisions, beside our saddle-bags of clothes. Through the course of the day nothing material transpired till very late in the afternoon, say less than an hour before sunset, when passing up a stony hollow from Richland creek, at the head of which was the war-path from the northern Indians to the southern tribes, we heard, just over the point of a hill, a noise like a child crying in great distress. We soon discovered there were Indians there, and the reason why they used that stratagem to decoy us was, that a few days before they had defeated a company, known for a long time as M'Farland's defeat, and a number were killed, and several children supposed to be lost in the woods. We immediately put whip to our horses, and in a few minutes crossed the ridge and descended to Camp creek about sunset, when we called a halt to consult on what was best to be done; and on putting it to vote whether we proceed on our journey, every one was for proceeding but one of the preachers, who said it would kill his horse to travel that night. The Bishop all this time was sitting on his horse in silence, and on the vote being taken he reined up his steed and said, "Kill man kill horse, kill horse first;" and in a few minutes we made our arrangements for the night. The night being dark, and nothing but a narrow path, we appointed two to proceed in front, to lead the way and keep the path, and two as a rear guard, to keep some distance behind and bring intelligence every half hour, that we might know whether they were in pursuit of us; for we could not go faster than a walk. They reported that they were following us till near twelve o'clock. We were then on the Big Laurel river. We agreed to proceed, and alighted from our horses and continued on foot till daybreak, when we arrived at the Hazel Patch, where we stopped and fed our horses, and took some refreshment. We were mounted, and on our journey by the rising of the sun; but by this time we were all very much fatigued, and we yet had at least between forty and fifty miles before us for that day. That night about dark we arrived at our good friend Willis Green's, near Stanford, Lincoln court-house, having been on horseback nearly forty hours, and having traveled about one hundred and ten miles in that time. I perfectly recollect that at supper I handed my cup for a second cup of tea, and before it reached me I was fast asleep, and had to be waked up to receive it. Part of us remained at Mr. Green's over Sunday, and preached at several places in the neighborhood. The Bishop and brother M'Henry proceeded on next morning to attend a quarterly meeting at brother Francis Clark's, on the waters of Salt river, six miles west of Danville.

On the 15th of April, 1793, the conference met at Masterson's Station. Preachers present, Francis Asbury, bishop; Francis Poythress, Henry Burchet, Jacob Lurton, James Ward, John Page, John Ball, Richard Bird, Benjamin Northcott, and William Burke. Barnabas M'Henry, from the Holston district, and Henry Hill, who traveled with Bishop Asbury, were also present. Nine preachers in all for Kentucky and Cumberland included, Nashville and the three counties of Davidson, Sumner, and Robinson, including a few settlements in Kentucky, in the neighborhood where Russelville is now situated. We received our appointments at the close of the conference, and separated in love and harmony. I was this year appointed to Danville circuit, in charge, and John Page as helper. We entered upon our work with a determination to use our best endeavors to promote the Redeemer's kingdom. The circuit was in but a poor condition. Discipline had been very much neglected, and numbers had their names on the class-papers who had not met their class for months. We applied ourselves to the discharge of our duty and enforced the Discipline, and, during the course of the summer, disposed of upward of one hundred. We had some few additions, but, under God, laid the foundation for a glorious revival, the next and following years. The bounds and extent of this circuit were large, including the counties of Mercer, Lincoln, Garrard, and Madison; the west part of the circuit included the head waters of Salt river, and Chaplin on the north, bounded by Kentucky river south and east, and extended as far as the settlements—taking four weeks to perform the round. There were three log meeting-houses in the circuit; one in Madison county, called Proctor's Chapel; one in the forks of Dix river, Garrett's meeting-house; and one on Shoenea run, called Shoney run. Not far from Harrod's Station, in Mercer county, during the course of this year, a new meeting-house was erected in Garrard county, considered the best meeting-house in the country, and they named it Burke's Chapel. I remained on Danville circuit till the first of April, 1794, and on the fifteenth our conference commenced at Louis's Chapel, in Jessamine county, in the bounds of Lexington.

Previous to the meeting of the conference we raised a company of twelve persons to proceed to the seat of the conference, for the purpose of guarding Bishop Asbury through the wilderness. We met a company at the

Crab Orchard, the place where we usually met by advertisement, circulated for the purpose of collecting a sufficient number for mutual protection against the Indians. The company, when assembled, consisted of about sixty, all well armed. We organized that night, and I was appointed commander. In the morning, all things being in readiness for our departure, we proceeded through the wilderness. The day previous there had started a large company, and among the number there were four preachers, two Baptist and two Dunkards. The company, with whom they traveled, had treated them in such an ungentlemanly and unchristian manner during the first day and night, that on the morning of the second day they all four started in advance, and had not proceeded more than one mile before they were surprised by a party of Indians, and all four killed and scalped, and their horses and all they had taken off by the Indians. We camped the first night not far from Big Laurel river, and next morning passed the place where the dead bodies of the preachers were thrown into a sink-hole and covered in part with some logs, and the wild beasts had torn and mangled them in the most shocking manner. That day we crossed the Cumberland river, and passed up the narrows to Turkey creek, and camped on the bank. I had not slept on any of the two preceding nights, and that night I intended to take a good sleep. Accordingly, after placing out the sentinels and securing my horse, I spread my saddle-blanket and my saddle and saddle-bags for my pillow, and laid me down close to my horse, and was, in a few minutes, sound asleep. It was not an hour before the company was alarmed. Some said they heard Indians, others affirmed that they heard them when cutting cane for their horses, and heard their dogs barking at their camp up the creek; and before they awakened me the greater part of the company were on their horses and had left the sentinels at their posts. Such was the panic that I immediately harnessed up my horse and mounted him, and had the guards brought in. The night was very dark, and we had to cross the creek immediately. The bank was very steep, and we had to cross in Indian file; and before all passed over the bank became very slippery, and the horses would get nearly to the top and slide back into the creek again. I was in front, and the word would pass along the line, "Halt in front." At length all got safely over, and we proceeded about four miles to Cannon creek. The night being very dark, and finding great difficulty to keep the path, I ordered a halt, and directed every man to turn out to the left and alight and hold his horse by the bridle. They accordingly did so, and I threw the reins of my bridle over my arm and laid down at the root of a beech-tree, and was soon asleep. I had previously given orders that we should form one hour before daybreak and be on the road, in order to elude the Indians, should they be in pursuit of us. We did so, and crossed the Cumberland Mountains early in the morning, and that night arrived at Bean's Station, near the Holston river, where we met the intelligence that Bishop Asbury, in consequence of ill health, could not attend the conference in Kentucky.

A large collection of emigrants was already met for the purpose of crossing the wilderness. The number was about one hundred and twenty, together with a great number of pack-horses. On the next morning we started in Indian file, pack-horses and all, making a line about a mile in length. It was determined by the company that the guard which had come through to meet the Bishop should bring up the rear. Nothing transpired through the course of the first day or night worthy of notice. Early on the second day we came to the ford of the Cumberland river; it was very much swollen, and when the front of the company arrived at the bank of the river, a party of Indians being on the opposite shore fired upon them; but the distance was such that no injury was done. None had courage to attempt crossing over, and when we, who were in the rear, came up, the whole company was crowded together, and many, both men and women, were as pale as death, and some weeping, not knowing what course to take. I immediately called out for volunteers, who would venture to cross the river. Out of the whole company we could only get eleven to undertake the hazardous duty. On our arriving at the opposite bank we alighted from our horses and took trees and awaited the approach of the Indians. None appearing we proceeded to the top of the bank; finding the course clear we beckoned them to proceed crossing, while we stood guard. No accident occurred through the remainder of that day. At night we encamped in an unfavorable position—a heavy thunder-shower passing over us forced us to stop. In that situation, after we had tied up our horses and built up our fires, we proceeded to place out the guards, when many who had not been used to such fatigue made themselves as comfortable as the nature of things would admit, and laid down to rest. I found from the manner in which the horses behaved that Indians were about with the intention of stealing some of our horses. Consequently, I kept on my feet the whole night, passing round and through the camp. The night passed off without any interruption. The third day at night we arrived at the Crab Orchard, and on the fourth day I proceeded to the conference at Louis's Chapel. We had at this an increase of two preachers—John Metcalf, who had come through the wilderness with us from the Virginia conference, and Thomas Scott, now Judge Scott, of Chilicothe, from the Baltimore conference. The presiding elder, F. Poythress, presided in the conference. The business having been gone through, I was dispatched to the Virginia conference with the proceedings of our conference, and to receive deacon's orders. The conference met at Joseph Mitchel's, on James river. Here we met Mr. Asbury, who had partly recovered from his sickness.

At this conference, which was held on the 26th May, I received my appointment on Hinkston circuit, Kentucky. This circuit included Clark county, Bourbon, and Montgomery; bounded on the north and east by the frontier settlements, on the south by the Kentucky river, and on the west by Lexington circuit. It was a three weeks' circuit, that had been taken off from Lexington; here I was alone. At my first quarterly meeting I was removed to Salt River circuit—the preacher having left—and put in charge. Here I remained two quarters under very embarrassed circumstances, it being the summer of Wayne's campaign, and great numbers were out in the service. This was the most difficult circuit in the bounds of the conference. It was a four weeks' circuit, and between four and five hundred miles round. It included Washington, Nelson, Jefferson, Shelby, and Green counties; bounded on the north by the Kentucky river, on the east by Danville circuit, on the south by the frontier settlements on Green river, including where Greensburg and Elizabethtown are now situated, and on the west by the Ohio river. Nothing worthy of record occurred, except hard times. I was reduced to the last pinch. My clothes were nearly all gone. I had patch upon patch and patch by patch, and I received only money sufficient to buy a waistcoat, and not enough of that to pay for the making, during the two quarters I remained on the circuit. After the second quarterly meeting I was changed, by the presiding elder, to Lexington circuit. This was the best circuit in the bounds of the conference, both for numbers and liberality. In this circuit I met

4*

with many good friends, and they supplied all my wants. Nothing special occurred during the year. Wayne's expedition having ended, the people returned to their homes and became more settled, and we had a gradual increase in the societies. Lexington was a four weeks' circuit, and tolerably compact. It contained the counties of Fayette, Jessamine, Woodford, Franklin, Scott, and Harrison; bounded on the east and north by Hinkston circuit, on the west by the frontiers. Frankfort, now the seat of government, was then a frontier station. The southern boundary was the Kentucky river, which is peculiar for the high cliffs of limestone rocks, which present a wild and grand appearance, in many places from four to five hundred feet high.

In the county of Jessamine, situated on the cliffs, was Bethel Academy, built entirely by subscriptions raised on the circuits. One hundred acres of land was given by Mr. Lewis, as the site for the Academy. The project originated with Mr. Asbury, Francis Poythress, Isaac Hite, of Jefferson; Colonel Hinde, of Nelson; Willis Green, of Lincoln; Richard Masterson, of Fayette; and Mr. Lewis, of Jessamine. A spacious building was erected, I think eighty by forty feet, three stories high. The design was to accommodate the students in the house with boarding, etc. The first and second stories were principally finished and a spacious hall in the center. The building of this house rendered the pecuniary means of the preachers very uncertain; for they were continually employed in begging for Bethel. The people were very liberal, but they could not do more than they did. The country was new, and the unsettled state of the people, in consequence of the Indian wars and depredations, kept the country in a continual state of agitation. The Legislature, at an early period, made a donation of six thousand acres of land to Bethel Academy. The land was located in Christian county, south of Green river, and remained a long time unproductive; and while I continued a trustee, till 1804, it remained rather a bill of expense than otherwise. In 1803 I was appointed by the Western conference to attend the Legislature and obtain an act of incorporation. I performed that duty, and Bethel was incorporated, with all the powers and privileges of a literary institution. From that time I was removed to such a distance that my connection with the Academy ceased. Rev. Valentine Cook was the first that organized the academical department; and at first the prospect was flattering. A number of students were in attendance; but difficulties occurred which it would be needless to mention, as all the parties concerned have gone to give an account at a higher tribunal; but such was the effect that the school soon declined, and brother Cook abandoned the project.

The Rev. John Metcalf, who had married and located, was next introduced, and kept a common school for some time. On his leaving the place vacant, Rev. Nathaniel Harris moved, with his family, and occupied the building as a dwelling, and kept a school for the neighborhood. On his leaving the premises, it was soon in a dilapidated state. The land on which it was built fell into the hands of Mr. Lewis's heirs, the house was taken down, so that not one stone was left upon another, and the whole was transferred to Nicholasville, and incorporated into a county academy, which is still in operation; but the Methodist Church have no more interest in it than other citizens of Jessamine county.

In the spring of 1795 I had traveled all the circuits in Kentucky except Limestone. This circuit lay on the north side of Licking river—a considerable wilderness intervening between Hinkston and Limestone circuits. It included Mason and Fleming counties. It was a small circuit; bounded on the east, south, and west by the frontier settlements, and on the north by the Ohio river. Taking it all in all, these were days, in the west, that tried men's souls. From the time that the first Methodist missionaries entered this new field of labor up to this spring, there had been one continued Indian war, while the whole frontier, east, west, north, and south, had been exposed to the inroads and cruel depredations of the merciless savages. This spring—1795—was the noted Nickajack expedition, which terminated the Cherokee war; and Wayne's treaty at Greenville, Ohio, put an end to the Indian wars, and the whole western country, for once, had peace. There is one thing worthy of notice, and that is, that notwithstanding the constant exposure the traveling preachers were subjected to, but two of them fell by the hands of the savages, and both of them by the name of Tucker. One was a young man, descending the Ohio on a flatboat, in company with several other boats—all were family boats, moving to Kentucky. They were attacked by the Indians near the mouth of Brush creek, now Adams county, Ohio. Several boats were taken possession of by the Indians, the inmates massacred, and the property taken by them. Every man in the boat with Tucker was killed, and Tucker wounded mortally. The Indians made attempts to board the boat, but, notwithstanding he was wounded, the women loaded the guns and Tucker kept up a constant fire upon them, and brought off the boat safe; but before they landed at Limestone he expired, and his remains quietly repose somewhere in that place. Brother James O'Cull assisted in burying him, and is the only man now living who could designate the spot. I think the Kentucky conference should erect a monument to his memory. The other was shot near a station south of Green river, not far from the present town of Greensburg.

The conference for the year 1795 met at Ebenezer Earnest's neighborhood, on Nolachucky, the last week in April. We passed through the wilderness this year without much apprehension of danger. The most of the preachers from Kentucky met their brethren on Holston district. This was the largest annual conference we had ever seen in the west. Bishop Asbury attended, and it was a conference of considerable interest. At this conference I was ordained to the office of an elder. My parchment bears date 30th April, 1795, Western territory. At this conference I was requested by the Bishop to preach the ordination sermon for the deacons. I did so, from the words of Paul to Timothy: "Study to shew thyself approved unto God a workman that needeth not to be ashamed, rightly dividing the word of truth." We had a most harmonious and blessed time. I received my appointment this year to Cumberland, Mero district, Western territory. The circuit included Davidson, Sumner, and Robinson counties, in the territory, and part of Logan county, Kentucky, lying on the waters of Red river, and extending out to the neighborhood where Russelville now stands; in a word, it included all the settlements in that region of country. In order to reach my destination I had to return through Kentucky, and to take my colleague, who was a young man, received at this conference, by the name of Peter Guthrie. He was a man of deep piety, but of slender preaching abilities. We made the best of our way for Cumberland, passed on from Lexington through Danville circuit and Salt River; and on the first night after we left the bounds of Salt River circuit, we stopped at the last house, on the edge of the barrens, on the south side of Green river, at Sidebottom's ferry. After we had put our horses up circumstances made it necessary, by an occurrence in the family, that we should camp out; and we accordingly made our fire in the woods and laid us down to rest; and, all things considered, we had a comfortable night's rest. We now had a vast barren track to pass through of between eighty and ninety miles, with but one house—M'Fadden's Station, on Big Barren river, not far from where Bowling Green is now situated. The next day we arrived in the settlement, on the waters of Red river. On the following day we arrived at Nashville, and in the evening at James Hockett's, about two miles west of town. He was a rich planter, and had formerly resided in the Choctaw nation. At this time he was a member of the Methodist Episcopal Church, and his house was a home for the traveling preachers. In this neighborhood I staid several days, and collected what information I could about the state of the circuit. Moses Speer, one of the preachers that traveled the circuit the preceding year, and had married in the neighborhood of Nashville, and a young man by the name of Joseph Dunn, were traveling on the circuit when we arrived.

On inquiry I found that James Haw, who was one of the first preachers that came to Kentucky, had located and settled in Cumberland, and embraced the views of O'Kelly, and by his influence and address had brought over the traveling and every local preacher but one in the country to his views, and considerable dissatisfaction had obtained in many of the societies. Under these circumstances I was greatly perplexed to know what course to take—a stranger to every body in the country, a young preacher, and Haw an old and experienced preacher, well known, a popular man, and looked up to as one of the fathers of the Church, and one who had suffered much in planting Methodism in Kentucky and Cumberland. After much reflection and prayer to God for direction, I finally settled upon the following plan; namely, to take the Discipline and examine it thoroughly, selecting all that was objected to by O'Kelly, and those who adhered to him, and then undertake an explanation and defense of the same. I accordingly met brother Speer at Nashville, and after preaching requested the society to remain, aud commenced my work. When I concluded my defense, I took the vote of the society, and they unanimously sustained the positions I had taken. Brother Speer also asked the privilege of making a few remarks. He stated to the society that he would consider the Church as a house that he lived in; and notwithstanding the door was not exactly in the place he should like it, or the chimney in the end that best pleased him, yet he could not throw away or pull down his house on that account; and, therefore, he concluded that he would not throw away the Church, although some things, he thought, could be improved in the Discipline. In consequence of this victory on my first attempt, I took courage, and proceeded with my work in every society; and, to my utter astonishment, I succeeded in every place, and saved every society but one small class on Red river, where a local preacher lived by the name of Jonathan Stevenson, who had traveled the circuit two years before, and located in that neighborhood. Haw and Stevenson appointed a meeting on Red river, and invited the Methodists all over the circuit to attend the meeting, for the purpose of organizing the new Church. The result was, that only ten or twelve members offered themselves, and the most of them had formerly belonged to the Baptist Church. Having failed in every attempt to break up the societies, the next step was to call me to a public debate. I accepted his challenge, and the day was appointed to meet at Station Cap, one of the most popular neighborhoods, and convenient to a number of large societies. Notwithstanding I accepted the challenge, I trembled for the cause. I was young in the ministry, and inexperienced in that kind of debate. He was an old minister, of long experience, and of high standing in the community. I summoned up all my courage, and, like young David with his sling, I went forth to meet the Goliah. The day arrived, and a great concourse of people attended. The preliminaries were settled, and I had the opening of the debate. The Lord stood by me. I had uncommon liberty, and before I concluded many voices were heard in the congregation, saying, "Give us the old way!" Mr. Haw arose to make his reply very much agitated, and exhibited a very bad temper, being very much confused. He made some statement that called from me a denial, and the people rose up to sustain me, which was no sooner done than he was so confused that he picked up his saddle-bags and walked off, and made no reply. This left me in possession of the whole field, and from that hour he lost his influence among the Methodists, and his usefulness as a preacher. In this situation he remained till 1801; and when the great revival began in Tennessee among the Presbyterians and Methodists, he connected himself with the former, and ended his days among them as a preacher. Benjamin Ogden, the colleague of Haw when they first came to Kentucky, married a Miss Easland, on Danville circuit, and located; in 1792 or 1793 joined O'Kelly. He resided in Hardin county, Kentucky. He remained many years unconnected with any Church; but several years before his death became again connected with the Methodist Episcopal Church, and ended his days among the Methodists. After the difficulties with Haw subsided, we had a considerable revival on the circuit, and some additions to the societies, and every thing moved on harmoniously. On the ninth day of January, 1796, I was married to Rachel Cooper, in Sumner county, Tennessee. I lost but one single appointment in consequence of my marriage, but pursued the even tenor of my way. The presiding elder never once visited the country during the whole year. A few weeks after I was married, the presiding elder sent down a preacher to relieve me, with directions for me to return to Kentucky. I immediately started, and visited the circuits where I had traveled in Kentucky, and remained between five and six weeks, and then returned to Tennessee, where I remained till we started for conference, about the tenth of April.

The conference this year was at Nelson's, in the neighborhood of Jonesboro, Western territory. In order to reach this conference we had a long and tedious journey through the wilderness of upward of one hundred miles, without a house. We had to pack on our horses the provisions necessary for ourselves and horses for three days and nights, and to camp out in the open air. The company consisted of James Campbell and Joseph Dunn, preachers, myself and wife, and a nephew of my wife. The last night we encamped we were very apprehensive that the Indians would rob us; consequently, some of us kept awake through the night; but we had no interruption, and the next day we reached the settlement in the neighborhood of where Knoxville is now situated. The day after we entered the bounds of Green circuit, where I had traveled in the year 1792, and were now among our old friends. We arrived at Nelson's the day before the conference commenced, and met Bishop Asbury. The business of the conference was done in peace and harmony. I shall always remember what Mr. Asbury said while my character was under examination before the conference and before I withdrew. He stated to the conference that brother Burke had accomplished two important things the past year—"the defeat of the O'Kellyites, and he had married a wife." It was well known to the preachers in those days that Mr. Asbury did not approve of their marrying, and if they did marry, that it was necessary to locate; but notwithstanding the opposition of the preachers and people, I felt it my duty to travel as long as Providence opened my way. Accordingly, I received my appointment that year on Guilford circuit, North Carolina. I immediately proceeded for my appointment, my wife accompanying me.

We arrived in the bounds of the circuit about the first of May. I made my home at my father's, near the High Rock ford, on Haw river, Rockingham county. It was a year of great distress in that section of country. For the want of breadstuffs numbers perished from want. As soon as the fruit could be eaten the people resorted to that as a means of subsistence, which brought on the flux and other complaints, that hurried many off the stage of action. During the summer and fall we had some considerable move among the people in different parts of the circuit, and some additions to the societies.

In the beginning of October I left the circuit to attend the second General conference, which assembled at Baltimore on the 20th of October. Dr. Coke and Bishop Asbury presided. The business of the conference was conducted with great harmony. At this conference the Chartered Fund for the relief of the superannuated preachers, and the widows and orphans of preachers, was established by a rule of the General conference. It is, perhaps, not known to many of the preachers now living how the funds were made up at the beginning to set the institution on foot. We had for many years previous a preachers' fund for the same purpose. This fund was created by a payment by each traveling preacher, when received into full connection, of twenty shillings, and every year after, at the annual conference, two dollars. The fund, which at this time was pretty considerable, was used by John Dickens, the first Book Steward, for printing books for the connection in America. The process was as follows: The money was used to pay for the printing. The books were sold by the preachers, and the principal was returned to the preachers' fund, and the profits retained to lay the foundation for a book fund. At this General conference the preachers' fund was merged into the Chartered Fund, and the residue was raised by subscriptions and donations from the members. In this way originated the Charter Fund and the Book Concern of the Methodist Episcopal Church in these United States; and this was brought about when the preacher's allowance was only sixty-four dollars, including all his presents and marriage fees.

There were several important events which transpired this year in the bounds of Guilford circuit that require a passing notice. A few years previous brother Simon Carlisle, quite a talented young man, was stationed on Caswell circuit, the circuit adjoining Guilford. He had been acceptable and useful, and completed his year to the satisfaction of all. In those days it was the custom for the preacher to select some place in the circuit which he considered his home, where he deposited for safe-keeping his surplus books and clothes, etc. He had made his home at a brother Harrison's, not far from Dunn river; and on the morning he was about to leave the circuit for the annual conference, he packed up his things in his saddle-bags, and left them in his room unlocked, and went out to see something about his horse. In his absence a wicked young man, son of brother Harrison, put a pocket pistol into his saddle-bags. On his return to the room, without making any examination, he locked his saddle-bags, and left for conference. When he arrived at his mother's, on the way to conference, on taking his things out of his saddle-bags he found a pocket pistol. He could not account for its being there; but leaving it he proceeded on to conference. During the year the pistol was taken to a shop on the road to have some repairs done to it, and a person passing challenged the same as being the pistol of young Harrison, and the same was traced to brother Carlisle. At the next annual conference, in 1794, he was charged with the fact of taking the pistol, and excommunicated from the Church, and so returned on the Minutes of that year. During the summer of 1796 young Harrison was taken sick and died; but just before his death he made a full confession of his having put the pistol into the saddle-bags of brother Carlisle, with the intention of injuring him; and I had the pleasure of restoring brother Carlisle again to the bosom of the Church, to his great joy. He has remained a minister in good standing ever since, and has been living for many years in Middle Tennessee, and has in old age connected himself with the traveling connection in the Tennessee conference.

On the 4th day of March, 1797, I set out for the western country, and met the conference on Holston. Mr. Asbury was at the conference. I received my appointment on the Holston circuit again, having been absent for five years. Brother William Duzan traveled with me that year. Nothing of importance transpired during that conference year. We had a gradual increase in the societies. I visited Clinch and Green circuits in the course of the year, and attended several quarterly meetings, which in those days of Methodism were the only popular meetings where the preachers, when they could leave their circuits, met to help forward the good cause. In the spring of 1798 Bishop Asbury met the conference on Holston, and I was appointed to Cumberland again, having been absent two years. I traveled this year alone, and had not the pleasure of seeing the face of a traveling preacher through the entire year. The circuit had become very large; the country was settling very fast; and many additions to the Church made by certificate. During this year many local preachers emigrated, and settled in the bounds of the circuit. Rev. John M'Gee settled at Dickson's Spring; Rev. Jesse Walker settled on White's Creek. This year I became acquainted with J. A. Grenade, who moved from the lower part of the state of North Carolina. He had in Carolina professed religion; but on coming to Tennessee he had fallen into a strange state of mind. He was in constant fear of hell, and despaired of ever being restored to the favor of God again. I did every thing in my power for his recovery. He traveled with me considerably, and sometimes he would have lucid intervals—seasons when he appeared perfectly rational, and expressed a hope; but suddenly he would relapse into melancholy and despair again.

During this year I had to pay nearly a hundred dollars for a horse, and I found it hard to raise the money, and support myself, and pay the board of my wife; however, I economized in every way. I borrowed a blanket, and wore it instead of a great-coat through the winter, and by that means paid my debts. Upon the whole, I spent this year very agreeably, and with some success. I left the circuit in the spring of 1799 for conference in Kentucky, at Bethel Academy. This year I received my appointment on Danville circuit for the second time, having been absent for seven years. Part of this year I had Henry Smith for my colleague, who, I believe, is yet living in Maryland. I had many difficulties to contend with, being the first married preacher that had ever attempted to travel with what the people and preachers called the incumbrance of a wife; and every thing was thrown in my way to discourage me. The presiding elder thought I had better locate; for, he said, the people would not support a married man. But I determined to hold on my way, and my wife encouraged me. She wrought with her own hands, and paid her board, and clothed herself; and I divided equally with my colleague, and by this means kept every thing quiet.

This year began my war with the Baptists. Having had some small revival, the Baptists did all they could to draw off our members and get them into the water; and I began with lecturing every time I baptized an infant, which greatly roused up the Baptists, so much so that I received a challenge from the Rev. Thomas Shelton, the champion of the whole Baptist denomination. I accepted the challenge, and the day was appointed at Irvin's Lick, in Madison county. We met according to appointment, and settled the preliminaries of debate, each to speak fifteen minutes. Brother John Watson was appointed by me to keep time and call to order, and a Baptist preacher appointed by Mr. Shelton for the same purpose. We proceeded about four hours to debate the subject. I had the close, when Shelton observed to the immense congregation that he believed I was an honest but a mistaken man. I proceeded to administer the ordinance of baptism on the spot, and Mr. Shelton stood by and witnessed the same. From that day the tug of war began, which continued till 1811, when I left the state. At that meeting Elisha W. Bowman was present, and a young speaker in the Methodist Episcopal Church, who immediately entered upon the study of the subject and became a warm auxiliary in the cause. William J. Thompson also took up the subject. He was a strong man and rendered efficient service. After 1800 John Sale and William M'Kendree engaged with me in the contest. We kept up a constant fire upon the Baptists, and the Methodists began to gain confidence and to make a respectable stand among the denominations of Christians.

The year 1799 I expected would terminate my labors in the western country. At the request of Bishop Asbury, all the preachers that had been in the west for any considerable time were to leave the country and attend the General conference at Baltimore, on the sixth day of May, 1800, and to receive their appointments in the old states, and a new set to be sent to the west. We all accordingly set out early in April. The following were the preachers that left: Francis Poythress, Thomas Wilkerson, John Page, John Watson, John Buxton, Henry Smith, John Kobler, and William Burke. Bishop Asbury had formed the intended plan of appointing a presiding elder to take charge of all the west in one district; namely, Kentucky, Tennessee, and all that part of Virginia west of New river and the North-Western territory, including the Miami and Scioto Valleys. He used his utmost endeavors, during the General conference, to engage a man for that purpose, but failed; for when they understood the extent of the territory they would have to travel over, they uniformly declined to undertake it. Before the close of the conference he applied to me to know if I would consent to return to Kentucky and take with me all the papers appertaining to the annual conference and Bethel Academy, and do the best I could for the work in that part of the field. I consented, and he appointed to go with me John Sale, Hezekiah Harraman, William Algood, and Henry Smith; for the Holston country, James Hunter, John Watson, and John Page; and for Cumberland, William Lambeth. John Sale and H. Harraman proceeded with me immediately for Kentucky. Hezekiah Harraman was appointed to Danville circuit, John Sale to Salt River and Shelby, William Algood to Limestone. I was appointed to Hinkston, and to superintend the quarterly meetings where there was no elder. William Algood never came to his appointment. I prevailed on Jeremiah Lawson to supply his place on Limestone circuit, and I placed Lewis Hunt on Hinkston, and spent the most of my time on Lexington, Hinkston, and Limestone circuits. My labors, during that summer, were very arduous, and to accomplish my work I rode down two good horses.

During that year the annual conference was changed from the spring to the fall; and on the first of October, 1800, the conference met at Bethel Academy. Bishops Asbury and Whatcoat attended, and they brought with them William M'Kendree, from the center district of Virginia, to take charge of the whole of the western country. Mr. Asbury wished me to go and take charge of the district that M'Kendree had left, but I told him it was out of the question; that I had returned to Kentucky, at his request, from Baltimore, in the spring; that I had rode down my horses; that I had worn out my clothes; that I was ragged and tattered; and last and not least, I had not a cent in my pocket, and, therefore, could not go. He yielded to the necessity of the case. At that conference Benjamin Lakin was readmitted and William Marsh admitted. I was appointed on Lexington and Hinkston united, with Thomas Wilkerson and Lewis Hunt. Wilkerson did not come on from Baltimore circuit till late in the spring of 1801.

CHAPTER III.

AUTOBIOGRAPHY CONTINUED.

I now enter upon a new era in the history of western Methodism. I consider this the proper place to give a description of the men and means employed in the establishment and progress of Methodism in this western country, and the difficulties and hardships encountered in the work. As early as the year 1785 the first traveling preachers visited the Holston country; their names were Richard Swift and Michael Gilbert. The country at this time was new and thinly settled. They met with many privations and sufferings, and made but little progress. The most of the country through which they traveled was very mountainous and rough, and the people ignorant and uncultivated, and the greater part a frontier exposed to Indian depredations. They were followed by Mark Whitaker and Mark Moore, who were zealous, plain, old-fashioned Methodist preachers, and calculated to make an impression. Their labors were successful, and they were instrumental in raising up many societies. Mark Whitaker in particular was a strong man, and maintained Methodist doctrine in opposition to Calvinism, which was the prevailing doctrine of that time. He laid a good foundation for his successors, and was followed by Jeremiah Matson and Thomas Ware, and after them in succession Joseph Doddridge, Jeremiah Able, John Tunnell, John Baldwin, Charles Hardy, John M'Gee, and John West. Under God these men planted the standard of the cross in the frontier settlements of the French Broad, and numerous societies were raised up, so that in 1791 the societies numbered upward of one thousand. About this time I arrived in the Holston country. These fathers of Methodism, most of whom have gone to their reward, will be long had in grateful remembrance. But two of them are lingering on the shores of mortality—Charles Hardy and John West. The most of them died in connection with the Church, and are now reaping the reward of their labors and sufferings. Joseph Doddridge received orders in the Episcopal Church of England, and settled in the Monongahela country, and there died. Jeremiah Able joined the Presbyterians, and lived and died in the Green river country, not far from Greensburg, Green county, Kentucky.

The pioneers of Methodism in that part of western Virginia and the Western territory suffered many privations, and underwent much toil and labor, preaching in forts and cabins, sleeping on straw, bear and buffalo skins, living on bear meat, venison, and wild turkeys, traveling over mountains and through solitary valleys, and, sometimes, lying on the cold ground; receiving but a scanty support, barely enough to keep soul and body together, with coarse home-made apparel; but the best of all was, their labors were owned and blessed of God, and they were like a band of brothers, having one purpose and end in view—the glory of God and the salvation of immortal souls. When the preachers met from their different and distant fields of labor, they had a feast of love and friendship; and when they parted, they wept and embraced each other as brothers beloved. Such was the spirit of primitive Methodist preachers.

There were but few local preachers at that time in that part of the western country, and they were like angels' visits, few and far between—one local preacher on West

New River circuit, a brother Morgan, whose labors were confined principally to a small circle; but one on Holston, old father Ragen, in the Rich Valley, not far from the Salt-Works. He was a man much respected, and, in some degree, useful in his neighborhood, but circumscribed in his operations as a preacher. At an early time brother Benjamin Vanpelt, a local preacher of considerable talents and usefulness, moved from Alexandria, Virginia, and settled on Lick creek, Green county, Western territory. He labored extensively, was very useful, and was made an instrument, under God, of doing much good. Several societies were formed by his ministry, and he may be considered one of the fathers of the Church. His memory will be long had in remembrance by the people of the French Broad country. He was the old and particular friend of Bishop Asbury, and one of the first meeting-houses built in that country was Vanpelt's meeting-house. I have been in company with the Bishop at his house, and heard him preach in the meeting-house as early as 1792. Brother Stilwell, another local preacher from Virginia, settled in the same neighborhood and united with brother Vanpelt, and they labored harmoniously in the good work. After the conclusion of the Indian war, in the spring of 1795, there was a great influx by immigration. Some of the traveling preachers married and settled in the country. James O'Conner settled on Watauga, Mark Whitaker near Jonesboro, Stephen Brooks in Green county, and many others, both preachers and members, settled in different sections, and some new preachers were raised up, and the work was enlarged; new circuits were formed, and some useful and talented young men entered into the traveling connection. Among the first was Francis Acuff, of precious memory, who, at an early period, fell a victim to disease, and died in the triumphs of faith on Danville circuit, Kentucky.

Nathaniel Massie, David Young, Henager, and Porter, in succession were raised up in that section of country, whose labors and usefulness are known among the thousands of Israel; and the few who remain to witness the spread and triumph of the Redeemer's kingdom are ready to exclaim, "The Lord hath done great things for us, whereof we are glad."

We now turn our attention to Kentucky. This country began to be settled by adventurers soon after the commencement of the Revolutionary war. It was completely insulated, being a vast wilderness to the south from the frontiers of Virginia and the Western territory, of one hundred and thirty miles on the eastern boundary; an uninhabited country till you arrived on the frontiers of Virginia and Pennsylvania; a few settlements being scattered through Brook county, Virginia, and on the Monongahela, and on Greenbriar river, and the head waters of James river, and on the north by the Ohio river; and the whole country extending to the lakes without inhabitants, except the Indians, who were the friends of the British, and under their influence, and kept up a constant warfare on the whole of the settlements in Kentucky. The first families that emigrated to Kentucky was in the year 1773, and the first station established was Boonsboro, on the Kentucky river, situated in what was afterward called Madison county. The next stations were Harrod's and Bryant's. Harrod's Station was situated on the south side of the Kentucky river, below the mouth of Dick's river; and as the settlements spread the stations were multiplied. Every new settlement had a station; one at Ruddell's Mills, at Georgetown, Millersburg, Mays Lick, Washington, Frankfort, Louisville, Middletown, Masterson's Station, Burnt Station, and numerous others formed as the country settled. The frontier settlements kept up the stations and block-houses till the treaty of Greenville, in the spring of 1795. In the first settlement of Kentucky the denomination of Baptists were the most numerous. Among the first preachers of that order were the Craigs, the Bledsoes, and Bailey, etc. There were a few Presbyterian ministers that settled in different sections of the country. Old father Rankin, of Lexington, Rev. Mr. Rice, from Virginia, settled in the forks of Dick's river, and the Rev. Robt. W. Finley at Cane Ridge. After the conclusion of the Revolutionary war the emigration was very great to Kentucky; and the Presbyterians sent out numbers of missionaries, who traveled and preached through the country, and settled down wherever they could establish a congregation. Among the first was the Rev. Messrs. James Blythe, Lyle, Welch, M'Namer, Stone, Reynolds, Stewart, and several others not recollected.

They established congregations in Fayette, Clark, Bourbon, Scott, and Woodford, and M'Clelland, in Mercer, and Washington. The Baptists still continued the most numerous; but at an early period, say about 1789, or 1790, they had a division in the Church. A numerous party arose among them calling themselves Separate, or by some denominated Free-Will Baptists. The Free-Will Baptists held in common the doctrines of the Methodists, except the unconditional final perseverance of the saints, and baptism by immersion as the only mode, while the Regulars held to the doctrine of predestination, as set forth in the Philadelphia Confession of Faith; but they were subject to another division. Rev. John Bailey and Bledso embraced the doctrines of Winchester, and were denominated Universalists. They were popular preachers among the Baptists, and made great inroads in many of their Churches; and the controversy was carried to great lengths, and conducted with much acrimony. At this period the Separatists took the lead. They successfully preached against the doctrine of predestination and decrees, enforced experimental and practical religion, formed Churches, and established separate associations, and became very numerous; but they have long since ceased to exist as a separate denomination. They gradually united with the Regular associations, and are now known as Baptists generally. At the commencement of these controversies the Methodists were few and far between.

Soon after the conclusion of the war with Great Britain, Francis Clark, a local preacher from old Virginia, settled in the neighborhood of Danville, Mercer county, and was among the first Methodists that emigrated to the country. He was a man of sound judgment, and well instructed in the doctrines of the Methodist Church. As a preacher he was successful, and was made the instrument of forming several societies, and lived many years to rejoice in the success of the cause that he had been the instrument, under God, of commencing in the wilderness. He died at his own domicile, in the fall of 1799, in great peace, and in hope of a blessed immortality. I attended his funeral in connection with the Rev. Francis Poythress, and at his request I preached from these words: "For to me to live is Christ, but to die is gain." The Rev. William J. Thompson emigrated at an early day from Stokes county, North Carolina, and settled in the same neighborhood. He became also a useful auxiliary, and preached with acceptance and success. He afterward joined the traveling connection in the Western conference; and when he moved to the state of Ohio became connected with the Ohio conference, where his labors and usefulness are held in remembrance by many. He still lives in good old age, in Clermont county, Ohio. The next local preachers that came to the country were Nathaniel Harris, from Virginia, Gabriel and Daniel

Woodfield, from the Redstone country. Harris settled in Jessamine county, and the Woodfields in Fayette county; and not long after Philip Taylor, from Virginia, settled in Jessamine county. These were considered a great acquisition to the infant societies. Nathaniel Harris and Gabriel Woodfield were among the first order of local preachers, and they were highly esteemed, and labored with success. They have been connected with the itinerancy, and labored in that relation with acceptance. Gabriel Woodfield afterward settled in Henry county; but before his death removed to Indiana, in the neighborhood of Madison, where he lived to a good old age, and died in peace among his friends and connections. Brother Nathaniel Harris still lives, at the age of nearly four-score years. He is still actively engaged in the good cause, and lives in the midst of his friends, highly esteemed and useful. Joseph Ferguson, a local preacher from Fairfax county, Virginia, moved to Kentucky at an early time, and settled in Nelson county, and was among the first preachers that settled in that section of the country. He was an amiable man, possessed good preaching talents, and was rendered very useful. He was highly esteemed, blessed with an amiable family, and his house was a home for the traveling preachers, who were at all times welcome guests. Brother Ferguson was subject at times to great depression of mind; but when in the company of the traveling preachers he was always cheerful and happy. He lived to a good old age, at the place where he first settled, and died in peace and in the triumphs of that Gospel which he had proclaimed for many years. Ferguson's meeting-house was one of the first that was built in that part of the country; and at one time there was a large society at that meeting-house, and when I was last in the neighborhood, in the fall of 1811, they still maintained a respectable standing.

One of the oldest meeting-houses in Madison county was Proctor's Chapel, not far from Boonsboro. That part of the country shared largely in the blessings of the Gospel, and Methodism flourished to a very great extent in that county. There were a number of respectable local preachers, whose labors were extensive and successful. Charles Kavanaugh, John Cook, R. Baker, and J. Proctor, were all early emigrants to that part of the country. Charles Kavanaugh was a preacher of splendid talents and great usefulness. He was an able defender of the doctrines of the Methodist Church, and was highly respected by all denominations. There were several families of that connection. Williams Kavanaugh was raised in that neighborhood, and was a cousin to Charles. Williams Kavanaugh and Lewis Garrett were both raised on Danville circuit, and both entered the traveling connection in the spring of 1794, and traveled that conference year together on Green circuit, now East Tennessee, then the Western territory. Of these two young men we shall hereafter have something more to say. Charles Kavanaugh, after having made full proof of his ministry in Kentucky, removed, in 1796 or 1797, to the neighborhood of Nashville, Tennessee, where I found him settled in 1798. He there commenced the practice of medicine, and was celebrated as a cancer doctor. Of his labors and usefulness in that country, and the manner in which he closed his life and labors, we hope some friend will furnish the account.

We must now turn our attention to the introduction of the traveling missionaries into the state of Kentucky. The first traveling Methodist preachers that ever set foot on Kentucky soil was James Haw and Benjamin Ogden. They were stationed in Kentucky, 1786—James Haw elder; and at the end of the year they returned ninety in society. This was the commencement of Methodism in the great west. In order to show the progress of Methodism, and the means and instruments employed, I shall give you the numbers of increase of members and traveling preachers in 1788. Number, 539. Circuits: Lexington, Thomas Williamson, Peter Massie, Benjamin Snelling; Danville, Wilson Lee; Cumberland, David Coombs, Barnabas M'Henry. In 1789: Number, 1,088. This year Francis Poythress was appointed presiding elder, and a regular district was formed. Lexington, James Haw, Wilson Lee, Stephen Brooks; Danville, Barnabas M'Henry, Peter Massie; Cumberland, Thomas Williamson, Joshua Hartley. In 1790: Number, 1,366. Francis Poythress presiding elder. Danville, Thomas Williamson, Stephen Brooks; Cumberland, James Haw, Wilson Lee, Peter Massie; Madison, Barnabas M'Henry, Benjamin Snelling, Samuel Tucker, Joseph Lillard; Lexington, Henry Burchet, David Haggard. In 1791: Number, 1,969. Francis Poythress presiding elder. Limestone, Peter Massie; Danville, Thomas Williamson, J. Tatman; Salt River, Wilson Lee, Joseph Lillard; Lexington, Henry Burchet, David Haggard; Cumberland, Barnabas M'Henry, James O'Cull. In 1792: Number, 2,235. Francis Poythress presiding elder. Limestone, John Ray; Lexington, John Sewell, Benjamin Northcott, John Page; Danville, Wilson Lee, Richard Bird; Cumberland, John Ball, J. Stephenson; Henry Burchet, Isaac Hammer, Salt River.

We shall now notice the state of religion. The first two years were principally taken up in seeking the lost sheep that had been scattered in the wilderness. In 1798 there was a new recruit of preachers sent out. Thomas Williamson, Wilson Lee, and David Coombs came from the Redstone country, which at that time was connected with the Baltimore conference as missionary ground; but soon afterward, as early as 1791, Bishop

Asbury held a conference at Uniontown, not far from the foot of Laurel Hill, in Pennsylvania. This new recruit consisted of young men, and all well qualified for the work of missionaries. They had no other object in view but to push forward the Redeemer's kingdom, and to enlarge the borders of Zion.

The same year Barnabas M'Henry, then quite a youth, and one of the early fruits of Methodism in the Holston country, came out into the field. His parents resided in the Rich Valley not far from the Salt-Works, Washington county, Virginia. He also penetrated the wilderness, and came to the help of the Lord against the mighty. This band of young, resolute soldiers of the cross united under two old and experienced veterans—Francis Poythress and James Haw. Providence opened their way, and they began to make some favorable impressions upon the minds and hearts of the people. They occupied the whole ground, and, with the assistance of the few local men who had been there before them, they carried the war into the camp of the enemy, and in a short time a powerful and extensive revival took place. Hundreds were added to the Church; and considering the situation of the country, surrounded by a wilderness, and the Indians continually making depredations on the frontiers, and the people constantly harassed and penned up in forts and stations, it may be considered among the greatest revivals that was ever known. In this revival a number of wealthy and respectable citizens were added to the Church—the Hardins, Thomases, Hites, Lewises, Easlands, Mastersons, Kavanaughs, Tuckers, Richardsons, Letemors, Browns, Garretts, Churchfields, Jefferses, Hoards, and numbers of others of respectable standing in society; and out of this revival was raised up some useful and promising young men, who entered the traveling connection, and many of them made full proof of their ministry, and lived many years to ornament the Church of God. I will name a few of them. Peter Massie, who was termed the weeping prophet, was among the first-fruits. He was made an instrument of great good wherever he went, scattering the holy fire. His labors were so great that his race was but short. He literally wore himself out in a few years. The zeal of God's cause literally consumed him. He was great and mighty in prayer, and always wished that he might die suddenly, and without lingering in pain. He labored faithfully for three years; and on the 18th of December, 1791, he was sitting in his chair at brother Hodge's, a station six miles south of Nashville, Tennessee, where he suddenly expired, in the morning about nine o'clock. So ended the labors of brother Massie. His remains lie near the Old Station, unhonored by a single stone, and to the present generation entirely unknown; but he rests from his labors in hope of a resurrection, while his immortal spirit is in the world of bliss and of glory. Others well known to the present generation of Methodists were also thrust out into the vineyard—John Ray, Benjamin Northcott, Joseph Lillard, and Joseph Tattman. In the year 1791 Henry Burchet and David Haggard, from the Virginia conference, and James O'Cull, from the Redstone country, were sent out as a reinforcement, and united in carrying on the work, which was still in progress, notwithstanding the campaigns that were carried on against the Indians; for during this time Harmar and St. Clair had both been defeated on the north of the Ohio river, and the country constantly kept in a state of agitation. Still Methodism held up her head, and presented a bold front. The societies maintained their ground. In 1792 the number was 2,235, and the number of traveling preachers eleven—about two hundred members to one preacher. The reader may have some kind of an idea what kind of pecuniary support they had. Traveling and preaching, night and day, in weariness and want; many days without the necessaries of life, and always without those comforts that are now enjoyed by traveling preachers; with worn and tattered garments, but happy and united like a band of brothers. The quarterly meetings and annual conferences were high times. When the pilgrims met they never met without embracing each other, and never parted at those seasons without weeping. Those were days that tried men's souls.

Thomas Williamson was a very successful and laborious preacher. He literally wore himself out in traveling and preaching, but ended his days in peace in the state of Kentucky, not far from Lexington. Wilson Lee was one of the most successful preachers among those early adventurers. He was a man of fine talents, meek and humble, of a sweet disposition, and not only a Christian and Christian minister, but much of a gentleman. During his stay in Kentucky, from 1787 to 1792, he traveled over all the settlements of Kentucky and Cumberland, much admired and beloved by saint and sinner. In the spring of 1792, in company with Bishop Asbury, he crossed the wilderness from Kentucky to Virginia, where I met him at conference on Holston, and from thence to the eastward, and attended the first General conference at Baltimore, November 1, 1792, and remained in the bounds of the New York, Philadelphia, and Baltimore conferences till he departed this life, in 1804, at Walter Worthington's, Ann Arundel county, Maryland. The last time I had the pleasure of seeing him was in Georgetown, District of Columbia, on my way to the General conference of May 1, 1804. He was then in a very feeble condition. His affliction was hemorrhage of the lungs, of which he died. During the time he traveled in Kentucky he passed through many sufferings and privations, in weariness and want, in hunger and nakedness; traveling from fort to fort, sometimes with a guard and sometimes alone; often exposing his life; for the savages were constantly in quest of plunder and of life; and scarcely a week passed without hearing of some one falling a prey to them; and what we say of brother Lee may be said of all the traveling preachers, as it respects their exposure and suffering, till the year 1794—the year of Wayne's campaign—when the northern Indians were held in fear and finally subdued.

In 1791 Henry Burchet was sent from the Virginia conference and stationed on Lexington circuit; in 1792 on Salt River. On both those circuits he was eminently useful. He was very zealous, and declined no labor or suffering, but offered himself a willing sacrifice to the cause of his Redeemer. He was among the first preachers in the west who took a deep interest in the rising generation. In every neighborhood where it was practicable he formed the children into classes, sang and prayed with them, catechised them, and exhorted them. For this work he had a peculiar turn, and was successful in carrying out his plan of instruction. Many years after I have heard the young people in Kentucky and Cumberland speak in the highest terms of Henry Burchet. At the conference held at Masterson's Station, in May, 1793, our beloved brother Burchet was in a poor state of health. He had labored the preceding year on Salt River circuit, the most extensive in the district, requiring more labor and suffering than any other in the country. Before the close of the year he felt a great weakness in his breast and spitting of blood. At the conference it appeared that Cumberland must be left to be provided for hereafter. Brother Burchet said, "Here am I, send me." His friends remonstrated against his going; the distance was great; considerable danger from Indians; the small-pox prevailing in the country—all was urged against his going; but after asking the consent of Bishop Asbury and the conference, he said, "If I perish who can doubt of my eternal rest, or fail to say, Let me die the death of the righteous, and let my last end be like his!" He labored with great success in Cumberland. Though weak and much afflicted in his breast, he held on his way till late in the fall, when he was obliged to stop traveling. He was a welcome guest at the house of a rich planter, two miles west of Nashville, by the name of James Hockett, where he remained, enjoying the hospitality of the family and the visits of his numerous friends, till the month of February, 1794, when he departed this life, in hope of eternal blessedness in the kingdom of God. At his request he was wrapped in white flannel and committed to the silent grave. I often visited his grave in 1795 and 1798; but I suppose since that day strangers are in the possession of the premises, and every vestige of the spot where he lies is obliterated, and, with the exception of a few, his name is forgotten. It is now forty-five years since Henry Burchet ceased to labor and to live. "Blessed are the dead that die in the Lord from henceforth, saith the Spirit; for they rest from their labors, and their works follow them."

James Haw must next claim our attention. He was the first traveling Methodist preacher that entered on the field in Kentucky in 1786. He was an able and successful laborer in the Lord's vineyard. Numerous were the sufferings and hardships that he underwent in planting the standard of the cross in that wild and uncultivated region, surrounded with savages, and traveling from fort to fort, and every day exposing his life; and, notwithstanding every difficulty and embarrassment, the good work progressed. In the years 1787, 1788, and 1789 the holy flame spread all over Kentucky and Cumberland. Haw, Poythress, Wilson Lee, and Williamson were the chief instruments in carrying on this great work. We may gather something from a letter written by James Haw to Bishop Asbury in the beginning of the year 1789.

It reads: "Good news from Zion; the work of God is going on rapidly in the new world; a glorious victory the Son of God has gained, and he is still going on conquering and to conquer. Shout, ye angels! Hell trembles and heaven rejoices daily over sinners that repent. At a quarterly meeting held in Bourbon county, Kentucky, July 19th and 20th, 1788, the Lord poured out his Spirit in a wonderful manner, first on the Christians, and sanctified several of them powerfully and gloriously, and, as I charitably hope, wholly. The seekers also felt the power and presence of God, and cried for mercy as at the point of death. We prayed with and for them, till we had reason to believe that the Lord converted seventeen or eighteen precious souls. Halleluiah, praise ye the Lord!

"As I went from that through the circuit to another quarterly meeting, the Lord converted two or three more. The Saturday and Sunday following the Lord poured out his Spirit again. The work of sanctification among the believers broke out again at the Lord's table, and the Spirit of the Lord went through the assembly like a mighty rushing wind. Some fell; many cried for mercy. Sighs and groans proceeded from their hearts; tears of sorrow for sin ran streaming down their eyes. Their prayers reached to heaven, and the Spirit of the Lord entered into them and filled fourteen or fifteen with peace and joy in believing. 'Salvation, O the joyful sound; how the echo flies!' A few days after brother Poythress came and went with me to another quarterly meeting. We had another gracious season round the Lord's table, but no remarkable stir till after preaching; when under several exhortations some bursted out into tears, others trembled, and some fell. I sprang in among the people, and the Lord converted one more very powerfully, who praised the Lord with such acclamation of joy as I trust will never be forgotten. The Sunday following I preached my farewell sermon and met the class, and the Lord converted three more. Glory be to his holy name forever!

"The first round I went on Cumberland the Lord converted six precious souls, and I joined three gracious Baptists to our Church; and every round, I have reason to believe, some sinners are awakened, some seekers joined to society, and some penitents converted to God. At our Cumberland quarterly meeting the Lord converted six souls the first day, and one the next. Glory, honor, praise, and power be unto God forever! The work still goes on. I have joined two more serious Baptists since the quarterly meeting. The Lord has converted several more precious souls in various parts of the circuit, and some more have joined the society, so that we have one hundred and twelve disciples now in Cumberland—forty-seven of whom, I trust, have received the gift of the Holy Ghost since they believed; and I hope these are but the first of a universal harvest which God will give us in this country. Brother Massie is with me, going on weeping over sinners, and the Lord blesses his labors. A letter from brother Williamson, dated November 10th, 1788, informs me that the work is still going on rapidly in Kentucky; that at two quarterly meetings since I came away, the Lord poured out his Spirit, and converted ten penitents and sanctified five believers, at the first, and twenty more were converted at the second; indeed, the wilderness and solitary places are glad, and the desert rejoices and blossoms as the rose, and, I trust, will soon become beautiful as *Tirza* and comely as *Jerusalem*.

"What shall I more say? Time would fail to tell you all the Lord's doings among us. It is marvelous in our eyes. To him be the glory, honor, praise, power, might, majesty, and dominion, both now and forever, amen and amen!

"P. S. Some of our responsible members of Cumberland have formerly lived at a place called Natchez, on the Mississippi river, then under the British, now under the Government of Spain. There are, they say, six or seven hundred American families there who have no Protestant minister of any kind, and I fear are perishing for want of the bread of life. I expect to know by the spring if there be free and full toleration for the Protestant religion there, and if there be to make the report to the conference."

The conference year of 1789 closed the labors of James Haw in Kentucky. The superintendence of the work was now altogether under the direction of F. Poythress, both in Kentucky and Cumberland. The circuits were well supplied in 1790: Danville, Thomas Williamson, Stephen Brooks; Cumberland, Wilson Lee, James Haw, Peter Massie; Madison, Barnabas M'Henry, Benjamin Snelling; Limestone, Samuel Tucker, Joseph Lillard; Lexington, Henry Burchet, David Haggard. Methodism still found favor in the eyes of the people, and the good work progressed, and numbers were added to the societies; and the circuits were enlarged in proportion as the immigration increased and new settlements were formed. In the course of three years the increase was rising one thousand. In 1794, the year of Wayne's campaign, the work declined very much, and many turned aside from the right way. Discipline was strictly attended to, and many expelled from the societies. The Indian war having terminated the people began to scatter in every direction. New settlements were formed, and Ohio and Indiana began to settle rapidly, and the societies many of them were broken up, and we had not preachers sufficient to follow the tide of emigration to their new settlements; consequently, we had a considerable decrease of members in the year 1795 and till 1801, when the great revival commenced and spread throughout all the western country; so that at the end of the conference year 1802, we had doubled our numbers from that of 1795. The revival also produced a great increase of local and traveling preachers.

The conference year of 1801 commenced a new era in the west. Mr. Asbury changed the name of the conference from that of Kentucky to that of the Western conference, which embraced all the western country then occupied by the Methodists; and William M'Kendree was appointed presiding elder. The circuits that composed the conference, and the preachers stationed this year, were as follows: Scioto and Miami, Henry Smith; Limestone, Benjamin Lakin; Hinkston and Lexington, William Burke, Thomas Wilkerson, and Lewis Hunt; Danville, Hezekiah Harraman; Salt River and Shelby, John Sale and William Marsh; Cumberland, John Page, Benjamin Young; Green, Samuel Douthel, Ezekiel Burdine; Holston and Russell, James Hunter; New River, John Watson. In the commencement of this year the appearance was rather gloomy in different sections of the work. The district was very large, and the presiding elder could not perform his round in less than six months.

The spring of 1801 the quarterly meetings in Kentucky were held without the presiding elder. The quarterly meeting for Hinkston circuit was held early in June, at Owens's meeting-house, Four-mile creek, commencing on Friday and breaking up on Monday morning. At this meeting was the first appearance of that astonishing revival to which we have alluded. Several professed to get religion, and many were under deep conviction for sin, and the meeting continued from Sunday morning till Monday morning, with but little intermission. From thence brother Lakin and myself proceeded in company, on Monday morning, to a Presbyterian sacrament, at Salem meeting-house, in the neighborhood of Col. John Martin's. The Rev. Mr. Lyle was pastor of that Church. There had been during the occasion more than ordinary attention and seriousness manifested. I arrived on the ground before the first sermon was concluded, and during the interval they insisted on my preaching the next sermon; and, notwithstanding I was much fatigued from the labors of the quarterly meeting, I at length consented, and commenced about two o'clock, P. M. I took for my text, "To you is the word of this salvation sent;" and before I concluded there was a great trembling among the dry bones. Great numbers fell to the ground and cried for mercy, old and young. Brother Lakin followed with one of his then powerful exhortations, and the work increased. The Presbyterian ministers stood astonished, not knowing what to make of such a tumult. Brother Lakin and myself proceeded to exhort and pray with them. Some obtained peace with God before the meeting broke up. This was the first appearance of the revival in the Presbyterian Church. From these two meetings the heavenly flame spread in every direction. Preachers and people, when they assembled for meeting, always expected the Lord to meet with them. Our next quarterly meeting was for Lexington circuit, at Jesse Griffith's, Scott county. On Saturday we had some indications of a good work. On Saturday night we had preaching in different parts of the neighborhood, which at that time was the custom; so that every local preacher and exhorter was employed in the work. Success attended the meetings, and on Sunday morning they came in companies singing and shouting on the road. Love-feast was opened on Sunday morning at eight o'clock, and such was the power and presence of God that the doors were thrown open, and the work became general, and continued till Monday afternoon, during which time numbers experienced justification by faith in the name of Jesus Christ. The work spread now into the several circuits. Salt River and Shelby were visited, and Danville shared in the blessing; also the Presbyterian Church caught the fire. Congregations were universally wakened up: M'Namer's congregation on Cabin creek; Barton Stone's at Cane Ridge; Reynolds's near Ruddell's Station and in Paris; Rev. Mr. Lisle at Salem; Mr. Rankin, Walnut Hills; Mr. Blythe at Lexington and Woodford; and Rev. Mr. Walsh at Cane run; likewise in Madison county, under the ministry of the Rev. Mr. Houston. The work extended to Ohio at Lower Springfield, Hamilton county; Rev. Mr. Thompson's congregation and Eagle creek; Rev. Mr. Dunlavey's congregation, Adams county. The Methodist local preachers and exhorters, and the members generally, united with them in carrying on the work, for they were at home wherever God was pleased to manifest his power; and having had some experience in such a school, were able to teach others. The Presbyterian ministers saw the advantage of such auxiliaries, and were pressing in their invitations, both for the traveling and local preachers, to attend their sacraments through the months of July and August. The Rev. Barton Stone was pastor of the Church at Cane Ridge. I had been formerly acquainted with him when he traveled as a missionary in the Holston and Cumberland country, previous to his settling at Cane Ridge; and we agreed to have a united sacrament of the Presbyterians and Methodists at Cane Ridge meeting-house, in August. The meeting was published, throughout the length and breadth of the country, to commence on Friday. On the first day I arrived in the neighborhood; but it was a rainy day, and I did not attend on the ground. On Saturday morning I attended. On Friday and Friday night they held meeting in the meeting house; and such was the power and presence of God on Friday night that the meeting continued all night; and next morning, Saturday, they repaired to a stand erected in the woods, the work still going on in the house, which continued there till Wednesday, without intermission. On Saturday the congregation was very numerous. The Presbyterians continued to occupy the stand during Saturday and Saturday night, whenever they could get a chance to be heard; but never invited any Methodist preacher to preach. On Sunday morning Mr. Stone, with some of the elders of the session, waited upon me to have a conference on the subject of the approaching sacrament, which was to be administered in the afternoon. The object in calling on me was, that I should make from the stand a public declaration how the Methodists held certain doctrines, etc. I told them we preached every day, and that our doctrines were published to the world through the press. Come and hear, go and read; and if that was the condition on which we were to unite in the sacrament, "Every man to his tent, O Israel;" for I should require of him to make a public declaration of their belief in certain doctrines. He then replied that we had better drop the subject; that he was perfectly satisfied, but that some of his elders were not. I observed that they might do as they thought best; but the subject got out among the Methodists, and a number did not partake of the sacrament, as none of our preachers were invited to assist in administering.

There is a mistaken opinion with regard to this meeting. Some writers of late represent it as having been a camp meeting. It is true there were a number of wagons and carriages, which remained on the ground night and day; but not a single tent was to be found, neither was any such thing as camp meetings heard of at that time. Preaching in the woods was a common thing at popular meetings, as meeting-houses in the west were not sufficient to hold the large number of people that attended on such occasions. This was the case at Cane Ridge.

On Sunday morning, when I came on the ground, I was met by my friends, to know if I was going to preach for them on that day. I told them I had not been invited; if I was, I should certainly do so. The morning passed off, but no invitation. Between ten and eleven I found a convenient place on the body of a fallen tree, about fifteen feet from the ground, where I fixed my stand in the open sun, with an umbrella affixed to a long pole and held over my head by brother Hugh Barnes. I commenced reading a hymn with an audible voice, and by the time we concluded singing and praying we had around us, standing on their feet, by fair calculation ten thousand people. I gave out my text in the following words: "For we must all stand before the judgment-seat of Christ;" and before I concluded my voice was not to be heard for the groans of the distressed and the shouts of triumph. Hundreds fell prostrate to the ground, and the work continued on that spot till Wednesday afternoon. It was estimated by some that not less than five hundred were at one time lying on the ground in the deepest agonies of distress, and every few minutes rising in shouts of triumph. Toward the evening I pitched the only tent on the ground. Having been accustomed to travel the wilderness, I soon had a tent constructed out of poles and papaw bushes. Here I remained Sunday night, and Monday and Monday night; and during that time there was not a single moment's cessation, but the work went on, and old and young, men, women, and children, were converted to God. It was estimated that on Sunday and Sunday night there were twenty thousand people on the ground. They had come far and near from all parts of Kentucky; some from Tennessee, and from north of the Ohio river; so that tidings of Cane Ridge meeting was carried to almost every corner of the country, and the holy fire spread in all directions.

Immediately after this meeting the last round of quarterly meetings commenced for that conference year, and they were appointed for four days, to commence on Friday. The work continued, and quarterly meetings were attended by thousands, and generally continued night and day with but little intermission; and during the week, at appointments in different parts of the country, we had to preach in the groves to thousands of people. We gave invitations to all the Presbyterian ministers to unite with us at our quarterly meetings; but they generally pleaded as an excuse that they had appointments to attend, and Friday, Saturday, and Sunday would pass off without any aid from them; but on Monday we generally saw some of their ministers in the congregation, but having our plans filled up for that day we consequently paid no attention to them; for we were fully satisfied that they only wanted the Methodists to shake the bush, and they would catch the birds. My advice to our official members in quarterly meeting conference was, to quietly withdraw from their meetings, and mind our own business. They did so, and no difficulty occurred in any of our societies. This conference year ended with the greatest prospects that had ever visited the far west.

In the year 1801 the Presbyterians had some gracious revivals in Sumner county, Tennessee, and Logan county, Kentucky. The two M'Gees, John—an old traveling preacher, who had located and settled on the Cumberland river—and his brother William, a Presbyterian minister, with two other Presbyterians, Messrs. Rankin and Hodges, in connection with brothers Page and Wilkerson, were united in carrying on the work both among the Methodists and Presbyterians; but the conference of 1802 opened with greater prospects, and the work became universal in Tennessee. The Presbyterians appeared to have forgotten that they had any Confession of Faith or discipline, and the Methodists had laid aside their Discipline, and seemed to forget that they were bound to observe the rules contained therein, and as established from time to time by the General conference.

I visited the old stamping-ground, Sumner and Davidson counties, where I had labored in 1795, and again in 1798, and found a great change. The class meetings were free to all; the love-feasts open to all; and they were mixed up in such confusion that it was impossible to tell to what Church or denomination they belonged. The Western annual conference for the year sat at Strauther's, in Sumner county, Tennessee. Bishop Asbury presided. There was a general attendance of the preachers, and the conference sat in the house of brother Strauther, and the public exercises were in the woods at a stand in hearing of the house. The conference and the public exercises were of the same mixed character. To my astonishment, on the first day of the conference several of the Presbyterian clergymen were introduced into the conference, and remained during that day. When the conference adjourned I took brother M'Kendree aside, and stated to him my views on the impropriety of the course pursued in breaking down all our rules and regulations as Methodists; but especially in our annual conference, I observed to him, that many of our local brethren, and some who had been traveling preachers for years, were excluded a seat among us, while those ministers of another denomination were admitted and not objected to. I insisted on him, as the presiding elder, to enter his objection when we met the next morning. He admitted it was wrong, but said he could not broach the subject, as Mr. Asbury appeared to entertain such favorable notions of the union that then prevailed. I observed that I was no enemy to union and communion with any denomination upon proper principles, and if he declined I would bring the subject before the conference, and accordingly did so on the sitting of the conference next morning. I stated my objections at length, and cited our Discipline, and insisted that our rules established class meetings and love-feasts as wise and prudential means, and that they were peculiar to the Methodist Church. Other denominations did not consider them either wise or prudential, or they would introduce them into their Churches; and why should they wish to intrude on our privileges, while they, by their own showing, considered them no privilege? and in regard to the annual conference, the Discipline clearly pointed out who had the right to a place in their sittings, etc. Mr. Asbury decidedly opposed my views, and stated to the conference that I was but a young man, and referred the conference to some of Mr. Wesley's views and conduct on like occasions. No member of the conference took sides with me, but all remained silent; and when Mr. Asbury concluded his remarks, I made my rejoinder, and acknowledged that I was but a junior, but thought I understood Methodist Discipline, and that as a Church we were not to be governed by Mr. Wesley's views or the views of any other man, however aged, but by the rules laid down by the General conference; and if the Presbyterians, or any other denomination, had a desire to enjoy what we esteemed privileges, let them adopt them in their Churches, and then we would reciprocate, and not till then. When I concluded my observations I requested Mr. Asbury to give me my appointment in this country, and I assured him I would soon put a stop to the present mode of doing business. He observed that I was too cold for that climate; that I should go further north. And here our controversy ended; but we had no more Presbyterian ministers during the sitting of conference. Mr. Asbury was at that time not able to walk alone, from a rheumatic affection in his feet, and brother M'Kendree had to accompany him to the Holston country; and after they arrived in the settlement in the neighborhood of Knoxville, the subject of what I had said at conference was brought up, and Mr. Asbury acknowledged that I had taken the proper ground, and wrote me on the subject, stating that reciprocity was the true doctrine. He also wrote to Mr. Rankin and Mr. Hodges his views, and at the next conference at Mount Gerizim, 1803, he preached that doctrine to the conference.

From the conference at Strauther's, October, 1802, I received my appointment on Limestone circuit alone. I was appointed at the conference to attend the Legislature of Kentucky and obtain an act of incorporation for Bethel Academy. I performed that duty and arrived on my circuit late in November. I took with me Adjet M'Guire, a young man that had been lately licensed to preach, and employed him as a helper, which was afterward sanctioned by the presiding elder. When I entered upon my circuit, I found that, to a very great extent, the people were prejudiced against a married preacher, and I could find no house open at which I could board my wife, either for love or money. In this state of affairs I was brought to a stand. I had some little money, and found a few friends; and in those days I considered myself equal to any emergency, and immediately set about cutting logs for a cabin, and a few friends assisted me in getting them together, and I purchased some plank and brick, and in the course of a few weeks had a snug little room fitted up adjoining brother L. Fitch's, about three miles from Flemingsburg. During the time I was building my cabin I attended my Sunday appointments, and through the week attended to my work and collecting materials to fit out my cabin; and having accomplished that business, I entered regularly upon my work. The circuit had been much neglected the past year, and religion was at a low ebb, and we commenced in good earnest. The winter was severe and the congregations but small. On the opening of spring I commenced two days' meetings, and called together the local preachers to my aid. Early in June we had a two days' meeting at Union meeting-house, not far from Germantown; and on that occasion it pleased God to manifest his power in a very singular manner on Sunday, and the first-fruits was the conversion of brother Petticord's oldest daughter. Brother Petticord was one of the first race of Methodists from Frederick county, Maryland, and a relative of Caleb B. Petticord, who was admitted on trial as a traveling preacher in 1777. This meeting continued on Sunday night and part of Monday, and numbers were seriously affected. From this meeting the holy flame spread in every direction, and the work became general throughout the circuit, at Bracken meeting-house, and Shannon, and Flemingsburg, and Locust meeting-house, and at private houses, and our congregations became crowded night and day.

In August we had a four days' meeting at Shannon meeting-house. This was a time that numbers still living well remember. This meeting continued night and day, without intermission. I was employed night and day without sleeping for three nights. Brother M'Kendree preached on Monday morning, and while he was preaching the power of God rested on the congregation; and about the middle of his sermon it came down upon him in such a manner that he sank down into my arms while sitting behind him in the pulpit. His silence called every eye to the pulpit. I instantly raised him up to his feet, and the congregation said his face beamed with glory. He shouted out the praise of God, and it appeared like an electric shock in the congregation. Many fell to the floor like men slain in the field of battle. The meeting continued till late in the afternoon, and witnesses were raised up to declare that God had power on earth to forgive sin, and many did say he could cleanse from all unrighteousness. From this meeting the work went on with astonishing power; hundreds were converted to God; and one of the most pleasing features of this revival was, that almost all the children of the old, faithful Methodists were the subjects of the work.

Our last quarterly meeting was at Flemingsburg, at which brother Nicholas Snethen and brother M'Kendree attended, and preached in the power and demonstration of the Spirit. It was a time long to be remembered. There was one peculiar circumstance which I will relate. Old father Duzan, who had raised a numerous family of sons and daughters, and then had a son in the traveling connection, was surrounded by his family and engaged in prayer on the ground. Presently he was seen supporting his youngest son, and proclaiming aloud to those around, "Glory to God, he has converted my last child. Now let me, thy servant, depart in peace; for my eyes have seen thy salvation." This conference year closed with an increase for Limestone circuit of about five hundred. The people were anxious for my return for the next year. There were now houses enough open to receive me to live in and cost me nothing. The preachers who united in carrying on this work, were Benjamin Northcott, James O'Cull, Jarvis Taylor, Joshua Sargent, Jeremiah Lawson, Hugh Barnes, and Richard Tilton, together with many exhorters and leaders, who entered heartily into the work. This year ended the happiest days of my itinerant life; for the happiest days of a Methodist preacher is to be on a circuit where he can pursue a regular course and preach every day. I had the honor of lodging the Bishop one night, in the log-cabin I had built, while on his way to conference.

The conference this year was at Mount Gerizim, October 2, 1803. At this conference Mr. Asbury insisted that I should cross the Ohio and take upon me the formation of a new district in that new and wilderness country, and act as presiding elder. I took several days to think on the subject, and gave him for answer, that I considered myself not sufficiently qualified for such a responsible undertaking; but he would not take no for an answer, but appointed me presiding elder of Ohio district, which included all the settlements from the Big Miami up to the neighborhood of Steubenville, which was then called West Wheeling circuit, running down the Ohio, including Little Kanawha and Guyandotte circuits, in Virginia, and some settlements on Licking, in the state of Kentucky.

I entered upon my work about the last of October, 1803. The first quarterly meeting was at Ward's meeting-house—a new house built of rough beech logs—on Duck creek, Hamilton county, near where Madisonville is now situated—John Sale and Joseph Oglesby were the circuit preachers. This was then called the Miami circuit, and included all the settlements between the Miamis and as far north including the settlements on Mad river, as high up as the neighborhood where Urbana now stands, and east of the Little Miami as high up as the settlements on Bullskin, and all the settlements on the East Fork of the Little Miami, and a few settlements in Campbell county, Kentucky. This route the preachers accomplished in six weeks. We organized two quarterly meetings in the bounds, so that the presiding elder was two weeks in the bounds of the circuit, preaching nearly every day. The most easterly appointment was at brother Boggs's, on the Little Miami, a few miles from the Yellow Springs. From that point we generally started at daylight for the settlements on the Scioto, having between forty and fifty miles, without a house, to the first inhabitants at old Chilicothe. The Scioto circuit included all that tract of country inhabited on Paint creek out to New Market, Brush creek, Eagle creek, and Ohio Brush creek, and up the Ohio to the mouth of Scioto, and then up the Scioto to the Pickaway Plains, including Chilicothe and the settlements on White's creek, a four weeks' circuit. From thence one day's ride to the settlements in Hocking Valley, which was called Hocking circuit, which laid principally on that river and its tributaries, and a few settlements on the waters of Walnut creek. From New Lancaster we generally took two days and a half to reach the bounds of West Wheeling circuit, in the neighborhood where St. Clairsville is now located. This was a four weeks' circuit, including the settlements on the Ohio river, and extending back to the frontier settlements on the West Wheeling and Short creeks, etc. From this point we returned by the same route to New Lancaster, and then down the Hocking to Sunday creek and Monday creek, and then over to Marietta circuit. This circuit was up and down the Ohio from Marietta as low down as the settlements were formed, and up to the head of Long Reach, and up the Muskingum river as far as Clover Bottom and Wolf creek, and so down to the neighborhood of Marietta, and over the Ohio into Virginia on the waters of the Little Kanawha. This was called the Muskingum and Little Kanawha circuits. It was but a three weeks' circuit, and had one preacher. From the neighborhood of Marietta we started down the Ohio river by way of Graham's Station to the mouth of the Great Kanawha, and down to Green Bottom—brother Spurlock's—which was the first appointment on Guyandotte circuit. This circuit contained all the territory south and west of the Great Kanawha, and down to the mouth of Big Sandy and the settlements back from the Ohio river. This was a field of labor that required about eleven weeks to accomplish, and many privations. The Methodists were, in those days, like angels' visits, few and far between, and we were half our time obliged to put up in taverns and places of entertainment, subject to the disorder and abuse of the unprincipled and half-civilized inmates, suffering with hunger and cold, and sleeping in open cabins on the floor, sometimes without bed or covering, and but little prospect of any support from the people among whom we labored, and none from any other source; for there was no provision in those days for missionaries. But, notwithstanding all the privations and sufferings that we endured, we had the consolation that our labor was not in vain in the Lord. We were gratified in having souls for our hire, and rejoiced to see the wilderness blossom as the rose. New societies sprang up in various places, the circuits were enlarged, immigration increased, and the forest was subdued, and comforts multiplied. In the fall of 1805 I was removed from the Ohio district to the Kentucky district, and brother John Sale was appointed my successor. The Western conference for this year was held at brother Houstin's, in Scott county, Kentucky, October 2d. Bishops Asbury and Whatcoat attended at this conference. Our borders became greatly enlarged. We now included in the Western conference five districts, stretching from the Muskingum, in Ohio, to the Opelousas, in Louisiana.

The two years that I presided in the Ohio district laid the foundation for the future success of Methodism. We had been successful in introducing our doctrines into almost every neighborhood, and this formed a nucleus for the immigrants that were constantly arriving in the country. Numbers of Methodists from Virginia, Maryland, Pennsylvania, New Jersey, and the eastern states, settled in the Miami, Scioto, Hocking, and Muskingum Valleys, and a goodly number of valuable local preachers settled among them, and united with us in carrying on the good work of God, under the superintendence of divine Providence. Numbers of young men were raised up in different sections of the western country, and entered the missionary field full of zeal, and eminently pious, and by this means we were enabled to follow immigration and the wide-spread settlements.

In 1804 the number of circuits in the Western conference was twenty-six, and the number of preachers stationed was thirty-seven, and but one district in Ohio. In 1810, which included brother Sale's four years on Ohio district, the work had extended, and there were three districts north-west of the Ohio river, and twenty-one circuits; number of preachers, thirty-one. The number of circuits for this year in the Western conference was fifty-nine, and the number of preachers stationed was eighty-one. In 1804 the number of members in the Ohio district was one thousand, two hundred and fifteen, and in the bounds of the Western conference, nine thousand, seven hundred and eighty. In 1810 the number in Ohio was eight thousand, seven hundred and eighty-one; and in the bounds of the Western conference, twenty-two thousand, nine hundred and four. Compare this with 1798. Number of preachers in Ohio, John Kobler;

number of members, ninety-nine. Number of preachers in the bounds of the Western conference, fourteen; and the number of members, two thousand, five hundred and ninety-five. To compare the present number in the bounds of Ohio, in fifty-six years they increased from ninety-nine to at least one hundred and fifty thousand. Surely this is the Lord's doing, and it is marvelous in our eyes. In 1798 was the first introduction of itinerancy north-west of the Ohio; and one solitary pilgrim passed over the brook hunting up the lost sheep of the house of Israel; and now behold them spread into bands, not only in Ohio, but Indiana, Illinois, Michigan, Wisconsin, Iowa, Missouri, Arkansas, Mississippi, Louisiana, Texas, Minnesota, Nebraska, Salt Lake, Oregon, and California, all of which at that time was comparatively a vast howling wilderness!

The exposure and labor incident to my appointment brought on severe attacks of bilious fever. At one time my life was despaired of; and in the fall of 1805 Mr. Asbury thought best to remove me to the Kentucky district. Here I was among my old friends with whom I had fought many a battle sore, and dried up Enon, near to Salem, and caused the doctrines of unconditional election and reprobation to become a stench in the nostrils of those who calmly investigated the subject. I spent four years in that district with great satisfaction to myself, and also to the people whom I was sent to serve. There were but a few things that interrupted our harmony and peace. One was, that in consequence of my illness I could not attend a meeting where the sacrament was to be administered. I sent a deacon with instructions to administer, which was called in question by some, and complaint entered against me; but I sustained the position I had taken, on the ground that the deacon was directed to assist the elder in such cases, and I succeeded in my justification. The other was, the part I took with the local preachers in advocating their right to elder's orders, which was finally successful. In 1807 there was a meeting of the local deacons at my house, at which Bishop Asbury was present, and favored the plan. The agitation after this meeting settled down quietly, and my opponents remained quiet.

I was next appointed to the Salt River district, where I remained two years, during which time another difficulty arose. A traveling elder was accused of immorality; and among the charges and specifications were some of improper words. I examined the charges, and for improper words I, as his presiding elder, acted upon them officially, and did not submit them to the committee, for which they charged me at conference with maladministration; but the conference sustained me. We had in general very good times throughout the district; but the field was a large one, including a very extensive territory; consequently, at the end of two years I was willing to have some better situation, and received my appointment to the Cincinnati circuit. Here I had for my helper John Strange. We passed an agreeable year; and at the conference held at Chilicothe, in the fall of 1811, I was appointed to Cincinnati station, it being the first station in the state of Ohio. I organized the station, and many of the rules and regulations that I established are still in use. We had but one church in the city, and it went under the name of the Stone Church. I preached three times every Sunday, and on Wednesday night; and while stationed in that house my voice failed me. The Methodists being too poor to buy a stove to warm the house in winter, and on Sunday morning it being generally crowded, their breath would condense on the walls, and the water would run down and across the floor. The next conference I did not attend, but was appointed supernumerary on the Cincinnati circuit. I was not able to do much, but to give advice in certain cases. This year I closed my itinerancy, and sold my horse, bridle, saddle-bags, and saddle, and gathered up the fragments, and the fortune that I had made from twenty-six years' labor amounted to three hundred dollars. From the 9th of January, 1796, I traveled as a married man, no allowance being made for the wife. Part of the time sixty-four dollars was allowed a traveling preacher, and he must find his own horse and fixins, his own wardrobe and that of his wife, together with her board; and the other part of the time it was eighty dollars, still nothing for wife. I was the first married preacher in the west who traveled after marrying. I met with every discouragement that could be thrown in my way. Preachers and people said, "You had better locate." I shared equally with the single men when they were on the circuit with me, in order to keep peace. I bore all the murmurings and complainings from every quarter, and appeared at conference every year ready for work. One winter I had to use a borrowed blanket instead of a cloak or overcoat. That year my wife was among her relations, and well taken care of. Now a man is no preacher except he has a wife and family, whose allowance is one hundred dollars, and wife the same, and children provided for; house rent, fuel, and table expenses; the bishops' salaries to the full secured, and for presiding elders so much is apportioned among the circuits and stations. The allowance to many of the preachers of the present day varies from eight hundred to fifteen hundred dollars per year, while the poor superannuate must find his own house, pay his rent, furnish his own table, etc., and receive from the conference steward sometimes fourteen and twenty dollars, and sometimes as high as forty dollars; and how can a superannuate keep soul and body together on that dividend? I am superannuate in the

Southern division, and know not how I shall make out to live. My labors and sufferings to cultivate and prepare the way for my brethren in the Kentucky, Tennessee, and Ohio conferences, are all known to God and the Church, and my testimony is in heaven. None seem to care for my circumstances now. I am at present in my eighty-fifth year, and can not stay much longer in the tabernacle; but, through riches of grace in Christ Jesus, I have for me prepared "a building of God, a house not made with hands, eternal in the heavens."

CHAPTER IV.

MICHAEL ELLIS.

In sketching the life of this great and good man—we say great, because all true greatness must have goodness for its basis, and this he possessed in an eminent degree—we regret that history furnishes us no record of the date and place of his birth, except that he was born in the state of Maryland. He was among the first that embraced religion in that state through the instrumentality of Wesley's missionaries. The field was then white unto harvest, and laborers were much needed to gather that harvest; hence, they were thrust out in the order of God's providence, in a way that the wisdom of the men of the present day would hardly allow to be proper. But God's ways are not our ways, neither are God's thoughts our thoughts. He who with "a worm can thrash the mountains," can make the feeblest instrumentality and agency accomplish the mightiest results. Thus, in the early days of Methodism, men were called to preach the Gospel, and thrust out into the field, that even the Methodist Church at the present day would object to as not possessing the necessary qualifications for such a work. Young Ellis was thus called; and feeling that woe was him if he did not preach the Gospel, he commenced soon after his conversion to call sinners to repentance. In the year 1784 he was admitted on trial as a traveling preacher; and the first appointment which appears on the Minutes was the city of Baltimore. He may have been traveling under the elder some time previous to the above date, as that was the time of his appointment to Baltimore, but of this we have no information. At the same conference where Bishop Asbury was ordained to the episcopal office, he was ordained a deacon. This was in the year 1785, and the presumption is, that he was admitted in the year 1783.

The next year, which was 1786, he was appointed to Frederick circuit, and the following year to Fairfax, in the state of Virginia, where he was instrumental, under God, of accomplishing much good in the enlargement of the Redeemer's kingdom. In the year 1788, for want of that support for his family which the Church could not or would not give, he was obliged either, according to apostolic instruction, to "deny the faith and become worse than an infidel in not providing for his own," or to leave the ministry and serve tables to keep his family from starvation. One duty can never crowd out another; and his first duty being to feed and clothe his wife and children, he could not have been either called of God to preach and travel to their neglect, nor would God have blessed his ministrations while thus engaged. A great many zealous and efficient ministers of the Gospel have been compelled to close their mission on this account, throwing the responsibility upon the Church, where it properly belongs. If they that preach the Gospel shall live of the Gospel, according to the ordination of heaven, that Church which will muzzle the ox, or, in other words, withhold its support from the minister, will be held accountable in the day of eternity, if not in time, for its gross neglect and dereliction. In the providence of God, however, such Churches are usually visited in time like those of Asia, as Churches like nations are judged in time. Does it not meet the observation of every one, that those individual Churches who supply most liberally the wants of their pastors, and engage most heartily in all benevolent enterprises, are the most blessed with spiritual prosperity? With what heart, let us ask, can a minister of the Gospel dispense the word of life and distribute spiritual things to a Church full of riches and increased in goods, when his heart is borne down with care and anxiety about the next meal for his poor wife and children? It would take a faith greater than Abraham's to enable him to pour forth bright, glad streams from such a troubled fountain. We know it is said, "Let him trust in God. He ought not to be anxious about what he shall eat or wear. His treasure is in heaven; and, beside all this, his great Master had not where to lay his head." All this is well enough, but God will not send the ravens to feed him, nor command the stones to be made bread, when there is a Church abundantly able to supply his wants, and God has commanded that Church to give the laborer his hire.

Thus it was with Michael Ellis, and thus it has been with hundreds in the ministry of the Methodist Church. Finding that he must look out for himself, he removed, with his family, to Ohio, and settled in Belmont county. Here he went to work with his own hands, toiling hard all week and going out on the Sabbath to preach the Gospel to the destitute in his neighborhood. By his own industry he was enabled to rear a large and interesting family; and one of his sons is now, and has been for the last twenty years, a traveling preacher in the Ohio conference.

It was not till the year 1809 that we became acquainted with this father in Israel. His influence for God and religion, like that of the patriarch Abraham in Mamre, spread all over the country where he resided, and is felt even to this day. His family having grown up, so that by his oversight and the industrious, frugal management of his amiable and pious wife he could see his way again opened to enter the itinerant field, he accordingly, on the first of November, 1810, was readmitted into the traveling connection, and appointed to West Wheeling circuit, in the bounds of which he had labored for many years as a local preacher with great acceptability and usefulness. The next year he was returned to the same circuit, and such was his increasing popularity, even in the vicinity of home, that he would have been gladly received another year but for disciplinary restrictions. Some preachers soon wear out in their fields of labor, and their sermons become stale and tiresome to their hearers. Under such circumstances the congregations look with anxiety for the close of the year, when their appointments will terminate and they can have a change. Though some are disposed to think—and it may be rightly enough—that our economy, in removing preachers every two years, is calculated to produce a restlessness in the minds of the people and a desire for frequent changes, yet we know, as a general thing, that no minister who devotes himself to study, that his profiting may appear to all, being thus enabled to bring out of the well-stored treasury of his mind that rich variety which the themes of the Gospel so abundantly furnish, will be at all likely to wear out, or cause his congregation to wish for his removal at the expiration of two years. Instead of this, they become increasingly interesting, and are enabled the more effectually to adapt their discourses to their audiences, so as to give to saint and sinner their portion in due season. The desire for a change may arise, however, from other causes beside want of devotion to study. The preacher may render himself unpopular from an uncouthness or unpleasantness, not to say boorishness, of manner, or from a want of sociality or common sense in his judgment of men and things; that, though he possessed the learning of a Clarke, or the eloquence of a Whitefield, he could not, without that necessary combination of requisites in a preacher, make himself useful to the people of his charge. Every minister should study the character of his hearers; and thus, while in his ministrations he would "study to show himself approved unto God a workman that needeth not to be ashamed, giving to all their portion," he would gain favor in sight of all the people. Alas! with too many preachers all the ambition they seem to have in preparing for the pulpit, is to commit to writing or memory a few skeletons or sketches that they have taken from Simeon or Hanam, which are as likely to be as full of Calvinism as any thing else; and thus, as mere parrots, they "mount the pulpit with a skip," repeat their memoriter harangues, and then "skip" down again. The hungry sheep look up and are not fed. Instead of taking their Bibles and going into their study, if they have one, and if not, to the woods, and there, by prayer and close, laborious thought, after finding a subject adapted to their hearers, study it out in all its connections and bearings, filling their minds and hearts full of the theme, and then going, baptized with the Holy Ghost, into their pulpits, or school-houses, or log-cabins, and pouring out the garnered truths with their full hearts, alas! how many have not a single thought of their own, and are the mere automata through which others speak! But, again, there are others who are so wonderfully enraptured with any thing of a metaphysical or transcendental cast, that the plain, home, heart-searching truths of the Gospel are lost sight of, and, consequently, the hearers who wait upon such a ministry do not "*taste* the good word of God." It is so festooned with the flowers of rhetoric, or scented with the phrases of metaphysics, or incased with the technicalities of logic, that the mind neither comprehends, appreciates, nor enjoys the preaching, if it may so be called. We once heard Bishop Asbury say to a class of young candidates for orders, "When you go into the pulpit, go from your closets. Leave all your vain speculations and metaphysical reasonings behind. Take with you your hearts full of fresh spring water from heaven, and preach Christ crucified and the resurrection, and that will conquer the world."

Although brother Ellis could not be called a learned man in the sciences, yet he was a Bible student, deeply versed in the science of salvation, and one of the soundest, clearest doctrinal preachers we ever heard. He studied divinity in the school of Christ, and was trained under the professorship of Wesley and Fletcher. His heart was deeply imbued with the grace of God; and having attained the fullness of the blessing of the Gospel of Christ, the perfect love that swelled his heart rolled out to bless mankind. We doubt whether he ever preached a sermon in which he did not introduce the doctrine of Christian perfection as taught in the Bible, and preached by Wesley and Fletcher. It was the plain, old-fashioned, unvarnished doctrine of entire sanctification, without any reference whatever to the philosophy of the intellect, the emotions, and volitions; a simple faith that brought into the soul the life and love of God. One of his favorite texts, in the latter days of his ministry, was, "Jesus Christ, who is made unto us wisdom and righteousness, sanctification and redemption." His mode of treating it was, if we recollect rightly, something after this sort. After explaining how Christ is made to the believer wisdom, he would divide his subject into three parts; namely, justification, sanctification, and eternal redemption. These doctrines he compared to a ladder, the foot of which rested on earth, and the top of which entered heaven: justification, sanctification, and redemption were the three successive rounds of this ladder, over which the soul passes in its course to heaven. He would clearly describe the doctrine of justification by showing the nature and condition thereof, and its attestation by the Holy Spirit. Then he would describe the nature and condition of sanctification, and finally what the Bible teaches in regard to redemption and glorification in heaven. He seemed to be the living impersonation of his theme, passing through all the progressive stages of his subject till its close, when he would give a shouting peroration that would make every heart feel that the preacher knew and felt whereof he spoke.

Such preaching would not be likely to tire a congregation hungering and thirsting after righteousness, and such a preacher would not be likely to wear out. His heart was full of the love of God, and when he would pour out that heart, it was refreshing and fructifying as the "dews of heaven that descended upon the mountains of Zion, where the Lord commanded his blessing, even life for evermore."

In the year 1812 he was appointed to Knox circuit, and it was a year of great labor and comfort to the old veteran of the cross. His predecessor had sown the seeds of Arianism broadcast all over the circuit, and they had taken deep root and were springing up, choking the plants of evangelical piety. Six of the local preachers had embraced the error, and some of the most active and influential members had been beguiled from the faith as it is in Jesus. Such was the confusion and division occasioned by this heresy, that it seemed as if the whole circuit would be broken up unless it were speedily arrested. Ellis went to work with the sword of the Spirit, and, proclaiming the truth in love with its two-edged power, it soon separated falsehood from the pure Gospel, and soon all were enabled to discern the fallacy of Arianism and cling to the divine doctrine. In the year 1813 we were appointed to Barnesville circuit, and had the pleasure of having this eminent servant of God for our colleague. This was a year of great prosperity and blessing to the Church. The circuit, like all circuits of that day, was large, embracing part of Virginia, and lying on the waters of Duck creek, north-east of Marietta. On it there was no leading road, and nothing by which we could reach the settlements but a bridle path. The inhabitants, like all backwoods people in those days, lived by the chase; yet we have often seen in their rude log-cabins as powerful exhibitions of the power of Christianity as ever we witnessed in the more refined circles of society. The fare on a great portion of this circuit was too rough for an aged man like father Ellis, and we chose to do all the work during the winter, and let him attend the appointments where the fare was better and the traveling more easy. In the spring he greatly desired to go into this wilderness portion, and to gratify him we consented. At breakfast we said, "Eat hearty, father Ellis; we fear you are going into the wilderness to be tempted by the devil. You must prepare to eat raccoon, opossum, or bear meat, and, indeed, in some places you may not be able to get that." Nothing intimidated, the old soldier penetrated the wilderness, and, ere he returned, won many trophies for the cross of Jesus.

In the year 1814 he was appointed to the West Wheeling circuit, and the year following to Fairfield, where he continued to do the work of an evangelist, preaching a full and free salvation to all. On this circuit lived old father Walker, the father of Rev. George W. Walker, of the Cincinnati conference; and under the labors of Ellis and his colleague—Samuel Brown—the family were converted to God and joined the Church. The old gentleman was a stanch Roman Catholic, and raised his children in that faith; but there was a power in the pure, unadulterated Gospel, as preached by this venerable herald of the cross, that cut its way through the superstitions and dead forms of that corrupt Church, and brought the soul away from all priestly mediation and absolution directly to Jesus Christ, the great high-priest, for pardon and salvation. In the year 1816 he was appointed to Pickaway, and the following year reappointed. In this and all the fields of his toil, he was in labors more abundant, and many souls were gathered into the fold of Christ, being made the happy partakers of saving grace. But his work, as an itinerant, was done. In the year 1819 he received from the conference a superannuated relation, and continued therein, preaching whenever he was able, till his Master summoned him away from the field of his toil and conflict, to that eternal glory and reward he had so often described. He had taken up his abode in the town of Rehoboth, Perry county, Ohio, and there, full of faith and the Holy Ghost, he breathed out his soul into the hands of that Savior whom living he loved, and whom dying he went to embrace forever.

Brother Ellis was a man of fine personal appearance, dignified and courteous in his manners. He was a pleasant speaker, and there was an unction attended his sermons which commended them to every man's conscience in the sight of God. His example and influence will be felt in the Church for many years to come.

CHAPTER V.

ORIGIN AND PROGRESS OF METHODISM IN CINCINNATI.

Though Methodism is evidently a pioneer religion, admirably adapted in its economy to the early settlements of the country, and is generally found far enough in advance of all other religious denominations, yet, as it regards the early settlement of Cincinnati, the Presbyterian Church takes precedence. This may be accounted for by the fact that the original proprietors of the town were Presbyterians. In laying out the town they appropriated the south half of the square bounded by Main and Walnut, Fourth and Fifth streets, for the use of said society. In the autumn of 1790 the Rev. James Kemper organized a Presbyterian society, and the congregations met regularly every Sabbath on this square, under the shade of the trees with which it was covered, to listen to the word of God. After a few years on this spot the society erected a stout frame building, forty feet by thirty in dimensions. It was inclosed with clapboards, but neither lathed, plastered, nor ceiled. The floor was made of boat plank, laid loosely on sleepers. The seats were constructed of the same material, supported by blocks of wood. They were, of course, without backs; and here our forefather pioneers worshiped, with their trusty rifles between their knees. On one side of the house a breast-work of unplaned cherry boards was constructed, which was styled the pulpit, behind which the preacher stood on a piece of boat plank, supported by two blocks of wood.

In 1792 the Presbytery of Transylvania was held in this church, and it was the first ecclesiastical body ever held in the place. No other Church was organized in Cincinnati till seven years after the organization of the Presbyterian Church. The next Church was probably the Baptist, which was organized in the town of Columbia, about six miles above Cincinnati, and now forming the eastern suburb. We have seen a sketch of the old house as it stood a few years ago, and as it stands yet, for aught we know, with its clapboards falling off, windows broken, and dilapidated walls and chimney. Here the Baptist denomination, in early times, gathered together, from all parts of the Miami Valley and the adjoining state of Kentucky, to listen to the word of life and witness the celebration of their beloved ordinance in the waters of their western Jordan. For days their solemn associations have been held on this spot; and though the old sanctuary has gone to decay, and the adjoining grove has given place to streets and squares, occupied with dwelling-houses, still it is a green and sunny spot in the memory of every Baptist of the olden time.

In the year 1798 the Rev. John Kobler, a Methodist preacher, and one of the early pioneers, visited Fort Washington. He quaintly describes his first visit to the town of Cincinnati. We are indebted to the Western Historical Society for this description, as it is a reply to said Society in regard to the question, "When and by whom was the first class formed at Fort Washington?" Without giving any information in regard to the point from whence he started, he says, "I rode down the Miami river thirty-six miles to explore this region of country. I found settlements very sparse indeed, only now and then a solitary family. About four o'clock in the afternoon I came to an old garrison called Fort Washington, situated on the bank of the big river, [Ohio,] which bore very much the appearance of a declining, time-stricken, God-forsaken place. Here are a few log buildings extra of the fortress, and a few families residing together, with a small printing-office just put in operation, and a small store, opened by a gentleman named Snodgrass. This, I was told, was the great place of rendezvous of olden time for the Federal troops when going to war with the Indians. Here, alas! General St. Clair made his last encampment with his troops before he met his lamentable defeat; here I wished very much to preach, but could find no opening or reception of any kind whatever. I left the old garrison to pursue my enterprise, with a full intention to visit it again, and make another effort with them on my next round; but this I did not do for the following reasons; namely, when I had gone a second round on my appointment, and further explored the settlements and circumstances of the country, there were some places where the opening prospects appeared much more promising than what I had seen in Fort Washington; and I was eager to take every advantage of time and things, by collecting what fruit was already apparent, by forming societies and building up those already formed; so that in a few rounds I had nearly lost sight of old Fort Washington, and finally concluded that it would be most proper for me, under existing circumstances, at least for the present, to omit it altogether; so that in this statement I am sorry to say it is not in my power to lay before the honorable Historical Society that information for which they have inquired with so much solicitude, *When and by whom was the first class formed at Fort Washington?*" The immediate successors of Kobler, the Revs. Lewis Hunt and Elisha Bowman, did venture to visit the old Fort and preach occasionally; with what success, however, history does not inform us, and no living man can tell. But these were not the only Methodist sermons that were preached at Fort Washington in that early day by wandering itinerants, who ventured to lift up their voice to the inhabitants. It was visited by a man who is still living, and sits by my side in his parlor, on Longworth-street, who preached in the court-house as presiding elder of the district in 1804, and preached in the house of Mr. Newcome, a Methodist, on Sycamore-street, but a short time after the society was formed.

Thus it will be seen that fifty-six years ago there were no Methodists known in Cincinnati, though our Presbyterian brethren had a congregation and a place of worship. Cincinnati was then a country village, containing a few hundred inhabitants, and they of that class which usually congregate around military encampments. Those who were in any way interested on the subject of religion would not, in consequence of belonging to the Presbyterian or Baptist Churches—both of which were strongly Calvinistic—be likely to invite a Methodist preacher to come into their midst, especially in those early times.

At that time the name of Methodist was not known in the place, though the sequel will show that shortly after there were some residing within the limits of the town who were not only sympathetically inclined to Methodism, but had been members of the Church elsewhere. An opportunity was soon after afforded to develop the Methodist element that slumbered in the heterogeneous mass of which the society at Fort Washington was composed.

Away up on the East Fork of the Little Miami, in the wilderness, there lived a young and sprightly farmer. His place of residence, or, rather, the neighborhood, had proven a genial soil for Methodism; and here it took root and flourished like the vines and cedars of Lebanon. Here was a stronghold for Methodism; and from this point as a center went out Methodist influence over the land. Here were congregated together, at quarterly and camp meeting occasions, the thousands of our Methodist Israel scattered abroad. On the occasion of these holy convocations many a young and zealous member of the Church was called to exercise his gifts as an exhorter, while many an exhorter has, on the ground of gifts, grace, and usefulness, been raised to the more exalted and responsible station of a local preacher. The young farmer of whom we have made mention was a local preacher of more than ordinary talents. It became necessary for Mr. Collins—for that was his name—to visit Cincinnati, for the purpose of purchasing some salt. Being in the store of Mr. Carter, he asked that gentleman if there were any Methodists in the place. To this the storekeeper responded, "Yes, sir; I am a Methodist." The local preacher was taken by surprise at the joyful intelligence, and, throwing his arms around his neck, he wept. He then asked him if there were any more Methodists in the place. The response to this was equally full of joyous intelligence: "O yes, brother, there are several." This caused the heart of the sympathetic Collins to leap for joy. "O," said the zealous young preacher, "that I could have them all together, that I might open to them my heart!" "In this you shall be gratified, my brother, as I will open my house, and call together the people, if you will preach."

The upper room of brother Carter's house was fitted up by the introduction of temporary benches, while every effort possible was made to give the appointment an extensive circulation. What was the astonishment of all when night came to find that there were only twelve persons present! It seemed that Methodism could neither awaken opposition nor contempt. At other times and places it has been regarded either as a stern and stubborn error that must be put down by fair and lusty argument, or when in the event reason failed, and it must be plied with ridicule, it has been called "the wildest vagary that ever sickened the imagination of a fool;" but the first sermon that was preached in Cincinnati by a Methodist preacher became neither the butt of reason nor of ridicule.

One of that number was our beloved and lamented sister Dennison, the daughter of brother Carter, at whose house the first sermon was preached. She recollected distinctly the meeting and all the incidents connected with it, and related to the writer of this many interesting facts a short time previous to her death. Though she was then but quite young, she was a professor of religion, and was with the little band assembled in that upper room on Front-street, between Walnut and Vine. She realized the good word of God, and the powers of the world to come. It was a memorable time for Methodism in Cincinnati. It was as the planting of a handful of corn on the tops of the mountains, the increasing and ever-multiplying products of which were to shake with the fruitage of Lebanon. It was the first time the Gospel, unfettered by decrees, sounded its clear notes in this then rising village. A small class was formed, which constituted the nucleus of the Church, as the few houses scattered here and there constituted the nucleus of a mighty city—the Queen City of the West. The formation of that first Methodist society was the introduction of a new element—not as it was in the old country, to rouse the stagnant forms of religion, and stir them into ife, but the introduction of an element into a new and ctive state of society, growing up under the cold and tereotyped forms of a religion from which all animal eeling was excluded, thus destined to rouse or control, and dapting itself, without changing its principles, to all the hases of social life.

The young preacher being greatly refreshed by the interview he had with the Methodists of Cincinnati, returned home; and some short time after he was regularly admitted into the traveling connection, and for many long years of hard service in the itinerant field he proved himself one of the most eloquent, talented, and successful ministers of the Gospel the west has ever known. Were it not that a biography of this distinguished and eloquent divine has already been written, and that by a gifted pen, we would feel constrained to record some touching, unwritten incidents of his life.

The next sermon preached to this infant Church was in a house on Main-street, between First and Second streets. The preacher was the Rev. John Sale, at that time traveling on the Miami circuit. This sermon, however, was preached under different circumstances from the first, and the congregation was increased to thirty or forty persons. After preaching a proposition was made to organize a society in the usual way, and according to the Discipline of the Church. Accordingly, a chapter was read from the Bible; then followed singing, prayer, and the reading of the General Rules of the society. All then, who felt desirous of becoming members of the society, and were willing to abide by the General Rules as they had been read, came forward and gave in their names. The number who came forward on that occasion was only eight, consisting of the following; namely, Mr. and Mrs. Carter, their son and daughter; Mr. and Mrs. Gibson, and Mr. and Mrs. St. Clair. Mr. Gibson was appointed the leader.

A regular Church being organized, arrangements were made to have preaching regularly every two weeks by the circuit preachers. The society received an accession in the ensuing spring by the arrival in town of two Methodist families; namely, those of Messrs. Richardson and Lyons, and subsequently by the arrival of Messrs. Nelson and Hall, and their families. This little band of Christians were closely attached to each othér, and were one in opinion, sentiment, and action. The cords of brotherly-love bound them together so strongly, and the natural affinities growing out of their relationship to each other as Methodists were such, that no spirit of discord was ever allowed to break in upon the harmony of their society, or for a moment interrupt the even tenor of its joyous way. With Christian charity they bore each other's burdens, and with Christian zeal and fidelity they watched over each other for good. Each one seemed to be the insurer of the other's reputation, and felt himself as responsible for his upright character as though he was his special guardian: hence, every thing that indicated, in the slightest degree, a departure from the path of holy rectitude, would at once awaken the liveliest apprehensions and interest on the part of the rest. If any one of the members was absent from class meetings, they were immediately inquired after, and as much care and solicitude manifested as if it had been the unexpected absence of some member of a family.

This mutual interest in the spiritual welfare of each member of the Church was what constituted the true secret of the early character of Methodism; and the great success which marked its progress in every country where it has been established, is to be attributed more to the recognition of this wholesome, social regulation than to any other peculiarity of doctrine or Church government.

Meetings were held in the little old log school-house below the hill, and not far from the old Fort. The location of this school-house was such as to accommodate the villagers; and as its site was somewhere not far from the intersection of Lawrence and Congress streets, it is presumed that this portion of the town was the most thickly inhabited. Sometimes the rowdies would stone the house; and on one occasion Ezekiel Hall, a zealous Methodist, and one who always was present to lead the singing, was taken by the rowdies, after meeting, and carried to his home on Main-street, where, after giving him three hearty cheers for his zeal and fortitude, they left him. The rioters were followed by two very strong young men, who were members of the Church, and had determined, at all hazards, to protect their feeble brother. The young men were Benjamin Stewart, now living near Carthage, in this county, and Robert Richardson, now living on Broadway in this city. Mr. Hall was the father of our late postmaster, and his wife is still living, an estimable member of the Methodist Church.

The first love-feast ever held by the Methodists in Cincinnati, was during a quarterly meeting in 1805. It was held in the court-house. There being no permanent place for holding meetings, and the society being greatly annoyed by many changes, it was at length resolved that efforts should be made to build a church, that Methodism might not only have a name but a local habitation. Accordingly, a lot was procured between Sycamore and Broadway, on Fifth-street. This was a large lot, and the rear part of it was appropriated, like that in the rear of the Presbyterian Church, for a cemetery—a very injudicious arrangement; but no one at that time would, for a moment, have entertained the idea that the crowding, pressing, teeming thousands of the city would make such encroachments as have been made upon the resting-places of the dead. The idea of burial in the city, whether judicious or not, is not so much the question as the fact, the broad, staring, standing fact, of man's avariciousness, and the disposition to appropriate to his interest even what belongs to the dead.

The society having procured the lot, commenced, in

the year 1805, to erect a stone church. This church was finished and dedicated to the worship of God the following year. From this point the society increased rapidly, and it was not long till the native eloquence of the backwoods preachers and the zeal of the membership attracted large congregations, and the church was too small to hold the crowds that collected there to hear the word of life. The building, however, was but small, only being about twenty feet wide and forty long. To accommodate the increasing masses who crowded to the "Old Stone," the rear end was taken out and twenty feet of brick added to it. Notwithstanding this enlargement, still there was not a sufficient room, and it was resolved to make arrangements for other enlargements. It was concluded to take out the sides of the brick part and extend the building out each way twenty feet, thus giving the church the form of a cross. After some time this last improvement was made; and though the congregations still continued gradually to increase with the ever-increasing population, yet it was many years before any movement was contemplated to meet these wants. At length, however, it was resolved to tear down and build on the site of the Old Stone a mammoth church, which would not only be the parent Methodist church in Cincinnati, but which would be sufficiently large for all occasions.

Colonies had already gone out from the old parent church, and had located preaching-places in several parts of the city. One of these was located on the corner of Plum and Fourth streets. Here the brethren erected a plain, substantial brick church, which, in process of time, was called the "Old Brick," to distinguish it from the "Old Stone;" and it was also designated by a certain class as "Brimstone Corner." This was doubtless in allusion to the fact, that here the sinner was visited with the terrors of the law, and Sinai's thunders were made to play upon his guilty ears. The Methodist preachers of those days preached the law as well as the Gospel, and they aimed, in every discourse, to give to saint and sinner their portion in due season, even if, in doing so, they should violate the unity of the subject. Indeed, it mattered but little what were the subjects selected, they usually had enough of repentance, and faith, and earnest invitation to Christ in their sermons to save a soul. Another charge was formed in the northern portion of the city, which was called Asbury, and also one in Fulton, denominated M'Kendree Chapel.

The time had at length come for the erection of a large central church, and the arrangements being made, the "Old Stone," with its brick appendages, was torn down, and from its ruins rose a mighty structure, denominated Wesley Chapel. It was dedicated in 1831; at that time the largest church in the place, and at the present time capable of holding a larger congregation than any building in the city. On account of its capacity as well as its location in the very heart of the city, it is selected on all great occasions. The address of the Hon. John Quincy Adams, on the occasion of laying the corner-stone of the Astronomical Observatory, was delivered here. Here the various large benevolent societies hold their anniversaries. It was here to listening thousands the eloquent Bascom delivered his lectures on the evidences of Christianity; and it was in this old cradle of Methodism the logical and earnest Rice delivered his course on the subject of Romanism. Here the Wesleyan Female College holds its Commencements, and annually crowds every seat, and aisle, and avenue, and gallery with eager listening thousands. But the time would fail to tell of all the associations that have met and mingled in old Wesley. Many have been the joyous shouts that have echoed from its venerable walls, and many have been the seasons of refreshing here enjoyed by God's people during the years of its existence. Here the General conference has held its sessions, the Parent Missionary Society and the Sunday School Union their anniversaries; and here the tribes of our Israel may repair from the east and the west, the north and the south, in all time to come.

The "Old Brick," of which we have already spoken, was built in 1822; but after several years, during which it became a place of hallowed memories, on account of the numerous conversions which had been witnessed at its altars, it was necessary to enlarge the borders of our western Zion in this place, and hence preparations were made to erect a new church. In the mean time, however, a colony had gone out from Fourth-street and had built a fine church edifice on Ninth-street. Instead of tearing down and rebuilding, it was determined to purchase a lot on Western Row, between Fourth and Fifth streets. Here the congregation built a very neat and commodious church, which was denominated "Morris Chapel," in honor of our beloved western Bishop. No congregation in the city has enjoyed more uninterrupted prosperity than this enterprising charge. Its leading members are men of energy and activity; and whatever good work their hands find to do, they do it with all their might. The Sabbath school and missionary causes have claimed their undivided and earnest attention; and, perhaps, no charge in our whole connection more vigorously or systematically engages in carrying out all the benevolent enterprises of the Church. The Sabbath school connected with this charge sent out, several years ago, a missionary to Germany, from whom regular communications were received, from year to year, which were read to the school, and had a great tendency to foster and increase the missionary spirit among the teachers and scholars of the school. For the present it is engaged in supporting a missionary among the Waldenses, under the direction of the Rev. Dr. Cooke, of the French conference.

But Methodist enterprise did not stop here. Asbury Chapel, in the northern part of the city, was consumed by fire, but the zealous brotherhood erected near its ruins a new and handsome edifice. Colonies from Morris Chapel and Ninth-Street went out, having among their number some of the most zealous and efficient of their membership, and founded Christie Chapel, and Salem, York-Street, and Park-Street Chapels, all having now energetic and active memberships; and last, not least, in that direction, from these, in their turn, was formed Clinton-Street Chapel, a young but vigorous branch of Methodism. In the mean time Bethel Chapel was founded by a colony from old Wesley and M'Kendree, and the trustees are now engaged in erecting a new and beautiful church on Ellen-street. Nor do we stop here; colonies from the different charges have founded societies and erected churches on Walnut Hills, the Mears neighborhood, and Mount Auburn.

We must not omit to mention, in our short sketch of the Methodist Church in Cincinnati, Union Chapel, the only pewed Methodist church in the city. It was originally composed of a few members of different charges, who, preferring family sittings to the old mode of separate sittings, associated together and purchased Grace Church, on Seventh-street, formerly belonging to the Episcopalians. They asked for recognition by the authorities of the Church, and for a pastor to supply them with preaching; and this being denied them they employed a local preacher, organized a Sabbath school, and set up a provisional government. They continued to make application for recognition, from time to time, to the bishops and the annual conference, but were denied, on the ground that it was contrary to Discipline, though it was urged that the same rights and privileges were enjoyed by numerous Methodist Churches elsewhere. Their case was finally submitted to the General conference, and that body struck out of the Discipline all portions pertaining to the advisory regulation, "let the men and women sit apart, without exception, in all our churches." So soon as this action was had Union Chapel was recognized, and a preacher sent to organize the congregation into a regular society. This Church has gone on gradually increasing in numbers and prosperity. The trustees have enlarged and remodeled their house of worship, and it now presents one of the most chaste and beautiful Gothic fronts in the city. Its interior is also elaborately and beautifully finished. The society deserves all praise for the enterprise manifested, not only in securing a church which is an honor to Methodism in the city, but for the zeal which it has shown in the Sabbath school and missionary cause; having, according to the showing of the Society of Religious Inquiry, the largest Sabbath school in the city, and having pledged itself to sustain a missionary to Rome, whenever the way shall be opened by the grant of a toleration from the Pope equivalent to that so liberally enjoyed by his subjects in this country.

While we speak thus of Union Chapel, we would not pass in silence other charges. They have all done well and deserve praise. We have already spoken of "Morris," and we might say the same of Ninth-Street, Bethel, Asbury, Christie, and Park-Street, and the sister charges, and, indeed, we doubt whether any denomination in the city, in proportion to ability, has done more than the Methodist Church in supporting the various benevolent institutions of the day. If we despise any body, it is the croaker who is ceaselessly howling about the Church having lost her primitive simplicity, and power, and influence in the world. We believe this day, under God, she is doing more for the conversion of the world than she ever did; and while there is quite as much zeal as was manifested in olden time, there is a thousand-fold more liberality. We have every thing to say favorably of Methodism in Cincinnati; and though she has not made that advancement she should have made, and might have made, yet she has far outstripped, in this respect, all other Protestant denominations, and those, too, who occupied all the ground before her.

We are not yet done with Methodism in Cincinnati. There are other Churches bearing the name which, though not exactly under the same ecclesiastical government, are, nevertheless, branches from the old stock, vigorous and healthy, and partaking of the nature and fatness of the root from whence they sprang. The Protestant Methodist Church, on Sixth-street, is a large, intelligent, and enterprising society, supporting one or two mission Churches in the city. The Methodist Episcopal Church South has also a large and flourishing congregation. This society is composed of some who were originally the stanchest friends of the old Church—intelligent, benevolent, and enterprising, and ready for every good word and work; and though we exceedingly regret the occasion which prompted them to a separate organization, still we look upon them as members of the family, having one grand patronymic, and we shall ever hold them as brethren beloved. God forbid that the time should ever come when we shall be so cramped by a headless and heartless bigotry, destitute alike of thought and feeling, that we can see no good beyond our narrow domicile, and have no emotions of brotherly kindness for those of another fold.

There is another interesting item connected with the history of Methodism in Cincinnati which, although we have not yet alluded to it, constitutes, if we judge correctly, the crowning glory of Methodism in the city, if not in the entire west. The establishment of a mission to the German population in our midst, among the thousands of infidel Rationalists and semi-infidel Roman Catholics from Germany, was the beginning of an enterprise which has been attended with the most grand and glorious results.

As commenced Methodism in Cincinnati, in an upper room, with but twelve hearers, fifty years ago, so commenced the German mission eighteen years ago, in the upper room of a shanty in a dark alley. The preacher was a professor of Greek and oriental literature, from the halls of Tubingen, a fellow-student of the infidel Strauss; but who, in the wilds of the west, among the Methodists, found salvation in the name of Jesus, and leaving his professor's chair, in the halls of Kenyon, went out the called of God to preach the Gospel of salvation to his dying fellow-countrymen. Though, like his livine Master, he came to his own, and his own received iim not, but persecuted him, and cast out his name as vil, he still persisted, and with a zeal and perseverance haracteristic of the German, when once convinced that e is right, he labored on, and God blessed the word to ie awakening and conversion of his countrymen. The ission from time to time received reinforcements from ie number of the converted, and one after another, as me progressed, God called the Germans into the field. ne of the early converts, who was a learned infidel, beme a bright and shining light, and carried the Gospel m Cincinnati to his brethren in Missouri, where mul-udes were converted; and that same minister is now at e head of a successful mission in Germany. Others nt every-where preaching the word, as the disciples nt out from Jerusalem; and first in the large cities, n in the villages and country places of the west and south, wherever there were Germans, these messengers carried the glad tidings of salvation. Nor did the mission stop in the west; it went back to the east and the large cities and towns, as far as Boston; had missionaries sent to them, and societies were organized all over the land from Maine to Louisiana. From this mere handful of corn what a mighty harvest has already been gathered! In Cincinnati there are four churches, some quite large; and in almost every large town where there are Germans, churches have been erected. No mission was ever established since the days of Pentecost that has been attended with greater success. There are now in the United States and Germany upward of one hundred ministers, and twelve thousand members—a larger number of ministers and members than was embraced in the entire west fifty years ago. In connection with the operations of the German Church, through the indefatigable labors of Doctor Nast, a German Methodist literature has been gotten up, consisting of translations of standard works on theology, Christian experience, biography, etc.; and the Doctor is now employed in writing a Commentary on the Bible adapted to Methodist theology, for the use of the ministry and membership. For many years the Doctor ha been editor of the Christliche Apologete, which has large circulation. Doctor Jacoby, of Bremen, also edit and publishes a religious sheet in that city. But as w propose only a sketch—a mere outline, we must close.

The next thing of a denominational character to whic we invite attention, as serving to show the enterprise (Methodism in Cincinnati, is the establishment of female college. In the fall of 1840 Doctor Elliott ga an account of his travels in the east, in the Advocate, which he called the attention of the Church to the i portance of female education, and continued to urge t subject till the year 1842, when, at his suggestion, meeting was called for the purpose of devising ways and means for establishing a female collegiate institute. The following are the official proceedings of the meetings held on the subject:

"At a special meeting of the preachers of Cincinnati, held in the editors' office of the Western Christian Advocate, May 4th, 1842, the following persons were present: L. L. Hamline, C. Elliott, J. L. Grover, G. C. Crum, W. H. Lawder, A. Miller, W. Nast, T. Harrison, L. Swormstedt, J. P. Kilbreth, and W. Herr. The meeting was organized by calling L. L. Hamline to the chair, and appointing W. Herr Secretary. At the request of the Chair the object of the meeting was explained by C. Elliott; namely, to consult on the expediency of taking measures to establish in this city a female institute of the highest possible grade. The following resolutions were presented and adopted.

"*Resolved*, That in the opinion of the meeting it is deemed advisable to call a public meeting to consider the practicability of establishing in Cincinnati a female institute.

"*Resolved*, That a committee, consisting of Messrs. Elliott, Hamline, Herr, Kilbreth, Wright, Grover, Crum, Lawder, Miller, Neff, H. Decamp, Thomas, Williams, and Nast, report a plan of the institute to be laid before the general meeting.

"On motion, it was agreed that the committee on the plan meet on next Wednesday, at 4 o'clock, P. M., at the editors' office.

"On motion, the meeting adjourned.

"L. L. HAMLINE, *Chairman*.

"W. HERR, *Secretary*.

"*May* 11, 1842.

"The committee on the plan met pursuant to adjournment: present, S. Williams, C. Elliott, J. L. Grover, T. Harrison, and W. Herr.

"S. Williams was called to the chair. The report of the committee was called for, which being read by C. Elliott, Chairman, was unanimously adopted.

"*Resolved,* That W. Herr and J. L. Grover be a committee to fix on the time and place for a public meeting, in order to submit the plan of a female institute in Cincinnati, and give due notice of the same.

"There being no further business, on motion the committee adjourned.

"S. Williams, *Chairman.*

"W. Herr, *Secretary.*

"Pursuant to public notice given, a meeting was held in Wesley Chapel, May 20th, 1842, in order to consult on the practicability of establishing in Cincinnati a female collegiate institute. L. Swormstedt was called to the chair, and W. Herr was appointed Secretary. After prayer, C. Elliott, Chairman of the committee, appointed in the primary meeting to report on the subject of a female institution, presented the following plan, detailing the general principles of the institute:

"At a meeting of the undersigned persons, held May 11, 1842, the following proceedings were had:

"Whereas, There is great need for improvement in the system of female education, as it respects the extent and accuracy of the course; and whereas, the members of the Methodist Episcopal Church in Cincinnati, both need and are able to maintain a female literary institute of the first order, of the following description, with such other marks of excellency as time, experience, and circumstances will point out; it is, therefore, important that such be established as soon as possible.

"The contemplated institution should embrace all the branches of female education, from the highest to the lowest, to such a degree as not to be exceeded, if possible, by any similar institution in the whole world.

"It should comprehend the following departments: 1. The common English department, embracing all those branches comprised in a thorough course of primary instruction.

"2. The collegiate department, which should comprise a good collegiate course of instruction adapted particularly for females.

3. "The Normal department, in which pupils will be prepared to become efficient teachers for schools of every grade, particularly the common schools, and female academies.

"4. The department of extras, in which those various branches, not necessary for all, yet useful for some, should be taught.

"The following branches, in connection with such others as are connected with a thorough course of instruction, should be taught:

"Reading; Writing; Arithmetic; Geography; History; Grammar; Rhetoric; Logic; Book-Keeping; Needle-Work in all its branches; Drawing and Painting; Music, vocal and instrumental; Mathematics, Natural Philosophy, Astronomy; the Natural Sciences, embracing Zoology, Botany, Mineralogy, Geology, Chemistry; Languages, as English, Latin, Greek, Hebrew, German, French, etc.; Mental Philosophy; Moral Philosophy; Biblical Studies, such as the Chronology, History, Geography, Antiquities, Evidences, etc., of Christianity. Other branches, not mentioned, will be arranged with the foregoing, in systematic order, so as to form a most complete course when put together.

"The following are some of the general principles, or characters, which should designate the institution:

"It should be a Methodist institution to all intents and purposes, so that the principles of Christianity, as taught by the Methodist Episcopal Church, would be constantly inculcated; and a full course of sound Biblical instruction should be learned by all; and all Methodist children should, without exception, go through this course thoroughly, in view of their becoming good Sabbath school teachers after they leave the institution, and as far as their services are needed while they continue in it. Yet children whose parents do not approve it, need not commit our catechisms, nor receive our peculiar views; but they must conform to our mode of worship and general regulations.

"The ornamental branches, as Music, Painting, etc., will be pursued in reference to utility and the practical purposes of life; and in accordance with just but enlightened views of the pure religion of Christ.

"It will be desirable that the institution should furnish all the aid in its power toward the education of poor female children and girls, both for their individual benefit, and the good of the public, in preparing them to be efficient teachers.

"A boarding-house would be necessary for the purpose of accommodating those pupils who would come from a distance; while the children of the citizens would be taught both as day scholars and as pursuing any one branch of study taught in the institution, yet under proper and salutary regulations.

"The city of Cincinnati possesses peculiar advantages for such an institution. By the public conveyances centering or touching here, the intercourse from any point is easy. The advantages of city institutions would be esteemed by many. Important aids could be derived from literary gentlemen in filling up some of the professorships.

"It might be sufficient public endowment to furnish the necessary buildings and literary apparatus, leaving the tuition to support the teachers, if possible; except that room be left to make provision for poor female children and girls.

"The undersigned believe that the members of the Methodist Episcopal Church in Cincinnati need such an institution, both for the literary and religious improvement of their children. It is also confidently believed that they are abundantly able to undergo the expense both of tuition, building, and apparatus. And though the present times are unfavorable in reference to the erection of buildings, the remedy to this would be to rent for the present, and afterward to purchase a lot and build at a time more favorable for procuring funds than the present.

"Entertaining the views stated above, we whose names are annexed, deem it advisable to call a meeting of the members and friends of our Church, for the purpose of examining the subject more thoroughly, in such way as they may think proper, for the purpose of adopting immediate measures toward the speedy and complete establishment of a high female literary institute.

CHARLES ELLIOTT,	WM. H. LAWDER,
L. L. HAMLINE,	ADAM MILLER,
WM. HERR,	WM. NEFF,
J. P. KILBRETH,	HARVEY DECAMP,
J. F. WRIGHT,	N. W. THOMAS,
J. L. GROVER,	S. WILLIAMS,
G. C. CRUM,	W. NAST.

Cincinnati, May 11, 1842.

"Whereupon it was moved that the report just read be adopted.

"On motion a committee of twenty-three was appointed, with instructions to proceed forthwith to establish, as soon as practicable, an institution according to the plan. The following persons composed the committee: Bishop Morris, Chairman; J. L. Grover, W. Neff, J. Lawrence,

Wesley Chapel charge; W. Herr, J. G. Rust, H. Decamp, Fourth-street do.; G. C. Crum, W. Woodruff, A. Riddle, Ninth-street do.; W. H. Lawder, S. Williams, G. W. Townley, Asbury do.; M. G. Perkiser, Burton Hazen, Mr. Litherberry, Fulton do.; W. H. Raper, J. F. Wright, L. Swormstedt, C. Elliott, L. L. Hamline, W. Nast, and A. Miller.

"It was moved that the proceedings of the several meetings, properly signed, be forwarded for publication in the Western Christian Advocate.

"On motion, the meeting adjourned with benediction.

"L. SWORMSTEDT, *Chairman.*

"W. HERR, *Secretary.*"

A house was rented on Ninth-street, from Mr. Woodruff, for the beginning of the school; but being found too small, the committee the following year procured the large and beautiful residence of Mr. John Reeves, on Seventh-street, for the rent of which ten brethren became individually responsible. In a short time the committee, through Dr. Elliott, procured the services of the Rev. P. B. Wilber and lady, from Virginia, and the Institute was commenced under favorable auspices. In November, of the same year, the committee published the course of study in the Preparatory and Collegiate Departments, embracing a thorough literary and classical course, requiring six years to complete it. The next month the Advocate announced the names of the Board of Instruction, as follows: Rev. P. B. Wilber, Principal; Mrs. C. Wilber, Governess; Miss Mary De Forest, Assistant; Miss Emeline Tompkins, Assistant in the Primary Department; W. Nixon, Professor of Music. A building had been erected on the grounds of the Reeves mansion for the accommodation of the pupils, and the school was represented as in a flourishing condition.

In the month of February, 1843, it was announced,

through the columns of the Advocate, that the second session of the Institute would commence in the new and elegant college building, on Seventh-street, with a large increase of students. The following spring session was opened with a still greater accession of pupils; and during the preceding winter the Legislature of Ohio granted an act of incorporation, conferring all the powers and privileges necessary for an institution of the highest grade. To the faculty were added two additional assistants; namely, Miss Stagg and Miss Harmon. Arrangements were also made for procuring a philosophical and chemical apparatus. At the close of the session lengthy and highly-commendatory articles, relating to the examination of the classes, appeared in the Cincinnati Gazette and Cincinnati Chronicle. The next session commenced with still an increase of boarding and day scholars, and at its close the number amounted to one hundred and fifty. The Cincinnati Chronicle contained the reports of the several Examining Committees, consisting of E. P. Langdon, A. N. Riddle, S. Lewis, W. Green, O. M. Mitchell, S. Williams, J. Stille, R. S. Foster, S. A. Latta, J. P. Kilbreth, S. Morrison, and Thomas Biggs, all of whom expressed their entire satisfaction of the thoroughness of the young ladies in their respective studies. At the same time a letter appeared from the pen of Professor Merrick, commending the Institute to the patronage of the public. The Commencement exercises of 1845 constituted a brilliant era in the history of the institution. They were held in the Ninth-Street Methodist Episcopal Church, which was crowded in every part. B. Storer, Esq., delivered an eloquent address before the Young Ladies' Lyceum, after which the graduates read their compositions, and received their degrees as Mistresses of English and Classical Literature. The plan of the original proprietors was now no longer an experiment, and the Female College from this point started out on its high and glorious career.

The boarding-house and college edifice, notwithstanding enlargements had been made, being inadequate to accommodate the numerous pupils that flocked to the institution from various parts of the country, it was resolved by the Board to purchase the large mansion owned by Henry Starr, Esq., on Vine-street. This property extended from Vine to College-street, and the grounds around it being large and tastefully ornamented, it was considered the most desirable location in the city. The purchase was in due time made, and a large college edifice erected on College-street sufficient to accommodate five hundred pupils. From year to year the college has sent out scores of graduates to all parts of the country; and the numbers enrolled on the catalogue have gradually increased, till now there are nearly five hundred. Large as are the preparations which were made to accommodate the pupils, yet during the past year the Board found it necessary to put up an additional building, and to purchase additional grounds. Under the superintendence of Mr. Wilber and his lady, the institution, from the beginning, has gone on prospering, and its patronage is greater than all other institutions of a similar character in the city combined. From a small school, with two or three teachers, the Wesleyan College has now nearly five hundred pupils, and nineteen teachers in the various departments of study.

It may not be improper to notice in this connection the Wesleyan Cemetery, located on an eligible and beautiful tract of ground, about four miles from the city, up the Millcreek Valley. The old cemetery in the city, belonging to the Church, having been filled, or nearly so, with the remains of the dead, it was not only deemed advisable, but necessary, to seek a burial-place elsewhere

Accordingly, the selection above alluded to was made; and in the year 1842 the ground was laid out and dedicated to the purposes for which it was designed—a peaceful resting-place for the dead. Many tasteful improvements have been made on this rural spot since it was laid out into burial-lots. In the center, on an elevation, which commands a fine view, is the Cemetery vault, surrounded by a circular, graveled carriage-way, with roads leading in every direction through the grounds. The numerous monuments, family-vaults, and inclosures of this Cemetery present a fine appearance; and when we gaze upon these quiet and beautiful resting-places the grave is robbed of half its terrors. To have a lot in this city of the dead, removed from the din and strife of business, and the avaricious hand of man, which would even invade the sacred precincts of the grave itself to gratify its lust for gain, is a pleasant reflection. Here affection and friendship in quietude may drop their tears and plant their flowers over the graves of their beloved.

To show the reader the improvements which have been made on the grounds, as well as those which are contemplated, we subjoin an extract from the report of the Directors of the Cemetery, recently presented. It is as follows:

"The carriage-ways have been, wherever practicable, widened from being only twelve to twenty feet, and well graded and graveled. The grounds have been cleared of weeds and bushes, and smoothed, so as to show a neat, pleasant, grassy surface. At the rear, in the western part of the grounds, a romantic grove of natural growth, of stately beeches, overshadows some secluded dells. Through these dells wind well-graded and, where necessary, paved roads, inviting to pensive walks. A new preachers' lot, thirty-two feet square, has been beautifully located, and is to be well inclosed and adorned. Trees and shrubbery have been set along the ways, and it is intended to have and keep all the footwalks of the Cemetery well graded and sodded, and skirted with shrubs and flowers. A provision has been made to have a nursery at the ground, for a variety of trees and shrubbery and flowering plants, to readily supply persons using the Cemetery for interment. This is done by leasing an acre, to the right of the main entrance, for such purpose, and under contract to furnish such supply. A new, two-story brick sexton's house has been erected, and is now occupied, at the left of the main entrance. This house is built in a rural style, which has so pleased the eye that at least one model of it has been already taken for imitation. It is also in negotiation to have a new brick Methodist Episcopal chapel erected, at the right of the nursery before mentioned, on low ground rather unfit for interments, one hundred feet in front, by one hundred and fifty feet deep from the center of the turnpike, or highway, to be exchanged for the present high grounds of the chapel, of very good quality for interments, and from which there is an extensive and beautiful landscape view, at the north-west corner of the Cemetery tract. A committee is appointed to examine the project of such exchange, and, if feasible, effect it. It is also intended further to grade and smooth the Cemetery tract, and to set and cultivate entirely around it a hedge of Osage orange; and, in fine, completely to improve and embellish the grounds, as much as the best taste and the funds of the Directors will admit."

CHAPTER VI.

FRANCIS POYTHRESS.

We have no means of ascertaining the time, or the place of the birth of the above-named pioneer preacher. From the Minutes we learn that he was received on trial, in the traveling connection, at the conference held in Baltimore in May, 1776. The conference was at that time in ecclesiastical connection with the British conference, and the preachers were all bound to yield implicit obedience to Mr. Wesley's authority, taking the doctrines and Discipline, as contained in the Minutes, for the sole rule of their conduct. The preachers were forbidden to administer any of the ordinances, and the people were required, with their pastors, to attend the Episcopal Church and receive the ordinances there, particularly those who resided in Maryland and Virginia. No preacher was allowed to reprint any of Mr. Wesley's books without his consent.

Some of the conversations which occurred at the conferences, and are recorded in the Minutes, are worthy of observation. Among others were the following: No preacher, who sustained the relation of a helper or assistant, was allowed to make any alterations in the circuit, or take in any new preaching-places, without consulting his superior. Every exhorter was prohibited from going to any place to exercise his gifts, except where directed. The preachers were required to meet the children once a fortnight, and examine the parents with regard to their conduct toward them. No local preacher was allowed to preach without having a written permit every quarter. All preachers were required to rise at four o'clock—at the latest five o'clock. They were required to continue in close connection with the Church; that is, the Church of England, and request the clergy to administer the ordinances to their people. Traveling preachers who held slaves were required to give promise of freedom. All members who distilled grain into liquor were disowned. In regard to singing, all the preachers who had any knowledge of the notes were required to improve it by learning to sing true themselves, and keeping close to Mr. Wesley's tunes and hymns.

After his admission, young Poythress was appointed to Carolina circuit. In 1778 he was appointed to Hanover circuit, and the succeeding years, up to 1784, to Sussex, New Hope, Fairfax, Talbot, and Alleghany. In 1785, which was the year following the conference at which a separate ecclesiastical organization was agreed upon, and the societies assumed the name of the Methodist Episcopal Church, he was stationed in the city of Baltimore. In the year 1786 he was appointed presiding elder of a district composed of the following circuits; namely, Brunswick, Sussex, Amelia, Williamsburg, Orange, Bedford, and Hanover. The succeeding year he was presiding elder of a district composed of Guilford, Fairfax, New Hope, and Caswell circuits. In 1788 he was associated with James Haw as elder of a district embracing Lexington, Danville, and Cumberland. The following year he was alone on the above district, and continued from year to year, the district being enlarged from time to time by the addition of new circuits, till the year 1797, when, from excessive labors, occasioned by the most fatiguing travel and hardships, such as would break down any man of the present day, he was placed in supernumerary relation, and John Kobler succeeded him on the district. In 1797 he again entered the effective ranks, and was appointed elder of a district composed of New River, Russell, Holston, and Green. We give the names of the circuits composing the districts at that early day, because the districts had no name by which they could be otherwise designated. The practice of naming the districts was not adopted till the year 1801.

The next year he was sent back to his old district. In the year 1800 he was sent to a district in North Carolina, embracing fifteen circuits. His removal to a new field, among strangers, and the subjection, if possible, to greater hardships than he had endured on his former fields, alone and friendless, without a companion, save the companionship which he found at different and distant points among his brethren, preyed heavily upon his system, shattering his nerves, and making fearful inroads upon a mind naturally of a too contemplative, if not somber cast; and seasons of gloom and darkness gathered around him. He should at once have desisted, and sought that rest and society for which he so much longed, among the friends and companions of his youth; but, alas! the necessity that rested in those days upon a Methodist preacher, stern as fate, kept him at his post, and he toiled on till his shattered frame, like the broken strings of a harp, could only sigh to the winds that swept through it; and his mind, in deep sympathy with his brain, became alike hattered and deranged. The next year he came back to Kentucky, but the light of the temple was gone, and the ye which shot the fires of genius and intelligence, now wildly stared upon the face of old, loving, long-tried riends as though they were strangers. Here he remained till death released him and sent his spirit home. Poor Poythress! Bravely didst thou toil and endure ardness on the well-fought field. A campaign of twen--four years of incessant toil in the gloomy wilds of the west, away from friends and loved ones at home, proved too much for thy nature to bear. But thou art gone "where the wicked cease to trouble, and the weary are at rest."

The Rev. Thomas Scott, a personal friend of the deceased, and himself one of the early pioneers of western Methodism, has furnished, among other interesting biographical and historical sketches, an account of some personal reminiscences connected with the melancholy fate of this zealous and indefatigable itinerant, which we subjoin:

"Our acquaintance with him commenced in April, 1794, and continued without much interruption for about six years, during which period we learned from him the following particulars: On the death of his father he inherited a handsome personal and real estate; and being, in early life, thus left, without any one to control his actions, he yielded to the impulses of his passions, which were violent, and rushed into all the follies and vices of youth. The circumstance which brought him to review his past life, was the reproof of a lady of elevated standing in society. Her reproof carried conviction to his heart. He left her house in confusion, and on his way home resolved to mend his ways. He commenced reading the Scriptures and praying in secret—soon saw and felt the exceeding sinfulness of sin, and groaned to be released from its galling chain. That led him to inquire after those persons whom he supposed capable of instructing him in the right way; but for a long time he sought in vain. At length he heard of the Rev. Deveraur Janet an Episcopalian clergyman of learning and deep piety then residing in a remote part of Virginia, whom he visited, and with whom he remained a considerable time hearing and receiving instruction. Having at length obtained redemption in the blood of Jesus, he soon becam sensible of his call to the ministry. He conferred not with flesh and blood, but immediately commenced his itinerant career, preaching the Gospel of the grace of God to all who would hear. This was prior to the time in which our Methodist preachers reached that part of Virginia in which he lived. On one of his preaching excursions through the southern parts of Virginia and North Carolina, he fell in with one of our traveling preachers—whose name we have forgotten—with whom he formed an acquaintance, who furnished him with the doctrines and Discipline of our Church, as drawn up by Mr. Wesley. These he read and attentively considered, and being convinced they were based on the Scriptures of divine revelation, he applied for admission, and was received into union and fellowship in the Church.

"The Minutes of the several annual conferences show all the circuits he traveled, except one, and districts over which he presided. They are as follows: 1776, Carolina. We are unable to name the circuit he traveled the following year; but from the facts that in 1778 he was received into full connection, and appointed to the charge of Hanover circuit, we infer that he traveled some circuit in 1777. In 1779, Sussex; 1780, New Hope; 1781, Fairfax; 1782, Talbot; and 1783, Alleghany. In that year, we believe, he extended his ministerial labors across the Alleghany Mountains on to the waters of the Little Youghiogheny. In 1784, Colvert; and 1785, Baltimore. In 1786 he was ordained an elder in the Church, and presided over the district composed of Brunswick, Sussex, and Amelia circuits. From the fact that in 1786 he was ordained an elder, we infer that in 1785 he was ordained a deacon; and if so, he was among the first of our American preachers who were ordained to that office. In 1787 he presided over the district composed of the circuits of Guilford, Halifax, New Hope, and Caswell, and in 1788 he was transferred to Kentucky; and, in conjunction with the Rev. James Haw, appointed to preside over the district composed of the Lexington, Danville, and Cumberland circuits. Haw, we believe, presided over the latter, and Poythress over the two former of these circuits. In 1799 Haw's functions as presiding elder ceased, and Poythress presided over the entire district. In 1790 Madison and Limestone circuits were formed, and added to his district. In 1791 the circuits south of the Kentucky river were reformed, the name of Madison being dropped, and that of Salt River substituted; and brother Poythress continued to preside over the district. In 1792 the following circuits were added to his district: Greenbrier, Cowpasture, Bottetourt, and Bedford. In 1793 the four circuits last named were taken from his district, but Hinkston circuit, then formed, was added to it. There was no other change made in the bounds of his district during the years 1794, 1795, and 1796, except that in this last-named year Shelby circuit was formed, and, together with Logan and Guilford, added to it. In 1797 Shelby circuit was dropped, and the Rev. John Kobler was appointed presiding elder, and the Rev. Francis Poythress supernumerary, over the district. In the fall of that year brother Kobler crossed over on the north-west side of the Ohio river, and formed the Miami circuit, and brother Poythress resumed his station on the district, over which he continued to preside till the end of that year. In 1798 the Rev. Francis Poythress and Jonathan Bird were appointed presiding elders of the district composed of New River, Russell, Holston, and Green circuits, and Rev. Valentine Cook was appointed presiding elder over the Kentucky district. Shortly after brother Cook's arrival in Kentucky—and we feel quite sure it was before he had completed one round on his district—he received instructions from

Bishop Asbury to take charge of Bethel Academy, then on the decline for want of a suitable teacher, and brother Poythress was instructed to take charge of the district. Cook, therefore, took charge of the Academy, Poythress of the district, and Bird remained on the station to which he had been appointed. In 1799 New River, Holston, and Russell, Green and Miami circuits were added to the Kentucky district, and brother Poythress was appointed presiding elder over it. Late in the fall of that year his bodily and mental powers gave way and fell into ruins. In 1800 he was, however, appointed presiding elder of the district composed of Morganton and Swanino, Yadkin, Salisbury, Haw River, Guilford, Franklin, Caswell, Tar River, Newbern, Goshen, Wilmington, Contentney, Pamlico, Roanoke, Matamuskeet, and Banks, but his affliction rendered it impracticable for him to take the station assigned him.

"Upon inspecting the bound Minutes, page 245, it will be seen that the Rev. William M'Kendree was, in that year, appointed presiding elder of the district composed of Greenbrier, Bottetourt, Bedford, Orange, Amherst, Williamsburg and Hanover, and Gloucester circuits, and that no presiding elder is named for the Kentucky district. So soon as Bishop Asbury received information of the malady under which brother Poythress was suffering, he gave instructions to brother M'Kendree to proceed to Kentucky and take charge of the district; and about the latter end of the summer of that year brother M'Kendree came on to the district. In 1802 and 1803 the name of brother Poythress stands recorded in the Minutes among the elders, but without any station being assigned him; after which we anxiously sought for his name, but it was not there. We have heard that he died many years since, but when and how he died we are uninformed.

"Bishop Asbury visited Kentucky for the first time in 1790, after which he never visited that state—if we rightly remember—till subsequent to the year 1800; and during these periods brother Poythress presided over each annual conference which sat in Kentucky, and the stationing of the preachers and government of the societies within his district were almost exclusively confided to him by the Bishop.

"Bishop Asbury was an excellent judge of men. He was intimately acquainted with brother Poythress; and the stations to which he appointed him furnishes conclusive evidence of the estimate he set upon him as a man and Christian minister.

"Brother Poythress was grave in his deportment, and chaste in his conversation, constant in his private devotions, and faithful in the discharge of his ministerial duties. We have no recollection of his having ever disappointed a congregation, unless prevented by sickness or disease. As often as practicable he visited from house to house, instructed and prayed in the family. Among the preachers he, like most other men, may have had his particular favorites, but all were treated by him with due benevolence and Christian respect. He was unwearied in his efforts to unite the traveling and local ministry as a band of brothers, so that their united efforts might be exerted in furthering the cause of God. As the weight of all the Churches in his district rested upon him, he sensibly felt the responsibility of his station, and put forth his utmost efforts to discharge, with fidelity, these important trusts which had been confided to him. The education of the rising generation he deemed to be intimately connected with the interests of the Church, and the result of that conviction was the erection of Bethel Academy. The erection of that institution, we are quite certain, met the approbation of Mr. Asbury, and a majority of the traveling and local preachers of that day.

"The conversational powers of brother Poythress were not of a high order; yet when he did engage in general conversation, he maintained his part with propriety, evincive of an extensive knowledge of men and things. His rank as a preacher was not much above mediocrity. He was, however, sound in the faith, in doctrine, in purity. There are many words in common use which he could not pronounce correctly; this we attributed to the loss of his teeth.

"He was—if we rightly remember—about five feet eight or nine inches in hight, and heavily built. His muscles were large, and when in the prime of life, we presume, he was a man of more than ordinary muscular strength. He dressed plain and neat. When we first saw him, we suppose, he had passed his sixtieth year. His muscles were quite flaccid, eyes sunken in his head, hair gray—turned back, hanging down on his shoulders—complexion dark, and countenance grave, inclining to melancholy. His step was, however, firm, and general appearance such as to command the respectful consideration of others. He possessed high, honorable feelings, and a deep sense of moral obligation. In general, he was an excellent disciplinarian. He endeavored to probe to the bottom each wound in the Church, in order that a radical cure might be effected; but would never consent to expel from the bosom of the Church those who evidenced contrition and amendment. And when free from the morbid action of his system, to which it becomes our painful duty to refer, we esteemed him to be a man of sound discriminating judgment. We, however, claim not for him exemption from error, the common frailty of man, and therefore concede to our excellent friend Daviess, of Kentucky, that he may have inflicted a wound on the character of the Rev. Benjamin Ogden. But we can not concede it as a fact that brother Poythress was influenced, in his conduct, by an impure or wicked motive. We were too long and intimately acquainted with him to harbor, for one moment, an idea so uncharitable and derogatory to his Christian character.

"We never had the pleasure of personal acquaintance with brother Ogden, but having heard him preach his last sermon east of the Mountains, in 1786, when on his journey, as a missionary to Kentucky, we read, with great satisfaction, Mr. Daviess's vindication of his character. We, however, thought there were, in that vindication, some expressions a little too harsh, and calculated to lead others to an erroneous conclusion respecting the character of brother Poythress.

"Symptoms of insanity were, at times, discoverable in brother Poythress several years prior to the time he ceased to travel and to preach, and such may have been his situation at the time the unpleasant circumstance occurred to which brother Daviess refers. We, therefore, put it to him to say whether the vail of Christian charity ought to be drawn over actions induced by a morbid excitement of the system, materially affecting, at the time, his intellectual faculties.

"During the latter part of the summer, fall, and winter of 1794 and 1795, brother Poythress, at times, exhibited the appearance of a man whose mind was drawn off from surrounding objects; and in that situation he would remain for one or more hours, when his system appeared to react, and he would engage in conversation as usual. At other times he complained of giddiness and pain in his head, and his stomach and bowels appeared to be affected with flatulency and acrid eructations. A general listlessness, irksomeness, and disgust seemed to overwhelm him. His countenance appeared sad and sullen, and he evinced an utter aversion and inability to engage in business of importance. At such times, he usually betook himself to bed, but did not appear to sleep soundly. These symptoms became more frequent during the forepart of the year 1795, and would sometimes last for hours. Near the close of the summer of 1795 the Rev. Aquilla Sugg, who traveled the Lexington circuit, in consequence of bad health was rendered incapable of performing effective service; and, at the request of brother Poythress, we took charge of the circuit till the ensuing spring. Our first quarterly meeting was held in a small log meeting-house, not far from Versailles, Woodford county. On Saturday brother Poythress arrived just before the time for commencing the public exercises—complained of being exceedingly unwell, and went to bed. In a few minutes he called, and said, 'Brother Scott, you must conduct the quarterly meeting, I can take no part in the public exercises.' On returning from meeting we found him still in bed, but finally prevailed on him to get up. We then walked out together, but had not proceeded far out of the hearing of others, when he suddenly stopped, and said, 'Brother Scott, I am a ruined man; a conspiracy has been formed against me by my sister Prior, Mr. Willis Green, and brother Simon Adams. My sister Prior charges me with having kept back part of the price of some negroes I sold for her several years since; Mr. Willis Green accuses me with having embezzled part of the money I collected for Bethel Academy; and brother Adams accuses me with having taken advantage of him in the purchase of a horse; the officers of justice are now in pursuit of me. I shall soon be incarcerated in prison, my character ruined, and the Church disgraced.' I assured him I knew each of those individuals to be his fast, adhering friend, and incapable of harboring a suspicion injurious to his character, and that he might rest assured that they had not formed a conspiracy against him. But all I said had no effect, and he pertinaciously insisted that what he had said was true, and said, 'they were then engaged in drawing others into their conspiracy.' During that conversation his countenance exhibited a ghastly appearance, and his whole frame trembled. On returning to the house he again retired to bed, where he remained—if we rightly remember—with his head generally covered, till the next Monday morning, when he was again prevailed on to get out of bed. After he had taken some refreshments, we again walked out together, and I urged him to return home to his sister's, assured him no conspiracy had been formed against him, and that if all he imagined were true, it was far better for him promptly to meet the danger than to attempt to flee from it like a coward. That advice seemed to strike the right chord, it immediately vibrated, and after a few minutes he answered, 'It is, perhaps, best promptly to meet the danger, but I can not do so, unless you attend and conduct the quarterly meeting for me at Browder's meeting-house, near Bardstown, on next Saturday and Sunday. That meeting must not be neglected.' We promised to comply with his request, and he returned to his sister's. That was the first clear and unequivocal evidence of partial insanity which we recollect of having noticed in brother Poythress—insanity as it respected three most intimate friends; for the conspiracy, and the causes leading to it, which he supposed to exist, had no existence except in his own heated imagination, and, for the time being, it was found to be impracticable to remove those delusive ideas from his mind.

"We were confident no conspiracy had been formed against him, as he imagined, and still we entertained fears that, in the particular cases named, he had yielded to the temptations of the archenemy of souls; and that a conviction of his crimes, and fear of detection had produced the effects we witnessed. Having, however, since that time, acquired some little knowledge of the symptoms which often exhibit themselves in partial insanity, the fears we then entertained have entirely vanished. We mention this, in order to show how extremely careful we ought to be, not to suffer suspicions injurious to the character of another to make a lodgment in our minds.

"Agreeably to promise, we attended the quarterly meeting, and in meeting brother Poythress he exclaimed, 'Why, upon earth, did you suffer me to leave you? It was all delusion. My sister met me as usual.' Early in the year 1797 he was confined by affliction; but whether his mind was affected during his affliction we are entirely uninformed. The last time we saw him was in the forepart of the winter of 1800. The balance of his mind was lost, and his body lay a complete wreck. His labors in the Church militant were at an end, but the fruits of his labors still remain.

"We are not aware that any hereditary taint existed, which, in its ultimate range, dethroned his reason; but we can readily imagine that the seeds of that dreadful malady were sown in his system by the constant exposures and sufferings during the war of the Revolution, and the twelve years he traveled and preached in the then almost wilderness of the west. Among the eight pioneers of Methodism in Kentucky and Tennessee in he year 1788, the name of Francis Poythress stands preminent. By those intrepid heroes of the cross the foun-ation of Methodism was laid in those states, on which thers have since built, and others are now building. heir names ought to be held in grateful remembrance y all who love our Lord Jesus Christ in sincerity and truth; but among all, we are inclined to the opinion, there is not one of them to whom the members of our Church, in those states, owe a greater debt of gratitude than to Francis Poythress."

In some notes appended by Samuel Williams, Esq., making a few alterations in the above narrative in regard to some dates and places, we have an item or two relating to the close of his life, which it may be proper to give. At times, we learn from these notes, he would converse rationally upon many subjects, while on other subjects he was hopelessly deranged. He was taken to his sister's, who lived twelve miles south of Lexington, Ky., where he remained till he died. He has gone, we trust, to that world where, in bright, unclouded intellect, he now gazes upon the scenes of eternal life.

CHAPTER VII.

BARNABAS M'HENRY.

The Rev. Barnabas M'Henry was among the first apostles of Methodism in the western country. He entered the itinerant connection in the year 1787. He was then but a youth, scarcely having reached his majority. Considering the dangers and hardships to which wandering itinerants were exposed at that early day in the west, the leaving all the endearments of a happy home, must be considered as an act of moral heroism of which but few would be capable at the present day. But as God raises up the men for the times in which they live, we must not be too exact in running our parallels or contrasting the past with the present. If we have not the men for scenes of toil, and hardship, and danger, it may be a comfortable reflection, at least, to know that they are not wanted, and the circumstances of the times do not demand them. We believe there is as much genuine zeal and devotion in the Church now as there ever was, even in the days of the apostles and primitive Christians, though not as generally diffused among the membership. If Methodist preachers in those days had, in the language of President Harrison, to live just as though they had taken the vows of poverty upon them, and had to face the dangers and difficulties that beset their path alone and unattended, we should rejoice that though the offense of the cross has not ceased, yet the times have been so wonderfully changed by the mild, humanizing, and ever progressive spirit of Christianity, that none are called to pass through the same trials and persecutions for Christ's sake. In those early days Methodism was a thing of contempt, and a Methodist preacher was considered as a special object of ridicule. Every conceivable method was resorted to for the purpose of caricaturing the preachers and their doctrines. Songs were written and sung, while specimens of Methodist sermons, perverted and distorted, were published broadcast, to bring odium upon the society. Grave preachers and pious deacons and elders were found, who would engage unscrupulously in this work. We knew ourselves a reverend divine who, at parties, would amuse his flock by getting up a mimic class meeting, interspersing it with occasional ditties and a shout. We do not say this because we wish to revive unpleasant memories, or to show up the conduct of those who claimed all the religion, and learning, and decency of the land; but simply as a specimen of the general contempt which prevailed in certain quarters for these "rude, uneducated circuit riders." Sometimes the very almanacs would be filled with songs and caricatures of Methodist preachers; and they were in as great demand as Davy Crockett almanacs were a few years ago. We were taught to believe that Methodism was of the devil, and no better than witchcraft. Here is a specimen of the sermons preached by Methodist preachers, and believed by many to be genuine. We found it in the almanac:

"Breathren, breathren, breathren! The word breathren comes from the tabernacle, because we dwell therein. If you are drowsy I will arouse you. I will beat a tattoo on the parchment cases of your consciences, and will whip the devil about like a whirligig among you."

It cost something in those days to be a Methodist, and especially to be a Methodist preacher. Young M'Henry, however, counted the cost, and joined the despised people. In process of time he was licensed to preach, and, being admitted into the traveling connection, was appointed to Yadkin circuit, North Carolina. In the year 1788 he was appointed to the Cumberland circuit, on the very borders of the white population. Here we find him, in company with a few others, occupying the entire field, and following the tides of immigration to their most distant homes for the purpose of preaching to them the Gospel of Jesus Christ. Traveling, in those days, was attended with great danger as well as difficulty. The Indians, on seeing their hunting grounds invaded by the pale faces, were wrought up to the greatest fury, and would, in revenge, mercilessly attack their invaders. The missionary band was obliged to take their lives in their hands and risk all in the great enterprise in which they were engaged. They had no missionary society, with its funds and sympathies, to support and cheer them in their toilsome work; but the best of all was, God was with them, and hundreds of those wanderers from civilization were happily converted to God, while the cabin and block-house were made to resound with the praises of the Almighty, and the wilderness and solitary places often resounded with the shouts of the converted.

Speaking of this band the eloquent Bascom once said, in reference to a narrative of their deeds: "To give the story an intense and thrilling interest, it need only be told true to nature and to the actual developments of experience. There is something so fresh, so racy, so charming in calling up the historical reminiscences of by-gone days, that in whatever form or garb I meet the facts, it is only to wonder and admire. How little is known of the courage and heroism of the early apostles of Methodism in the western world! What a mere tithe of information has even the Church respecting her worthiest sons! The modern methods of missionary toil throw very little light upon this subject. More is *said* now and less *done.* We report to the full amount of our achievements, and facts are often anticipated by a detail of hopes. Not so with these early pioneers; they labored, suffered, and triumphed in obscurity and want. No admiring populace cheered them on. No feverish community gazetted them into fame. Principle alone sustained them, and their glory was that of action. Many of these men had minds of no common mold, and richly stored with varied knowledge. Even a century in a single community produces few such men as Barnabas M'Henry and Valentine Cook. They were men by themselves, and their memory would adorn the history of any Church in any age. The same is true of others; and I am anxious that the recollections, as far as practicable, concerning them, may be saved from oblivion. How much worthless stuff is now recorded, while incidents of so much interest are looked upon as unworthy of record or inquiry! Do not too many prefer the shallow and the meager, if it be modern, to the deep and lofty traits of character belonging to an era anterior to ours? Is there much hope that really great men will multiply among us, unless we duly appreciate and study the character and elements of greatness in those by whom we have been preceded? If I have been of any service to the Church, or to the world, much of the result is owing to the study of character in early life. Providentially thrown into the pulpit and upon the field of ministerial action at the age of sixteen—the mere dawn of manhood—I taught myself to learn the formation of character, in view both of goodness and greatness, by observing closely the striking characteristic both of the living and the dead claiming these attributes.'

The father of the writer of this sketch once preached a thanksgiving sermon, in which he said, "We backwood people ought to thank God most heartily for two things namely, the Indians and the Methodist preachers; for in the settlement of this great country the Indians kept the white population from scattering into clans and taking possession of certain districts of country, claiming it, and forming a government of their own, and finally going to war with each other, thus confining them to the government of the country. While the waves of population rolled out westward the Indians rolled them back again, and kept them together. Then the itinerant Methodist preachers, in the true spirit of their Master, followed up the emigrant from block-house to block-house, and from station to cabin and camp, and the voice of mercy and salvation was heard, and the Sabbath regarded." To this work M'Henry addressed himself with a zeal and devotion worthy of so great a cause.

In the year 1789 he was appointed to the Danville circuit, in company with Peter Massie as a colleague. While on this circuit he encountered much opposition from the Baptists, who verily thought they were doing God's service in making the most extraordinary efforts to hedge up the way of Methodist preachers. The preachers of that denomination published, from their pulpits and elsewhere, the most exaggerated and ridiculous statements imaginable about Methodist doctrines and usages, and every means was resorted to to prevent the people from going out to hear the preachers; but the very course they took only excited their curiosity to hear, and thus brought them into notice. Thus the foolishness, if not the wrath of man, was made the means by which hundreds were brought to hear the Gospel of a free salvation, and multitudes embraced its provisions and were saved. Persecution always has failed, and ever will fail, to put down the truth. The history of Paganism and Romanism is abundant proof of this. The apostle says, "We can do nothing against the truth but for the truth;"

and we have often known systems of error themselves dragged into notice, and made an object of sympathy, solely on account of a mad, misguided opposition. The best way in the world to put down error is to preach up the truth. The fire that a crazy zealot would call down from heaven to consume the adversaries of his peculiar faith or practice, will be as likely to consume himself as his opposers.

So it was, all the opposition these "free-grace preachers," as they were termed, met with, only served for the furtherance of the Gospel; and like the persecutions against Paul, which carried the Gospel to Rome, and introduced it to the palace of Cesar himself, so were the persecutions of the early Methodist preachers made the instrument, in the Divine hand, of bringing the doctrines of repentance, and faith, and salvation, to many who would not, in all probability, have heard them as dispensed by itinerants.

In the year 1790 M'Henry was sent to the Madison circuit. This field of labor was at that time said to be the most stubborn and unpromising, occupying, as it did, the most uncivilized portion of Kentucky. It seemed to be a place of grand rendezvous for fugitives from justice from the older states. The whole district of country was missionary ground, as this was the first time it was found upon the Minutes. In this field the laborious itinerant did the work of an evangelist. Though men may be guilty of crimes which may send them abroad from the haunts of justice and civilized society, yet it would be difficult for them to flee to any place where the Methodist preacher would not find them, and in their dark retreats offer to them the blessings of pardon and salvation. They might escape from the law and the rigor of justice, but the Gospel, with its offers of pardon would find them out, and their sin-burdened souls would be invited to partake of its full and glorious provisions. Those upon whom others were disposed to look as reprobates, shut out from the pale of God's mercy, and doomed by an irreversible decree to death and hell, were regarded by these heralds of the cross as redeemed by the Son of God; and though their crimes were of the deepest dye, even unto "scarlet and crimson," yet the blood of Jesus could wash them white as mountain snow. It was, doubtless, on account of this indiscriminate offer of salvation that their preaching was so obnoxious to the reigning orthodoxy of that day. Many a dark, unrighteous heart was changed through the instrumentality of such preaching, from nature and sin to grace and holiness, and lawless men were made obedient subjects of government and respectable members of society, who otherwise might have continued the enemies of God and man. As the result of his labors this year, there were left on the circuit at its close two hundred and twelve white members and eight colored.

The following year the subject of our sketch was appointed to the Cumberland circuit. Here he labored with great success and usefulness. The population was quite sparse, and the rides long and fatiguing. Notwithstanding all this, however, he girded himself for the work, and labored on in faith and hope. The Methodist preacher then had but one work, and he devoted himself exclusively to that. Being fully impressed with his call to preach the Gospel, he could not turn aside to engage in land and stock speculations, or enter into the noisy, wrangling field of politics, nor even sit down to the more honorable and useful employment of teaching school or taking a professorship or presidency in a college, or an editorship or agency, however important; the Holy Ghost had moved him to call sinners to repentance, and the great work of saving souls was all in all to him. Nor had he any time for writing books, and precious little for reading any but his Bible and Discipline. Being shut up to these to a great extent, as John Bunyan, in Bedford jail, was confined to an old Bible and a Concordance, like that man of God, he could map out the path of life, and picture the glories of heaven and the glooms of hell with a vividness and a power that made all hearts feel their reality. The preachers of those days did not suffer themselves to be carried away into the endless mazes of metaphysical speculation, or to be lost in the fogs of an occult philosophy; but bathing their vision in the eternal sunshine of God's truth, they came down, like Moses from the burning mountain, full of love and radiant with glory.

In the year 1792 M'Henry was appointed presiding elder of the Holston district, including Green River, New River, and Russell circuits, embracing an extent of country that would now cover a half dozen conferences. Here he was exposed to the savages and all the difficulties of traveling, without roads, bridges, or ferries to cross the streams; yet he would, with the most indomitable zeal, urge his way through the tangled thicket and dense forest, and across the rapid rivers and over the craggy mountains, preaching Christ and him crucified to the dwellers in the log-cabins of the most desolate regions. Burning with a love to save souls for whom his Master died, he was borne onward in his glorious career, and many precious seals to his ministry will hail him on the shores of immortality as the instrument of their conversion to God. The succeeding year he was appointed to the charge of a yet larger district, including Bedford, Bottetourt, Greenbrier, and Cowpasture circuits. It is almost incredible, at this day, for one to be told the labors and hardships of the early pioneers of Methodism. We fear that the zeal of the preachers of the present day would be severely tested, if they were required to cultivate similar fields; and yet such is our faith in the power of Methodism, under God, that we believe if the field were here there are men of God who would say to the bishop, "Here am I, send me." They labored, and we have entered into their labors. God be praised that the Church had such men for such times! The two succeeding years find him on Salt Creek circuit, the latter of which he was the third man, giving a strong indication that, through his excessive toils and hardships, his vigorous constitution had been impaired, and he was, from overtaxed exertions, declining in strength. Such was the fact; for in the following year he was obliged to cease from his labors as an itinerant, and take a local relation. During the years in which he continued in this relation his zeal for the cause of Christ did not in the least abate, as he continued to preach whenever opportunity would present itself, and his health would permit. In the great revival of 1800 he took an active part, and was very efficient in leading on the sacramental hosts of God's elect to glorious war.

In 1819 he re-entered the traveling connection, and again took rank with his brethren in the itinerant field. He was appointed presiding elder of the Salt River district, Tennessee conference, where he labored with great success through the year, and at its close was reappointed. His constitution, however, was too much broken down to enable him to continue long in his much-loved employ as an itinerant. Like an old soldier, he only felt at home on the field; and it was with the greatest reluctance that he was obliged, at the close of the year, to lay down his charge, and retire from the itinerant ranks; yet he did not cease to preach. With trembling frame and faltering tongue he would, like the beloved John, gather around him the disciples of Jesus, and exhort them as dear children to love one another. But the day of his departure at length came. That dreadful scourge, the cholera, which spread lamentation and mourning throughout the length and breadth of our land, visited the region where he lived, and was made God's messenger to open to him the gates of life. On the 16th of June, 1833, after this man of God had preached the Gospel for half a century, he was called from labor to reward. The full salvation which he preached to others, and so richly enjoyed in his own soul, sustained him in the dying hour, and fitted by grace he was admitted to heaven. He spent a laborious but happy life, and died a blessed death. He fought his last battle, and finished his course.

"Life's labor done, as sinks the clay,
Light from its load the spirit flies,
While heaven and earth conspire to say,
How blest the righteous when he dies!"

Brother M'Henry possessed a high order of intellect, and for the opportunities enjoyed in those days he had acquired a good share of learning. As a pioneer Methodist preacher, he thoroughly understood the doctrines of the Church, and took great pleasure in their exposition to all with whom he was brought in contact. He also loved the spiritual and temporal economy of the Church, and labored for their defense. To our young brethren in the ministry, who may read this rapid and imperfect sketch, suffer us to exhort you to study the character, and endeavor to imitate the virtues, and zeal, and self-sacrificing devotion of this faithful itinerant. You have entered into his labors. For God's sake, suffer not the work so well begun, and successfully carried on by the pioneers of Methodism, to die in your hands. To carry on this glorious work no self-indulgence can be tolerated for a moment. Let a zeal for God and a love for souls burn in your heart and urge you onward. Courage, and zeal and perseverance are as much demanded now, and perhaps more so, than at any former period in the Church's history. Study, therefore, to show yourselves approved of God, workmen that need not to be ashamed; then you will truly share in their labors on earth and their rewards in heaven.

CHAPTER VIII.

THOMAS SCOTT.

THE sketches of Western Methodism would be incomplete, at least so far as pioneer preachers are concerned, without a biography of Judge Scott, who is the oldest living preacher now in the west, being one or two years the senior of the venerable Burke in the itinerant ranks. This aged minister is now engaged in writing a history of his life and times in the Western Christian Advocate, which will serve as a valuable monument of the past, and be read with interest by present and future generations. We are happy in being able to furnish our readers with an interesting sketch, drawn up by Samuel Williams, Esq., of Mount Auburn, an old and intimate friend of the Judge. In the sketch the young reader will see vividly portrayed the trials and struggles which young men had to encounter in the early settlement of the west; and young men of the present day may draw from these scenes of trial and discouragement incident to border life, courage and hope from the example furnished, that "*labor et perseverantia omnia vincet.*" But to the sketch.

"Thomas Scott, familiarly called Judge Scott, from having been several years a judge of the Supreme Court of Ohio, has been a resident of Chillicothe more than fifty-one years, where he still resides, enjoying a green old age, having just completed the eightieth year of his earthly pilgrimage. He was born at Skypton, near the junction of the north and south branches of the Potomac river, Alleghany county, Maryland, October 31, 1772. His father's parents were Scotch-Irish, and emigrated from Ireland

and settled in Berks county, Pennsylvania, shortly after the battle of the Boyne, in 1690. They were Protestants, and had sustained heavy losses by the Catholics previous to that battle.

"Before the age of fourteen years Mr. Scott embraced religion, and became a member of the Methodist Episcopal Church, when there were only a little over twenty thousand members in its communion, and about one hundred and seventeen preachers. He has, therefore, been a member of the Church more than sixty-six years. At the conference at Leesburg, Virginia, in April, 1789, when only *sixteen and a half years old*, he was admitted on trial in the traveling connection, and appointed to Gloucester circuit, Virginia, together with those distinguished ministers, Lewis Chasteen and Valentine Cook. The following year he was appointed to Berkely circuit, with Lewis Chasteen preacher in charge. Soon after they commenced their labors, Mr. Chasteen was seized with the small-pox, which injured one of his eyes so much that he could labor but little till near the close of the year. This devolved nearly the entire labor, as well as the administration of discipline, upon the youthful Scott, yet only eighteen years old. At the conference in May, 1791, he was received into full connection, and ordained deacon by Bishop Asbury, who appointed him in charge of Stafford circuit, Virginia, with Samuel Hitt, late of Champaign county, Ohio, as his helper. In 1792 he was appointed to Frederic circuit, Virginia, with Thomas Lyell as his helper.

"Mr. Lyell, although young, and only in the second year of his ministry, had already acquired great fame as a very eloquent and popular preacher. This, together with his amiable disposition, his polished manners, his fascinating conversation, and his fine personal figure, conspired to make him a great favorite, both with the preachers and people. For many successive years he was stationed in the most populous cities, and caressed, and, perhaps, flattered wherever he went. In 1804 he located, and afterward took orders in the Protestant Episcopal Church, and was settled in the city of New York as rector of a populous and wealthy parish, which he served with great acceptance till his death, at an advanced age, a few years since. It is said that he preserved, to the last, a friendly attachment to the Methodist Episcopal Church and her ministry. But to return from this digression.

"At the conference held at the place of Mr. Scott's nativity, in June, 1793, he was ordained elder by Bishop Asbury, and appointed to the Ohio circuit, in charge, with the Rev. Robert Bonham as his helper. This circuit was of great extent, and much of which lay along the frontier settlements on the Ohio river, in Western Virginia and Pennsylvania, and exposed to the attacks of the Indians.

"In the spring of 1794, in pursuance of instructions from Bishop Asbury, Mr. Scott descended the Ohio river to join the Kentucky conference, which convened on the 15th of April. Embarking at Wheeling, on a flat-bottomed boat, ladened with provisions for General Wayne's army, he descended the Ohio river to Brook's landing, above the mouth of Limestone creek, where Maysville now stands. The settlements along the Ohio river, at that period, were few and far between, and the intervening wilderness was occupied by hostile tribes of Indians, to whose attacks descending boats were continually exposed. Floating with the current, the voyage was necessarily tedious, and the boat often passing along very near to the shore, those on board were in great danger from the unerring rifle of the Indian. But Mr. Scott, unconscious of his danger, was accustomed daily to sit, for hours together, on the top of the boat, reading, even while the boat was floating along close to the shore covered with bushes, from which the savage tomahawk of the practiced Indian might have been hurled to his destruction. He has oftentimes since reflected with surprise upon his own imprudence, and ascribed his preservation to a merciful and overruling Providence. Having sent his horse on to Kentucky a few days ahead, Mr. Scott, on landing there himself, immediately proceeded to the home of his parents, on the head waters of Bracken creek, Mason county, with whom he spent a few days, and then repaired to the seat of the Kentucky conference, near Bethel Academy, Jessamine county, where he received an appointment to Danville circuit, on which he continued to labor during the conference year. At the conference in May, 1795, he located for the purpose of attending to important temporal business in Pennsylvania. But sickness and other circumstances prevented his going to Pennsylvania. To accustom himself to hard labor, he turned in to cut down and strip the bark from large trees for his brother James, who was a tanner. When the season for this work was over, he went to school about a month to acquire a better knowledge of arithmetic. Every Thursday afternoon he walked three miles to meet a class, of which he was leader, and had his appointments to preach on Sabbath, one of which places was in Maysville, and it is probable he was the first Methodist minister who ever preached the Gospel in that town. In the latter part of the summer, at the request of the Rev. F. Poythress, the presiding elder, Mr. Scott took charge of the Lexington circuit, in place of the Rev. Aquilla Sugg, whose health had failed, and he continued on that circuit till the meeting of the Kentucky conference in the spring of 1796, from which time his labors as an itinerant minister in the Church ceased.

"On the 10th of May, 1796, Mr. Scott married Miss Catharine Wood, a pious young lady, whose parents had long been Methodists, and soon after settled in Washington, Mason county, Ky., where he obtained employment as a clerk in a dry goods store. In a few months the merchant failed in business, and Mr. Scott thereby lost nearly half his earnings. After this he devoted a small portion of his time to reading the elementary principles of law, and copying and memorizing the forms of entries in civil and criminal proceedings in the courts. This he did in expectation of being appointed clerk of the courts in a new county about to be set off from Mason; but which office, although his superior fitness for it was admitted by all, was, through the treachery of pretended friends, given to another. He now determined upon the study of law, with the view of practicing at the bar, and, therefore, declined several very favorable offers of eastern merchants to engage in the mercantile business. But in what way he was to support himself and family, while pursuing his legal studies, was now the question. Various plans were considered; and as 'necessity is the mother of invention,' he finally resolved upon opening a tailor's-shop in Washington, so soon as he could gain sufficient practical knowledge of the business to follow it. His father was a tailor, and when a boy he had often assisted him on long winter nights, and wet or stormy days, and was expert in the use of the needle, but was ignorant of the art of cutting, and of joining the parts of garments together. To acquire this knowledge, he worked awhile as a journeyman in an extensive shop in Washington. But the proprietor, aware of Mr. Scott's intention to commence business himself, never allowed him to be present when he took the measure for garments or cut them. He was obliged, therefore, to get the requisite knowledge from a tailor in the country.

"He had never yet had any practice in measuring, or cutting, or fitting garments, and might well have been deterred, by his fears, from attempting to open shop and commence. But relying upon his own native genius, and his patient, untiring perseverance in whatever he undertook, he did open a shop and commence business. He spoiled the first coat he attempted to cut. But, nothing daunted, he tried again and succeeded. His neighbors kindly encouraged him, and work soon came in so fast that he had to employ journeymen. The late Mr. John Watson, well known in Chillicothe and elsewhere as an able hotel-keeper, worked some time for Mr. Scott as a journeyman.

"Anxious to proceed in his legal studies, and yet having no time that he could devote to it, he adopted an expedient which none but an indomitable spirit, like his, would have thought of resorting to. Mrs. Scott was an excellent reader, and as she had a hired woman to do the domestic work, she devoted her leisure time to reading to Mr. Scott, while at work on his shop-board, Blackstone's Commentaries, and other law books; and as she read, he treasured up in memory, and reflected on the contents read. The reading was often succeeded by singing, as they were both good singers; and while both were busily engaged in plying the needle, they would beguile the time by singing some of the sweet songs of Zion, and thus they cheerily passed the day.

"In the fall of 1798 Mr. Scott removed, with his family, to Lexington, where he commenced a regular course of law-reading under the late honorable James Brown, deceased. In the winter of 1800, before he had completed the extensive course of legal studies which he had anxiously desired, he was obliged, from pecuniary necessity, to desist; and having obtained license to practice law, he removed to and settled in Flemingsburg, Fleming county, where he was appointed prosecuting-attorney. Here, and in the counties of Mason and Bracken, he obtained some little practice, but did not succeed well in either of those counties. Although well versed in the principles of law, he had never yet read any book which treated of practice either in courts of law or equity. While at Flemingsburg he commenced a course of mathematical studies.

"In March, 1801, he visited Chillicothe, by advice of the late General Nathaniel Massie and other friends, and upon consultation with his old friend, Dr. Edward Tiffin—whom he had known and taken into the Church eleven years prior to that time, in Virginia—he concluded to remove to and settle in that town, which he did the following month, and has continued to reside there to the present time—a period of over fifty-one years. Before leaving Kentucky he went to Cincinnati and was examined before the General Court of the North-Western Territory—Judge Burnett, Mr. M'Millen, and Attorney-General St. Clair examiners—and admitted to the degree of counselor at law. During the summer of 1801 he wrote in the clerk's office for Doctor Tiffin, and engaged in such other business as he could to obtain a scanty subsistence, as he could not practice as counselor at law till he had resided two years in the territory. The succeeding winter he was employed as engrossing and enrolling clerk during the session of the Territorial Legislature. On the assembling of the convention for forming a constitution for the state, Mr. Scott was elected Secretary to that body. Dr. Tiffin being a candidate for governor, under the new constitution, he resigned the clerkship of the several courts which he then held, and Mr. Scott was appointed in his place by the acting governor. At the first township election in Chillicothe, under the constitution, he was elected a justice of the peace, and was the first one commissioned under the state government. At the session of the first General Assembly, under the constitution, Mr. Scott was elected Secretary of the senate, to which office he was annually appointed till 1809, in February of which year he was elected, by the Legislature, one of the judges of the Supreme Court, and the year following was re-elected and commissioned chief judge of that Court. This office he held till July, 1815, when, finding the salary insufficient for the support of himself and family, he resigned his seat on the bench and resumed the practice of law.

"In October, 1815, Judge Scott was elected one of the representatives of Ross county, in the Legislature, and in 1822, he and the late Judge Francis Dunlevy and Thomas Ewing, Esq., were commissioned by Governor Morrow, under a law of the state, as a board of revision, to revise the general laws of the state, and to report the same to the General Assembly at its ensuing session. The Board had not quite completed their work when the Legislature met; and one of the first things done by that body was to dissolve the Board, so that no report was made. In March, 1829, he was appointed, by the President and senate, Register of the Land-Office at Chillicothe, which office he held, by successive appointments, till March, 1845, when he was removed by President Polk.

"The foregoing sketch of our old friend and neighbor is condensed from a more extended one recently drawn up by himself, and kindly furnished to us. We have devoted more space to it than we can well spare, and yet have been obliged to omit many incidents and facts which would have lent additional interest to the narrative. Many of his friends have, with us, regretted that the Judge ever exchanged his high and holy calling of an embassador of Christ for the bar, or the bench, or political life, with its turmoil and strife. 'Tis true, he possessed superior qualifications for the bar, and the bench, and the various other offices he has held. But his fitness for the ministry was of a still higher order. And had he remained at his post therein, he would, doubtless, long since have ranked with the most talented and distinguished ministers in the Church; nay, might possibly now be filling the dignified office of its senior superintendent. It is but justice, however, to add, that he considered himself forced, by 'dire necessity,' to take the course he did. 'For,' said he, 'had the Church at that period been able to support myself and family, I would have spent my whole life in the ministry. But the Church was then too poor to do it.' It is much to be lamented that many others of the ablest and most useful ministers in the Church, in former times, were, from the same cause, compelled to retire from the work."

CHAPTER IX.

JOHN KOBLER.

If we were to hear of a minister of Jesus who had preached the first sermon in what is now the state of Ohio, and spread the first table of the Lord that was ever spread in this wilderness, would it not awaken a thrilling emotion in our hearts and create a romantic interest to hear something of his wonderful history? What adventure could be connected with more stirring incident than the adventures of such a man in braving the perils of the wilderness, and preaching the Gospel, and administering its ordinances in these wilds more than fifty years ago? We have his history, gentle reader, and the incidents connected with his heroic Christian life.

The subject of our sketch was born in Culpepper county, Virginia, on the 29th of August, in the year 1768. He was blessed with pious parents, and particularly a pious mother—one of the greatest blessings to mortals; for to the mother more than to any other, and, in fact, all other influences combined, apart from the grace of God, is the child indebted for its character. A mother's smile, and gentle word, and kind hand do more to mold the character and fix the destiny of the child than all other agencies combined. "Give me," said Madame de Stael, "the first seven years of a child's ife, and I care not who afterward shall have its training." This, as a general principle, will hold good, as the period lluded to constitutes, to a great extent, the forming tage of human character. During that time it receives its bent and direction for time and eternity. Having a mother whose mind and heart were thoroughly imbued with the principles and graces of religion, young Kobler was early trained in the path of virtue, and fortified against the assaults of vice and sin. The example and teachings of that godly mother were accompanied by ardent prayer and the impressive and awakening influence of the Holy Spirit. Thus, at a very early period in his life, he was led to feel the importance of religion. Drawn by the Spirit, and yielding up his young heart to its genial influences, he was led away from the noisy sports of life to the place of retirement, where he would read his Bible and pour out his young affections to the great Father in heaven. Under the influence of such agencies, human and divine, as were at work on his heart, he was soon led into the possession of that regenerating grace which filled his heart with the joys of salvation.

In the nineteenth year of his age we find him a professor of religion, and happy in the love of God. This profession he maintained by a consistency of conduct which would do honor to a mature Christian. He was, however, evidently designed for a higher service than that of exemplifying the Gospel of Jesus in the private walks of life; and it could be seen by his peculiar fervency and the train of his thoughts, that the Spirit was calling him to the work of the ministry. Moved by that Spirit in a way he could not mistake for the motions of his own heart, he obeyed the Divine call, and in the twenty-first year of his age he gave up home, and friends and earthly comforts and prospects, and entered the rough and rugged field of itinerant life. Shortly after his entrance upon the work of an itinerant, there being a loud call for preachers in the far west, he enlisted as a volunteer and went out as a pioneer to the North-Western territory. Here, in these wilds, he encountered toils privations, and hardships incident to the life of a pioneer preacher. He lived and labored in this region amid scenes of danger, and was personally acquainted with many an adventure, and could relate sufferings which had been endured by the early settlers which would seem almost incredible at this day. In Powell's Valley he became acquainted with a lady who had been captured by the Indians, and who related to him her sufferings, an account of which he gave to Bishop Asbury when on a visit to his circuit. The maiden name of the lady was Dickenson. She had married a gentleman by the name of Scott, and was living in the valley. On a certain evening, her husband and children being in bed, eight or nine Indians rushed into the house full of threatening and slaughter. Startled by their terrific yells, Mr. Scott sprang from the bed and instantly every gun they had was fired at him. Although badly wounded he broke through them all, and ran out of the house into the woods. Several of them immediately started in pursuit, and soon overtaking him, being faint from loss of blood, they butchered him and took off his scalp. The mother gathered her helpless children in her arms, and, convulsed with fear, awaited the result. Soon they returned, and, wresting her children from her grasp, they cruelly murdered them before her eyes. They then plundered the house and took her prisoner. From the cabin they went ut into the depths of the forest, and, kindling a fire, hey spent the night in drinking, shouting, and dancing. he next day they divided the plunder among themselves s equally as possible. Among the number of articles aken was one of Mr. Wesley's hymn-books. For this hey had no use, and, no one seeming to care for it, the istracted woman, by signs, desired that it might be given her. To this they assented, and taking the book, from hose appropriate hymns she had often derived courage and comfort, she opened its pages and began to read. When the Indians saw this they were greatly displeased, and snatching it from her, they gave her to understand that they believed her a conjurer. After this they started in the direction of the Indian towns, and traveled several days through the wilderness. The grief and sorrow of this afflicted woman were so great that she could scarcely realize the horrid scenes through which she had passed, and thought she was dreaming. To aggravate that grief, if possible, these fiends took the scalps of her husband and children and hung them around her neck. Thus she walked along through tangled thickets and over rugged mountains, almost fainting from fatigue, and worn down with anguish. When they saw her panting for breath, and almost ready to sink from exhaustion in her weary marches, they would laugh at her calamity and mock her feebleness. Every spark of humanity, however, was not extinct in this savage band. There was one Indian who, in the hour of her extremity, procured for her some water to quench her burning thirst, and when she was ready to sink made the remainder stop for her to rest. For eleven days they traveled on, and when almost famished with hunger they called a halt, and committing her to the care of an old Indian they started off to hunt for food. After resting awhile the old Indian went to work to dress a deer-skin. Mrs. Scott observing that his mind was wholly absorbed in his employment, walked about from place to place, and watching her opportunity she fled, and was soon out of sight in the forest After running for some time she came to a cane-brake and entering it was securely hidden. The Indians, o returning at night and finding their prisoner gone, starte out in pursuit of her. It seems that they had taken th direction in which she had gone; for during the nigh she frequently heard them searching for her, and answe ing one another with an owl-like hoot. In the darkness of the night, alone in the wilderness, and hunted by the savages like a beast of prey, this poor woman fell upon her knees, and poured out her soul in supplication to her Father, God. She spent the night in prayer, and the savages not being able to find her hiding-place, left for other parts. In the morning she started in the direction, as she supposed, of Kentucky, almost despairing of ever being permitted to look upon a white face again. One day, while wandering in the wilderness, not knowing whither she was going, almost ready to sink from want of food and rest, having nothing to subsist upon but roots, young grape-vines, and sweet cane, she heard, not far from her, a loud yell and a tremendous noise, like the furious tramping of many horses. She instantly secreted herself in a thicket close by, and in a few moments, from her hiding-place, she saw a large company of Indians rush by with a drove of horses, which they had stolen from the whites. When the sound had died away, and all was still, she left her retreat, and journeyed on. After traveling a short distance, she came in sight of a huge bear, who was devouring a deer, and so pressed was she with hunger, that she drew near in hopes of getting some. At her approach the bear looked up and growled hideously. Fearing an attack she hastened away. At length night came on and she laid down, and all through its gloomy hours she dreamed of eating; but morning came, and she was sick and faint with hunger. As she pursued her journey she came to a rocky region, and finding a cave, in which there were some leaves, she concluded, as all hope had nearly deserted her, to go in and lie down, and resign herself to her fate. For several hours she occupied this den of wild beasts, and wept and prayed for deliverance from her pain and sorrow. Her whole system was racked with pain, so much so that she could not rest, and she was obliged to rise and pursue her journey. She thought of home, and the dear ones who had been rudely snatched from her embrace, and the fountains of her grief were opened afresh, while her moans and lamentations waked the echoes of the wilderness, and reached the ears of her Father in heaven.

Day after day she traveled on, and she finally came to the spot where the Cumberland river breaks through the mountains. She crawled down the cliffs a considerable distance, till the darkening defiles around her filled her with dismay. Far down below her rolled the rapid river. Around her were craggy rocks, and above her the steep, precipitous cliffs, which her insensibility to fear had enabled her to descend, but which her strength would never allow her to scale. She was now on the edge of a frightful precipice, formed by a rock which rose up perpendicularly from the bank of the river. To go back she could not, and to descend that precipice would crush her by the fall. But it was the only alternative; and falling upon her knees she prayed most fervently, and commended her soul to God. Then rising, she seized a bush which grew out of the fissures of the rock, on the very edge, and letting herself down as far as it would reach, she let go, and fell to the bottom on the jagged rocks. Wonderful as it was, she was not killed; but bruised and mangled, she lay in a state of insensibility for several hours When she revived she considered that her end was near and soon her sufferings would end with her life. Bu her time had not yet come, and she was immortal til that hour. A sensation of thirst came on her that wa insupportable. The waters were before her, dashing thei spray almost at her feet, but in her wounded and helples condition how could she reach them? Feeling that sh must drink or die, she made an effort, and by slow an painful progress she at last crawled to the brink, an quenched her burning thirst. This greatly revived her, and after a short time she was able to get up and walk. Following along the bank of the river, she came to a path, and, entering it, she pursued it a short distance, when it branched off in two directions. One direction of this path led back into the wilderness; the other to the settlements. Which path to take she knew not. She, however, unfortunately determined to take the one leading to the wilderness. Before proceeding many steps, a little bird, of a dove color, flew close by her face, and fluttered along into the other path. She stopped, and gazed upon it, when it flew toward her, and then returned to the path a second time. Taking this to be a Providential interference, she took the path of the bird, which flew on before her, and was at length among the abodes of humanity and civilization.

Soon after, under the preaching of the Gospel pioneer, she embraced religion, led a consistent life, and died in the triumphs of the Christian faith. Brother Kobler preached her funeral discourse, in which he related the wonderful trials and deliverances of this pioneer mother.

There being a field open in the region north-west of the Ohio, and laborers being wanted, Kobler went over to travel the wilderness where we now live, and preached the Gospel of Jesus to the scattered inhabitants. A sketch, furnished by him for the Western Historical Society, in August, 1841, we will insert, as it will serve to show, in his own language, what was the state and condition of the country upward of fifty years ago. It begins as follows:

"In the year 1798, the writer of this article was sent by Bishop Asbury, as a missionary to this region of country, then called the North-Western territory, now Ohio state, to form a new circuit, and to plant the first principles of the Gospel. In passing through the country he found it almost in its native, rude, and uncultivated state. The inhabitants were settled in small neighborhoods, and few and far between; and little or no improvement about them. No sound of the everlasting Gospel had as yet broken upon their ears, or gladdened their hearts; no house of worship was erected wherein Jehovah's name was recorded; no joining the assembly of the saints, or those who keep the holy day; but the whole might, with strict propriety, be called 'a land of darkness, and the shadow of death,'

'Where the sound of a church-going bell,
Those vales and rocks never heard
Ne'er sighed at the sound of a knell,
Nor smiled when a Sabbath appeared.'

"The site on which Cincinnati now stands, was nearly a dense and uncultivated forest. No improvement was to be seen but Fort Washington, which was built on the brow of the hill, and extended down to the margin of the river; around which was built a number of cabins, in which resided the first settlers of the place. This fortress was then under the command of General Harrison, and was the great place of rendezvous for the federal troops, which were sent by the government to guard the frontiers, or to go forth to war with the Indians. In this state of things the writer left this country forty years ago, and never saw or visited the state of Ohio till the third day of July last, at which time he came from aboard the steamboat Bristol, and walked through a considerable part of the city of Cincinnati; but he has nc language to express his reflections, and the peculiarity of thoughts which rushed upon his mind, while comparing the past state of things with the present. After passing from street to street, and from square to square for more than half a mile, he came to the conclusion that no city in the Union could vie with it in beauty and magnitude considering its short growth. Having, since arriving in Cincinnati, traveled over many parts of his old missionary ground, he finds a most astonishing change and improvement has taken place. Where formerly there were indistinct paths, sometimes only trees being blazed to direct our course from one house or settlement to another, now there are highly-improved roads, and turnpikes, and and every facility for public conveyance. And where there stood unbroken forests, now there are numerous villages and large towns, numbering their thousands. The farms and farm-houses are equal in convenience, beauty, and taste to any in the Union. But the best and most encouraging of all is, to see a large proportion of the inhabitants of the country, both in villages and cities, truly religious; men and women who fear God, and work righteousness. The writer of this article can not help here adverting to the time when he spread the first table for the sacrament of the Lord's supper, that was spread north-west of the Ohio. When the communicants were called to approach the table, the number did not exceed twenty-five or thirty; this was the sum total of all that were in the country. Now the Minutes of the annual conferences of Ohio return one hundred thousand regular Church members; so mightily hath the word of God run and prevailed! Where we once preached in log-cabins, we now see stately churches erected, whose spires point toward heaven, and whose solemn bells announce the arrival of the Christian Sabbath, and call the attention of the multitude to the house of God. This is indeed the Lord's doing, and a circumstance of the deepest regard to its original founder; and we would pray that this land may continue to be greatly blessed of the Lord, and continue to be a people with whom God may delight to dwell. I should judge from the locality of the country, the richness of the soil, salubrity of climate, and the industry of the inhabitants, that in a few years this state will be equal in wealth and number, if not superior to any of the eastern states. The Church, in her present onward course, is spreading a divine influence which deeply affects all states and conditions, sects and orders of men. Look in any direction and you will see her rising up in all the power and majesty of divine grace, the righteousness thereof going forth with brightness, and the salvation thereof like unto a lamp that burneth. Our Congress and legislative halls have in them their Obadiahs—a number who are not ashamed to confess 'that they fear the Lord greatly;' and while they sit at the helm of government, and guide the destinies of our wide-spreading republic, we see them fully awake to the interests of the Church, under the conviction that 'righteousness exalteth a nation, while sin is a reproach to any people.' But whence is this divine knowledge derived? Certainly from the Bible; that book which is sending forth a flood of divine light and truth into every department of Church and state. While we as ministers and members of the Church enjoy those invaluable privileges, it is our duty to lay them deeply to heart, that we may duly appreciate and wisely improve them. Your aged servant, the writer of this article, has been standing on the walls of our Zion for fifty-five years; and while, with unwearied vigilance, he has been guarding and laboring for the interests of the Church, he has been making strict observations on circumstances and things connected with the Church; and from long observation he has been fully convinced, and, of late, more so than ever, that it is the doctrine which we preach, the discipline which we have exercised, and the system by which, as a Church, we are regulated, that have produced those happy results, in the conversion and sanctification of so many thousands. Our doctrines are: First, free salvation; so that wherever the minister meets his congregation, be they many or few, he feels no hesitancy in offering salvation to every soul present, and accordingly tells them, 'that Jesus Christ, by the grace of God, tasted death for every man.' Secondly, we preach a present salvation; which is salvation by faith alone, as the condition, and the only condition, of our justification before God. Thirdly, the doctrine of holiness, as the Christian's highest privilege, and most indispensable duty. St. Paul terms it, 'The mark and prize of our high calling, which is of God in Christ Jesus,' and exhorts all believers to press to its attainment. To the doctrines of the everlasting Gospel we owe all our spiritual achievements; and, as a people, all that we have and are. Our system of doctrine and discipline has been well and long tried. It has stood the fiery ordeal of one century, and has come forth as gold and as 'silver tried in a furnace of earth, and purified seven times.' Here, then, I would say to our ministers and to the Church, whereunto we have already attained, let us walk by the same rule; let us mind the same things; never lose sight of the spirit and practice of Gospel holiness in all its hights and depths, as the leading and essential qualification for the Christian ministry. The herald of mercy and grace may speak with the tongue of angelic eloquence rather than men; but if he lacks love—the constraining principle, 2 Cor. v, 14—he will be only as 'sounding brass, or as a tinkling cymbal.' St. Paul saith, 'The love of Christ constraineth us.' O, who can tell the force, the power, and the eloquence of constraining love! This alone can carry fire to frozen hearts, and make the terrified sinner to cry, 'What must I do to be saved?' When one of those master-spirits, from the sacred desk, draws the Gospel bow at a venture, his arm is nerved with an almighty energy; the arrows of the

Almighty will be sharp and powerful in the hearts of the King's enemies, whereby the people will fall under Him. Dear brethren in the ministry, let us press on to a higher state of holiness; let us be 'men of one Book,' studying closely the Bible—men mighty in prayer, having deep communion with God; let us go from our knees into the pulpit, and there, with enlarged hearts and open mouths, and losing all sight of self, and every shadow of self, preach as a dying man to dying men, holding up the Lord Jesus Christ as the Great Expedient for a lost and ruined world. Let holiness be in every composition, and make a part of every sermon. Blessed is that minister that shall be found so doing. Though his preaching abilities may be small and lightly esteemed by a misjudging world, yet, clad in Gospel panoply complete, and having on the armor of righteousness, on the right hand and on the left, he will 'turn many to righteousness,' and shine as the stars forever and ever. Let us not only teach our Church publicly, but from house to house, visiting their families, and encouraging and praying with them; by which means they will be strengthened, and made to walk in the fear of God, and in the comforts of the Holy Ghost. By this means you will be instruments in 'strengthening the weak, binding up that which was broken, and bringing back that which was driven away.' Meet the class, if possible, after preaching. In the early stage of Methodism the class meeting was our bond of union. O, with what warm hearts did the dear people go to the class-room; and there, with sobbing hearts and flowing eyes, would tell over their trials, and what God had done for their souls; and all this in such a melting strain that the hardest heart could not remain unmoved. O, let us take heed to ourselves, and to all the flock over which the Holy Ghost hath made us overseers, to feed the Church of God, which he hath purchased with his own blood. As the dew upon Mount Hermon, and as the dew that descended upon the mountains of Zion, so may the Lord command his blessing upon his people, even life for evermore."

Though Kobler was possessed of a constitution naturally of more than ordinary strength, the privation and toil, accompanied with the necessary exposure of a Methodist missionary at that early day in the history of our country and the Church, gave to that constitution a shock from which it never recovered. Endowed with abilities, as a preacher, above mediocrity, and fired with a zeal worthy his high vocation, for a period of eighteen years he labored with great success in the itinerant field, and many souls were converted through his instrumentality. Being completely prostrated by disease, in the year 1809 he was induced to locate, and settled in the neighborhood in which he was born.

Unsought by himself, in the year 1836 the Baltimore annual conference placed his name on the list of its superannuated ministers. Fond of meeting with the redeemed of the Lord, as age grew upon him, and as he was unable to visit distant circuit appointments, he sought for a residence in a place where he could assemble with the people of God, and be useful; and hence he removed to Fredericksburg, Virginia. In that place his saint-like spirit, exhibited in Christian conversation, his dignified ministerial bearing, and his untiring labors in preaching, exhorting, praying, visiting the sick and imprisoned, did more, under God, to give character and permanency to Methodism in that place than any other human agency. The Church in Fredericksburg was small and poor, and the house in which the members worshiped was dilapidated and situated in an out-of-the-way place. The membership resolved to better their condition, and thereby increase their facilities for doing good by building a new church. To aid them in this undertaking, father Kobler was not only one of the most liberal subscribers, but he started out, in the seventy-fourth year of his age, on an excursion, appealing to the Churches of the west, the early field of his itinerant toil, for assistance. During this tour he visited the Ohio conference, and met with success in his undertaking. He seemed, like good old Simeon, to wait for the completion and dedication of this house of the Lord; and when the day at length arrived, and the Lord was invoked to take possession of the newly-erected temple, while all the lovers of Methodism were joyful, the old patriarch was transported. The object for which he had ardently prayed and labored was accomplished, and he was ready to say, "Now, Lord, lettest thou thy servant depart in peace; for mine eyes have seen thy salvation." His days, however, were lengthened, and he was permitted to witness one of the most interesting and powerful revivals in that church. The glorious work had hardly abated ere disease laid its destroying hand upon him. During his affliction he was perfectly happy, and the light of heaven beamed on his happy countenance. Without a murmur he suffered the will of his Master. Often was he heard to say, "Living or dying, I am the Lord's." On his friends asking him if he had any thing he desired them to pray for, he replied, "Pray for the Church, that God would abundantly pour out his Spirit upon it, and take it into close keeping with himself." On one occasion he said, "I have dug deep, and brought all the evidence to bear, and I find I have a strong confidence, which nothing can shake; but all is through the infinite merits of my Lord and Savior. I wish it to be known to all, that the principles which I have believed, and taught, and practiced in life, I cling to in death, and find they sustain me. I have tried all my life to make my ministry and life con sistent." About half an hour before he died he was asked, "Is Jesus precious?" "O, yes, very precious!" and then he uttered, as his last words on earth, "Come, Lord Jesus; come in power, come quickly!" In a few minutes he was no more; the spirit had gone to heaven. Having left the tabernacle which it had occupied for three quarters of a century, it went to its building of God above.

CHAPTER X.

BENJAMIN LAKIN.

THIS western pioneer was born in the state of Maryland. When quite young his parents removed to the state of Pennsylvania; but not being satisfied with the country, they continued their peregrinations westward till they arrived at the state of Kentucky. It was in the early settlement of that country that they made their home among its cane-brakes. Young Lakin, sharing the fortunes of his father, amid the scenes of the dark and bloody ground, could not be expected to have received much literary or religious training. In that day there were few who knew any thing about experimental religion, what there was consisting more of a mere form than any thing else. Indeed, there was precious little even of that. Still the country was not wholly destitute for a wandering Methodist preacher, whose circuit, like the track of a comet, swept over the whole space of the country, would touch at the different and distant neighborhoods, and pour from his heart, richly filled with the treasures of experimental religion, the soul-saving truths of the Gospel. Under the influence of such preaching young Lakin was brought to feel his need of a Savior and, after seeking with great earnestness for the blessing of pardon and salvation, he at length was enabled, through faith, to behold and embrace the "Lamb of God, wh taketh away the sin of the world." It was not long afte his conversion that he felt called to take up his cross an follow his Savior, in bearing the messages of mercy to hi dying fellow-men. There was nothing in those days to render an itinerant life in the least degree inviting. Every step of such a mission was connected with danger and toil; and it was not likely that any would enter the ministry except from the firmest convictions of a duty the most pressing and imperative in its nature. It seems to us, though we may be wrong—if so, God forgive us—that such has been the change wrought upon the face of the country and society in general, making the post of a Gospel minister rather desirable than otherwise, that many do not feel that awful sense of responsibility connected with the calling which it is just as important to feel now as then, and that we find young men entering upon this work about in the same way, and with no greater anxiety or interest than they would enter upon any learned or business profession for the purpose of honor and emolument; and the danger of mistaking the call is increased, from the fact that so much stress is laid upon mere literary training and scholastic attainments connected with the wonderfully-restless desire the present generation has for learned ministers. We know of nothing that would tend more effectually to bring back the dark ages upon the Church than such a disposition to exalt learning at the expense of the zeal and wisdom of our fathers in the ministry. They perhaps knew little about Latin, Greek, and Hebrew, or Biblical literature, in the critical sense of that term, but they were thoroughly versed in the Bible; and hence, in the language of Luther, "*Bonus textuarius, bonus theologus*"—he is always the best divine who is best acquainted with the Scriptures. They were men of the Bible; men of faith and men of prayer; and coming to their congregations with an unction from the Holy One, the word of God was like "a fire and a hammer, which broke the rock in pieces." We would not decry knowledge; God forbid! Let the minister of the present day study all the branches of theological literature, and all collateral sciences, posting himself up thoroughly in all departments; but above all, let him, when he comes to feed the flock of God, come from the deep fountains of eternal Truth, and from the foot of the cross. Let his visits be frequent to Tabor and Olivet, as well as Gethsemane and Calvary, and, filled with the Spirit of Jesus, he will be mighty, through God, to the pulling down of the strongholds of infidelity and sin. We do not believe, now that the days of miracles and inspiration are passed, that God will prepare sermons for drones, or that he will convert a dull and stupid intellect into a bright one. Such extraordinary manifestations we are not to look for; and hence we judge with the Church, that with "grace" must be connected "gifts." We recollect distinctly when, if a father had three sons and was able to give then an education, he selected the brightest for a lawyer, the next for a doctor, and the dullest of all for a preacher. We would reverse this arrangement, and judge that the last should be first and the first last. But to our sketch.

Young Lakin was called to preach, and, conferring not with flesh and blood, he entered the itinerant ranks in the year 1794, and traveled under the presiding elder, Francis Poythress. In the following spring he was admitted on trial and appointed to Green River circuit. In 1796 he was appointed to Danville circuit, and in 1797 he was admitted into full connection, ordained a deacon and appointed to Lexington circuit. During this year he married an excellent wife and located. Such was the prejudice that existed in the Church, at that day, against married preachers, that it was almost out of the question for any man to continue in the work if he had a wife. They were not exactly obliged to take the Popish vow of celibacy, but it almost amounted to the same thing; an there being such a high example for single life, as exhibited in the cases of the bishops, if a preacher married he was looked upon almost as a heretic who had denied the faith. Besides, no provision was made for the wife, and she was regarded, on all hands, as an incumbrance. Whether this opposition arose from the poverty or parsimoniousness of the Church, or from the belief that a man with a wife was not sufficiently disentangled from the world, and hence unfit for the work of an itinerant, or, perhaps, from all combined, we know not; but such was the fact, that but only one or two had courage and endurance enough to travel when married. We recollect that within the last twenty years, in the Ohio conference, young men have been discontinued who married within two years, though there was nothing else against them.

Under such a state of things Lakin located, and laboring with his own hands during the week, to support his family, he preached from place to place on Sabbath with zeal and power. Having to support himself there was no objection to his preaching; for of all denominations of Christians we ever knew, the Methodists, in general, are most attached to a *free* Gospel; that is, one that costs them nothing; and, humiliating as it may seem, we have heard some thank God for it. The time came, however, when brother Lakin, being able, after some sort, to support his family, re-entered the traveling connection, and was appointed to Limestone circuit. In the year 1802 he was appointed to travel Scioto and Miami circuits combined. We request our reader to look at the map and see the extent of the field of this one man's labor—a tract of country including all southern Ohio. It was during this year we became acquainted with this pioneer. We met him as he was moving from Kentucky to the field of his labor. The point where we met him was on the eastern side of the Little Miami, the track of the railroad now occupying the spot. Then there was nothing that deserved the name of a road—a kind of a trace. We were surprised to see a man and woman in a cart drawn by one horse—surprised, because this was a superior way of traveling, not known to the settlers, who traveled and carried their movables on pack-horses. As we came up we halted to look at his vehicle. As we stopped he inquired how far it was to the next house. This we were unable to tell, for the road was uninhabited. We then had the curiosity to ask him who he was, where he was going, and what was his business? He quickly and kindly replied, "My name is Lakin; I am a Methodist preacher, and am going to preach the Gospel to lost sinners in the Miami and Scioto country." Filled with strange imaginings we parted, and the preacher drove on.

What would the young preacher of the present day think of taking his wife in a cart and starting out without money, home, or friends and traveling through the wilderness seeking for the lost? Yet such trials and hardships your fathers endured. God be praised that the times have changed, and that you are not subjected to the same toils and sufferings! After filling up this year brother Lakin was sent to Salt River circuit, in Kentucky, and in all probability returned with his family and all in that little cart. In 1804 he was appointed to Danville, and in 1805 to Salt River and Shelby united. In 1806 and 1807 he was sent back to Miami, and traveled successively the following circuits; namely, Deer Creek, Hockhocking, Cincinnati, Whiteoak, Union, Limestone, Lexington, and Hinkston. At the close of his year on this circuit, his health failing, he was returned supernumerary, and the next year—1819—continuing to decline, he was placed on the superannuated list, where he remained till the day of his death.

We have thus given a brief and rapid outline of the

labors of this faithful and devoted servant of Jesus. He was one of the ministers of those days who stood side by side and guided the Church through that most remarkable revival of religion, which swept like a tornado over the western world. In the greatest excitement the clear and penetrating voice of Lakin might be heard amid the din and roar of the Lord's battle, directing the wounded to the Lamb of God, who taketh away the sins of the world. Day and night he was upon the watchtower, and in the class and praying circles his place was never empty—leading the blind by the right way, carrying the lambs in his bosom, urging on the laggard professor, and warning the sinner in tones of thunder to flee the wrath to come. While he was in the relation of a worn-out preacher he never had a dumb Sabbath, always having his appointments ahead, except when quarterly or camp meetings would intervene. He was always on hand at these, and would preach and labor with all his remaining strength. Great success attended his labors, and he was universally accepted and beloved as a minister of Jesus. We knew him well, and loved him as a father in the Gospel with a pure heart fervently. His visits to our family, once a year, were looked for with great solicitude, and he was made a blessing to all the children. Father Lakin did not suffer his calm, benignant features, in his last days, to be wrinkled with a sour godliness. There was no howling or whining about every thing going wrong in the Church and among the preachers. He had a contempt for croakers, and would look up and thank God for a good conservative progress in all the departments of Methodism. Quiet, and peaceful, and glorious, as when the descending sun throws his last rays on a receding world, tinging the trees and mountains with his mellow light, did this venerable servant of the cross pass down to the grave. He preached his last sermon in M'Kendree

Chapel, Brown county, Ohio, on the 28th day of January, 1848. On Tuesday he returned home to Point Pleasant. The next two days he complained some of indisposition, but on Friday he started on horseback—his usual mode of traveling—to quarterly meeting, at Felicity, O. After riding six miles he reached the house of sister Richards in usual health, and enjoying a very happy frame of mind. He conversed freely and cheerfully with the family till about seven o'clock, when looking at his watch he stepped out of the room door and fell. The family, supposing he had fainted, used all the means in their power to revive him; but his work was done, and his happy spirit had fled to the mansions above. Thus, in the eighty-second year of his age, and the fifty-fourth of his ministry, this devoted, self-sacrificing preacher of the Gospel

"Ceased at once to work and live."

CHAPTER XI.

JOHN SALE.

IF, as one has said, "history is philosophy teaching by examples," we may add, with equal propriety, biography furnishes the examples which history records. No department of literature can be more interesting than truthful narratives of human life—certainly none can be more instructive; and hence it is that we grasp with eagerness and read with avidity sketches of the life and times of those who have gained notoriety by worthy or adventurous deeds.

The subject of our narrative was a western man. He was born in the state of Virginia, on the 24th of April, 1769. History furnishes us no account of the precise place of his birth, or of his parentage. In early life he was awakened and converted to God, through the instrumentality of Methodist preachers who visited the neighborhood where he resided. He soon joined the Church, and, for a youth, became a devoted and exemplary Christian.

It is worthy of remark, that so many of the early preachers were converted in their youth. It seems to have been the order of Providence, since the days of Samuel, who was called when a child to the service of the sanctuary, to take the young and susceptible mind and early train it, by grace, for the great work of the ministry. If the reader will look over the biographical sketches which we have written, he will find that nearly all who were called to preach the Gospel were, in early life, made the subjects of converting grace.

When young Sale became religious he was surrounded by worldly and wicked associations, and it cost him an effort, such as those only can make who have firmly resolved, by God's grace, to break up all unhallowed associations, and start out, at all hazards, in the path of life, who, putting their hand to the plow and counting the cost, have crossed the chasm that separated them from the world of sin, and cut away the communication. To become a Methodist at that time, which of all the forms of Christianity was most despised by the wicked, was to enter upon a profession which would insure the contempt and scorn of the ungodly, and, not unfrequently, of many professors of another faith. The most opprobrious terms were heaped upon Methodists in that day, and they were called "fanatics, swaddlers," etc. Young Sale, however, had Christian courage and nerve enough to breast the storm of ridicule which he met, and bravely stood his ground, fully identifying himself with the despised number of God's children. With zeal and courage he took up the cross, despised the shame, and boldly espoused the cause of his divine Master. He passed through many and severe conflicts of mind in regard to his call to preach the Gospel; but after much prayer and profound consideration in regard to what was his duty, he finally yielded to the movings of the Spirit and was licensed to preach, and in due time received on trial in the traveling connection, at the conference held at Salem Chapel, in the state of Virginia, on the 24th of November, 1795. The first circuit to which he was sent was Swanino, in the wilds of Virginia, where he had his courage and fidelity tested in breasting the dangers and hardships of a pioneer preacher. His next circuit was the Mattamuskeet, in the lowlands of the above state. Added to the necessary hardships connected with traveling this circuit, it was a very sickly region and much dreaded by the itinerant; but as no scenes could disgust or dangers deter the preachers of those days, wherever, in the providence of God, their lot was cast, Sale went, in the name of his Master, and entered upon the work assigned him ready to do or die.

After finishing his labors on this field, he was sent over the mountains to the Holston circuit. Here, in the west, he had the same hard fare; but he had, as a good and faithful soldier, enlisted "during the war," and felt no disposition to lay down his arms till the great Captain of his salvation should grant him a final release from conflict and suffering below. In the year 1799 he traveled the Russell circuit, and the two succeeding years he labored on Salt River and Shelby circuits. The next year he traveled the Danville circuit, where, as on all the circuits named, he was made a blessing to multitudes. Many will hail him on the shores of immortality as the honored instrument of their conversion to God.

In the year 1803 he was sent to the North-Western territory, and stationed on Scioto circuit, which embraced a large extent of country. The following year he was appointed to Miami circuit. These two circuits then embraced all the south and west portions of the now state of Ohio. It was while traveling this circuit that he organized the first society of Methodists in Cincinnati, mention of which the reader will find in the chapter which relates to the origin and progress of Methodism in Cincinnati. The conference which had been held at Mt. Gerizim the preceding year, organized the Ohio district, which was the first in the state, and the Rev. William Burke was appointed the presiding elder, as his autobiography will show. For the purpose of giving the preachers of the present day some idea of the extent of the fields of labor, and the manner in which they were supplied, we will give a list of appointments: Muskingum and Little Kanawha, George Askins; Hockhocking, James Quinn, John Meek; Scioto, William Patterson, Nathan Barnes; Miami, John Sale, J. Oglesby; Guyandotte, Asa Shinn. When we take into the account the sparseness of the population, the distance between the appointments without roads, rivers to be crossed without bridges, it must be obvious that none but such as felt a necessity laid upon them to preach the Gospel would be likely to engage in such a work. In the year 1805 he returned to Kentucky and was appointed to the Lexington circuit. Here he labored with success in cultivating the vineyard of the Lord, and at the expiration of the year was sent to the Ohio district, where he labored with untiring zeal for two years. At this time the district was divided, and he was appointed to the Miami district. It was during his labors on this district that we first became acquainted with him, and from his hand in 1809 we received our first license to preach the Gospel. He had employed us to travel on the circuit four months previous to the date of our license, and with his permit we endeavored to preach Christ and his salvation around the circuit. From the camp meeting on Paint creek, where we received license to preach, without any recommendation from a class meeting or quarterly conference we were recommended to the annual conference for admission, and accordingly received. A short time since we visited this consecrated spot. But the grand old woods were gone. The trees, which spread their giant branches and screened us from the sun, affording the most refreshing shade, have been leveled by the axman's stroke, and there, ir that cornfield where we stood, had been gathered thou sands of men and women, from all parts of the country to listen to the words of life. A thousand recollection rushed upon us as we stood there and wept to think ho many of that assembled throng had passed away. Her stood the Rev. Dr. Tiffin, and the eloquent Monett, and the zealous Collins, of the Baltimore conference—father of the late Rev. John Collins—the presiding elder, and the aged father of the writer of this sketch, and with full and fervent hearts proclaimed God's love to perishing sinners, many of whom tremblingly fled to Christ for mercy, and found pardon and salvation. But preachers and people have alike gone to that bourne from whence no traveler returns, these to answer for the manner in which they discharged their duty as ministers of the Gospel, and those to render an account for the manner in which they received that Gospel from their lips. What a solemn reflection, that in a few years all the old pioneers who preached the Gospel in the west will be gone, and nothing left to tell of their toils and sufferings but a few hasty sketches!

In this field of labor brother Sale was quite successful, and prosperity attended his labors in all parts of the district. The next four years he labored on the Kentucky district, and the two following he was back again on the Miami district. In 1817 he traveled Union circuit, and the following year Mad River; and in 1819 he is again n the Miami district. The year following, in consequence of loss of health, he was obliged to take a superınnuated relation, in which he remained for five years, at he expiration of which time, his health improving, he vas made effective, and appointed to the Wilmington cir-uit. The next year he traveled Union circuit, and the ollowing Piqua, where he closed his labors with his fe.

How rapidly have we passed over the labors of the last n years of his life, all summed up in a few lines; and ow meager the whole of our sketch of this pioneer reacher! And yet how can it be otherwise, where nothg is left, not even a page, from which to gather a history of his labors? Indeed, were it not for the printed Minutes, which contain his appointments from year to year, not even this much could be saved from oblivion If "blessings brighten as they take their flight," and we are not disposed to appreciate them till they are removed from us, how assiduously should we labor to gather up the reminiscences of our aged brethren, and how fondly should we cherish those recollections of their heroic achievements in the cause of their Lord, which endear them to us!

On the 15th of January, 1827, while on the Piqua circuit, at the house of his friend and brother, Mr. French, he was called to yield up his spirit into the hands of God. We visited him a day or two before his death, and although his sufferings were intense, yet he had great peace in believing. His faith enabled him to behold the land that was afar off, and to rejoice in the sight of his distant heavenly home. He was frequently heard to say, "I am nearing my home. My last battle is fought, and the victory sure! Halleluiah! My Savior reigneth over heaven and earth most glorious! Praise the Lord!" On my second visit we were accompanied by Colonel William M'Lean, one of his warm, personal friends. We found him very happy, just on the verge of heaven. When on rising to leave, we took his hand, and bade him farewell. He said, "My son, be faithful, and you shall have a crown of life." We left the dying herald of the cross strong in faith, giving glory to God for a religion that

"Can make a dying bed
Feel soft as downy pillows are,
While on his breast he leaned his head,
And breathed his life out sweetly there."

Worn down with the toils and sufferings, as the necessary and always concomitant attendants of an itineran life, he was ready and prepared to enter into the rest of heaven.

"Servant of God, well done,
Rest from thy loved employ;
The battle's fought, the vict'ry won,
Enter thy Master's joy."

Brother Sale was about five feet ten inches high, of great symmetry of form, dignified and courteous in his manners. He had a dark eye, which, when lighted up with the Gospel themes, would flash its fires of holy passion, and melt at the recital of a Savior's love. But he has gone where anxiety, and toil, and tears come not.

Brother Sale was not a very vehement speaker, and yet he was far from being dry or uninteresting. He indulged very little in declamation, his chief aim being to preach the doctrines of the Gospel, and enforcing the practice thereof; so that while his hearers were thoroughly indoctrinated in regard to all matters of belief, they were urged to the performance of all duties, and thus a life in the soul was produced which fitted them for heaven. No one excelled him in the judicious administration of discipline and the government of the Church. We never knew a better manager. He seemed to govern without design, and so thoroughly did he acquaint himself with the disposition and temperament of men, that all yielded to his advice and direction without feeling themselves under any constraint. He was a great favorite of Bishop Asbury, and was, when able to attend, elected, from time to time, as a delegate to the General conference. After marrying he settled in the neighborhood of Xenia, at a place called Union, one of the early strongholds of our western Zion. His family of sons and daughters embraced religion in early life. One of his sons is now a traveling preacher in Indiana, and we trust is following in the footsteps of his father. His pious and venerable consort still lives, full of faith and good works, waiting with patience for the hour to arrive when her divine Lord shall call her to mingle with the departed in the world of bliss.

CHAPTER XII.

THE FIRST METHODIST CHURCHES IN OHIO.

We have already given a description of the "Old Stone," in Cincinnati; but before its day there were here *and there scattered over the state*, in different places, round and hewed-log, and frame churches, which had been erected and dedicated to the worship of God. Though rude they answered the purpose for which they were erected, and were suited to the times. Some of these yet stand as mementos of the past; and though they may be unoccupied, or devoted to other purposes, or have fallen into decay, and no longer resound with the clear, full voice of the early pioneer itinerant, or echo the sound of praise and prayer, still their memory is precious, and a thousand hallowed associations gather around their fallen timbers and dilapidated walls. Could histories of all these early churches be written by some master hand, what thrilling memories would come up from the forgotten past, as the hallowed scenes of other days would crowd upon the vision. Our fathers are gone. Only here and there, like the rude churches they occupied, are they left. As the trees of the mighty forest they have fallen around us, and every year witnesses their departure from our midst.

In the Advocate of 1840 the reader will find the following from the pen of the Rev. H. Smith, a western pioneer, whose letter to the Historical Society is not only descriptive of early times in Ohio, but shows the difficulties the first preachers had to encounter in getting congregations and places to preach. It was written to Mr. Samuel Williams, the Secretary of said Society; and among the interesting items which it contains the reader will find an allusion to a log meeting-house, on Scioto Brush creek, supposed by him to have been the first Methodist church in the North-Western territory:

"As I have been solicited by several of my brethren, in the west, to write something for your society, I ventured to make a beginning in a letter to my old friend, the Rev. William Burke, about the first of August. I do not know whether it was received, or how disposed of, if received, as I have had no Western Christian Advocate from the 17th of July to the 28th of August. What I do in this way I must do quickly. I am the more encouraged to write as your Society gives great latitude, and seems to be disposed to exercise indulgence.

"Lewis Hunt, a young man, traveled Miami circuit in 1799; but we had heard that he was broken down, and I was sent to take his place. On the 15th of September I set out, in company with brother Francis M'Cormick, to meet brother Hunt, on Mad river. We met him at brother Hamer's, and found him so far recovered as to be able to go on in his work. My instructions were, that if he should be able to continue in the work, to go up the Scioto, and form a circuit there. We consulted our friends, and formed a plan, uniting Scioto to Miami, making a six weeks' circuit. This plan was, however, abandoned, on account of the great distance between the two circuits, and the dismal swamp we would have to pass through every round.

"On the 18th of September I left brother Hunt, and returned to brother M'Cormick's, and on Sunday, the 22d, I, for the first time, heard the Rev. Philip Gatch preach. He was truly a very fine sample of primitive

Methodist preachers, simple, plain, and powerful; his reliance for success appeared to be wholly upon power from above. I found him a meek-spirited, agreeable old man, always willing to give counsel when asked, but never intruding. But the old veteran has gone to his reward, and I trust his praise is still in the Churches in the west. I had the pleasure of giving an exhortation after the good old man, and the Lord was with us indeed, in public and in class meeting. Some were much refreshed, and my own soul among the rest.

"Monday, 23d. I was unwell, but rode about ten miles toward my new field of labor, and lodged with a poor but pious Methodist family.

"Tuesday, 24th. I pursued my journey up the Ohio river, and put up with James Sargent, an old Methodist friend from Maryland, who received and treated me with all the kindness of an old Maryland Methodist. Here I left two appointments for my next round.

"Wednesday, 25th. I still pursued my course up the Ohio river, but had a very intricate path, and, indeed, sometimes none at all; but by the good hand of the Lord upon me, the evening brought me to the house of a kind Presbyterian family. We spent the evening in conversation on religious subjects. The old gentleman asked me to pray with them in the evening, and again in the morning, and pressingly invited me to call again whenever I came that way. I thanked them for their hospitality, but never had another opportunity of calling upon them.

"Thursday, 26th. I left this kind family at the mouth of Red Oak, and started for Eagle creek, and began to inquire for Methodists, but could hear of none. I took up Eagle creek, and being directed to a family where I could get some information, I rode up to the house, and asked the good man of the house if he could tell me where any of the people called Methodists lived. He said he could give me no information. But his wife formerly belonged to the society, and invited me to alight and come in. I did so; and while my horse was eating, I told them who I was, and my business. I entered into conversation about spiritual things, and requested the man to call his family together, and I prayed with and for them, and was much drawn out. I gave them a short exhortation, and left them all in tears. I rode about eight or nine miles, and inquired for Methodists again, and was directed to a poor man's cabin. I found him and his wife Jane in the cornfield. I called to him, and inquired if he could tell me where I could find any of the people called Methodists. He leaped over the fence, ran to me, and took me by the hand with all the cordiality of a true Irishman. I told him my name and business, and he received me with every expression of joy, called to Jane, and conducted me in triumph to the cabin. Jane came out of the field in cornfield habiliments, it is true; but she soon washed and changed her dress, and appeared to make me as welcome to their cabin as her husband. Such a reception was worth a day's ride. If I was but poorly qualified for a missionary in every other respect, I was not in one thing; for I had long since conquered my foolish prejudice and delicacy about eating, drinking, and lodging. I could submit to any kind of inconvenience where I had an opportunity of doing good, for I thought myself honored in being permitted to labor in any part of the Lord's vineyard. My call was among the poor, and among them I could feel myself at home. Jane gave me something to eat, and we ate our morsel with gladness, and talked about Jesus. In time of family prayer the melting power of God came down and filled the place with glory. The merciful people had taken their poor horse in with them the previous winter, and of course it could not be very agreeable; but poor Jane brought out of her chest as clean white sheets as ever came from Ireland, and spread them on my bed, and I slept sweetly, and arose refreshed. Here I was informed there were four or five Methodist families still higher up the creek, who had formed themselves into a society, and met on Sundays for prayer and class meeting.

"Friday, 27th. I rode to old brother John Foster's, and the dear family received me with open arms, and sent out word to their neighbors, and I preached on Saturday the 28th, to about eighteen or twenty persons with a degree of life, and the word seemed to find way to their hearts.

"Sunday, 29th. I preached at Peter Rankin's, four miles down the creek, to a small but very attentive congregation—this was the place where the small society met—and the poor starving sheep fed freely upon the word of life.

Monday, 30th. I rode to a brother Wormsley's, on Ohio Brush creek. With this family I had been acquainted in Kentucky, and we had an unexpected but joyful meeting. In family worship the Lord was present in power, the dear family were melted into tears, and the room appeared to be filled with glory and with God. We sang and talked about Jesus, and shouted aloud for joy. And who would not shout for such an unexpected, but seasonable visitation of mercy? Word was sent out, and preaching appointed at William Bushill's.

Tuesday, 31st. I attended, our congregation was small, the country was sparsely settled, and the notice short. I stood up among them, and cried, 'I Am hath sent me unto you.' Some poor sinners were deeply affected, and seemed to feel as if the Lord had sent me to them, and the Lord's poor mourning children had no doubt of it. O, it was worth while to suffer a little to meet with such a scene, and such a reception! Here a society was already formed by Joseph Moore, from Scioto Brush creek; and Simon Frilds was their leader.

"Wednesday, October 1st. I rode to Joseph Moore's, Scioto Brush creek. Here I found a considerable society already organized by brother Moore. Here I had some success, and the society increased, so that on the sixth of August, 1800, we proposed building a meeting-house; for no private house would hold our week-day congregation. But we met with some opposition, for some wanted a free house. But as no one seemed to care 'for their souls' but the Methodists, it appeared to me like foolishness to build a house for other denominations, before they came and wanted a house. We, however, succeeded in building a small log-house, but then large enough for the neighborhood, the first Methodist meeting-house on the circuit, and perhaps the first in the North-Western territory. I did not stop to preach here on my first visit, but left an appointment for my next, and pressed onward toward Pee Pee, on the Scioto.

"Friday morning, 4th. I rode through a heavy rain to Pee Pee, and called at the house of Snowden Sargent, a kind-hearted old Methodist from Maryland. I was wet, hungry, and brought plenty of company with me, from a bear-skin, my bed the night before. I introduced myself, and met with a cordial reception by a very kind family.

"Saturday, 5th. I rested and refitted; and truly rest was needful, as well as desirable. Here I met with several friends with whom I had been acquainted, and among them the Rev. William Talbott, who had preached at my father's when he first began to itinerate. But his zeal and excessive labors soon broke him down, and he retired from the itinerancy, and tried to provide for himself and rising family. He, however, preached occasionally. I heard him preach afterward at our quarterly meeting, at Pee Pee, with divine unction.

"Sunday, October 6th. I preached for the first time at Pee Pee. All were very attentive, and some felt the word. After preaching I called together a few who had been in society in various places, and organized a class, and the Lord was truly among us. One shouted aloud, and the most of the professors appeared to be much quickened. In those days I was always at home in a class meeting, and if I did not succeed in public I was almost sure to come out in class. I preached again at night; the people were all attention. I lodged with my friend Talbott. O, how ought those to be esteemed who have sacrificed their health, and almost their lives, in the cause of God! but this is not always the case, for some end their days in obscurity and poverty."

We have before us also a communication from one of the pioneers of Methodism in Ohio—the Rev. John Meek—which will furnish the reader an account of some of the first meeting-houses of his day. These reminiscences of olden time are not only interesting in themselves, but they serve to show how small and seemingly insignificant were the beginnings of Methodism in this western valley, and what astonishing progress has been made in the increase of membership, and the building of churches all over the land:

"In the year 1805, when the Miami Valley, from Cincinnati to the settlement two miles from the spot of ground where the beautiful town of Urbana is built, extending and spreading from the Big Miami river to White-oak creek, into what is now called Brown county, at brother Davis's, near where Georgetown is now growing, I was appointed to that circuit. The above territory was my field of labor in that year—1805—which was the year alluded to by brother Simmons, in which Hopewell meeting-house was built, at the dedication of which the small Church in that part of the wilderness was blessed by the labors of our beloved M'Kendree, of precious memory, and brother William Burke, who was then presiding elder of the Ohio district, together with brothers Amos and Patterson. I believe brother Burke preached from 2 Corinthians iii, 18: 'But we all with open face,' etc.; and brother M'Kendree followed with, 'Now the Lord is that Spirit, and where the Spirit of the Lord is there is liberty'—17th verse. The anointing of the Holy Spirit appeared to be upon them; 'the power of God was present to heal;' the slain of the Lord were many; the cry of the wounded, and the shout of them that were made whole 'was heard afar off;' and, blessed be God! I expect to meet some in heaven that were converted to God at that meeting. I will here say, those were the happiest days of my life—log-cabins to preach in, puncheon floors to sleep on, long rides, corn-bread and milk to eat, a constant succession of kind friends to make welcome, and the love of God in the soul, a home high up in heaven in prospect, and the blessed promise of, 'Lo I am with you always, even unto the end of the world,' gave the mind a most pleasing variety, and caused our time to move on most agreeably. But where have I wandered from what I intended when I sat down to write?

"But to old Hopewell log meeting-house. I will say to brother Simmons's inquiry, a log meeting-house was erected in West Wheeling circuit, on Indian Short creek, called Holmes's meeting-house, some time in the year 1803, in the immediate neighborhood of which there followed one of the most powerful revivals of the work of God, in the awakening and conversion of sinners to God, that I recollect ever to have witnessed; and I think I will be safe in saying, that from the time that Holmes's log meeting-house was erected, more than one hundred souls were happily converted to God, and on their way to heaven, ere Hopewell meeting-house, of which my beloved Simmons speaks, was ever thought of. And in the year 1804 there was a log meeting-house commenced, raised, and covered at old brother Thomas Odle's, a local preacher, on Eagle creek, in Scioto circuit, though it was never finished. So you see the pioneers of the Miami were not the first in Ohio to build meeting-houses."

CHAPTER XIII.

SAMUEL PARKER.

THAT eminent servant of the Lord Jesus Christ, whose name stands at the head of this chapter, in consequence of his relation to the west and the labors and privations he endured in planting the Gospel from the Muskingum and Ohio to the Missouri and Mississippi, deserves a prominent place in the annals of western Methodism. To give our readers a sketch of his laborious and useful life is the object of this chapter.

Samuel Parker was born in the state of New Jersey in the year 1774. His parents were religious, and, of course, respectable. Indeed, none need wish to trace their genealogy to a higher or more honorable source; for a Christian is emphatically "the highest style of man," and the only respect of persons with God himself is that which has for its basis a religious character. Young Parker was early put to a trade, that he might learn, by a lawful and honorable employment, to gain a respectable living in the world. It is said he possessed a remarkable natural genius, and made great proficiency in the mechanic art in which he was employed.

The most remarkable event that transpired in relation to him, in the days of his youth, was his conversion to God, and the sudden abandonment consequent thereon of his wicked practices and ungodly associates. Among the young and frivolous, in scenes of mirth and revelry, his presence was always the most agreeable, and his company was sought for on all occasions, being a general favorite among all classes. He had a voice of unusual sweetness as well as of compass and power. Added to this peculiar gift, as a child of song, was an urbanity of manners and a suavity of disposition that prepossessed all hearts in his favor. When he joined the Church and broke up his old and wicked associations, of course his former wicked friends forsook him. The line of demarkation was much more strongly marked between the Church and the world then than at the present time, and professors of religion were distinguished by peculiarities which made them known and read of all men. One has said, in speaking of the wonderful similarity between the most of professors of religion at the present day and the world, that it would take the eye of an angel to distinguish them; but it was not so then. A profession of religion created a chasm between the professor and the world, which, though not as broad and deep as that which separated Abraham from Dives, yet was impassable to all but those who would willingly take up their cross and, despising the shame, enroll themselves under the banner of the Prince of Life. Young Parker had deliberately crossed over to the Lord's side, and was ready, having counted the cost, to "hail reproach and welcome shame" for the sake of Jesus and his cause. For twelve years he continued a private member of the Church, faithfully devoted to all her interests, and ready to engage in any work that his Master might assign him. There was one work, however, concerning which he had much solicitude, and that was the fearfully-responsible work of the ministry. During all this time he was greatly exercised in mind in regard to his call. He would not rush suddenly into a place where angels are not permitted to enter, nor would he shrink from a responsibility clearly imposed, however great. He wanted full proof that he was called of God to proclaim salvation to his dying fellow-man, and having that he was ready to give up all for Christ, and enter whatever field of labor might be assigned to him.

We are of the number of those who believe that there are more who refuse to yield to this divine call to the ministry than of those who presumptuously rush uncalled into the holy place, and that the providence of God has much to do, not only in preparing the way for the one but in restraining the other. Fully impressed, after years of conflict, that he had a call to preach the Gospel, and that if he did not yield the Divine displeasure would rest upon him, he at length gave himself up wholly to the Lord in the work of the ministry, and in the year 1800 was duly licensed as a local preacher in the Methodist Episcopal Church. While he continued in this relation he exercised his gifts at every opportunity, and engaged in a course of preparatory study, the more effectually to prepare himself for usefulness, should Providence open his way into the itinerant field. During this time he made rapid progress in literary and theological knowledge, and was thus enabled, in the year 1805, to enter the itinerant ranks with advantages of literary and theological training vastly superior to many of his cotemporaries. His, however, was not that knowledge that puffeth up. He brought all his literature, and science, and theology to the foot of the cross, and there had his attainments and himself baptized with the meek and holy spirit of his Master. He was received on trial, as a traveling preacher, in the Western conference, held at Mt. Gerizim, Kentucky, in the fall of the year above specified, and was appointed to Hinkston circuit, where he remained traveling from appointment to appointment, doing the work of an evangelist and striving to make full proof of his ministry. In the year 1806 he was appointed to the Lexington circuit, and the year following to Limestone circuit, both in the state of Kentucky. In

1808 he was appointed to the Miami circuit, in the state of Ohio, Cincinnati being one of the appointments. On this circuit he was the messenger of glad tidings to many a despairing sinner. Multitudes were awakened and converted to God through his instrumentality, and throughout the Miami Valley there are many who were brought into the kingdom of grace through his instrumentality, and yet stand living witnesses for Christ and the power of the Gospel to save.

We have already remarked that brother Parker possessed a voice of unusual melody, and was excelled by few, if any, in the power of song. Many were attracted to the Church to listen to the divine strains which he would pour forth upon his enraptured and weeping audiences. He was not only gifted with a remarkable voice, but he had brought it under a high state of cultivation, and it was said he was a perfect master of music. We were told by Bishop M'Kendree that when he was on the Hinkston circuit, at one of brother Parker's quarterly meetings, he mentioned to him a tune which he had heard in the southern part of Kentucky that so interested and thrilled him, that it had been sounding in his mind ever since. The Bishop was deprived, like many others, of the wonderful gift of song, though he had an exquisite ear for music, and was said to be a connoisseur. Brother Parker told him he thought he could produce it, and for this purpose they both retired to the woods. The plan for its production, or, rather, reproduction, was this. The preacher sounded the various notes, and the Bishop would tell him when a note accorded with the tune. Thus he continued till he had written every note of the entire piece. The time for preaching having arrived they went into the congregation, and to the utter astonishment of the Bishop the tune was sung to appropriate words, but with a melody and a power, which not only affected the Bishop, but the whole congregation, to tears.

But his musical powers were not all, though to hear him would remind one of the melody of heaven; he had an eloquence and power in the pulpit that were irresistible, and wherever he went wondering and weeping audiences crowded to hear him. Many came a great distance to listen to him, so wide-spread was his fame as a pulpit orator. On one occasion an aged and very pious German brother came a considerable distance to hear him. When he arrived the preacher had taken his text and was making his introduction. The old brother took his seat and listened to the slow and measured words of the preacher, as he proceeded to advance his propositions. Not being able to discover any thing extraordinary, either in the matter or manner of the preacher, the honest old German would drop his head, giving it a significant shake, and say to himself, "Dis bees not Barker: dis be not him surely." After he had progressed some time in his discourse, and began to warm up a little with his theme, and occasionally flash out a bright and beautiful thought, the Dutchman, with a meditative look, and head a little inclined, would say, "May be dis is Barker." The preacher at length got fairly under way; his soul was on fire, and impassioned strains of eloquence, like full bursts of glory from the upper sanctuary, fell upon the rapt multitude. The old German rose to his feet, and was moving unconsciously forward, charmed with the eloquence of the preacher. He was lost to all surrounding objects, and lost to himself; for so intently was his attention fixed that he dropped his hat. When the preacher closed, the old man was at the altar, as near as he could get to the pulpit, and, drawing a long breath, he turned round, exclaiming, in a loud voice, "Mine Got, vot an outcome dis Barker has got!"

It is related of this old German brother, that being in court one time when a young lawyer, a member of the Methodist Church, was pleading most eloquently and feelingly the case of a poor, unfortunate girl, so much so that the judges and jury alike began to shed tears, he rose from his seat and exclaimed, "Mine Got, send more power; send more power to these sinners' hearts!" The good old man imagined that they were awakened by the exhortation of the Methodist lawyer, and that they would soon all be at the mourner's bench crying for mercy.

At the conference which was held in the year 1809, brother Parker was elected and ordained to the office of an elder in the Church. Having used the office of a deacon well, and having obtained a good degree and great boldness in the cause of his Master, and having given full proof of his efficiency as a minister, he was deemed worthy of promotion to the more responsible, but yet more arduous office of a presiding elder. His district embraced the whole of the state of Indiana, and the states of Illinois and Missouri. For vastness of territory, and for the amount of labor required to travel it, we think this must have been the banner district of those times. Notwithstanding the extent of the field, the amount of labor necessary to be expended in its cultivation, Parker's zeal and enterprise were adequate to the great undertaking. Buckling on the harness, if possible, with a steadier nerve and greater firmness of purpose, he turned his face toward the setting sun, and was soon lost to sight in the depths of the wilderness on the errand of his Master. In traversing this vast wilderness of woods, prairies, swamps, and rivers, inhabited principally by savage men and beasts of prey, exposed to the northern blasts of winter and the scorching heats of summer, God was with him. In the rude log-cabins of the west he found hard fare, but harder still when no cabin opened its friendly door, and he had to lie down supperless among the leaves of the wood, or the grass of the prairies, and not unfrequently upon the snow, with nothing but heaven's canopy for his covering. From the Whitewater, in Indiana, to the farthest settler in Missouri, did this faithful herald of the cross go to proclaim the glad tidings of salvation in the name of Jesus. For four years did the indefatigable Parker cultivate this vast field, and with such success "so mightily grew the word of God and prevailed," that it was necessary, at the expiration of this period, to divide the district, and call more laborers into the vineyard of the Lord. When he entered upon the field there were but three hundred and eighty-two members in all its bounds; but at the expiration of four years, under his superintendence, there were upward of two thousand.

An incident occurred at the conference which was held in Cincinnati, in 1813, which, in this connection, we will relate. There being no church on Sabbath large enough to hold the congregation, or rather the vast crowds which attended upon the ministrations of the occasion, we adjourned to the Lower Market Space, on Lower Market-street, between Sycamore and Broadway. The services commenced at 11 o'clock. The Rev. Learner Blackman preached from the third petition of the Lord's prayer: "Thy kingdom come." He was followed by brother Parker with a sermon on the fourth petition of the same prayer: "Thy will be done." After he had concluded, brother James Ward gave an exhortation after the manner of olden time. Then followed brother John Collins, who, from the same butcher's block whereon the preachers had stood, commenced, with a soft and silvery voice, to sell the shambles—as only John Collins could—in the market. These he made emblematic of a full salvation without money and without price. It was not long till the vast assembly were in tears at the melting, moving strains of the eloquent preacher. On invitation a large number came forward, and kneeled down for an interest in the prayers of God's people. We joined with them, and other ministers who were present, heartily in the work, and before that meeting closed in the market-house, many souls were happily converted to God.

This year brother Parker was appointed to labor on the Deer Creek circuit, which included all the settlements on that stream, as well as those on Darby, Scioto, and the North Fork of Paint creek, extending to Chillicothe, then the metropolis of the state. In this less extensive but still laborious field, his efforts to advance the kingdom of his Lord were wonderfully blessed. It was in the palmy days of camp meetings, before such meetings had lost their sheen and power, and the region where he labored was blessed with these annual seasons of religious interest. One of the most powerful camp meetings ever held in the west was in the bounds of this circuit, at White Brown's, on Deer creek. Here were collected the thousands of our Israel from all parts of the country, while the ministry was represented by the best talent in the Western conference. Among the preachers present on this occasion were John Collins, J. Quinn, Alexander Cummins, R. W. Finley, Hellums, Strange, Crume, and others. While one after another of these pioneer preachers would hold forth the word of life to listening, attentive thousands, the Spirit would apply the truth with demonstrative power to the heart, and hundreds were awakened and converted to God. Many that came out of an idle curiosity had an interest awakened in their hearts, to them before unknown, while many who came to curse and oppose the cause of God, remained to pray and unite with the faithful in carrying it on. It was a time long to be remembered, and hundreds on earth and in heaven will call to remembrance, with grateful emotions, the hallowed scenes and associations at the Deer Creek camp meeting.

At the close of the year 1813 the conference was held at Steubenville, Ohio. From this conference brother Parker received his appointment to the Miami district, which at that time embraced all the country lying between the Ohio river and the Olentangy, and the Scioto and Great Miami. His labors on this field were arduous, but successful. A zeal for the cause of God, fed with an unquenchable fire from off God's altar, urged him on, and nothing could stop him in his burning course around his district. Many, in the day of eternity, will thank God for sending the messages of mercy through so eloquent and faithful a herald.

The next year, which was 1815, he was removed from the Miami district, and appointed presiding elder of the Kentucky district. He remained in this field of labor four consecutive years, during all which time he was in labors more abundant. He was universally beloved on the district, both by the preachers and people, and his labors were crowned with great success. He had now reached life's prime, being in the forty-fifth year of his age; and deeming it prudent to change his relation in life by taking to himself a companion, he accordingly sought and obtained the hand of Miss Alethia Tilton, the daughter of a venerable and useful local preacher of that name, who proved a most worthy and suitable partner for a Methodist itinerant, in those days of privation and hardship. This worthy lady enjoyed his society long enough to be sensible of the melancholy fact that there is no affliction incident to suffering humanity so exquisite as the loss of a companion, who united all the endearing qualities that nature and grace can combine in the person of a husband.

We come now to the most interesting, because the most trying, period in the history of our departed brother's life; one which not only served to develop his character even more fully than it yet had been developed, but which presents the Church and the world an example of moral heroism as worthy of imitation as it is of praise.

At the conference which was held in Cincinnati in the summer of 1819, the bishops felt the utmost solicitude in regard to finding a man of the requisite qualifications to fill a post of the greatest importance in the Mississippi conference. Before them were ministers from all parts of the great western field; and after scanning the whole, they found in the person of Samuel Parker the one that, in their judgment, was admirably adapted for the work. His experience in the work, and above all his commanding talents, fitted him, in an eminent degree, for the occupancy of that difficult and distant field. The only thing they could conceive of as being in the way of his appointment was, his delicate health, and that his wife must be torn away from the embrace of her friends to share the fate and fortunes of her husband—a stranger in a strange land. Besides the greatness of the distance and his feeble health, the country embraced in the field was regarded as quite sickly. When, however, the bishops intimated the demands which the Church, in the providence of God, seemed to have upon his labors and sacrifices, in the true spirit of a witness for Jesus, if need be, to the ends of the earth, he was ready to say, in the language of Paul, "I count not my life dear unto me, that I may finish my course with joy, and the ministry which I have received of the Lord Jesus, to testify the Gospel of the grace of God." He had laid all upon the altar of his Lord. He had endured hardness as a good soldier, and it was no time now for him to take back the offering, or to hesitate in the further fulfillment of the vows which he had made to please Him who had called him to be a soldier. Ready for every position which God, in his providence, might assign him, he said to the over-shepherds of the Church, "Here am I, send me."

The conference closed, and when it was announced by the presiding bishop that he was appointed presiding elder of the Mississippi district, a wave of sympathy rolled over the entire conference. We shall never forget the parting scene. When we took our dear Parker by the hand, and said, "Farewell, beloved brother, till we meet again," we felt that it would be in the communings of that world,

"Where no farewell words are spoken,
And no farewell tears are shed."

It seemed as though we were all engaged in the solemnities of a sacrifice where the victim was one of the most lovely and talented of our brotherhood.

The last days of summer were tinting with golden hues the plains of the sunny south, as the sweet-spirited Parker, with his lovely bride, was wending his way thither in the name of his Master. He had left his friends, and home, and kindred, and was going to a far-distant land, among strangers, to labor and die. The bishops fondly hoped that the genial winter-clime of the south might prove beneficial to his health; but, alas! how often has it proven true, that where one invalid passes the process of acclimation, and becomes convalescent, many die; and so it proved in this case. When he arrived at his destination, enfeebled and worn down with fatigue, his disease assumed, in a short time, a more malignant type, so that in November the most fearful apprehensions were excited that he would soon be called to exchange worlds. He never performed any labor on his district, and the only advantage resulting from his emigration to that distant and difficult post was the lesson which his example afforded, and the spirit and peace in which a Christian can suffer and die.

Thus he lingered on till the session of the Missouri conference, when he seemed to have slightly improved, and hopes were entertained by some that he might recover; but others, better acquainted with the nature of his disease, and the climate to which it was subjected, knew that they were as fallacious and transient as the fading hues of evening, which serve only to light the passage of departing day. Soon after conference he relapsed into a worse state than before, and he was rapidly brought down to the verge of the grave. In all these sufferings and changes through which he passed, this servant of the Lord was enabled to say, in perfect resignation, "Father, not my will but thine be done." On the sixth of December, when a holy quiet was reigning around, disturbed only by the sobs of an affectionate wife, which alone prevented one from thinking that the chamber where he lay was quite in the confines of heaven, the talented, faithful, and devoted Parker passed away to the bosom of his Savior and God.

Before his departure God had blessed him with an infant son, but the little one did not long survive. It was soon called to join its father in the blissful realms of the blest. The Sabbath after his decease his funeral sermon was preached, at Washington, Mississippi, by the Rev. William Winans, to a large and weeping congregation. The text was Revelations xiv, 13: "Blessed are the dead who die in the Lord; yea, saith the Spirit, that they may rest from their labors, and their works follow them."

The personal appearance of brother Parker was strikingly prepossessing. He was about five feet ten or eleven inches high, a slender but well-made form. He had a fine intellectual cast of countenance, expansive forehead, and black, piercing eye. He was one of the finest speakers we ever listened to, his voice being exceedingly musical, and capable of the softest, sweetest intonations. But that fine, manly form is mingled with the dust, and that voice, so entrancing, has been hushed upon earth forever. A volume might be written upon the labors and sufferings, and excellences of his character; but as we only design brief sketches, embracing important points in the lives of some of our pioneer Methodist preachers, to rescue them from oblivion, and hold up their example to the light of the present generation, we must bring our remarks, however reluctantly, to a close.

CHAPTER XIV.

LEARNER BLACKMAN.

THE subject of our present sketch was born in the state of New Jersey; but in regard to the exact date of his birth we have no opportunity of knowing. He was descended from pious parents, and many members of the family, at different periods of life, became religious. Our acquaintance with brother Blackman commenced in the year 1808. He was a brother-in-law of the Rev. John Collins, through whose instrumentality he was brought into the kingdom of grace, and made an heir of salvation. The personal appearance of Blackman was prepossessing, and impressed one, in looking upon his tall, slender form, and dark, flashing eye, that he had genius and eloquence; but when engaged in conversation, the brilliance and fascination of his manners would demonstrate that fact in a remarkable degree. To judge of his eloquence, however, he must be heard; and none who were permitted to listen to his silvery voice, when engaged in description, or its impassioned strains when in declamation, would go away without being impressed with his power over the heart. He may have taken the pathetic Collins for his model as a pulpit orator. Of this, however, we can not speak assuredly; but whoever was his model, or whether he had any that he copied after, one thing is certain, he was an eloquent divine.

We have been favored with a description of western preachers by one who has lived to witness what he calls the various phases through which the pulpit style has passed in his day. Among the first class of Methodist preachers there was a marked, if not an exclusive attention and devotion to doctrinal preaching. In all their sermons the distinctive doctrines of Methodism occupied the chief place. Repentance, faith, justification, sanctification, the possibility of falling from grace, with the doctrine of the atonement as contradistinguished from the Calvinian view, and occasional brushes at Church polity and ordinances as held by other denominations, formed the staples of the sermons of these early preachers. But not only was Calvinism attacked; Arianism, Universalism, and other forms of error were made to feel the lash of these sturdy pioneers of the faith of Wesley.

The next class which immediately succeeded these, in a great measure lost sight of polemic theology, and turned their attention to the graces of oratory. Their sermons were profusely interlarded with poetry, and some of the preachers possessed a peculiar *penchant* for blank verse. We recollect to have heard it said of one of the preachers of this class, that "he would break a square any time to make a jingle." Nicely-rounded periods, beauty of expression, and fine rhetorical flourishes, were regarded as of more importance than orthodoxy itself. Still, however, there were exceptions to this general rule, as also in regard to the first class.

This class had its day, and was followed by a third, and succeeding one, whose characteristic consisted in a didactic style of preaching. Their sermons, though not elaborately ornamented with poetry and flights of fancy, were, nevertheless, illustrated, from beginning to end, with anecdotes and incidents, some of which were so appropriate, that they are told by preachers of this class with thrilling effect, even to this day. A well-authenticated anecdote or incident, in the hands of a skillful preacher, will frequently accomplish more in arresting the attention and stirring up the soul to action, than the most powerful declamation itself. We shall have occasion, in another part of this book, to relate some of these.

This peculiar style of preaching, however, did not last always. It served its allotted time and gave way, not to a new class, but to the revival of an old one; and it seems that it did not stop in a medium in regard to its predecessors, but bounded back to the old stock, and revived the good old doctrinal style, mixing it up, however, with a little more of the historical and exegetical. How far this applies to the Methodist pulpit of the present day, your old friend will leave some graphic delineator of the times to describe. We do not profess to wield such a pen as would claim for us the qualification to enter upon the task of describing the Methodist pulpit of the present day, though were we to assume it we would not be disposed to consider it as being marked by any one striking characteristic distinguishing it from the pulpits of other denominations. We believe the Methodist pulpit to have vastly more learning at the present time than at any former period; but whether it possesses more zeal, and devotion, and wisdom, such as is adequate to win souls to Christ, is a question we shall not at present discuss, only so far as to say that our Church seems, in the hands of the present ministry, to be enlarging her borders beyond all precedent, in every section of the country.

But we ask pardon of our readers for having digressed so far from our subject, and shall resume our sketch of the young and talented Blackman. At the early age of nineteen he commenced his itinerant life. He was admitted on trial in the year 1800, and sent to Kent circuit. After this he traveled in regular succession Dover, Russell, New River, and Lexington circuits. Concerning his labors in these respective fields we have no information. In the year 1805 he was sent as a missionary to Natchez, thus passing rapidly over a vast extent of country.

The new field of labor to which he was destined was then the farthest west. To reach his appointment it was necessary for him to travel through a wilderness seven or eight hundred miles in extent, untenanted, except by savages and beasts of prey. But no, there were worse men than savages and beasts of prey—more cruel than the panther. We allude to those Indian traders who, to rob the red man of his skins and furs, would give them ardent spirits to drink and make them drunk, so that they would, in turn, rob and murder the traveler. It is the example of the white man that gave to the Indian character its desperate savageness; and as an old soldier and statesman, well acquainted with the history and policy of the nation, the other day remarked in Congress, "In every treaty that has been violated by the Indians the white man has been the aggressor."

Nothing daunted, our young hero missionary started on his journey. For fourteen days and nights he traveled alone and unattended through the wilderness. At night he would hitch his horse, and taking his saddlebags for a pillow and his blanket for a covering, he would lie down in the woods, commending himself to the keeping of his God. At length he arrived at the place of his destination. Methodism had scarcely gained an existence in the place. Yet there were a few who had been awakened and converted to God through the labors of Rev. Tobias Gibson, and they were struggling to keep alive the spark of grace in the midst of the superabounding wickedness. Notwithstanding there were some reputable persons friendly disposed to religion and morals, yet it was a lamentable fact that the vast majority were totally bankrupt in morals, and their proud hearts and vicious lives made them decided opponents of the Gospel of Christ; but their opposition was more strictly arrayed against those who preached it. At one time, when a plain, unlettered man was preaching, the wicked portion of the audience had great merriment on account of his ignorance of correct language. It seems that they had set themselves up to be *judges*, not hearers, of the word. We have such hearers at the present day. They will make a man offend for a word, and they will tax their shallow brains so much to recollect that, such is their anxiety to criticise, that if one should ask them about the division of the subject, or even the text itself, their feeble brains can not recall it. They are unable to hold but one idea at a time. At one time the grammar of this preacher was at fault, at another time his rhetoric, and then his logic, besides his gestures were awkward, etc. They did all they could to hedge up the poor man's way, and said he was not competent to preach. However, he was not to be intimidated by the laugh and sneer of his ungodly hearers. On one of his visits he took for his text the following: "Ye serpents, ye generation of vipers, how can ye escape the damnation of hell!" Then said he, in tones of thunder, "Gentlemen, is that grammar?" He was divinely assisted in his sermon, and having greatly the advantage of his censors, who sat as if taken by surprise, he kept it by pouring upon them passage after passage of divine denunciation upon the wicked, frequently asking the annoying question, "Gentlemen, is that grammar?" So successful was that effort, that ever afterward there was a studied silence in regard to the preacher's defects, and his grammar never afterward was called in question.

In the midst of such society young Blackman commenced his labors in that distant region. He was a stranger in a strange land, far from home and kindred. There were then no missionary funds to aid the itinerant in planting the Gospel in destitute places, and all the support upon which he could rely was the naked promise, "Lo, I am with you alway, even to the end of the world." He shared largely in the labors, privations, and reproaches incident to his calling, as a minister; but he realized the fulfillment of the promise in the presence of his Master, and the consolations of his grace. Occasionally the bright and happy scenes of home would flit across his memory, and the temptation to return to the loved ones he had left would be presented to his mind. "Surely," would the tempter say, "Your God is not a hard master, and he does not require you to preach the Gospel to those who will neither receive nor support it." But

> "The vows of God were on him,
> And he dare not turn aside to
> Pluck terrestrial fruit, or play with
> Earthly flowers."

What if they did not receive him; they also rejected his Master, and the servant must not be greater than his Lord; so in faith, and patience, and hope he labored on in the service of his King and Savior.

In the year 1806 he was appointed presiding elder of the Mississippi district. New laborers were brought into the field, which, while it proved a source of mutual encouragement, enabled them to present a stronger front to the enemy. The strongholds of sin and infidelity were attacked; errors, incrusted by time and fortified by custom, were destroyed; prejudices, the most inveterate, were driven away; and the light of the Gospel began to shed its cheering beams upon the long night of darkness which had reigned. Sinners were awakened and converted to God, houses of worship were erected, Churches organized, and the institutions of religion established; in fine, "the wilderness and solitary places were made glad, and the desert to rejoice and blossom as the rose," through the instrumentality of these faithful, self-denying heralds of the cross. In all the bounds of his present field of labor, when he first entered upon his work, there were but seventy-four whites and sixty-two colored members; and after three years' labor he was permitted to see embraced in the same field an entire district, with five circuits and a large increase in the membership.

But the itinerant system required him to cultivate other fields, and he left the lowlands of Mississippi, where he was beloved and respected by a numerous host of friends, whom God had raised up as the fruits of his labors, and went to Tennessee to preside on the Holston district. Here he continued two years, and from thence was removed to the Cumberland district, where he also remained two years, and at the expiration of which time he was placed, by the authorities of the Church, on the Nashville district. On all these fields he was in labors more abundant, and God crowned those labors with success, by making them effectual in bringing into the Church a rich harvest of souls. Perhaps under the labors of no one, in his day, were the borders of Zion more enlarged in the lengthening of her cords and the strengthening of her stakes. In the year 1815 he was reappointed to the Cumberland district. In the mean time he had married; and desirous of visiting his relations in Ohio, among whom was brother Collins, who had married his sister, he took a few days of spare time for that purpose.

He was again at his home and surrounded by the scenes of his youth—surrounded by the friends of other days, whose presence called up hallowed associations. After enjoying their society for a short time—for he could spare but a little while to turn aside and greet his friends—he bade them adieu and started for the field of his labors. Many tears were shed at parting, but none knew that they were the tears of a last farewell. None knew that in a few hours that tall, graceful form would be cold in death, and that dark but kindly eye, which beamed with such happiness, would close its light on earth forever. But the ways of God are inscrutable;

"Impervious shadows hide
The mystery of heaven."

The minister and his young, blooming bride, on their return, reached Cincinnati. Here they must cross the Ohio; but no proud steamer, as now, with its spacious guards spread out to the beach, is waiting to receive the passengers and ferry them over. A crazy craft, with sails and paddles, in that olden time, was all the means possessed for keeping up a communication between Ohio and Kentucky. Alighting from the carriage, the horses were driven into the flat, and it was pushed from the shore. Brother Blackman stood in front of his horses to hold them. When all was clear, and the boat was a short distance from the shore, the ferryman commenced hoisting his sails, the sight or flapping of which frightened the horses. Blackman made every effort to hold them, but before assistance could be had they plunged overboard, taking him with them. He had a strong arm and was a good swimmer; but, alas! neither strength nor skill can avail when the work of man is done. Till that hour he was immortal, but the time had come for the termination of his labors and his release from earth. He sank to rise no more a living man, till Jesus shall wake his saints from the sleep of death and call them up to heaven. Thus ended the laborious life of the young and talented Learner Blackman; and though the waters of the river, which roll yonder, quenched his life and drowned his dying words, yet we believe he sleeps in Jesus.

CHAPTER XV.

LOST CHILD; OR, "THE CAMP OF LYDIA."

To a denizen of a large city the words which stand at the head of this article produce but a faint impression when compared with that produced upon the mind of the villager. To the former it is a familiar sound, and he is accustomed by day and by night to hear the bellman's voice rising above the din of the city, or ringing out on the clear night air, "Lost child!" But when these words fall upon the ear of the dweller in the woods, or the inhabitant of the wilderness, a thousand frightful images at once rush upon the mind, rousing all to the most intense excitement. Once, while returning home about eleven o'clock on a cold winter's night, in a large city, we heard, at the corner of a square, an alarm bell, and we stopped to listen. Presently a despairing cry arose, "Lost children," accompanied by a description of their persons, and directions where to take them if found. Knowing it was not the old bellman, whose voice had become familiar to us in crying, "Lost child," we waited till the crier came up. When he reached the corner where we stood, he rung his bell and cried again. Just as he concluded, a whiskered animal, dressed in gentleman's clothes, coming along, exclaimed, "Try it again, old fellow!" "You heartless wretch!" said we, but he passed without noticing us. We then asked the crier whose children were lost. "Mine," said he, "and the child of a poor widow living close by me. We are not able to pay the bellman, and I started out myself to hunt the children." "O, God," we thought, "what a heartless world! Here is a poor man seeking his lost child at the dead hour of night, in the streets and alleys of a vast city, and not a soul to sympathize with or help him!" But to our story.

In the year 1805, when all the region of country bordering upon the Ohio river was a wilderness, and only here and there were villages, which had sprung up in the vicinity of forts—such, for instance, as Marietta, at Fort Harmar, and Cincinnati, at Fort Washington—and the savages roamed unmolested over the broad prairies and through the dense forests of the west, a scene occurred at a settlement about thirty miles north-east of Cincinnati, which produced the most astonishing excitement throughout the whole surrounding country. There lived at this settlement a family by the name of Osborn, which consisted of the father, and mother, and two daughters, the elder of whom was about eleven years of age, and the younger about seven. In those days of backwoods life every member of the family was employed, from necessity, in farming pursuits, and almost as soon as a child was able to walk it was taught to engage in some employment connected with rural life. While the father was engaged in attending his small patch of corn, and the mother was attending her domestic concerns, of cooking, knitting, spinning, or weaving, the children would be employed, if sons, in assisting the father in the field or barn; and if daughters, in helping the mother in domestic duties.

It was usually the duty of the younger boys to hunt the cows, which were left to run in the woods, and sometimes were difficult to find. As there were no boys in this family, it devolved upon the girls to search the ranges of the cattle, and drive home the cows. One afternoon in the latter part of summer, the little girls of the Osborn family started out on their accustomed pursuit. After finding the cows, which they were enabled to do by the tinkling of their bells, they started to drive them home. The elder girl, having become bewildered, supposed, from the direction the cows took, that they were going from instead of toward home. Fully impressed with this belief, she requested her little sister to stay where she was, and she would run and head them, and turn them in the right direction. But the cows, intent on going home, would not be diverted from their course. What to do she knew not; and fearing that her sister would be lost, she left the cattle, and started on hunt of her; but alas! how did her young heart ache when, after wandering about for a long while, and crying out her name in the woods, she could not find her! Sadly she started, without her sister, in the direction of home, as she supposed; but instead of this, the poor, bewildered child took an opposite direction from her father's cabin. The younger girl followed the sound of the cow-bells, and arrived safely at home; but Lydia—for that was her name—wandered on, and was lost in the wilderness.

Night came on, casting its darkened shadows over the forest, but she came not to greet the anxious eyes of her parents, which were growing sorrowful and dim with watching. No time was to be lost; their child was in the woods, exposed to the savages and wild beasts. The neighborhood was roused with the alarm of "Lost child!" The cry became general, like the cry of fire at night in a country village. Every heart was touched, and soon, in every direction, torches were seen flashing their light into the darkness of the forest. Bells were rung, horns were blown, and guns were fired through the woods, if, perchance, the sound might reach the ear of the lost one. The whole night was spent in a fruitless search. The news flew in every direction, and reached the settlement where we resided, and as many as could leave home turned out to seek for the lost child. This day was also spent in vain, though some signs of her tracks in crossing branches and miry places were discovered, all, however, indicating that she was going farther into the wilderness. On the third day the famous backwoodsman and hunter, Cornelius Washburn, arrived, with about five hundred others. Washburn was accompanied by his noted hunting-dog, of which it was said he would follow any scent his master would put him upon. At length the night of the third day arrived, but still no intelligence of the lost child. We were now deep in the wilderness, and we all made preparations for camping out that night. After lighting our fires, and taking some refreshment, we retired to rest by lying down upon the ground by our camp-fires. At daybreak we were up again, and ready for our search; but as the collection of people was so numerous, we concluded it was best to form ourselves into companies, and take different directions, and meet at night at a place designated, and report in relation to our discoveries. Money was collected and sent to the settlements to buy provisions, to be brought to the place of rendezvous. Every day we received accessions to our numbers, so that on the seventh day it was supposed there were more than a thousand persons gathered from all parts of the country, and many from Kentucky. The seventh night was spent on the head waters of the East Fork of the Little Miami. Washburn reported that he had discovered where the little girl had slept for several nights. The place she had selected was where one tree had fallen across another, which was lying down, and afforded a good protection. He also saw where she had plucked and eaten some fox-grapes and whortleberries. To this place the whole crowd hurried. Nothing could have restrained them, so eager were they to find the lost child, or some clue that would lead to her discovery.

In all these journeyings the father was present, and so absorbed in grief at the loss of his dear Lydia, that he could neither eat nor sleep. Sorrow drank up his spirits, and he refused to be comforted. When hope was kindled in his heart that his child would be found, he seemed like one frantic, and flew in every direction, calling most piteously the name of his child; but she was not there, her little feet had borne her to some other quarter of the wildwood. It was agreed the next morning that all the company should start out abreast, about three rods apart, with a man in the middle, and one at each end of the line, whose duty it was to blow horns at certain intervals for the purpose of keeping the line in order. It was an immense line, extending for several miles. Each man was instructed to examine carefully every branch and wet place, and every hollow log and thicket, to see if any traces of her were discoverable.

Thus, day after day, and night after night, the search went on, till sixteen days were passed away in the fruitless endeavor to find her. In the mean time, some of the company having lost all hope of finding her, returned home, but others came and filled their places, so that on no day were there less than one thousand persons on the search. On the fourteenth day, accompanied by two others, we took across to the North Fork of Whiteoak, and carefully searched the banks of that stream for miles. On the morning of the fifteenth day we found where she had crossed, by her footprints in the sand, at the water's edge. These footprints appeared to be fresh, and greatly revived our hopes. We were now distant from the main body of men several miles; and while one of our number was dispatched to communicate the intelligence, we proceeded to follow up a fork of the creek which puts in just where her footprints were found. Here there was an opening on the bottom land, where there was a large blackberry patch nearly a quarter of a mile in length. Near this patch we found a neat little house, built of sticks, nicely adjusted. It was covered with sticks, and over these were placed, in regular layers, pieces of moss taken from the logs and sides of trees in the neighborhood. The cracks were all neatly stopped with moss. In the center, on one side, was a little door, and in the interior was a bed made of leaves, covered with moss, and decorated with wild flowers. All could see at once that it was the work of a child; and we may have been childish while gazing upon it; for the tears stole freely down our cheeks. Here, away in the wilderness, far from human habitation, had this lost child constructed this miniature house, and thus recalled the scenes of home, and sister, and mother, and father.

The child must have been here several days; for, from her little house to the blackberry patch, she had beaten quite a path, and some parts of the patch were picked quite bare. We imagined that we had at last found the place where the little wanderer had fixed her abode; but now that we had got in reach of the prize, how to take it was the question. To make a noise would frighten her away to some hiding-place where she could not be found; for children, when lost, become wild as the antelope in his native forest, and if caught will make every possible resistance, even looking upon their best friends as enemies. Supposing that she was not far off, and would return to her house, we removed to a short distance, where we would be unobserved, and sat down to wait her coming. But there were no signs of her returning, and fearing lest we might be discovered by the lost child, we stole softly under covert, from tree to tree, and cleared the opening. Ascending an eminence, where we had a full view of the blackberry patch, we carefully scanned every part of it, and were satisfied that she was not there. Returning again, and making a more thorough examination, we could discover no fresh signs of her presence, and we concluded to return to the main creek, and wait for the company, and prevent, if possible, the press of the eager crowd from rushing on and destroying what signs might yet remain undiscovered. It is said that there were more than a thousand men encamped along the creek that night. The encampment extended for half a mile.

Fearing the consequences of making a disclosure of what we had seen at the blackberry patch, we kept it a secret till morning, and then taking aside the best woodsmen in the company, we led them to the house of the child. We then returned and formed the whole company into military order, and marched them out into the opening, where, flanking out right and left, they surrounded the entire space, and formed a hollow square. At the sight of the little cabin a scene occurred which it would be impossible to describe. Here were brave, stalwart men, who had been subjected to the perils of the wilderness, contending for every inch with savages and wild beasts, whose hearts were never known to quail with fear, who, at sight of that little cabin, were melted into tears. Some, as if deeming it unmanly to weep, or to be seen manifesting so much human sympathy, turned aside, while others left the ranks to give vent to their feelings in solitude. But when the father came up to the little dwelling his own dear child had built for herself, and exclaimed, "O, Lydia, Lydia, my dear child, are you yet alive!" a thousand hearts broke forth in uncontrollable grief.

The result of the investigation made by the hunters was, that the signs were three or four days old. Horse-tracks were also found in the grass, supposed to be about the same age. The conjecture was, that she had been discovered and taken away by some hunters, or a party of Indians. It was agreed, however, to make another effort. The company was divided, and sent out in different directions, to see if any further signs could be found of hunters or Indians. Two miles from "Lydia's camp"—for so it is called to this day—her bonnet was found hanging on a bush, and eight or ten miles further off, an Indian camp was discovered, supposed to have been vacated for five or six days. The conclusion was that the child had been carried off by the Indians, none knew where. Further pursuit being considered useless, the company disbanded, and returned to their homes. Not so, however, with the father. The love of his child was to him sweeter than life. He never gave up the search, but penetrated the wildest solitudes, and sought for her among the Indians till the day of his death. The lost was never found.

CHAPTER XVI.

JAMES AXLEY.

THE following graphic and stirring sketch of the Rev. James Axley, the eccentric preacher, has been kindly furnished for us by the Rev. Thomas A. Morris, D. D., Bishop of the Methodist Episcopal Church. It consists mostly of personal reminiscences of that remarkable man, and such, indeed, in a majority of instances, is all that we can gather of the fathers of Methodism in the west. So far as a connected biography is concerned the most that we can find is the bare announcement, on the Minutes of the various fields of labor, occupied by the preachers from year to year, and then, at the close of their earthly labors, a short obituary, embracing but a meager outline of their life and labors, and the circumstances connected with their death. But even this is denied the toil-worn soldier, should he be found in the local ranks, when death calls to take him home.

"In 1804 the Western conference was reinforced by a class of young men, some of whom became very distinguished Methodist preachers—among them were Samuel Parker, Peter Cartwright, and James Axley. With the last-named I never enjoyed but one week's personal acquaintance, but that left on my memory an indelible impression of his person and character, of which this pen-portrait is but an imperfect reflection. He had mingled with scenes of excitement, toil, and peril, well calculated to develop his physical and mental energies.

Among his early fields of labor were Red river, Hockhocking, French Broad, Opelousas, and Powel's Valley. Subsequently he labored on Wabash, Holston, Green River, and French Broad districts as presiding elder. These widely-separated points in the Lord's vineyard, all included in the old Western conference, indicate that he had a pretty thorough breaking into the Gospel harness after the manner of our fathers, in the days of Bishop Asbury, when itinerancy was what its name imports.

"Long as I had been crossing the path of that notable man, and much as I had heard of him among the people, my first sight of him was not obtained till the autumn of 1837. That year the Holston conference met at Madisonville, eastern part of Tennessee, some ten miles from which brother Axley, then in a local relation, resided. The first day of the session after adjournment I was walking to my lodgings alone, when I heard a brother some forty steps behind me say to another, 'Yonder comes brother Axley.' Looking ahead, I observed a man advancing toward me whose person was imposing. He was perhaps five feet eight inches high; not corpulent, but very broad and compactly built, formed for strength; his step was firm, his face was square, complexion dark, eyebrows heavy, appearance rugged; dressed in the costume of our fathers, with straight-breasted coat, and broad-brimmed hat projecting over a sedate countenance. His wide-spread fame as a natural genius without any early education, and especially the numerous incidents I had heard of him as a western pioneer, had excited in me a greater desire for his personal acquaintance than that of any other living man I had ever seen, except Jacob Gruber. The sound of his name falling on my ear involuntarily quickened my pace, and we were soon together. As I neared him I held out my right hand and received his, when the following salutations were exchanged:

"'How are you, brother Axley?'

"'Who are you?'

"'My name is Thomas A. Morris.'

"Then surveying me from head to foot, he replied, 'Upon my word, I think they were hard pushed for Bishop-timber when they got hold of you.'

"'That is just what I thought myself, brother Axley.'

"'Why, you look too young for a Bishop.'

"'As to that, I am old enough to know more and do better.'

"Turning back with me, we walked to our lodging, being both quartered at the same place. Every hour that I could redeem from conference and council business was enlivened by his quaint but thrilling narratives of his early travels, labors, and difficulties. Unaccustomed to the free use of the pen, he kept all his records in his tenacious memory, much strengthened by use, and narrated with uncommon precision as to names, dates, and the order in which facts transpired. This he did leisurely and with perfect self-possession, but spiced the whole with such apt remarks and consummate good-humor that the attention of the company never faltered. Never was I better entertained or more instructed with the conversation of a fellow-sojourner in one week than with his. It was decidedly rich.

"Next morning I observed him seated near the door, remote from the business platform, and invited him forward to conduct the opening religious service of the conference. Then it was that some of his peculiarities were practically developed to me for the first time. His reading and prayer were brief and simple, yet quite impressive; but his singing took me entirely by surprise. He used no hymn-book, gave out no lines, but led off on a familiar hymn and tune in strains so exhilarating and devotional that both appeared to be new and superexcellent. Whether he had ever paid any special attention to tune-books is doubtful, as he was proverbial for his opposition to choir-singing. However that may have been, his voice embodied in itself more strength, more volume, more melody, and certainly more devotional influence, than that of an ordinary church-choir of a dozen select singers. He was invited to a seat on the platform.

"After the journal was read, an unimportant resolution was offered, over which there was a little sharp shooting by speech-makers. Our guest, though opposed to the motion, did not interfere in the discussion. The brethren, having fired their minute guns, came to a vote, expressed in the usual way by raising their hands: two hands were plainly visible, and another was partly elevated and then suddenly drawn down. Before the Chair had time to announce the decision, brother Axley vociferated, in a very quaint manner, 'Just two votes and a half for that!' The effect upon the risibles of the body-ecclesiastic was electrical; the gravest of the fathers were convulsed with laughter. Only the author of it seemed to be self-possessed.

"There were points of singular contrast in his character. His exterior was rough as a block of granite fresh from the quarry, and his manner of reproving disorderly persons at popular meetings over which he presided was said to indicate severity; yet his conscience was so tender and his moral sensibility so acute, that a mere suggestion from a friend that he had erred in any given case would draw from him prompt acknowledgment with a shower of tears. His dress and address indicated the rustic, probably perpetuated by the force of early habit; and yet in social intercourse he was both kind and attractive. His conversational talent was of a superior order. Without classical learning or much pretension to book knowledge, he was such a master in practical, every-day affairs that he could not only delight, but instruct sages and divines. He could so present even a common-place topic as to throw interest around it, and by his musical powers he conquered some who could be reached by no other means. I was informed that individuals who were at first his enemies and persecutors because of his profession as a Methodist preacher, on hearing him sing, became his warm friends; and I do not doubt it. Indeed, he told me of himself an instance in which he was relieved from great embarrassment by singing, without saying any thing as to the merit of the performance. It occurred while he was laboring on the Opelousas mission, in Louisiana, perhaps about the year 1807 or 1808. In order to supply some destitute neighborhoods with the Gospel by enlarging his mission, he went on a tour of exploration where he was a stranger to all. Some of his adventures during that expedition would, by the ministers of this generation, be regarded as specimens of moral heroism. But omitting other incidents, I shall refer only to the point in hand. One evening, after riding all day without any dinner, he called at a house where the family consisted of a widow lady, a grown daughter, a number of children, and some servants, none of whom were religious. The lady and her family regretted his coming, would not grant his request to remain over night, and clearly indicated, by looks and actions, that he was an unwelcome guest. The reader may ask why he did not leave immediately. The reason was, he knew, if defeated in obtaining lodging there, nothing remained for him but a berth in the dark wood, without food or shelter, at an inclement season of the year. As he lingered a little to warm himself and consider how he should manage to pass that dreary night, the thought of his forlorn condition as a homeless stranger, without money or friends, came like a dark cloud over his mind. His deep, sad cogitations proceeded in silence. Then, as was natural in his extremity, he turned his thoughts toward his heavenly Father's house above, where he hoped some day to find a home free from the ills of mortal life. Being a little cheered with the prospect, without leave, introduction, or ceremony, he began to sing one of the songs of Zion in a strange land. As he proceeded his depressed feelings became elevated; the vision of faith ranged above and beyond the desolate wilderness he had just been contemplating as the place of his night's sojourn; the family were soon all melted into tears; he took fresh courage, and sang on with the least possible pause, till he had finished, perhaps, the third song, when the lady called a servant, and ordered him to put the gentleman's horse in the stable; and the daughter added, 'Be sure to feed him well.' Thus a few strains of sacred melody, such as Axley could wield, removed all opposition and relieved the case.

"Brother Axley made every important interest of life a subject of prayer, as all Christian people should. Toward the close of our week's interview he incidentally alluded to his courtship and marriage, which occurred, I believe, after he had been a minister some years. He opened his mind to his intended by letter, inclosed in another letter to her brother, with whom she resided. To the brother he wrote, if he had any objection to the correspondence with his sister, to burn it, and that would end the matter. The letter, however, was delivered into her hand, containing a proposition of marriage, and a notice that he would be there on a given day to receive the answer. On the day appointed he came, obtained an interview, and opened the cause by stating he wished to talk over the subject alluded to in his letter; 'but, first of all,' said he, 'we must pray for direction.' They kneeled together, and he led in prayer. After prayer he wished to know whether she consented to the proposed union. She thought it would not be amiss for her to have longer time in which to decide; but he deemed that needless, as they were well acquainted, and insisted on a present and direct answer. The result was marriage.

"He was proverbial for his opposition to slavery and whisky. After he located he supported his family by the labor of his own hands as a farmer, and was wont to testify, on all proper occasions, that his logs were rolled, his house raised, and his grain cut without whisky; and though he had plentiful crops of corn, not the first track of a negro's foot was ever seen in one of his fields. Such was his version of facts, as I learned from some of his friends.

"I never heard brother Axley preach; but, according to popular fame, his pulpit performances were practical, forcible, and left a deep and abiding impression on the multitudes that thronged together to hear him. To this day we occasionally hear allusion made to a sermon he preached in the city of Baltimore, during the General conference of 1820, of which he was a member. It must have been a potent sermon to be remembered so distinctly for the third of a century. I have heard also very frequent allusions to his pulpit performances in different parts of the western country, where he had operated to good purpose as a traveling preacher, more particularly in Kentucky and Tennessee. But perhaps the effort which occasioned the most talk and obtained the greatest notoriety was the one said to have been made in his own section of country, and was commonly known as Axley's temperance sermon, though not so designated by any preannouncement. It should be known that east

Tennessee in those days was regarded as a great country for producing peach-brandy, and for a free use of it; also, that the New Lights abounded there, familiarly called Schismatics, and that Church members who rendered themselves liable to a disciplinary process would occasionally go over to them, as a city of refuge, where they felt safe from its restraints. With this preliminary, I proceed to recite a passage from the sermon, reminding the reader that my authority is not personal knowledge, but the verbal statement of a highly-respectable Methodist minister, Rev. Dr. G., of Tennessee. I write it substantially as I heard it:

"TEXT: 'Alexander the coppersmith did me much evil: the Lord reward him according to his works,' 2 Timothy iv, 14.

"Paul was a traveling preacher, and a bishop, I presume, or a presiding elder at least; for he traveled extensively, and had much to do, not only in regulating the societies, but also in sending the preachers here, there, and yonder. He was zealous, laborious, would not build on another man's foundation, but formed new circuits, where Christ was not named, 'so that from Jerusalem, and round about unto Illyricum, he had fully preached the Gospel of Christ.' One new place that he visited was very wicked—Sabbath-breaking, dancing, drinking, quarreling, fighting, swearing, etc., abounded; but the word of the Lord took effect; there was a powerful stir among the people, and many precious souls were converted. Among the subjects of that work there was a certain noted character, Alexander by name, and a still-maker by trade; also, one Hymeneus, who was his partner in the business. Paul formed a new society, and appointed brother Alexander class-leader. There was a great change in the place; the people left off their drinking, swearing, fighting, horse-racing, dancing, and all their wicked practices. The stills were worked up into bells and stew-kettles, and thus applied to useful purposes. The settlement was orderly, the meetings were prosperous, and things went well among them for some time. But one year they had a pleasant spring; there was no late frost, and the peach crop hit exactly. I do suppose, my brethren, that such a crop of peaches was never known before. The old folks ate all they could eat, the children ate all they could eat, the pigs ate all they could eat, and the sisters preserved all they could preserve, and still the limbs of the trees were bending and breaking. One Sunday, when the brethren met for worship, they gathered round outside of the meeting-house, and got to talking about their worldly business—as you know people sometimes do, and it is a mighty bad practice—and one said to another, 'Brother, how is the peach crop with you this year?' 'O,' said he, 'you never saw the like; they are rotting on the ground under the trees; I don't know what to do with them.' 'How would it do,' said one, 'to still them? The peaches will go to waste, but the brandy will keep; and it is very good in certain cases, if not used to excess.' 'I should like to know,' said a cute brother, 'how you could make brandy without stills?' 'That's nothing,' replied one, 'for our class-leader—brother Alexander—is as good a still-maker as need be, and brother Hymeneus is another, and, rather than see the fruit wasted, no doubt they would make us a few.' The next thing heard on the subject was a hammering in the class-leader's shop; and soon the stills in every brother's orchard were smoking, and the liquid poison streaming. When one called on another the bottle was brought out, with the remark, 'I want you to taste my new brandy; I think it is pretty good.' The guest, after tasting once, was urged to repeat, when, smacking his lips, he would reply, 'Well, it's tolerable; but I wish you would come over and taste mine; I think mine is a little better.' So they tasted and tasted till many of them got about half drunk, and I don't know but three-quarters. Then the very devil was raised among them; the society was all in an uproar, and Paul was sent for to come and settle the difficulty. At first it was difficult to find sober, disinterested ones enough to try the guilty; but finally he got his committee formed; and the first one he brought to account was Alexander, who pleaded not guilty. He declared that he had not tasted, bought, sold, or distilled a drop of brandy. 'But,' said Paul, 'you made the stills, otherwise there could have been no liquor made; and if no liquor, no one could have been intoxicated.' So they expelled him first, then Hymeneus next, and went on for compliment, till the society was relieved of all still-makers, distillers, dram-sellers, and dram-drinkers, and peace was once more restored. Paul says, 'Holding faith and a good conscience; which some having put away, concerning faith have made shipwreck; of whom is Hymeneus and Alexander; whom I have delivered unto Satan, that they may learn not to blaspheme.'

"Of course they flew off the handle, and joined the Schismatics.

"Now, in view of the peculiar structure of brother Axley's mind, and his characteristic habits of thought and expression, they who were best acquainted with him will be most likely to admit that the above outline may be substantially correct. I was anxious to have learned more items of the history of that good man; but at my next visit to Holston conference, in 1840, I had left me only the mournful pleasure of visiting his grave, in a rural cemetery, which, at that time, was without inscription or inclosure. If some one of our senior brethren, better acquainted with the subject of this brief notice than the writer, would favor the public with a reliable biography, and thereby rescue the name of James Axley from oblivion, he would confer a lasting benefit on the Church and the numerous friends of the deceased. Whatever is to be rescued from oblivion concerning the early pioneers of Methodism must be soon done."

To the personal reminiscences of the Bishop might be added others by those who knew Axley, and were privileged to wait on his ministry. In the autobiography of Samuel Williams, Esq., we find the following:

"The name of James Axley was rendered familiar to us by being carved by himself, during the sitting of the conference of 1807, on the back of the seat in front of the one in which we usually sat, in the little, old brick chapel. Our recollection of his person is rather indistinct; but we think he was tall and raw-boned, and a little awkward in his manners and movements. In the matter and delivery of his discourses there was a marked originality, a vein of humor, and even drollery, which, while it interested and frequently amused his hearers, often gave severe point and directness to his rebukes. He was, nevertheless, a preacher of very respectable talents and undoubted piety. And if he was not a 'polished shaft' in the quiver of the Almighty, yet the arrow was none the less sharp and keen. We have heard many anecdotes of his sayings and doings. The following, related to us about thirty years ago by the Rev. John Collins, we give the reader as a specimen:

"In one of his discourses Mr. Axley was descanting upon conformity to the world among Christians, particularly in fashionable dress and manners. To meet the pleas and excuses usually set up in behalf of these departures from the good old way, he held a sort of colloquy with an imaginary apologist, seated at the further end of the congregation, whose supposed pleas and excuses he would state on behalf of his man of straw, in an altered tone; then resuming his natural voice, he would reply and demolish the arguments of his opponent. After thus discussing the subject for some time, the opponent was made to say,

"'But, sir, some of your Methodist preachers themselves dress in fashionable style, and in air and manner enact the dandy.'

"'O no, my friend, that can not be. Methodist preachers know their calling better. They are men of more sense than that, and would not stoop so low as to disgrace themselves and the sacred office they hold by such gross inconsistency of character.'

"'Well, sir, if you won't take my word for it, just look at those young preachers in the pulpit, behind you.'

"Mr. Axley, turning immediately around, with seeming surprise, and facing two or three rather fashionably-dressed junior preachers seated in the rear of the pulpit, he surveyed each of them from head to foot for two or three minutes, while they quailed under the withering glance of his keen and penetrating eye; then turning again to the congregation, and leaning a little forward over the front of the desk, with his arm extended, and his eyes as if fixed on the apologist at the further end of the church, he said, in a subdued tone, yet distinctly enough to be heard by all present,

"'*If you please, sir, we'll drop the subject!*'

"Although the following additional anecdote of Mr. Axley may be familiar to many of our readers, we hope they will pardon us for inserting it, as it is worthy of a more durable record than the columns of a newspaper, from which we clip it. The late Judge Hugh L. White, who relates it, was a learned and able jurist and distinguished statesman, and for many years a conspicuous member of the United States senate from the state of Tennessee.

"On a certain day a number of lawyers and literary men were together in the town of Knoxville, Tennessee, and the conversation turned on preachers and preaching. One and another had expressed his opinion of the performances of this and that pulpit orator, when at length Judge White spoke up:

"'Well, gentlemen, on this subject each man is, of course, entitled to his own opinion; but I must confess that father Axley brought me to a sense of my evil deeds, at least a portion of them, more effectually than any preacher I ever heard.'

"At this, every eye and ear was turned, for Judge White was never known to speak lightly on religious subjects, and, moreover, was habitually cautious and respectful in his remarks about religious men. The company now expressed the most urgent desire that the Judge should give the particulars, and expectation stood on tiptoe.

"'I went up,' said the Judge, 'one evening to the Methodist church. A sermon was preached by a clergyman with whom I was not acquainted, but father Axley was in the pulpit. At the close of the sermon he arose and said to the congregation, "I am not going to detain you by delivering an exhortation; I have risen merely to administer a rebuke for improper conduct, which I have observed here to-night." This, of course, waked up the entire assembly, and the stillness was profound, while Axley stood and looked for several seconds over the congregation. Then stretching out his large, long arm, and pointing with his finger steadily in one direction, he said, "Now, I calculate that those two young men, who were talking in that corner of the house while the brother was preaching, think that I am going to talk about them. Well, it is true, it looks very bad, when well-dressed young men, who you would suppose, from their appearance, belonged to some respectable family, come to the house of God, and instead of reverencing the majesty of Him that dwelleth therein, or attending to the message of his everlasting love, get together in one corner of the house"—his finger all the time pointing as steady and straight as the aim of a rifleman—"and there, during the whole solemn service, keep talking, tittering, laughing, and giggling, thus annoying the minister, disturbing the congregation, and sinning against God. I'm sorry for the young men. I'm sorry for their parents. I'm sorry they have done so to-night. I hope they will never do so again. But, however, that's not the thing I was going to talk about. It is another matter, so important that I thought it would be wrong to suffer the congregation to depart without administering a suitable rebuke. Now," said he, stretching out his huge arm, and pointing in another direction, "perhaps that man who was asleep on the bench out there, while the brother was preaching, thinks I am going to talk about him. Well, I must confess it looks very bad for a man to come into a worshiping assembly, and, instead of taking a seat like others, and listening to the blessed Gospel, carelessly stretching himself out on a bench, and going to sleep. It is not only a proof of great insensibility with regard to the obligations which we owe to our Creator and Redeemer, but it shows a want of genteel breeding. It shows that the poor man has been so unfortunate in his bringing up as not to have been taught good manners. He don't know what is polite and respectful in a worshiping assembly among whom he comes to mingle. I'm sorry for the poor man. I'm sorry for the family to which he belongs. I'm sorry he did not know better. I hope he will never do so again. But, however, this was not what I was going to talk about." Thus father Axley went on, for some time, "boxing the compass," hitting a number of persons and things that he was not going to talk about, and hitting *hard*, till the attention and curiosity of the audience were raised to their highest pitch, when finally he remarked:

"'"The thing of which I was going to talk was *chewing tobacco*. Now, I do hope, when any gentleman comes to church who can't keep from using tobacco during the hours of worship, that he will just take his hat and use it for a spit-box. You all know we are Methodists. You all know that our custom is to kneel when we pray. Now, any gentleman may see, in a moment, how exceedingly inconvenient it must be for a well-dressed Methodist lady to be compelled to kneel down in a puddle of tobacco spit."

"'Now,' said Judge White, 'at this time I had in my mouth an uncommonly large quid of tobacco. Axley's singular manner and train of remark strongly arrested my attention. While he was stirring to the right and left, hitting those "things" that he was not going to talk about, my curiosity was busy to find out what he could be aiming at. I was chewing and spitting my large quid with uncommon rapidity, and looking up at the preacher to catch every word and every gesture—when at last he pounced upon the tobacco, behold, there I had a *great puddle* of tobacco spit! I quietly slipped the quid out of my mouth, and dashed it as far as I could under the seats, resolved never again to be found chewing tobacco in the Methodist church.'"

Axley must have been a thorough student of human nature, as was generally the case with the Methodist preachers of that day. Men whose profession calls them to travel in all sections of the country, and mingle with all classes of society, as Methodist preachers have to do, must be dull students and stupid observers of men and things, if they don't become thoroughly acquainted with men's hearts and lives. What the eccentric Axley learned in the wide field of labor before him he put to good account, and thus gave evidence that he was not like the sage of olden time, who mingled with the world only to learn its follies and then retired to his cell alone to weep over them.

CHAPTER XVII.

JOSEPH OGLESBY.

In sketching the life of this pioneer preacher, who, for fifty years, toiled in the wilds of the west; the first herald of the cross that ever penetrated the wilderness of Illinois and preached the Gospel to its scattered inhabitants, we are at a loss for materials respecting his early life and conversion. We find his name on the general Minutes as a probationer in the year 1804, when, as we have already seen, he traveled the Miami circuit with the Rev. John Sale. The Minutes show the work on the Ohio district as follows: W. Burke, presiding elder; Muskingum, George Askin; Hockhocking, James Quinn, John Meek; Scioto, William Pattison, Nathan Barnes; Miami, John Sale, Joseph Oglesby; Guyandotte, Asa Shinn.

In the year following he was sent into the wilderness in the then distant Illinois, almost beyond the reach of the white population. Having preceded Jesse Walker, a most interesting sketch of whose labors, in that distant region, is given by Bishop Morris in his "Miscellany," the reader has only to refer to that work to see what must have been the toils and hardships of Oglesby in planting Methodism among the semi-civilized inhabitants. The next year he was sent to Barren circuit, in the Cumberland district; in the year following to Shelby, in the Kentucky district. In 1808 he was sent to Nashville circuit, with David Young for his colleague, and the succeeding year to Maramack, in Indiana. At the close of this year he located. How long he remained in a local relation to the Church we are not able to say exactly. In the mean time he was engaged as a practitioner of medicine, in which profession, we are informed, he was quite successful. His zeal and industry were great, both as it regarded his professional engagements in the healing art, and his duties as a preacher, being ready at all times to do good to the bodies and the souls of men.

In the year 1849 we find his name on the effective list in the Indiana conference. That year he was stationed on the Martinsville circuit. The next year his name stands on the Minutes among the superannuated preachers, and the presumption is that his age and feebleness were such as to disqualify him from doing fully the work of an itinerant, and rather than be in the way of an effective man he would not insist on being regarded as fully adequate for the work when he was not. The year 1851 also finds him among the superannuated. Still he traveled extensively, and labored whenever opportunity presented; and frequently his pulpit ministrations were characterized with the pathos and power of a former day. In the Minutes of 1852, in answer to the question of the South-Eastern Indiana conference, "Who have died this year?" the name of Joseph Oglesby stands among the number. The following is the conference memoir, and though short, like the memoirs of the deceased preachers as found in the early Minutes, still it is expressive of his character and labors as a minister of the Lord Jesus, and serves to show the estimate put upon him as a member of the conference:

"Rev. Joseph Oglesby.—This venerable servant of God departed this life April 9, 1852, in the city of Louisville.

"We regret that the residence of his family, beyond the bounds of this conference, has prevented us from obtaining materials for as full a report as his meritorious life demands. But what needs it? His 'witness is in heaven—his record is on high.' There dwell many seals to his ministry, and there rests his happy spirit.

"He was a pioneer Methodist minister. Nearly fifty years ago he began his arduous toils. Ohio, Kentucky, Indiana, Illinois, and Missouri, he traversed, preaching every-where the 'Gospel of the kingdom'—'the word of this salvation.' No history of Methodism in the vast Mississippi Valley can be complete which does not speak largely of the labors of Joseph Oglesby. Much of it 'he was.'

"In the days of his strength he stood among the strong men of Methodism. 'He was an able minister of the New Testament.' As old age pressed upon him his zeal did not abate. He continued in his superannuated days to preach Jesus, almost every Sabbath, and often through the week.

"The last Sabbath before his short and fatal illness, he preached with great power from 'O that thou hadst hearkened to my commandments; then had thy peace been as a river, and thy righteousness as the waves of the sea.'

"He died with his armor on, and fell in sight of glory. Many shall rise up and call him blessed."

CHAPTER XVIII.

WILLIAM BEAUCHAMP.

Among the bright stars which shone in the galaxy of Methodism in the close of the eighteenth century, was the Rev. William Beauchamp. After filling several important stations, such as Pittsburg, New York, Boston, etc., he removed to the west, and settled on the Little Kanawha, in Western Virginia. Having, in early life, received a good English and classical education, he devoted himself, in his local sphere, to literary pursuits. With but few exceptions, there were not many literary men in the itinerant ranks in those days. Those were called, as a general thing, into the ministry, who belonged, like the early founders of Christianity, to the toiling classes of community. They were taken from the plow, the loom, the bench, and the anvil, and, with the broad seal of heaven's commission written on their hearts, they went forth to draw from their own experience, and the uncommented word of God, those soul-saving truths which brought the sinner to the dust, and raised the fallen to the blessings of pardon and salvation.

Still, as it was in the days of the apostles and the Reformation, there were some who were distinguished for profound literary attainments, and of this number was William Beauchamp. In the wilds of Virginia, removed from the toil of itinerant life, in which he had worn himself down, he passed his time in the congenial pursuits of a literary life, while his Sabbaths were occupied in preaching the Gospel to the scattered inhabitants in all the region round about. As the fruit of his literary toils, he published "Essays," in Marietta, in the year 1811, "on the Truth of the Christian Religion, or Evidences of Christianity." This work was written in a graceful, flowing style, and would do honor to the head and heart of any man. It gave evidence of genius and piety of a high degree, and was extensively read and deservedly popular. His production gained him a name as a writer in the west, and it was not long till his services were required as an editor of a religious periodical. A correspondence was opened between him and the Rev. Thomas S. Hinde, of Chillicothe, on this subject, an account of which, together with other circumstances, furnished by the latter, we will give in his own words:

"The writer of this memoir, with a number of his religious friends and acquaintances, had long lamented the prevalency of Arian and Pelagian doctrines, with which the Methodist societies at this time, *in places*, were much infested. The Rev. Samuel Parker, in 1811, 1812, and 1813, had traveled through the interior of Ohio. The distinguished talents of this minister of grace, connected with the sweet temper and disposition of the man, had enabled him to wield the scepter of the Gospel with such signal success that those doctrines, wherever he went, received a fatal blow; to make the victory full and complete, a periodical publication was thought to be absolutely necessary; through which medium the doctrines of the Church might be disseminated. Our Methodist Magazine had long since been discontinued, and no disposition appeared to be manifested to revive it. These circumstances had induced the writer, upon his own responsibility, to issue a prospectus for a periodical religious publication, to be published in Chillicothe, which was designed to batter down those absurd notions, so prevalent at this period. Brother Beauchamp was solicited to undertake it, and this, connected perhaps with other circumstances, induced him to remove to Chillicothe, Ohio, some time in the year 1815. The year following—1816—that excellent periodical work, 'The Western Christian Monitor,' was published monthly. Publications of this kind had sprung up in various parts of the United States, and the name of this forestalled; so that 'Western' was added by way of distinction. In this publication brother Beauchamp was aided by the writer of this memoir, but more by compilations and selections than in original matter; and at his request brother Beauchamp wrote a short commentary on the *articles* of religion of the Methodist Episcopal Church, which was published in numbers. The Monitor was extensively circulated, has done much good, and the bound volumes are now, and always will be, a valuable acquisition to any library. The infant state of the western country, the difficulties attending the distribution of the work, and, worse than all, the very ill state of brother Beauchamp's health at this time, all tended greatly to discourage him in the prosecution of it; and from these and other circumstances, which it is now needless to mention, at the end of the first year it was wholly discontinued.

"While brother Beauchamp resided in Chillicothe, he became extensively known, and to the Church in that place very useful; his persuasive eloquence and his solid piety gained him many friends both among professors and non-professors, who were so generally impressed with a sense of his real worth, that his name is now, and will long be had in remembrance; and but little doubt is entertained that his labors in this place paved the way for that great and glorious revival of religion, which commenced soon after he left it to remove to Mount Carmel, in Illinois.

"Those lucid intervals during the ministry of the writer's friends, Mr. Samuel Parker and Mr. William

Beauchamp—the one immediately succeeding the other in Chillicothe—in his associations with them around the country in different places, at various meetings, he now retrospects as the happiest period of his life! The tremulous motions of the late calamitous war had subsided, peace reigned, the Gospel spread most astonishingly; and it was his delight to hear, at one time, Parker as the Cicero, and at another Beauchamp as the Demosthenes, of the Church in the west. Pleasing, yet melancholy thought! their race is run, and these two ministers of the Church have left us to mourn *for ourselves!* One slumbers in the *valley* of the Mississippi, the other sweetly—for the present—reposes on the *hights* of Peoli, in Indiana!

> 'Thus the men
> Whom nature's works instruct, with God himself
> Hold converse; grow familiar; act upon his plan;
> And form to his the relish of their souls!' "

We have already seen that the subject of our narrative had closed his editorial labors and removed to Mount Carmel, Illinois. Having undertaken the agency of the new settlement, where a society was to be formed on the principle of elective affinity, he commenced the work of surveying the land, laying off the squares and streets, and public places of the town. The lands belonging to the company were exceedingly fertile, and the inducements offered were such that in a short time large numbers sought this El Dorado of the west. All was a wilderness, but active preparations were made for clearing and building. On the holy Sabbath the sound of a trumpet would bring the people together, and the eloquent Beauchamp would charm his listening auditors with the Gospel of Jesus. And they were a highly-favored congregation; for no preacher in the splendid churches of the large cities could discourse more eloquently. On winter evenings he would collect together the youth of the neighborhood and instruct them in the various branches of a solid education. His information was extensive and general, embracing all the useful departments of knowledge, and his services were sought on almost every subject involving the different professions, as well as the mechanic arts. He labored to make himself useful in all the departments of life, and his chief aim seemed to be to advance the happiness of all. Added to all, his services were gratuitous, and none could complain of exorbitant professional fees when his opinion or services were required. He literally preached and toiled for nothing, finding himself.

We once knew a preacher who was sent to a poor circuit in Ohio, where, at the first quarterly meeting, there was not money enough raised from all the classes to pay the traveling expenses of one of the preachers. The prospect was so gloomy, in regard to support, that the presiding elder gave him a dispensation that he might teach a school. He accordingly gathered together about sixty scholars, ranging from A B C up to mineralogy and Latin. From each scholar he received a small sum, to be paid in store goods at an exorbitant price; but as he had no rent to pay, being permitted to occupy an old log-cabin that was tenantless, he managed to get along. On Sabbath he would preach to the people of the neighborhood in the school-house. It happened that there came along a Universalist preacher, who was anxious to enlighten the people on the subject of religion, and he requested the privilege of preaching in the school-house, which was granted. The burden of his discourse was to expose the priestcraft of the orthodox clergy, and to convince the dear people that they were terribly priest-ridden; that these fat, sleek Methodist preachers cared more for the fleece than they did for the flock. On the next Sabbath, after the school-teacher had preached, an old local preacher, who lived in the neighborhood, and had been a colleague of Bishop Hedding on a New England circuit, was invited to close the exercises. He had heard the Universalist the Sabbath before, and was making a reply, at the Universalist's invitation, which would have completely demolished him, had not the meeting been broken up by a drunken man, who came in and ordered him out of the pulpit. On rising to give out a hymn, he said he wished to make a remark. "Last Sabbath," said he, "we heard much about priestcraft, and about our being priest-ridden, and all that sort of thing. Well, I don't think we have much reason to complain of being priest-ridden, for our preacher teaches our children, furnishes wood and candles, builds the fire, sweeps the house, attends our sick, buries our dead, and preaches for nothing—all for nothing—lives in a log-cabin and finds himself."

Thus it was with Beauchamp. He was surveyor, lawyer, physician, school-teacher, mechanic, and preacher; and his services, like the blessings of the Gospel, were without money and without price. His arduous labors preyed heavily upon his delicate constitution, and he was obliged, in 1821, to retire to his farm, about three miles from Carmel. Shortly after this he was called to part with his son—his only son—in the thirteenth year of his age. He was a bright and beautiful boy, tender and affectionate in his disposition, and beloved by all; but Death, who loves a shining mark, claimed him as his own, and he fell a blighted flower, and was gathered to the tomb. After this deep affliction, brother Beauchamp re-entered the itinerant ranks in the Missouri conference, and was stationed in the city of St. Louis. In this station he labored with great success for one year, at the expiration of which time he was appointed presiding elder of the Indiana district. His district was large, embracing eleven circuits, and covering a wide extent of territory, where he labored with zeal untiring in cultivating the vineyard of his Lord and Master. While on this district he was elected a delegate to the General conference. Such was the estimate put upon his talents by the members of the General conference, that he came within a few votes of being elected to the Episcopacy. His journey to Baltimore and the severe labor connected with the district, which embraced almost the entire state of Indiana, were too great for his constitution to bear, and the old complaint, under which he had suffered, returned. In a very feeble state of health he was taken to his fourth quarterly meeting, which was on the camp-ground near Peoli. Here he became worse, but gave advice and attended to some business. From this place he was removed to Mr. Craven's, and from thence to Mr. Peek's, at Peoli, where he would be more convenient to medical aid. All efforts that medical skill could make were, however, unavailing, and he continued to sink under the power of disease till, at the expiration of six weeks from the time of the attack, he yielded up his spirit into the hands of God. His death was tranquil, and, with the bright hopes of a faithful Christian, he passed over the swellings of Jordan. His funeral sermon was preached by Bishop Roberts from the text, "Precious in the sight of the Lord is the death of his saints." At the time of his death he was in the fifty-third year of his age.

The following description of his person and address, from the pen of his intimate friend, T. S. Hinde, will give the reader a correct idea of the learned and talented subject of our sketch:

"He was a man of common stature, about five feet ten inches in hight, light form, dark, or auburn hair, rather of a sallow complexion and thin visage. His features were remarkably regular and round; his head, forehead, and face were well proportioned; there was nothing striking in the appearance either of his nose or mouth, both exhibiting a quite common appearance, nor, at first view, was there any thing remarkable in the cast of his eye; like that of most geniuses it seemed to slumber in thought, till roused to action. But a strict observer, particularly a discerning stranger, would discover an indication therefrom of deep thought and a reflecting mind; and yet a reserve bordering on austerity. While his eye was watchful and vigilant, a strict and rigid observer of passing events, it was apparently hid and retired where caution and prudence were deemed necessary. This was its cast to a stranger; but to an acquaintance or a friend he was free and open. His gait was generally slow, but when in health his motions were more rapid. He was very uniform in his conduct, and systematic in his deportment; yet no man was ever a more pleasant and agreeable member of society, adapting his language and conversation to the state and capacities of each, being perfectly at home among the high or the low, the rich or the poor. Though apparently pensive and reserved, yet there was no man more pleasant, communicative, and cheerful. In a company of select friends he was in his element, and his soul then appeared expanded as at a mental feast. His dark hazel eye would rise from its apparent languor, and sparkle with beams of light. His countenance, like the sun breaking forth from a parting cloud, would assume a lovely sprightliness, as if to cheer the spirits of those with whom he delighted to be associated; for he took great pleasure in the society of his friends.

"Mr. Beauchamp in his friendship was steady and uniform, on no occasion yielding his regard for one till he was well satisfied that his confidence was misplaced. He had a little stoop of the shoulders, and when speaking in public his gestures were natural and easy. His voice was very uniform, remarkably soft in social conversation, but in argument energetic. In his preaching, when holding out the promises and the invitations of the Gospel, there was a soft tenderness, a sweetness in his voice, produced frequently by gentle breaks, as if the rising sympathies of his soul obstructed, in some degree, his utterance; when a gentle, thrilling sensation appeared to move a listening multitude, all bending forward to catch every sentence or word as it fell from his lips. This circumstance has frequently been admired. But when he became argumentative, and discussed doctrinal points, or when false doctrines were attacked, the tone of his voice was elevated, his whole system became nerved, and his voice assumed a deep hollow tone, and then soon became elevated to its highest key, and fell like peals of thunder on the ears of a listening assembly. On one occasion the force of his powerful eloquence was fully demonstrated; it was on a subject of controversy. His antagonist, who had sat and listened for some length of time to arguments too powerful for him to answer, began to look as if the voice which he now heard came from another world, through the shadow of a man; he rose, apparently with a view to leave the house, but being so overcome he staggered, caught by the railing, reeled, and fell to his seat, and there sat, overwhelmed and confounded, till the discourse was concluded, when he quietly stepped from the house. His manner of preaching was plain, seldom dividing his subject into different heads, but took the natural division of the text. He would indeed branch out on his subject, but it was so natural and easy, and done in such a way as appeared to unfold new beauties in the Gospel. His sermons were deep, and made a lasting impression upon the mind, because they were both practical and doctrinal. Holiness was his theme; there was seldom a shout raised in the assembly under his preaching, but always strict attention paid to his discourses, and every eye fixed upon the speaker; and, frequently, the people all bathed in tears."

CHAPTER XIX.

GOVERNOR TIFFIN.

THE following interesting sketch of the life of Edward Tiffin, the first Governor of the state of Ohio, has been kindly furnished us by Samuel Williams, Esq., to whose correct and graphic pen Methodism is largely indebted for historical recollections.

"Edward Tiffin was born in the town of Carlisle, Cumberland county, England, a few miles south of the border of Scotland, June 19, 1766. His education was limited to the ordinary branches of a common English course, as his parents were in moderate circumstances and unable to educate him better. At an early age he commenced the study of medicine; and in 1784, at the age of about eighteen years, before he had completed his medical course, he immigrated to the United States and settled in Charlestown, Berkley—now Jefferson—county, Virginia, whither his parents and all the family soon afterward removed. Having finished the study of medicine, under a distinguished physician, whose name I have forgotten, Mr. Tiffin, while yet very young, commenced the practice; and by his skill and success in his profession, he soon acquired a high character and standing as a physician.

"His natural buoyancy of spirit and great vivacity, his sprightliness of temperament and pleasing manners, together with his engaging conversational powers, and his active and agile movements, made him the favorite in the fashionable and gay circles around him, and the life and soul of the company wherever he was present. In 1789, when about twenty-three years old, he united in marriage with Miss Mary Worthington, daughter of Mr. Robert Worthington, near Charlestown, and sister of the late Governor Thomas Worthington, of Ohio. The year following Dr. Tiffin and his wife, were attracted by curiosity, perhaps, to hear the Rev. Lewis Chastain and Rev. Thomas Scott, the two Methodist preachers stationed that year on Berkley circuit, and whose fame brought out large congregations to hear them. Mr. Scott, by his preaching, and especially by his youthfulness—being then only eighteen years old—attracted particular notice. The truth reached the heart and conscience of the Doctor, and he was received into the Church as a probationer by Mr. Scott, who thus notices the circumstance in his 'Historical Recollections,' in the Western Christian Advocate of June 8, 1853:

"'After preaching at Hite's Chapel, the first round I took on the [Berkley] circuit, I was invited by Mr. John Anderson, grandfather of the late Rev. Mr. Anderson, of the Ohio conference, deceased, to preach in Charlestown, situated about four miles distant, the next time I came round. I consented and appointed to preach there on the Sabbath. Mr. Anderson and his wife belonged to the class at Hite's Chapel, but resided in Charlestown. In the interval between that and the time appointed for preaching, several prayer meetings were held at Mr. Anderson's, during which they were greatly disturbed by mobs.

"'The day named for the purpose was beautiful, and I preached to a large, attentive congregation, in a grove near the town. When I had concluded, I notified the congregation that it was my wish to form, on that day, a Methodist society or class in that town, and invited all who were determined to flee the wrath to come and be saved from their sins, to meet me at the house of Mr.

Anderson at an hour named. Before the hour had arrived Dr. Edward Tiffin came into the room where I was sitting and commenced a conversation with me. Being a stranger to me, and not knowing but that he had been one of those who had favored the mobs, I conversed with him cautiously. He, however, remained, and several others soon collected. After singing, prayer, and an exhortation, I gave an invitation to those who wished to become members to come forward and announce their names. The Doctor was standing on the opposite side of the room fronting me. I had not perceived that he was affected; but the moment I gave the invitation he quickly stepped forward, evidently under deep and pungent conviction, roaring almost with anguish, and asked for admission into our Church. He was admitted; and before I had completed that round on the circuit, he had preached several sermons.' In another place the Judge writes: 'Immediately after I had received Dr. Tiffin into the Church he became convinced of his call to the ministry. Conferring not with flesh and blood, and without waiting for a license, he immediately commenced preaching. One of the places selected by him for that purpose was Bullskin. There his ministerial labors, as also the labors of the Revs. Lewis Chastain and Valentine Cook, were greatly blessed. A very large class of lively, excellent members was formed, who met at the house of old Mr. Smith, father of the Rev. Henry Smith,' of Pilgrim's Rest, near Baltimore. Mr. Smith, in his 'Recollections,' speaks of Dr. Tiffin's preaching as 'pathetic and powerful.' But although the Doctor commenced preaching before receiving license for that purpose, it was evident that he had not run before he was sent. Not only did the love of Christ constrain him to proclaim the unsearchable riches of his Gospel, but the divine call to the ministry was so powerfully impressed upon his mind that he dared not, at his peril, disobey it. Yet the cross was almost insupportably heavy, and he had, at first, well nigh sunk under it. The Doctor told me himself, more than thirty-five years ago, that, attending at one of his appointments—perhaps one of the first that had been made for him—seeing the people flock in in multitudes, and knowing that mere curiosity to hear him preach had brought most of them out, his heart failed within him. He slipped out some half an hour before the time appointed for commencing the meeting, and hastily retired to a deep forest near at hand, with the intention of hiding himself till the congregation should become tired of waiting and disperse. But it would not do. He could not flee from the vivid conviction which seemed to sound in his ear like thunder, and thrill like lightning through all his soul. 'A dispensation of the Gospel is committed to me, and *woe is unto me* if I preach not the Gospel.' In his agony the perspiration fell in large drops from his face, and his garments were wet with its profuse flow. He felt almost involuntarily impelled to return to the house, which was now full to overflowing, and great numbers outside. Scarcely able to stand, the Doctor—like one of his distinguished predecessors in the ministry, the first time he preached at Corinth—commenced the service 'in weakness, and in fear, and in much trembling.' But he soon felt divinely aided, and threw off the incubus which seemed to press him to the earth, and he preached with great liberty; and if his 'speech and his preaching was not with enticing words of man's wisdom,' yet it was 'in demonstration of the Spirit, and of power;' for sinners were cut to the heart, and God honored his servant in the sight of all the people.

"About two years after Dr. Tiffin began to preach, he was admitted to the office of a deacon in the Methodist Episcopal Church, by Bishop Asbury, by whom he was ordained on the 19th of November, 1792, as appears by the Bishop's parchment of ordination, of that date, now before me. At that period the Discipline authorized the Bishop to ordain local preachers to the order of deacons, on a testimonial of the requisite qualifications, signed by three elders, three deacons, and three traveling preachers. But in the case of Dr. Tiffin—as I learned, either from the Doctor himself, or one of his sisters—this formality was dispensed with; and the good Bishop, who greatly loved the Doctor, on the occasion of a visit at his house, voluntarily and without the solicitation or suggestion of any one, conferred upon him, impromptu, by regular ordination, the office of deacon.

"In 1796 Dr. Tiffin removed to and settled in the village of Chillicothe, in the territory north-west of the Ohio river. That village had been laid out but a short time before by General Nathaniel Massie, and most of it was yet covered with a dense forest. The Doctor selected a four acre out-lot at the upper end of the town for his residence, and built thereon the first house erected in town which was graced with a shingle roof. He continued the practice of medicine in Chillicothe and the surrounding country, attending promptly, as far as practicable, to all calls for professional services, encountering often severe sufferings from the inclemency of the weather, in long and fatiguing rides on horseback, on dark nights over wretched roads, or, rather, no roads at all, crossing swollen streams with dangerous fords, and with the full knowledge, frequently, that the patient was too poor to make him any remuneration for his services and medicines. It was his custom, whenever practicable, to pray with his patients, and administer to them suitable religious counsel and instruction; and these exercises were usually accompanied with good effect. In obstetric cases this was especially his practice; and in protracted cases of this nature, he has been known to engage in fervent prayer with and for the patient twice or thrice, or oftener. His example of praying with his patients would be well worthy of imitation by all pious physicians. This, we believe, a portion of them do.

"Notwithstanding his extensive and laborious practice as a physician, Doctor Tiffin found time to labor much and zealously, and with great usefulness, in his Lord's vineyard. He had his regular Sabbath appointments for preaching in the country—for there was then no opening for it in town—and his ministry was signally blest to his congregations. One of his regular preaching-places was at Anthony Davenport's, on Deer creek, twelve miles north of Chillicothe. Here he had a large congregation, and organized a flourishing society long before any of the traveling preachers had visited that part of the country. The Rev. Henry Smith, in his 'Recollections of an old itinerant'—p. 326—who visited that society in October, 1799, speaks warmly of its prosperous condition. Mr. Smith, in the same connection, adds: 'Monday, October 4th. I rode down the river to Chillicothe, and put up with Doctor Tiffin, with whom I had been long acquainted, [in Virginia.] The Doctor had often preached in our neighborhood, and sometimes at my father's. He and his excellent wife received me as a messenger of Christ, and treated me with great kindness. Sister Tiffin was one of the most conscientious and heavenly-minded women I ever saw. She was a mother in our Israel indeed. About that time a report was put in circulation that the Doctor had given up his religion. He laughed at it, and said, "It would not do for me to backslide; for my wife would let me have no peace." The Doctor, however, refused to take any part in religious exercises in Chillicothe out of his own family. He had his reasons for it.' Those 'reasons,' it would seem, were considered by Mr.

Smith valid. They probably grew out of the 'report' mentioned by him, which, I suppose, 'was put in circulation' by some narrow-minded and malicious persons, through envy or jealousy, because of the Doctor's deservedly great popularity.

"About the time Mr. Smith speaks of—autumn of 1799—Dr. Tiffin was elected a member of the territorial Legislature. The North-Western territory then embraced all the country lying north-west of the Ohio river and east of the Mississippi; and delegates were in attendance from the isolated settlements of Kaskaskia, on the Mississippi, at Vincennes, on the Wabash, and at Detroit, in Michigan. Solomon Sibley represented the latter in the territorial Legislature. Mr. Sibley and the Doctor took prominent parts in the debates; and were frequently on opposite sides in the discussions. The former was cool, deliberate, and logical in debate; while the latter, though not less logical and conclusive in his argument, was exceedingly animated and ardent in his feelings, and would sometimes, unguardedly, expose himself to the keen retorts of his philosophic opponent. Some sixteen or eighteen years after this period, I was present when Mr. Sibley, on his return from a session of Congress, of which he was a member, paid a visit to Dr. Tiffin, in Chillicothe. Their service together in the territorial Legislature was alluded to, when the Doctor very pleasantly remarked, 'In our debates, Mr. Sibley, I wished a thousand times that I could have the same calm, philosophic, and imperturbable spirit which you possessed. I saw and *felt* the advantage which it gave you over me when we happened to come into collision.' 'I hope, Doctor,' replied Mr. Sibley, 'that I never said any thing, when replying to you, that was in any way personally offensive?' 'Not at all,' rejoined the Doctor; 'the marked respect which you always showed toward those opposed to you in debate, could not but command my admiration, and often filled me with keen regret at the unguarded expressions which escaped me in the heat of debate.' Mr. Sibley laughingly replied, 'I well remember, Doctor, how often I have wished that I could infuse into my remarks on the floor the same ardor of feeling which was displayed in your speeches.' The interview was a very pleasant one to both these gentlemen.

"Mr. Sibley was one of the early pioneers of Michigan, whither he emigrated from Massachusetts, his native state. He was a prominent, useful, and influential citizen, and held successively several important offices, both under the territorial and state governments. He died at Detroit some years since.

"In the autumn of 1802 an election was held to choose delegates to the convention which adopted the first Constitution, and formed a state government for Ohio. Dr. Tiffin was elected one of the delegates from Ross county; and on the meeting of the convention he was chosen its President, the duties of which office he discharged with much ability and great satisfaction. The members were chosen for their honesty and capacity. They came together as business men, and without wasting their time in speeches 'for Buncombe,' they went earnestly to work, and in thirty days framed an excellent Constitution, which served the state for nearly half a century, a monument of the wisdom of its founders.

"The next year, when the chief Executive of the state was to be chosen under the new Constitution, the eyes of the people were turned to Dr. Tiffin, and he was elected their first Governor without opposition, I believe. Two years afterward, when his term of service expired, he was re-elected to the same office.

"It was during Governor Tiffin's second term of office, near the close of 1806, that the conspiracy of Aaron

Burr was developed. His object was either a severance of the western states from the Union, or to seize upon that portion embraced in Louisiana, lately ceded by France to the United States. Burr had procured, at different points on the upper Ohio, a great number of flat-boats, and secretly freighted them with a large quantity of provisions and munitions of war. These boats were to rendezvous, at a given time, at Blennerhassett's Island. Governor Tiffin, on obtaining information of Burr's movements, promptly dispatched an express to the military commandant at Marietta, with orders to call out a strong militia force, armed and equipped for service, and post them, with all expedition, at a given point below Blennerhassett's Island, where the channel would oblige the boats to pass very near to the Ohio side of the river. The order was promptly executed; and before Burr had any knowledge of the movement, the armed force to intercept his fleet was at the narrows, with a small battery of light field artillery. To pass this battery was found impossible; and Burr was obliged to abandon the expedition, and make his escape to parts unknown. As an interesting fragment of history pertaining to this affair, I insert the following, clipped from the New York Standard, an old newspaper:

"'It is well known that Burr, defeated in his efforts to divide and crush the republican party, planned a conspiracy, having for its object the severance of the Union, and that in December, 1806, various parties of men collected by him, and brought over to his views, embarked upon the Ohio river, and were to rendezvous at Blennerhassett's Island, which was the great point of concentration and depot, whence the expedition was to go forth to accomplish its nefarious project. But Mr. Jefferson, then at the head of the Government, had not been an inactive observer of these proceedings. He dispatched a messenger, Mr. John Graham, into the western country, to put himself in communication with the executives and legislatures of the several states, and to urge the adoption of such measures as might be necessary to arrest the conspiracy. The authorities of Ohio immediately put themselves in action. A law was passed unanimously, for calling out the militia, and vesting all necessary powers in the Governor, and an address was transmitted to Mr. Jefferson, assuring him of the confidence of the people of Ohio in his administration, and of their determination to put down all efforts to sever the Union. The then Governor, Mr. Tiffin, acted with promptitude. The people responded by one simultaneous expression against the adventurer thus aiming a fatal blow at the liberties of our country. The militia were called out, many of the persons engaged in the enterprise were arrested, and the whole project was defeated.

"'We have lately turned to the files of the National Intelligencer, and found the following proceedings which it may not be uninteresting to read. The admirable letter to Mr. Jefferson can not fail to commend itself to the country, as well for its beautiful tone as for its truly-republican sentiments.

"'"CHILLICOTHE, December 26, 1806.

"'"On Thursday last Mr. Lewis Cass introduced the following resolution, which was agreed to, and passed both houses without one dissenting voice:

"'"*Resolved*, unanimously, by the General Assembly of the state of Ohio, that the Governor be requested to transmit to the President of the United States the following address:

"'"To Thomas Jefferson, Esq., President of the United States:

"'"SIR,—At a time when the public mind throughout the Union is agitated with alarming reports respecting the existence and designs of a party hostile to the welfare and prosperity of our country, we deem it a duty incumbent on us to express to the Executive of the Union our attachment to the Government of the United States, and our confidence in its administration. Whatever may be the intentions of desperate and abandoned men respecting the destruction of that Constitution which has raised us to our present elevated rank among the nations of the world, and which is our only security for the future, we trust they will find very few advocates in the state of Ohio. We express the feelings and opinions of our constituents, when we say that no arts of intriguing men—no real or visionary prospects of advantage, will ever induce us to sever that bond of union, which is our only security against domestic violence and foreign invasion.

"'"Believing that the fundamental maxims of rational liberty have guided you in the administration of our Government, we hesitate not to express our full and entire confidence in your councils and conduct. Enjoying every blessing which, as men and citizens, we could desire, and in a country fertile in nature's choicest gifts, we could deem it presumptuous, indeed, to hazard, by intestine dissensions, these incalculable advantages. We trust that public rumor has magnified the danger; but should the design in agitation be as destructive as represented, we have no doubt that all fears will shortly be dissipated before the indignation of our citizens. That you may long live to enjoy the confidence and attachment of the American people, is the sincere and unanimous wish of the Legislature of Ohio."

"'Reply of Mr. Jefferson to the Governor of Ohio:

"'"WASHINGTON, February 2, 1807.

"'"SIR,—The pressing business, during a session of the Legislature, has rendered me more tardy in addressing you than it was my wish to have been. That our fellow-citizens of the west would need only to be informed of criminal machinations against the public safety, to crush them at once, I never entertained a doubt.

"'"I have seen, with the greatest satisfaction, that among those who have distinguished themselves by their fidelity to their country, on the occasion of the enterprise of Mr. Burr, yourself and the Legislature of Ohio have been the most eminent; the promptitude and energy displayed by your state has been as honorable to itself, as salutary to its sister states; and in declaring that you have deserved most of your country, I do but express the grateful sentiments of every fellow-citizen in it. The hand of the people has given a mortal blow to a conspiracy which, in other countries, would have called for an appeal to arms, and has proved that government to be the strongest of which every man feels himself a part. It is a happy illustration, too, of the importance of preserving to the state authorities all that vigor which the Constitution foresaw would be necessary, not only for their own safety, but for that of the whole.

"'"In making these acknowledgments of the merit of having set this illustrious example of exertion for the common safety, I pray that they may be considered as addressed to yourself and the Legislature particularly, and generally to every citizen who has availed himself of the opportunity given, of proving his devotion to his country.

"'"Accept my salutations and assurances of great consideration and esteem.

[Signed,] "'"THOMAS JEFFERSON.

"'"His Excellency, GOVERNOR TIFFIN."'

"At the session of the Legislature in 1806–7, Governor Tiffin was chosen senator in Congress, in place of Thomas Worthington, whose term expired the 4th of

March following. Dr. Tiffin took his seat in the senate in December, 1807. Early in the following year he suffered a great bereavement in the death of his excellent and pious wife. Mrs. Tiffin embraced religion, and united herself to the Church at or about the same time with the Doctor. She was a most devoted and deeply-experienced Christian, loved and esteemed by all who knew her. She was a great favorite of the venerated Bishop Asbury, who speaks in the highest terms of her in his journal. This event probably determined the Doctor to retire from public life. Accordingly, after the close of the session of the Congress, which terminated on the third of March, 1809, he resigned his seat in the senate, and returned to the peaceful retirement of private life. Early in the spring of this year, after his retirement from the senate, he removed to his beautiful farm on Deer creek, about eight miles north of Chillicothe, where he enjoyed the sweets of rural life in the cultivation of the rich alluvial land on that stream. Soon after this he united in marriage with Miss Mary Porter, of Twin township, in the same—Ross—county; an amiable, pious, and highly-respectable young lady, who, by her estimable qualities, and sweetness of spirit, filled the measure of his domestic happiness.

"The Doctor, however, was not permitted a long respite from public life. At the general election in October following his retirement from the United States senate, his fellow-citizens of Ross county called him to represent them in the popular branch of the Legislature. The session was opened on the first Monday in December following. Dr. Alexander Campbell, of Adams county, who had been Speaker of the house of representatives for two or three sessions previous, was re-elected to that post. As Dr. Tiffin's seat in the United States senate was yet vacant, the two houses of the Legislature, soon after the session commenced, met in joint session, in the hall of the house of representatives, to elect a successor. Chillicothe was yet the seat of government, and the old stone court-house the capitol, in which the sessions were held. The building was very illy adapted for the purpose. The house occupied the court-room on the ground floor, a very uncomfortable, badly-lighted, and roughly-finished room, with a large fireplace at each end, and a wide, open stairway out of one corner, leading up to the second floor. All the wood which could be piled on the fires failed to heat the large room in winter. The senate occupied the grand-jury room on the second floor. This was a low room, with a platform for the Speaker's seat at one side, and long, roughly-made tables on the floor, with plain, Windsor chairs ranged behind them for the reverend senators.

"The two houses, as above stated, met in joint session. The senate, headed by their Speaker, Thomas Kirker, Esq., and their Secretary, Rev. Thomas Scott, descended the wide stairway before mentioned, and, on entering the 'bar,' were received by the members of the house, standing, and conducted to seats, the Speaker taking his seat at the right of the Speaker of the house. When all were seated and in readiness, the Speaker of the senate arose and said: 'Gentlemen of the senate, you will please prepare your ballots for senator in the Congress of the United States, to fill the vacancy caused by the resignation of Edward Tiffin.' The Speaker of the house then called upon the 'gentlemen of the house of representatives' to prepare their ballots for the same purpose. A teller from each house, named by their respective Speakers, collected the ballots in hats, and read them at the Clerk's table; each of the Clerks took down the votes given, and handed the result to their Speakers, by which it was shown that Doctor Alexander Campbell, Speaker of the house, was duly elected. This was, in due form, announced by Mr. Speaker Kirker to the 'gentlemen of the senate,' and was followed by the Speaker of the house, who, under evident embarrassment, but which he succeeded very well in overcoming, announced in the same form: 'Gentlemen of the house of representatives, it appears that Alexander Campbell, of Adams county, has been duly elected senator in the Congress of the United States, to fill the vacancy created by the resignation of Edward Tiffin.' On the retirement of the senate to their chamber, Dr. Campbell arose, and, after a few very touching farewell remarks, handed to the Clerk, Mr. Thomas S. Hinde, a written resignation of the Speakership of the house, and retired from the chair. The Clerk immediately arose, and read the resignation to the house, and, on motion, the house proceeded at once to elect a Speaker to fill the vacancy. Dr. Tiffin was put in nomination, and, I think, unanimously chosen Speaker; and, on taking the chair, presented his thanks to the house in a neat little speech.

"I was present during the whole of the proceedings which I have here given in detail, and record them now to show the reader of the present day how such things were done in that early period of our state's history, while yet in its primitive simplicity and purity. Let the reader contrast these simple, honest, and dignified proceedings with the disgraceful legislative caucusing, party drilling, corrupting influences, and bacchanalian orgies of some modern 'progressive' legislatures we wot of. We are strongly inclined to indulge in some further reflections here; but, lest it might give offense, we refrain.

"Doctor Tiffin was returned to the house of representatives the following year also—1810—and again chosen Speaker by that body. The seat of government having been, in the mean time, by order of the previous session, removed to Zanesville, the Legislature met and held its session in that town. For this removal of the seat of government, the town of Zanesville was indebted to the efforts and influence of its member, George Jackson. It remained there, however, but two or three years, and was removed back to Chillicothe, and soon afterward to Columbus, the permanent seat. Dr. Tiffin's intimate knowledge of the duties of the chair, and his habitual promptness and business tact, admirably fitted him to preside over a deliberative assembly; and as presiding officer he was deservedly popular, and gave great satisfaction.

"The Doctor's income from the rent of his house in town, and the products of his mill and farm in the country, being inadequate to the support of his family, he removed into town again, in the autumn of 1810, and resumed his practice as a physician, to which he devoted his whole attention; and his well-known skill and popularity in his profession brought him at once into an extensive and lucrative practice. In surgical operations he was equally successful. Some instances of important cases might be mentioned; but we will name but one or two. On one occasion, when visiting the sick, some fifteen or twenty miles from Chillicothe, on Deer creek, he was sent for to see a man who had cut his foot very badly with a scythe, when mowing. The Doctor found the patient's foot in a high state of inflammation, with mortification commenced and rapidly advancing, requiring immediate amputation. To have delayed till he could get his surgical instruments would have been fatal to the patient, as the weather was extremely sultry. In place of a tourniquet he used a silk handkerchief, which he drew tightly around the leg. Then using his penknife for a scalpel, and a common handsaw for sawing off the bones, he soon had the diseased part of the limb severed, the wound dressed, and thereby saved the man's life. At another time he was sent for to visit a woman, a few miles east of Chillicothe, who had an inflammatory disease in one of her breasts. Mortification having set in, the Doctor found it necessary, to save the woman's life, to amputate the entire breast. This critical operation he performed successfully, and the patient's life was saved.

"An act of Congress creating the General Land-Office was passed, April 25, 1812. This act provided for the appointment, by the President and senate, of a 'Commissioner of the General Land-Office,' with a salary of three thousand dollars, under whose direction and management the business of the office was to be conducted. In selecting a suitable man to take charge of this important office, President Madison, wholly unexpected and unsolicited by either Dr. Tiffin or any of his friends, conferred it upon him. His nomination, when sent into the senate, gave great satisfaction to that body, and elicited an expression of warm approval from several members. The nomination was immediately taken up and unanimously confirmed. The first intimation which the Doctor had of his appointment, was the receipt, by the next mail, of his commission, with a friendly private letter from President Madison, and complimentary letters from Mr. Worthington, then in the senate, and several other members. The gratifying manner in which the office was conferred determined the Doctor at once to accept it. A few days thereafter, leaving his family in Chillicothe, he mounted his horse—the only practicable mode of traveling at that time—and, accompanied by the Rev. Joseph S. Collins,* of Chillicothe, whom he took along as a clerk in the office, he set out for Washington, which

* The father of the Rev. John A. Collins, of the Baltimore conference. He still survives, at the advanced age of seventy-five years, and resides in Georgetown, District of Columbia.

he reached in about two weeks of diligent and weary travel. Here he immediately set about organizing the General Land-Office, and putting it in train for business. This was a laborious work, as the books, documents, papers, maps, etc., had to be gathered out of the several departments and bureaus of state, treasury, and war, and appropriately arranged for business in the new office. The Surveyor-General of the public lands, and the Registers and Receivers of the numerous land-offices in the west, were placed under the direction and control of the new Commissioner; and these were to be put in communication with him, and receive his instructions for their government in performing their duties.

"Early in the following autumn the Doctor returned to Chillicothe, for the purpose of settling up his affairs, and to remove his family to Washington City, which he did. He took a beautiful mansion on the summit of Meridian Hill—as it is called, I believe—on the northwest extremity of Washington, to which were attached several acres of ground, including garden and an orchard of choice fruit of various kinds. The Doctor devoted unremitted attention to the duties of his office, where he was always to be found during the hours of business.

"When the British army, in August, 1814, was on the march upon Washington City, and the order was given to remove the books, documents, and every thing pertaining to the public offices, to places of safety, in the country, he was the first officer to commence the work. By his prompt and efficient measures for the safety of his office, he succeeded in removing its entire contents to a safe place in Loudon county, Virginia, about ten miles from Washington; while several of the other offices in the departments lost much of their valuable documents, all the public buildings, with their contents, having been burned by the enemy.

The Doctor, who never relished much a residence in Washington City, where the technical formalities and customs in fashionable life were unsuited to his taste, had now a strong desire to return to the west. The office of Surveyor-General of public lands north-west of the Ohio river, was then held by Josiah Meigs, Esq., who kept the office at Cincinnati, and was paid a salary by Government of two thousand dollars per year. The Doctor conceived the project of effecting an exchange of offices with Mr. Meigs, provided the consent of the President and senate could be obtained. Early in the autumn of 1814 he wrote to Mr. Meigs, confidentially, making the proposition here named to him, who willingly consented thereto. The Doctor next brought the subject before the President privately, and satisfied him that the proposed exchange was mutually desired by himself and Mr. Meigs, and that the public interest would in no way suffer thereby. Mr. Madison obligingly assented to their wishes, and sent to the senate their nominations for that purpose, which were confirmed by that body.

The way being now open for the Doctor's return to his favored west, he lost no time in making his preparations for that purpose. Sending on his household goods in advance, he, with Mrs. Tiffin and their children and nurse, performed the tedious journey in the family carriage. He immediately removed the Surveyor-General's office from Cincinnati to Chillicothe, its location not being fixed by law at any one place. Here he fitted up the office in an old, one-story log building, which had been erected in the early settlement of the town, and stood on Water-street, in front of his dwelling-house, and, I believe, remains there yet, a relic of the olden time. The Doctor now went to work, with his characteristic ardor and assiduity, to acquaint himself minutely with the routine of the duties devolving upon him, and to ge-

'the run'—the history and present state of its business. This was a laborious task, one in which he derived little or no assistance from the only clerk whom he found in the office, who had been himself but a short time in it; Mr. Meigs having set out for Washington City about the time that the Doctor left it for Ohio. At that time no public surveys were being made, having been suspended by the presence of hostile Indians on the territory to be surveyed, and but little current business demanded attention.

"In the spring of 1814, before he had any thought of returning to Ohio, Dr. Tiffin, without any solicitation from me or my friends, had appointed me to a clerkship in the General Land-Office. Wishing to have me in his office at Chillicothe, the Doctor, in January following, made the proposition to me, and offered me the post of chief clerk therein. This offer I very willingly accepted, and in the spring of 1815 moved back to Chillicothe, and immediately entered upon the duties of my new employment. The business of this office being exactly suited to my taste and inclinations, it will not, I hope, be considered out of place for me to say that I devoted, unremittingly, what little energy and ardor I possessed to make myself thoroughly acquainted with the whole routine of duties devolving upon me, as well as those pertaining to the head of the office; for these, likewise, as the Doctor's health declined, he committed almost entirely to my management. It was, I will add, gratifying to me to know that the onerous duties, thus devolved by him upon his chief clerk, were performed to the Doctor's entire satisfaction, as well as that of the department at Washington, the head of which, in after years, spoke of the manner in which the business of the office had been conducted in very flattering terms.

"During the first three or four years after the Doctor's return from Washington, he occasionally preached in town; and, at one time, for several months, conducted the religious services of the little society of the Protestant Episcopal Church in Chillicothe, who had, as yet, no pastor. Besides the morning service of that Church, he usually read a sermon from some book, using for this purpose, mostly, 'Burder's Village Sermons.' He was a fine reader, and read from the pages of the book, which lay on the desk before him, with all the appropriate emphasis, cadence, intonation, and pathos of an extemporaneous discourse. On one Sunday he did venture to deliver one of his own extemporaneous sermons, and with such warmth and power that his congregation was thrown into great amazement. A committee appointed by them waited upon the Doctor the next day, and expressed their disapprobation of extempore sermons, desiring him, in future, to read only. Whether he ever officiated for them afterward I do not now recollect, but think he did not.

"The Doctor had long been subject to occasional paroxysms of severe nervous headache, which did not usually continue beyond a few hours. As he advanced in years these paroxysms became more frequent and severe, with painful disturbance of the whole nervous system, and great suffering. These afflictions gradually advanced upon him to the end of his life; and during the last four or five years of it most of his time was spent in his bed. I usually went to his room every morning, to see him before opening the office; and often has he said to me, 'I had a very bad night of it, and was in hopes that I would have died before morning!' And on more than one occasion he has added, 'O, how glad I would be if the Lord would only send the messenger, and release me from my sufferings! I fancy that when my exulting spirit would reach the ceiling it would turn a moment and gaze upon the lifeless body, and triumphantly exclaim, "Ha, you old diseased carcass, I am liberated from your loathsome prison at last! Farewell, till we meet again, when the trumpet shall awaken you from the tomb, and your mortal shall put on immortality!"' When well enough to leave his room, he would attend to some business in the office, or overlook the work in his garden, or other matters about the house; and, as often as practicable, he attended public worship and his class meetings. He read much even when unable to sit up. Hundreds of times have I found him on his bed with a book in his hand, the pages of which he was poring over with earnestness, although suffering much at the time. His reading was generally confined to religious works.

"The last few years of his life were but little diversified with incident. Disease and suffering were gradually wearing him down to the grave. He was mostly confined to his room and to his bed. And when his health permitted him to be out, he was soon obliged to return again to his room.

"Doctor Tiffin held the office of Surveyor-General for nearly fifteen years, enjoying the entire confidence of Presidents Madison, Monroe, and John Quincy Adams, and the departments at Washington, in his capacity, integrity, and faithfulness in office. On the accession of General Jackson to the Presidency, the new doctrine that 'to the victors belonged the spoils' was adopted, and carried out, through all the numerous offices of the Government, from the highest to the lowest, where the incumbents were not known to be political adherents and active partisans of the General and his administration. The Doctor had, for twenty years or more previous to this time, laid politics aside. He concerned not himself with, nor took any part whatever in, the political party movements of the day. He contented himself, when able to attend, by going to the polls and depositing his ballot. His name, of course, was enrolled high up on the list of the proscribed, and he was early removed from office by the new President. His successor was General William Lytle, of Cincinnati, a gentleman every way worthy of the appointment. On the 1st of July, 1829, General Lytle appeared, and laid before Dr. Tiffin, then on his death-bed, his commission, and an order from the department at Washington for the delivery of the office to him, as his successor. This was done very politely and promptly, and the office was at once removed by General Lytle to Cincinnati.

"The Doctor's health continued to decline, and he gradually sunk till Sunday evening, the 9th of August, 1829, a little over six weeks after his removal from office. He had been long sensible of his approaching end, and contemplated the solemn event not only with calm complacency, but with joyful anticipations of a triumphant admission into his heavenly Father's kingdom and to the society of 'just men made perfect.' This joyful confidence he gave frequent expression to when visited by his friends and brethren. He retained the full exercise of his reason to the last, and gently and calmly sunk into the embraces of death about sundown of the day above mentioned, aged sixty-three years and two months. I close this brief account of his death with the following appropriate obituary notice, which I clip from the Chillicothe 'Scioto Gazette,' of August 12, 1829:

"'Died, at his residence in this place, on Sunday evening last, the 9th inst., Dr. EDWARD TIFFIN, in the sixty-fourth year of his age.

"'The deceased was a native of England, but immigrated to America at an early period in life, and settled in Berkly county, in the state of Virginia, as a practicing physician. Shortly after this state—then a part of the North-West territory, so called—was opened for settlement, he removed to this town, then in its infancy, and erected the first house that was covered with a *shingle roof.* In 1799 he was elected a member of the territorial Legislature, in which capacity he continued to serve till he was chosen a member of the convention that formed the Constitution of Ohio, of which body he was President. When, in 1803, the Constitution of the state went into operation, he was called to the first executive office under it, by a very flattering vote of the people. This mark of the public confidence was again extended to him at the succeeding election of Governor. But before he had completed his second gubernatorial term, he was elected a senator in the Congress of the United States. In this distinguished station, he served the state till a heavy domestic misfortune compelled him, temporarily, to retire from public life. In the early part of the administration of President Madison, the General Land-Office was formed into a distinct bureau of the Treasury Department. In looking to the west for a suitable person to be placed at its head, the penetrating judgment of that great man selected the subject of this notice as its first Commissioner. He promptly repaired to the post, and faithfully devoted himself to the organization and discharge of the various, complicated, and arduous duties of the office, till he was appointed Surveyor-General of the United States, in which capacity he continued to act till the first of July last, when he was removed by President Jackson for his unbending honesty and independence as a politician; thus filling a life of almost continued public usefulness for upward of thirty years.

"'In the various relations of a parent, husband, Christian, neighbor, and private citizen, the deceased has been but rarely equaled, and perhaps never excelled.

"'As a public man, he was inflexibly just, upright,

independent, and firm. As a private citizen, he was emphatically an honest and conscientious man; and as a Christian, he was catholic in his religious opinions, and exemplary and practically pious.

"'He has left, to deplore his loss, a widow, five children, a number of other near relations, and an extensive circle of public and private acquaintances. On the succeeding afternoon his mortal remains were committed to the tomb, attended by a large concourse of the citizens of the town and of the adjoining neighborhood.'

"In stature Dr. Tiffin was about five feet six inches, with pretty full and heavy body, and light limbs. His head was large, and his face full and round, with florid complexion. Baldness had taken place long before he had reached the meridian of life; and, for the last fifteen or twenty years of it, he was obliged to wear a wig. His countenance was one of the most expressive I have ever seen, especially when lighted up with animation. He was remarkable for the activity and quickness of his movements, and whatsoever he did, he did with promptness and with his might. Dr. Monett—a physician of Chillicothe—used to say of him, that 'what he could not do quickly, he could not do at all.' It was his rule of action, 'never to put off till to-morrow that which could be done to-day.' In company, his conversation was generally animated, always engaging, and his manner full of life and vivacity, which often made him, on such occasions, the 'observed of all observers.'

"In his financial affairs—especially those in relation to the office, where large expenditures were annually made on account of the public surveys—he was particularly exact, making it a point to keep his accounts posted up every day, ready for settlement in case of his death. And when removed from office, having no instructions about paying over the balance of public money in his hands—some four or five thousand dollars—he gave the department at Washington no rest till he obtained an order to pay it over to his successor, which he instantly did.

"His benevolence to the poor and needy was bounded only by his inability farther to relieve them. I have known him to feel intensely when he had not the means at hand, or to spare, to supply the wants of the needy and destitute; and his known charity to the poor brought numerous calls from them for relief. In several instances, where he did not wish the recipients to know from whom the relief came, he has made me the almoner of his charity, and very probably often availed himself of similar services from others. The sufferings of the sick and poor always awakened his sympathies, and

"'His pity gave ere charity began.'

"After his appointment as Surveyor-General, being no longer engaged in the practice of physic, he kept always on hand a supply of medicines in common use for the use of the poor and those not well able to pay, and to all such who called on him, he distributed suitable medicines, with professional advice and instructions, free of charge. Calls of this description were numerous, chiefly from the country; and I have known him to be employed for hours together in attending to the cases of the sick, in inquiring into the symptoms, in giving advice, writing prescriptions and making up packages of medicines, even when he was scarcely able to be out of his bed, or actually confined to it.

"It should have been mentioned in its proper place, in the early portion of the Doctor's life, his filial care of his aged parents, for whom he provided a home in his own house, after their children were all settled in the world. He contributed in every way to their comfort and happiness, nursed them himself, with all tenderness and affection, when they were sick, and, to the extent of his power, smoothed their passage to the tomb. They both died, I think, about the year 1807.

"As a preacher, the Doctor's talents were much above mediocrity. He was methodical in the arrangement of his discourses, and always 'stuck to his text,' and presented his subject with clearness and force. His language was somewhat florid, but yet plain, and adapted to the easy comprehension of all. His action in the pulpit was highly impulsive, yet natural and graceful, and his countenance lighted up with expression. His discourses were delivered with great animation and with eloquence and power, and his appeals to the hearts and consciences of his hearers were pointed, forcible, and effective. In the country around Chillicothe, where the Doctor had so often preached, he was deservedly very popular, and his labors in the pulpit much sought after, and at quarterly and camp meetings he was always assigned one, at least, of the chief appointments on the Sabbath. Three of Dr. Tiffin's sermons, preached in 1817, have been given in the 'Ohio Conference Offering,' a collection of sermons published in 1851, by Rev. M. P. Gaddis. (See pp. 340–360.)

"To the active labors and influence of Dr. Tiffin, the Church is more indebted than to any other man for the introduction and establishment of Methodism in Chillicothe and the surrounding country.

"We may add, in conclusion, that the Doctor's excellent lady, whom he left a widow, survived him but a few years. His four daughters are still living. The eldest is married to Mr. Joseph A. Reynolds, and resides near Urbana; another married M. Scott Cook, Esq., of Chillicothe; and the youngest is the wife of Dr. C. G. Comegys, a talented and skillful physician of Cincinnati. The remaining daughter is unmarried. His only son, Edward

Parker Tiffin, chose the profession of medicine, and, after completing his studies and graduating, he spent two years in Paris, France, to perfect his knowledge of the healing art, and returned to the United States last autumn, and took the cars at New York on his route home. At one of the stopping-places on the way, where the passengers breakfasted, the train started before he had got on again, and in attempting to get on one of the cars when in motion, his foot slipped off the step, and he fell on the track, and was instantly run over by the wheels, nearly cutting off one leg and one arm, both near the body. He was taken back to New York, but survived only a few hours.

"Dr. Tiffin, it is to be regretted, left no papers nor any written memorial of his life. Most of the foregoing memoir is drawn from memory, and relates to matters occurring from twenty-five to almost fifty years ago. It is also to be regretted that the only likeness left of the Doctor is a small miniature, which bears but little resemblance to the original, and altogether fails to give the striking features and fine expression of countenance of the Doctor. I have been shown a portrait on some bank notes, which is said to be copied from the miniature above mentioned; but it fails to convey even what little trace of likeness is found in the miniature."

CHAPTER XX.

JOHN A. GRENADE.

A SHORT sketch of this wonderful man, written by our friend and brother, Dr. Baker, of the Cincinnati conference, containing some deeply-thrilling and interesting incidents, will be found below. The Doctor's sketch is prefaced by the following:

"DEAR BROTHER,—I am much gratified to learn that you are engaged in rescuing from the shades of forgetfulness the names, the labors, and privations of those pious dead, who, in the early stages of the settlement of the vast region of this now cultivated and truly 'great west,' went forth, bearing the precious seed of Gospel truth, and scattering it broadcast over the extensive field. They had, morally speaking, to fell the forest, to clear, break up, and reclaim a soil, wild and luxuriant, of a vitiated growth, and transform it into a fruitful field. How did those men toil and suffer privation! Surely their names, their labors, their sufferings, and their success should be stereotyped in the records of Methodism, and of the nation, in all coming generations. But, alas! even the names of some of them are almost forgotten. We hope you will gather up many of the fragments that yet remain. It is a work worthy of your pen; and the book will be hailed with joy by hundreds of the pioneers of Methodism who yet linger on earth, both in the north and in the south, and by thousands of their descendants.

"I send you herewith a few reminiscences of Rev. John A. Grenade, known, in the days of his itinerancy, as the 'wild man.' Some points in his character and history I have learned from others, but the pastoral visit I give from memory.

"God, in his wisdom, for the accomplishment of his purposes, has, in every age of the world, chosen such instrumentalities as were adapted to the times, circumstances, and state of society. This is illustrated and confirmed, as in numerous other instances, in the character of the early Methodist preachers of this country. Moreover, times and circumstances tend to develop the character, mold the habits, and shape the courses of men. Hence, 'men for the times' are the instruments God has provided to meet emergencies; and where they are obedient to their call, and with fidelity attend to the work to which they were destined, success ever has, and ever will honor and crown their efforts; and if some disobey, others will be called. Thus are the designs of God accomplished. Such men always leave their impress upon their age.

"Of several of the Methodist preachers who labored in the south-west in the days of my childhood, I have recollections more or less distinct. Samuel Douthet was hortatory and pathetic; Ralph Lotspeich, a weeping prophet; Thomas Wilkerson, a son of consolation, whose speech dropped like the gentle dew; John Crane, a warm, earnest, eloquent man. He, too, often wept in preaching. Crane was a slender man, apparently feeble, very zealous, and abundant in labors. He fell a martyr to his work in 1812, on Duck river, Tennessee, where he labored night and day, while God himself was warning the terrified inhabitants by 'terribly shaking the earth.' James Axley, droll, witty, argumentative, and often powerful. I heard him last at a camp meeting in Tennessee, in 1819. There are others of whom I could speak. Among them all, however, Grenade was the 'Son of Thunder.' The visit to my father's family, when he traveled the Holston circuit, impressed him upon my memory so as never to be forgotten.

"Of the parentage, nativity, or early life of Mr. Grenade I know nothing. When I saw him at my father's, in 1803, he was, as I suppose, near thirty years of age. He was about medium hight, but slender; of a quick and elastic step; formed for action. His voice was full and musical; his eye keen, *piercing;* and, when speaking, his jesticulations were violent. He was a man of respectable education, a physician, and a poet. His temperament was ardent, or, as Martin Luther said of himself, he was 'choleric by nature.'

"After his conversion, if my impressions are correct, he lost his evidence of justification and all his religious enjoyment, in consequence of refusing to preach. But the Spirit of God pursued him, and, though he tried to shake off his convictions of duty, he was brought to see and feel his perilous condition so sensibly as to excite the most fearful apprehensions and alarm. The enemy, taking advantage of his condition, suggested that his destiny was now sealed; that he had 'grieved the Spirit of God whereby he had been sealed;' that he had 'sinned against the Holy Ghost;' that his case was hopeless, and his doom unalterably sealed. He yielded to the temptation, and his spirit sank within him. Now it was he 'found trouble and sorrow;' yea, 'the pains of hell got hold upon him,' and now for a season the billows of the Divine wrath seemed to overwhelm him. He was brought to the verge of despair, and here he struggled long and hard. While thus drinking the 'cup of trembling,' the wormwood and gall, he wandered in forests and mountains, by day and by night, scarcely taking sufficient rest or nourishment to sustain nature, bewailing his lost—as he believed—his hopeless condition and fearful destiny.

It was in this state of mind he composed some of his mournful and penitential poems, as he doubtless thought and feared, the funeral dirges of all his hopes. But though bordering on despair, he continued to pour out his soul in prayer, still cherishing a faint hope that mercy might possibly yet be extended to him, and the vials of Divine wrath be turned aside. Often did he wrestle as in an agony, pleading with God for mercy. It was in consequence of his thus wandering alone, bewailing his condition, and refusing to be comforted, that he first obtained the appellation of the 'wild man,' which cognomen consorted equally well with his subsequent zeal and the character of his efforts as a minister.

"When he obtained deliverance it was sudden—instantaneous as the lightning's flash. As he lay alone upon the ground, looking up toward heaven with mingled hope and despair, a light from heaven shone round about him, dispelling his gloomy forebodings, and filling his soul with unutterable peace and joy. It was a complete triumph. The transition was so sudden, so great, that the morning of rapturous joy was now as overwhelming as had been the long, dark night of his sorrow. In the poem commemorative of this event, and which I heard him sing with the deepest emotions, are the following stanzas:

'One evening, pensive as I lay
Alone upon the ground,
As I to God began to pray,
A light shone all around.

Glory to God! I loudly cried,
My sins are all forgiven;
For me, for me the Savior died;
My peace is made with heav'n.'

"Having been thus severely schooled by experience in the evils of sin, and having tasted the joys of salvation, he became exceedingly zealous for the honor of that God whose mercy had so marvelously saved him, and, deeply concerned for the salvation of his perishing fellow-men, he immediately engaged in calling sinners to repentance.

"Mr. Grenade entered the traveling connection in 1802, in the Western conference, and was appointed that year to Green circuit, with Moses Floyd in charge. In 1803 he was appointed to Holston circuit, with Thomas Milligan in charge; but Milligan was afterward sent to Clinch, and Grenade was left in charge. The Holston circuit then embraced a large extent of country in East Tennessee, in the bounds of which my father then lived. Whether Grenade was left with or without a colleague, I know not; one thing is certain, however, he was abundant in labors, insomuch that his career as an itinerant was brief. His circuits were large, his rides long, and much of the time he labored both day and night; for where he had not regular appointments, his zeal and extraordinary labors rendered him so notorious that the people would throng him. Though often coy, shy, and fearful of approaching too near, yet they flocked to see and hear him; and he was ever ready to speak for his Master; ever ready to warn, to instruct, to comfort, to pray, or to sing, as opportunity offered or occasion required. He obeyed the injunction, 'Work while it is called to-day.' Such was his zeal for God, and his concern for the souls of men, that he seemed to have forgotten himself, or to disregard the effects of his excessive labors upon his own frail constitution; and his success may be learned from the official reports from the fields of his toil.

"At this time my father resided on Roseberry creek, a small tributary of the Holston river, in Knox county, Tennessee. About two miles distant was a preaching-place, where the family were in the habit of attending preaching, and where my two eldest sisters, about this time, joined the little society. It was during this year, I think, in the month of June, and about two months before my father's death, that Mr. Grenade made one of his primitive pastoral visits to our family. Though I was then but a child, I have a vivid recollection of this visit. Some of the family had been to hear him preach, and he came home with them. Soon after they returned from meeting word was sent to my uncle's family, who lived on an adjoining farm, and I think to some other near neighbors, that Mr. Grenade was there, and would be glad to see and converse with as many as could conveniently collect. Soon after dinner the family were collected. My uncle's family, with others, came in. All being seated in the largest room of the farm-house—we had no parlors in the country in those days—the table was set out a little distance from the wall, and the books placed upon it. The preacher then came from his room, was introduced to the company, and then took his station by the table, my father sitting by his side. He first read a portion of Scripture, sung a hymn, and prayed. Well do I remember the earnestness, fervor, and unction of his prayer. He then gave an exhortation, in which he waxed quite warm, frequently moving the table forward before him, till at the close of his exhortation it stood near the center of the room. His hearers, except my father and elder sisters, being unaccustomed to such stentorian addresses, kept as respectful and non-committal a distance as the dimensions of the domestic chapel would permit. And as to my little self, being among the youngest of his auditors, and extremely timid by nature, I was partly hid in the bushes in the fireplace. It was customary in those days, in the warm season of the year, to clean out this recess, paint the hearth, and adorn it with green bushes from the woods and flowers from the garden. The exhortation over he sang again, and then proceeded to speak personally to each individual present. Well do I remember what a chill ran over me when, in passing round the room in his earnest manner, rubbing his hands, he came opposite to where I sat, reaching forth his hand, and laying it upon my head, implored the blessing of 'Him that dwelt in the bush' to rest upon the child. At that moment my heart seemed to sink within me; but 'coupled with fear' was a reverence for the man. I wept, I loved him; for I really believed he wished us all to be saved. After conversing with, and earnestly exhorting all in the room, he came again to the place of beginning; and never shall I forget the attitude in which he stood before my father. Rubbing his hands briskly, lifting his feet alternately, and letting them down with no very slow or light tread, breathing deep inspirations drawn through his teeth, he almost literally danced, like David before the ark. After indulging for some moments in this ebullition of feeling, in which not a word was spoken, his full soul found vent in an outburst of blessing and thanksgiving to God that, though the harvest was large, and the laborers so few in that region, he had found one who was laboring faithfully in the wilderness to prepare the way of the Lord. He then walked the room for some time, singing hymns and spiritual songs, mostly of his own composing. His earnest manner, the shrill and musical tones of his voice, his speaking eye, now beaming with joy, and now suffused with tears, alternating with the varied emotions of his ardent soul, which seemed to be full of the mighty thoughts that were struggling within and seeking an utterance, made such an impression upon my heart at the time, that the lapse of half a century, with all its vicissitudes, has not erased. I even yet recollect some of the stanzas he there sung, especially those relating to his own experience, in which he so vividly portrays his condition, as when, in the anguish of his soul, he poured forth his wild and bitter wail of despair:

'O, that I were some bird or beast;
Some wolf, or stork, or owl!
Some lofty tree should bear my nest,
Or through the desert prowl.'

And then his joyful deliverance, as given above. This stanza is, I think, nearly *verbatim* from his experience, as originally versified by himself.

"At the close of these services, which, to the best of my recollection, lasted not less than two hours, the company retired with his blessing. This interview, I presume, was never forgotten by any who were then present. Such pastoral visits were seldom in those days, and such a one I have not witnessed since. The evening was spent by Mr. Grenade and my father in conversation on the all-important subject of their work—the work of saving souls. These were times that demanded and called into requisition all the wisdom, the fortitude, and the patient perseverance of the few and widely-scattered laborers then in the field.

"The next morning, after family worship and an early breakfast, these servants of God, with renewed vows of fidelity in their work, parted for the last time. In a few weeks from this time my father died suddenly of apoplexy. Though he fell unexpectedly, in high health, and in the strength of manhood, he fell with the trumpet at his mouth. It was on the Sabbath. He had an appointment to preach at eleven o'clock that day, but his work was done. About two o'clock in the morning he was heard breathing in an unusual and laborious manner. In a few moments a light was procured, and his family gathered around his bed. But he spoke not; death was doing its work in a summary manner; and he

'Ceased at once to work and live.'

"I have said Grenade was a poet. His poetry was characteristic of the man, and his style as a preacher bold, towering, often tinctured with the 'awfully sublime,' yet flowing with ease and naturalness, and sometimes extremely tender and pathetic. In my childhood I memorized many of his 'spiritual songs;' but have forgotten most of them. I have not seen any of them in their original dress for many years, and fear they are 'out of print.' Some vestiges of them, occasionally found in compilations, are so mangled and distorted that the author, if living, would hardly recognize them.

"Mr. Grenade labored but three years as an itinerant. His zeal carried him beyond his strength, and under his indefatigable labors and exposures in the new settlements his health failed, and he located. My last information of him was, that he was practicing medicine somewhere in south-western Tennessee."

CHAPTER XXI.

THE WESTERN METHODIST BOOK CONCERN.

A SKETCH of the history of this institution, so intimately connected with the interests of Methodism in the west, should perhaps have been embraced in our sketch of the origin and progress of Methodism in Cincinnati; but as the Western Book Concern never has been, and never was designed to be local in its operations, but to embrace the entire west and south in the sphere of its labors, we have thought it more appropriate to assign to it a separate chapter.

The General conference of 1787, having founded a Book Concern in Philadelphia, the proceeds of which were appropriated mostly to the establishment of Cokesbury College and district schools, and which underwent changes and modifications, from time to time, in its policy, till it was removed to New York in 1804, finally determined to devote the most of the profits to the enlargement of the Concern and the increasing of the facilities for the manufacture of books. Accordingly, in the year 1820, it was resolved that a branch should be located in Cincinnati, for the purpose of supplying the conferences west of the mountains with Methodist books. The books from New York were at that time wagoned to Philadelphia, and from thence to Pittsburg, where they were shipped on the Ohio river for Cincinnati.

If about the time of which we are writing, an individual had been passing along Elm-street, between Fourth and Fifth streets, he would have seen, on the corner of Elm and Fifth streets, a small office, over the door of which he could have read, on a small, rude sign, "Methodist Book Room." And it was a "room," sure enough; for in its fifteen by twenty capacity great operations were performed. Like the log-cabins of our fathers, in which the kitchen, dining-room, sitting-room, chamber, and parlor were all in one, this "Book Room" comprised the depository, packing-room, counting-room, and Agent's office. It was also, to some extent, like the present Book Room, a kind of preacher's exchange. But, as we were going to say, had the individual we have supposed passing along been disposed to have looked within, he would have found a plain but intelligent-looking man behind the counter, or at the desk, or bending over a box of books which he might have been packing or unpacking, ready to receive and wait upon him with words of kindness, proceeding from an open, generous heart. That man was Martin Ruter, afterward President of Alleghany College and the master spirit of the Texas pioneers, where he labored, suffered, and died, giving up his martyr spirit into the hands of the great Savior, who called him away from the halls of learning to traverse the wilds of Texas, and lay the foundations of the Church in that infant republic. But to return from our digression. In that small store, had the inquiry been made, there might have been found the works of Wesley, Fletcher, Clarke, and Coke, together with the Journals of Asbury and the Hymn-Book and Discipline. There, also, he might have subscribed for the Christian Advocate and Zion's Herald; and, had he desired to have become more intimately acquainted with the condition and prospects of the Church, he might have obtained a copy of the General Minutes. But stay, gentle reader, we are a little too fast. The oldest Book Agent now living is here by our side, and he will correct us by telling you that if you purchased any of these books, you were obliged to do it on the wholesale principle, as the idea of a *retail sales-room* was not thought of in that day. Whenever an individual member of the Church in the vicinity wished to obtain either of the books named, he would call at or send a message to the house of brother Ruter, close by the Book Room, where it could be had.

Such was the Western Book Concern in the year 1820, thirty-four years ago. What it has been since, and through all the progressive stages of its development till the present time, we shall endeavor briefly to describe. At first it was a mere depository, not even regarded as a branch of the parent Concern at New York, and, of course, it was neither expected nor desired that it should engage in the publication of any books. All that was published by Dr. Ruter, during his connection with the Concern, was a Scriptural Catechism and Primer; but these were on his own individual responsibility. Under all the embarrassing circumstances in which he was called to carry on the business, the Doctor managed it well; and, though the total receipts for the first year did not amount to as much as is now received sometimes in a few days, being little over four thousand dollars, yet, considering the times, it was a pretty good business.

At that time there was a specific rule in the Discipline which rendered an Agent ineligible to re-election after he had been serving in that office eight years. Dr. Ruter's term having expired by limitation in 1828, the General conference, which was held at Pittsburg, elected the Rev. Charles Holliday as Agent of the Concern in Cincinnati. As the successor of Dr. Ruter, he set himself to work to make himself acquainted with the business, which, though at that time was not very intricate, still required some knowledge of the book business.

Besides, at that time there were no clerks who had grown up in the establishment, like the Messrs. Kilbreth, Phillips, and Doughty, and others, to whom the Agents could look for information; and, hence, they had to begin with the A B C of the Concern, and study out its policy and operations as opportunity presented and as circumstances might require. In process of time it became necessary to remove the Book Room to another place, and, accordingly, brother Holliday rented a house on George-street, between Race and Elm, and appropriated the front room for the storage and package of books and every thing else belonging to the establishment. After occupying this location for upward of two years, it was thought best to make another removal, and the Concern was accordingly removed to the west side of Walnut, between Third and Fourth streets, in a stone building, which is still standing, on the north-west corner of Baker and Walnut streets, Mr. Henry Shaffer, who is still living in Cincinnati, being a clerk. Greater facilities were afforded here for carrying on the operations, as it was in a more business part of the city. The Concern occupied this location till the General conference of 1832, when it was determined that its operations should be enlarged by the appointment of two Agents and the removal to a still more conspicuous part of the city, and one more favorable to business facilities. Accordingly, the Rev. C. Holliday was re-elected Principal and the Rev. John F. Wright Assistant Book Agent, and the establishment was again removed, to the west side of Main-street, a few doors above Sixth-street, in a storehouse owned by Josiah Lawrence, Esq. Here the operations of the Concern were greatly enlarged, and its efficiency in supplying the western and southern country with Methodist literature became apparent to all. The demand for Hymn-Books and Disciplines, particularly, having greatly increased, and it being difficult at all times to supply this demand, in consequence of the difficulty connected with the modes of transportation, it was determined to publish these works in the west, which, in due time, was done, the Hymn-Book being the first book published by authority. In the spring of the year 1834 the publication of the Western Christian Advocate was commenced at the Concern, and the Rev. Thomas A. Morris was appointed Editor. This paper has been increasing its patronage subscription list from that time, during all the periods of its history, to the present day. No Church paper in the country has been more popular, or received a more extensive patronage, and had a greater circulation, than the Western Christian Advocate. But more of this anon. In the year 1836 the General conference struck out of the Discipline the provision which limited the office of Book Agent to eight years, and the Agents of the Western Book Concern were not required to act any longer in a subordinate capacity to the New York Concern, but to "co-operate with them." They were also authorized to publish any book in the General Catalogue when, in their judgment and that of the Book Committee, it would be advantageous to the interests of the Church; provided that they should not publish type editions of such books as were stereotyped at New York. The conference also appointed an Assistant Editor of the Western Christian Advocate. The persons elected were Rev. Charles Elliott, D. D., Principal, and Rev. William Phillips, Assistant Editor. The Book Agents were also authorized, with the advice and consent of the Book Committee, to procure a lot of ground, and erect thereon suitable buildings for a printing office, Book Room, and bindery; and for that end they were allowed to appropriate such moneys in their hands as they could spare from the Concern, together with any donations that might be made for that purpose in the west. At this conference Rev. J. F. Wright was elected Principal and Rev. L. Swormstedt, Assistant Agent. After much consultation, a lot on the corner of Eighth and Main streets, known as the St. Clair property, on which stood the mansion of General St. Clair, surrounded by lofty trees, was selected as the site. In its day this was regarded as a princely mansion, and even yet it presents the appearance of a venerable old pile. Around it, could its history be written, might doubtless be gathered many thrilling recollections of olden time. Here, doubtless, many a levee and soiree has been held by the officers of old Fort Washington and the army of General St. Clair. It stood back upward of a hundred feet from Main-street, in the center of the lot, and hence it was not necessary to remove it for the buildings which were to be erected. But more of this mansion hereafter.

Preparations were made as soon as possible for putting up the necessary buildings, and a printing office, in due course of time, was erected, on the rear of the lot, four stories high, and sufficiently large for all the purposes of printing. The first book printed and published by the Concern from manuscript was Phillips's Strictures, the publication of which was ordered by the Ohio conference. We have already made an allusion to this work in our sketch of its author. The next work was the Wyandott Mission, which was followed by Morris's Sermons, Life of Roberts, Power on Universalism, Tomlinson's Millennium, Shaffer on Baptism, History of German Missions, House's Sketches, Memoir of Mrs. Sears, Anecdotes of Wesley, Prison Life, History of Methodist Episcopal Missions, Ohio Conference Offering, Butler's Analogy with Analysis, Objections to Calvinism, Carroll's Exposition, Morris's Miscellany, Domestic Piety, Memoir of Gurley, Life of Quinn, Larrabee's Evidences, Life of

Collins, American Slavery, Wesley and his Coadjutors, Letters to School Girls, Lorrain's Sea-Sermons, Miley on Class Meetings, Life and Times of Wiley, Autobiography of Finley, Positive Theology, Asbury and his Coadjutors, Life of Gatch, etc. We may not have given these in the exact order of time in which they were published; but it is sufficient to answer all the purposes of a sketch, and the reader can see what has been done since 1836 in the publication of original works. Besides these, numerous reprints, both English and German, in the latter of which are several original publications, and a large number of pamphlets and tracts, too numerous to mention, have been issued from time to time. For many of the reprints duplicate stereotype plates were received from the Concern in New York.

In the year 1839 a charter for the Western Book Concern was obtained from the Legislature of Ohio. In the year 1840 the Rev. J. F. Wright was re-elected, and Rev. L. Swormstedt continued Assistant Agent, at which time the Agents were authorized to publish a monthly periodical adapted to the ladies. This work was commenced in January, 1841, with the title of "Ladies' Repository and Gatherings of the West;" and Rev. L. L. Hamline, Assistant Editor of the Advocate, was appointed its Editor. The Agents also had authority to publish any book which had not previously been published by the Agents at New York, when in their judgment, and that of the Book Committee, the demand for such publication would justify, and the interest of the Church required it. They were, however, prohibited from reprinting any of the larger works, such as the Commentaries, quarto Bibles, etc. They were also authorized to publish such books and tracts as were recommended by the General conference, and any new works which the editors should approve, and the Book Committee and annual conference recommend. This year a German paper, for the benefit of the German Methodists, was established at Cincinnati, entitled *Der Christliche Apologete*, and the Rev. William Nast was elected Editor. The Agents were also, by a rule passed at this conference, required to remit to the Agents at New York, as largely and frequently as their funds would allow, and to the full amount of stock furnished, if practicable. They were also required to remit all surplus funds not required for carrying on the business, to be added to the profits of the Concern at New York.

In process of time a lot adjoining the St. Clair mansion was purchased, and after the Book Concern proper was erected, a large four-story building was placed upon it, which is occupied by stores, the rent of which yields a handsome income. The entire lot, on which stand both of the buildings, is upward of one hundred feet, fronting on Main-street, and runs entirely back to the alley, inclosed on Eighth-street, from the Book Room to the printing office, by a high brick wall. The main building is upward of fifty feet front, and upward of a hundred feet deep, six stories high, two having been added the past year. The first floor in front is divided into a large sales-room and clerks' offices, in the rear of which is the office of the Agents. Immediately in the rear of the sales-room is a private room, fitted up with great neatness, for the Book Committee, or the transaction of any business connected with the Concern. In one side of this room has been built a substantial brick vault, with iron doors, for the safe-keeping of the account-books, etc. In the rear of the front rooms is the packing department, which extends the whole width of the building. On the second floor, over the front rooms, is the depository for the books of the General Catalogue, and the Sunday school publications are in the rear, as also the German publications and tracts. The rooms on the third floor are occupied by three embossing-presses, which are worked and heated by steam from the boiler under the yard of the printing office. In this room there are thirteen hands constantly employed. The fourth story is also occupied with the bindery, in which there are sixteen hands. The fifth story, which is exclusively occupied by females, under the superintendence of Mr. White, is devoted to those branches of the business included in the bindery appropriate to females, such as folding, sewing, stitching, gathering, collating, etc. In this department there are thirty-six girls. The sixth story is a general depository for stock. The whole establishment is heated with steam, which is conducted through pipes from the boiler all through the building. The first story is lighted with gas, which is often necessary during dark days, of which there are many in Cincinnati. The whole establishment has recently undergone a most complete and thorough repair and remodeling, and every department is reduced to a system of operations which would compare favorably with any similar establishment. The number of clerks employed at present in the Book Room is eight, beside two or three in the mailing department. The whole number of hands in the bindery, exclusive of the foreman, Mr. Vandewater, is sixty-four, of which twenty-eight are males and thirty-six are females.

We now come to describe the printing office; but before doing so, as it is on our way, we will ask our reader to pass with us out of the Book Room, on Main-street, and, turning to the right, enter with us an avenue between the last-mentioned place and the building appropriated to stores, which will conduct us to the old mansion, alluded to above. A fire having recently occurred in an adjoining building, which destroyed part of the roof of the "mansion," the heavy and elaborately-wrought cornice which once ornamented this ancient building has been removed, and the walls run up, the better to protect the building from such accidents in future. Before us is the spacious double doorway, in front of which is the massy door-stone, which has been pressed by the feet of many who have long since been gathered to the tomb. At the left, on entering, you will discover over the door, "Library." This room is nicely fitted up with cases for books on all sides; and here may be found a large, and, in some respects, rare and curious library. Many an ancient tome of Latin and Greek, over which the "old man learned" has pored, in the days when tied to the linguistic chair in college, or searching for the doctrines and rites of the Tridentine councils, that he might present to the world a true delineation of the Mother of Harlots or the Man of Sin. But this library is not rich in patristic lore alone; it embraces the whole range of Biblical literature, and a considerable of what may be called general and polite. The rooms on the right are occupied by Mr. Boyd, a gentleman connected with the Concern, while the rear below is occupied by the faithful Charles, the messenger. Let us now ascend the ancient stairway. Two flights and we reach the landing, in front of which is the room occupied by the Editor of the Ladies' Repository, Rev. D. W. Clark, D. D. To look at the Doctor's case, which stands to the left there, against the wall, with pigeon-boxes labeled to receive exchange periodicals, such as quarterlies and monthlies, and the most of which seem to be occupied, you would think the organ of order was strongly developed; and it may be for aught we know; but if you will cast a glance at his table you would be led to infer almost any thing else. Perhaps, like ourself, he is a great *lover* of order, but can't take the time always to put his odds and ends to rights. He is, however, quite good-natured, and, though he don't like to be bored much, yet will not become nervous and lose his balance at our prying looks. You will perceive, however, that he has a sanguine temperament, and it won't do to try him too much; so we will pass into the next apartment. It would be well enough, in passing, to say, that the Doctor is winning golden honors for the Repository, as the increase in the subscription list will abundantly show. This narrow room is occupied by Dr. Nast, the Editor of the Apologist, and the apostle of the Germans. There seems to be a German air diffused all around this apartment. The Doctor is at his desk writing an editorial, or perhaps translating, or it may be poring over German and Latin Commentaries, for the purpose of consulting authorities in making his Exposition. He is a kind, good-natured man, a fine scholar, and an earnest, evangelical preacher. His books, his papers, his assistant, and his very stove and table, all seem to be German; and, as we don't understand his language, let us go into the next room. On the right there, sitting on that rocking-chair, with one shoe off, and the other slip-shod, with a pile of old manuscripts and papers, and a stray old book or two, lying on the table in glorious confusion, sits Dr. Elliott. See how incessantly he nods and shakes his massy head as he reads on, with his spectacles on the top of his head! He is not angry nor excited, though he thus frowns and shakes his head; for he is good-natured and clever, but he is deeply engaged and interested. He is an intellectual giant; and though he looks rough and unpolished in regard to his personnel, yet, like the lumbering road-wagon of olden time, he bears a precious freight—all bullion.

Do you see on the left there, standing by a desk, with several slips of paper with different headings lying before him, and the latest papers, a foot or two thick, neatly piled up on the table beside him, a pale, attenuated-looking young man? In one hand is a pen, and in the other—fearing some official will carry them off—is clutched with nervous energy a pair of long, sharp-pointed scissors. Well, that is the Assistant Editor, to whom you are indebted for all the news-items, general and local, in the Advocate, appropriately arranged in the different departments. Poor House! he goes frequently to the gymnasium, on Third-street, besides walking to the side of Mt. Auburn twice a day, and preaching on Sabbath; but, notwithstanding all this exercise, he looks cadaverous and pale, as though he had been for years shut out from the light of day, in some monastic cell, engaged day and night with the pen. He bears it all, however, with great patience; and there, in his long, office-gown, from Monday morn till Saturday night, he stands like Patience on a monument.

But we must leave these editors alone in their glory. We will now go down the private stairway, and enter the printing office, in the yard of which you will see a brick building for wetting and pressing paper. On the first floor of the printing establishment are four Adams presses and one cylinder press, on which are printed the Advocate, Ladies' Repository, Apologist, Sunday School Advocate, and the various books of the Concern. These presses are fed mostly by girls. There are in this room eight hands. In the room above the mailing of all the Church periodicals is performed by seven hands. On the left is the German composing-room, with three or four hands. Above this, on the third floor, are the composing-rooms, in which, including the foreman of the establishment, Mr. R. P. Thompson, there are from twelve to fifteen compositors. The fourth floor is the drying and pressing department, in which there is one hydraulic and one screw press. Here there are three hands. In one corner of this room, partitioned off, is a smaller one, occupied by Mr. Gale, the very correct proof-reader for the Concern, to whom many a blunderer in orthography, etymology, syntax, prosody, and punctuation is indebted for making him appear respectable in the world of letters. Adjoining the printing office is a building erected for the carpenter, Mr. Hand, who is constantly employed in the manufacture of boxes, and in making repairs about the establishment. At the other end of the printing office is a building containing two vaults, in which are deposited the stereotype plates.

With your permission, gentle reader, we will pass out on Eighth-street, and return to the Book Room. We are not through yet. We wish to introduce you to the Agents, which, perhaps, we ought to have done first; but we can do that just as well now as at any other time, perhaps. They are, however, generally known, having to travel pretty extensively over the continent, in visiting the conferences for the purpose of collecting the debts due the Concern. The Rev. L. Swormstedt, the senior Agent, who has been so many years connected with the Concern, we will find in his office at the desk, looking over the letters received pertaining to all the business connected with the establishment, and which are quite numerous every day. So large a Concern requires his unremitting attention. Before introducing you, we will relate what was said of him by one of the Commissioners who went with him to Pittsburg in 1853, and furnished a description of his colleagues. Here it is:

"Our other friend is, in fullness and rotundity of person, somewhat like Falstaff. He seems to live in comfort; and so commanding is his person that he passes almost every-where for a bishop. He preaches with power; his enunciation is distinct; every word comes out like a dollar from the mint; he often utters strong thought, and never, I think, drops a foolish remark. He has great energy of character; he perseveres through all difficulties, and makes every thing bow before him. When he commenced his ministerial career he was a slender, fair-haired youth, neat in his appearance and gentlemanly in his manners. He had been a merchant clerk. Early in his itinerancy he was placed upon a circuit which did not pay the preacher. The amount due was estimated and divided among the different classes; the year rolled round, and the money was not collected. At a certain appointment was a large class. After preaching he detained it, and asked the leader how much was collected; and finding a large deficit, he stationed the leader at the door, and ordered him to let no one out till the whole amount due was paid. Taking the class-book, he commenced calling the names, and insisted on immediate payment of something from every one. Excuses were made at first; but the resolution of the preacher was not to be resisted, and there was a wonderful whispering and borrowing of change. Having gone through, a deficit was still remaining, and the names were called over again. Seeing the difficulty of the operation, one of the bystanders who were outside the cabin school-house, put his hand through a pane of glass, and offered the preacher fifty cents. 'That will not do,' he cried; 'you can not pay the way of these people to heaven.' Having gone through a second time, there was still something due. The outsider again presented himself at the broken pane with his half dollar, and so pressed the preacher that he took it, but observed that he should put it in the collection—that it could not be credited to the class—and then proceeded with the third call, which was an effectual one. I need not say that he was—as he deserved to be—*paid*. For many years the Church has wisely availed herself of his abilities as a collector and financier. With all his sternness and strength of character, he is noted for his generosity and kindness of heart. His house is the home of domestic comfort, well-ordered children, and hearty welcomes; his purse is always open, his ear attentive to the voice of distress, and his tongue ever ready to make confession if he finds himself in error. He is one of the few men who, with great capacities and facilities to enrich themselves, have chosen rather to serve the Church."

From the above description, one would think he would make an admirable Agent, at least so far as the collection of money was concerned; and woe betide you if you happen to find yourself at conference a delinquent to the Book Concern, without the needful to meet the demands. He seems to know no man after the flesh, but will ask you, at the conference room, if you have not already been to see him, and made payment or given your note, to walk up to his room and settle your account accordingly. We have more than once encountered him, and if we did not know that beneath all this seemingly-rough and threatening exterior, there was a kind and generous heart, we should have set him down as one of the most stern and unyielding men in the world. Still, we have very often thought he could get along quite as successfully if he were to put on a little more of the *suaviter in modo.* God has not constituted all men alike, however; and it is a blessed thing that he has not, as it would not do in nature to have no rough places. The overhanging, craggy rock is relieved by the peaceful vale which smiles in beauty at its base, and the storm-cloud, with its fierce lightning and hoarse thunder, only makes more pleasant and delightful the calm, when clouds and storms have passed away.

The Church could not well do without Swormstedt. Having been for so long a time engaged in the business of the Book Concern, he has acquired a thorough knowledge of all its departments and the general detail of business connected with each. We think him admirably qualified for the post which he occupies, and if it must needs be that the agency be confined to the itinerant ranks, we do not think the intereste of the Concern could be better attended to or its business carried on by a more efficient Agent than is the present incumbent. We are of the opinion that the policy of removing Agents just for the sake of rotation in office, is a very questionable policy, to say the least of it, and especially where such a responsible and complicated business is concerned. No man, however great his business tact or qualifications, can enter upon such an agency, and become fully acquainted with its duties short of one term; and when we consider that the habits of preachers are such as to lead the mind away from the commerce of the world, it can not be expected, in the very nature of the case, that they could hope to be qualified for such a post in so short a time. Hence, when integrity and ability are found to exist in those who are already employed in this department of the Church, it certainly is the most safe and judicious to continue them in office, and not remove them for any slight and transient causes, or simply from the desire of promotion to office.

Before describing the Assistant, that gigantic athlete who sits yonder by the desk in the packing-room, making an entry of a bill of books, we will go back and describe the old Agent, J. F. Wright, who is now the presiding elder of the East Cincinnati district, and who resides in a most lovely mansion on one of the beautiful slopes of Mount Auburn, concerning which Dr. Dixon remarked to us, on his visit here, that it reminded him more of England than any thing he had seen since leaving the favored isle. In the language of the friend who described brother S., "he is a little above the medium hight, stoutly built, a little stoop-shouldered, a silver-haired, sweet-faced, neatly-dressed man, of good business ability, sensible, safe. He has a fine sense of the ludicrous, and enjoys a joke as well as most men; but usually he is grave, and in his social intercourse engaging and discreet, dropping every now and then some useful remark. A smile generally plays upon his countenance; he rarely offends; always seeks to oblige; but is firm where principle is involved. He preaches plain, practical discourses; rarely declaims; and is to be ranked, perhaps, with the weeping prophets or the loving evangelists. He has written a book—a neat biography of one of our earlier preachers. Notwithstanding his business abilities, his extreme caution, and his forecast, he has been overreached, and has recently lost $28,000. He bears this with Christian resignation and calmness. He is one of those cases which prove that the race is not to the swift nor the battle to the strong. I am happy to say that he will not be left poor, his good wife having property which is not affected by his personal obligations." We should rather be disposed to take him for a bishop by far than the present senior incumbent of the Book Room; and, if comparisons were not odious, we might have something to say about his possession of some peculiar qualifications which Le Roi, the king, does not, in our judgment, possess, as well as some traits he does possess, which would not be very desirable in a Methodist bishop. And yet, if he were a bishop, he would, in our estimation, come as near to Wesley himself, and perhaps more so than Coke or Asbury. Certain it is, that whatever he would do in the episcopal office would be done in the fear of God and with the utmost conscientiousness; and, though some might be disposed to question his judgment, none would for a moment arraign his motives; for in regard to honesty and sincerity, he is one of God's noblest specimens.

It would be well enough, also, in this connection, to say a few things about the other Agents. After the resignation of Rev. J. F. Wright, in 1844, the Rev. L. Swormstedt was elected Principal and the Rev. J. T. Mitchell Assistant. Brother Mitchell had received a good training in the itinerant ranks in the wilds of the west, and, under the precepts and examples of his venerable patriarch father, himself a Methodist preacher, he came into the Concern having nothing to learn, either as regarded the doctrines, economy, or usages of Methodism. Having a good education and a ready wit, it did not take him long to make himself acquainted with the general business of the Concern, and had he been allowed to remain, he would, doubtless, have been a valuable acquisition to the Concern. At the close of his term, he took a transfer to the Ohio conference, and was stationed four consecutive years in Cincinnati. He is now stationed in Urbana, and is the Secretary of the Cincinnati conference, beloved and respected by all. His successor in office was the Rev. John H. Power, an old and valued member of the North Ohio conference, who has made himself known and felt in the religious and literary world as a preacher, polemic, and author. His works on Universalism have had an extensive sale. As a Christian and a minister, his character is strongly marked. His prejudices, if we may be allowed to use the word in an accommodated sense, are strong; and what he believes to be right, he will cling to with the utmost tenacity, if not doggedness, of purpose. He has the sharp, hard features of a Calvin; and yet we hardly think that he would consent to the burning of a Servetus, who might differ from him in opinion. Like his predecessor, however, he had to go by the board at the expiration of four years, and make way for the present incumbent. Since his retiracy he has been appointed by the Ohio, North Ohio, Cincinnati, and Kentucky conferences as Agent of the Tract Society; and he has entered upon that work with vigor; for one of his characteristics is to engage with all his might in whatever he undertakes.

We now come to speak of the Rev. Adam Poe, the present Assistant. As already intimated, he has a herculean frame, and none would doubt his being a descendant of the conqueror of the Indian Big Foot. Brother Poe is thoroughly a Methodist, and, though not yet beyond life's prime, has been a traveling preacher for many years. A faithful and devoted servant of the Church, he is no less faithful to the interests of the Book Concern, ever ready to spring into the harness and work at any post in the establishment. He seems determined to understand all the details of business and do the work assigned him by the General conference.

We have given the reader a rough and hasty sketch of the Book Concern; but, before closing, we must not omit to mention the extent of its present operations. We are informed, by reliable authority, that the amount of sales during the current year is greater than at any former period, and greater than all the sales effected during many of the first years of the existence of the Concern. In addition to the sales, the Concern issues twenty-six thousand copies of the Western Christian Advocate, eighteen thousand copies of the Ladies' Repository, thirty thousand copies of the Sunday School Advocate, six thousand copies of the Missionary Advocate, and five thousand of the German Apologist. In view of what has been accomplished during the thirty-four years of its existence, commencing with a small branch Depository, and gradually increasing to its present giant proportions as a wholesale establishment, what mind can calculate its future expansion, or the amount of good yet to be accomplished in the great work of spreading a pure literature and a Scriptural holiness over all these lands!

CHAPTER XXII.

JOHN COLLINS.

We have been importuned by several of our brethren to give a sketch of this eminent servant of the Lord Jesus Christ, embracing such incidents connected with his life, and such personal reminiscences as may serve, in conjunction with the biography already written, to preserve a memory of the man. The reader must allow us our own free and easy way of describing the life, labors, and character of this pioneer preacher.

Our first acquaintance with him was the result of an accident, and one which frequently happened to the pioneers of early times in the western country. It came to pass that soon after he had settled on the East Fork of the Little Miami, and had built a cabin, and was making preparations for farming, his horses strayed away, one of which, after traveling a distance of thirty miles through the wilderness, in a northerly direction, came to our cabin. Knowing it to be an estray, we availed ourself of all the facilities the country then afforded of giving it an extensive publication, which was done by telling all our neighbors, and requesting them to tell all their neighbors and every body they saw, that we had in our possession an estray horse, with such and such marks about him, which the owner could have by proving property. Not many days after a stranger rode up to our door, and asked us if we had an estray horse in our possession. We told him we had, and invited him to alight, hitch his horse, and walk in. Thanking us very politely, he did so; and, from the description he gave of the horse, we were satisfied it was his property. We were at once struck with the blandness of his manners and his pleasant address. He did not seem to have the roughness of the pioneer farmer about him, and we never would have supposed him engaged in such an occupation. He entered into a very agreeable and pleasant conversation about the country, the habits of the people, and other matters of interest. For the short acquaintance, we never met with any individual in all our eventful life who was more prepossessing in his manners. After having partaken of the humble fare of our cabin, he made some inquiries in regard to the religious privileges of the neighborhood; and, finding that there were no meetings held in that section, he expressed regret, and exhorted most affectionately, with tears, ourself and wife to seek God in the pardon of our sins, and embrace the Savior. When he concluded, he said: "I will preach in Hillsboro on such a Sabbath; will you not come to meeting?" We promised to do so. He then said, "My dear friend, if it will be perfectly agreeable to you, I should like to pray with you before leaving." "Certainly," said we, and the man of God kneeled down, and with a fervency and tenderness which broke up the great deep of our heart, he poured out his soul to God in our behalf. His prayer was such as only John Collins could make. Our heart was strangely and wonderfully drawn toward him, and we were won by his sweetness and gentleness. From that hour we loved him, and it continued unabated through a long ministerial life. We love him still in that heavenly world, where, by God's grace, we hope erelong to meet him, and enjoy his society forever. He left us with many a benediction upon his lips; and when the period arrived for him to preach at Hillsboro we were there, and for the first time heard him preach the Gospel of Jesus Christ to weeping multitudes gathered from all parts of the country. He had removed into the neighborhood where he then resided in the year 1803, and having received license to preach as a local preacher in New Jersey, he improved his gifts in traveling all round the country, as opportunity presented itself, preaching the Gospel of the kingdom. It was during the time he sustained a local relation to the Church that he preached the first Methodist sermon ever preached in Cincinnati—as the reader has already seen in our sketch of the rise and progress of Methodism in this city. Not only in Cincinnati, but in many other places was he the pioneer of Methodism. At Columbia, six miles above Cincinnati proper, he organized a class; and while he would labor with his hands during the week, he would start out on Saturday afternoon to some appointment, where he preached on the Sabbath; and the day of eternity only will disclose the amount of good accomplished through his instrumentality in bringing sinners from darkness to light, and building up the saints on the sure foundation of their faith.

After laboring on his farm for four years, during which time he had planted the Gospel in many settlements in the Miami Valley, and being prospered by Providence, he found himself in a condition, temporally considered, which enabled him to take a wider field of labor. He was admitted into the traveling connection in the year 1807. His first appointment was the Miami circuit, which, at that period, embraced nearly all the section of country now included in the Cincinnati conference. Here was a field of labor that might have made a soul of less courage quail; but he never hesitated at hardships and danger, and taking leave of his faithful, affectionate wife and little children, with the sword of the Spirit, relying upon the strength of Israel's God, he went forth in his name and power to do the work of an evangelist, and make full proof of his ministry. Encouraged by the promise, "Lo, I am with you, even unto the end of the world," his glad and courageous heart could sing,

"On these mountains let me labor,
In these valleys let me tell
How he died, the blessed Savior,
To redeem lost souls from hell.

Nor did the faithful herald labor in vain; hundreds heard the glad sound of salvation from his lips, and were converted to God through his instrumentality. His next appointment was scarcely less extensive. Starting from Snow Hill, in Clinton county, he traveled through Highland and Ross counties, including all the settlements of Paint creek and the Scioto river, down to the mouth, thence down the Ohio to the mouth of Eagle creek, including all the settlements on Sun-fish, Scioto Brush creek, Ohio Brush creek, including West Union and Manchester; thence across, by the Cherry Fork, to the place of beginning. This year he achieved much for our Zion in the wilderness, and multitudes were born into the kingdom of God. Methodist preachers in those days were no sinecures. They sought not ease, honor, or popularity; and as for wealth, that was entirely out of the question. Their hire was souls, and the hope of an eternal reward impelled them onward in the great work in which they were engaged. The next two years Collins traveled Deer Creek circuit, which included the town of Chilicothe and all the settlements west of Lancaster and on the Darbys. On this circuit lived an old veteran Methodist named White Brown, who immigrated to this western country in an early day, and was denominated by the Rev. J. Quinn the patriarch of the Scioto Valley. He opened his house for the itinerant, and his wide, generous heart, as large as a continent, embraced the entire

Church and all her interests. His house was the constant home of Bishop Asbury, in his annual visits, and on his farm was the great camp meeting ground, more famous in those days than all other places of a similar character, on account of the wonderful outpourings of God's Spirit upon the listening thousands that would annually congregate in its peaceful groves. White Brown and his camp-ground were known throughout the entire Methodist connection, and a narration of many of the scenes which had occurred at this consecrated spot had been communicated to other lands. Father Brown and his devoted companion have long since gone to mingle with the sainted Whatcoat, Asbury, George, M'Kendree, and others, in that bright world,

> "Where congregations ne'er break up,
> And Sabbaths never end."

The labors of Collins on this circuit were attended with unexampled prosperity. The Gospel river widened and deepened in its onward flow, and thousands stood upon its banks rejoicing in its fullness. He attended camp meetings far and near, and he was what might be called emphatically a camp meeting man. No preacher had the power of rousing the masses, and holding them by his eloquence and power, to so great an extent as the meek and sainted Collins. Often have we heard him relate the story of the lost child, describing with inimitable tenderness the feelings of the mother, whom he tried to comfort, but who, like Rachel, "would not be comforted, because her child was not;" and then, when the child was found, with the utmost pathos would he relate the joyous emotions of the mother. No tragedian ever succeeded better in transferring the feelings of a character to his audience in his impersonations, than did the inimitable Collins. So far was he from falling under the charge made by a tragedian to a minister of the Gospel of representing fact as if it were fiction, that he became the living embodiment of his theme, and with a soul on fire he poured out the living truth till every heart was moved. Often have we seen thousands borne down by his impassioned eloquence like the trees of the forest in a storm. And it was irresistible. Steel your heart as you might; summon all your philosophy and stoicism; and nerve up your soul to an iron insensibility and endurance, surrounding it with a rampart of the strongest prejudices, the lightning of his eloquence, accompanied by the deep-toned, awfully-sublime thunder of his words, which came burning from his soul, would melt down your hardness, and break away every fortification in which you were intrenched, while tears from the deep, unsealed fountains of your soul would come unbidden, like the rain. The only way to escape his power was to flee from his presence and hearing; for a Boanerges as well as a son of consolation was he. Perhaps no man ever combined the two elements here alluded to—power and pathos—more than Collins. But no pen is fully adequate to describe the man, and we doubt if any mind is competent to give an analysis of his character, as in it were blended strange contrasts and peculiarities, which rendered it altogether unique if not entirely *sui generis*.

Though apparently a compound of tenderness and sympathy, there were times when he would be severe, and use the rod. As an illustration of this we will relate an incident which occurred in the year 1809, at a camp meeting on the Scioto bottom, at Foster's. We have abundant reason for recollecting well the time, place, and circumstances. The Rev. Thomas S. Hinde and ourself, both young preachers, and boiling over with a zeal for the cause of God, impatient to see the work go on and carry every thing before it, concluded to take the matter pretty much into our own hands. Accordingly, we went out into the woods, a short distance from the encampment, and commenced singing, for the purpose of collecting the sinners around us, whom we intended to take by a storm of exhortation. It was not long till a large crowd was collected, and many left their tents to see what was the disturbance in the woods. The wicked feeling that they were not under the restraints that they would be were they on the encampment, listening to exhortation and prayer, as might have been expected, became noisy, and interrupted us exceedingly. We had raised a storm sure enough, but how to guide it was what had not entered into our calculations. There was no telling what would have been the result, as there were demons there in the form of men ready for every vile thing. Just at this juncture intelligence of this state of things reached the ears of brother Collins, and he ordered us forthwith to the preachers' tent, where he gave us such a trimming for our disorderly proceedings as boys do not get every day. This was a chastisement which, though severe, did not break our bones, and proved of great service to us in after life.

At this meeting great opposition was manifested by the wicked; but, notwithstanding, though it seemed all the spirits of darkness had gathered there from the knobs, the Sun-fish hills, and the Dividing Ridge, yet many were converted to God; and of this happy number many were young people. After the meeting ended, a party who were opposed to the revival, and were offended at the loss of their young companions who had embraced religion, got up a dance. A young man by the name of J. Fraley was the leader. The time at length came, and youth and pleasure met to chase the hours with glowing feet. But hark! in the midst of the revelry a cry! Some one has fallen in the dance, and he cries aloud,

"God be merciful to me a sinner!" It is Fraley, the leader. Consternation is spread over every face; terror fills every mind! Others join the cry, and then and there was hurrying in every direction from the scene of that gathered throng. Brother John Foster, a local preacher, was sent for, and the sound of mirth and revelry gave place to the sound of prayer, while the loud laugh was exchanged to louder cries for mercy. Then began a glorious work of God, and many in that ball-room were converted, and filled with greater joy than ever earthly pleasure could give. A joy and peace filled their souls,

> "Which nothing earthly gives, or can destroy;
> The soul's calm sunshine, and the heart-felt joy."

Young Fraley, when converted, gathered all that would go with him, and marched round from house to house, singing, shouting, and praying. We were then on the circuit, and witnessed the fruits of this glorious revival.

We will relate an incident connected with another camp meeting which we attended, in company with brother Collins. This camp meeting was held the same year of the one alluded to above. It was on Eagle creek. A large concourse of people had collected together from all parts of the country. The hour for preaching had arrived, and after the congregation was collected by the blast of a trumpet, brother Collins arose and gave out a hymn. From the manner of his reading it all could tell that his heart was filled with emotions too big for utterance. It was sung as only the Methodists in early times could sing at camp meetings. It seemed as if the soul of the entire encampment was in the sound, and went up to heaven as an offering of praise. When the last strains died away upon the solitudes of the surrounding forest, the man of God fell upon his knees, and poured out his full heart to the God of heaven.

An awful stillness reigned, interrupted only by an occasional sob or a suppressed amen. Presently the Holy Spirit was poured out, and like a rushing, mighty wind it came down upon the encampment. Five hundred fell prostrate to the ground, either screaming for mercy or shouting the high praises of God. The preacher's voice was lost, and God was all in all.

There was something in the person of Collins that would at once impress any beholder with the character of the man. He was above the medium hight—of slender form. His head was somewhat massy in its proportions; one would think rather too much so for his slender frame, as it generally was inclined upon his shoulder. His eyes were small, but keen and penetrating, though deeply sunken in his forehead beneath heavy, overhanging brows. His cast of countenance was Grecian. His motions were generally quick, but graceful, especially in the pulpit; and to see him walk along the street with his silver-headed cane, which he usually carried in his older days, you would at once be impressed with the dignity and refinement of his manners. It seemed that the God of nature and grace had made him for the great work to which he was called. His voice was the most musical and penetrating we ever heard, and, as we have already indicated, his manner was peculiar to himself. To those who were familiar with him there were certain movements about him which would indicate the state of his mind, just as coming events in nature cast their shadows before. When you would see his lips compress, and he would throw his head aside, slightly elevating, with a sort of shrug, his right shoulder, and the tear would start from his eye like the rain-drop which falls from the heat of the cloud, then you might know that the Spirit of the Lord was upon him, and might expect with certainty to witness displays of Divine power.

In the year 1811 he was appointed to Union circuit without a colleague. This circuit included the towns of Dayton, Xenia, and Lebanon. At the latter place he was instrumental, in the hands of God, in accomplishing a great work. His preaching was attended with the demonstration of the Spirit and power, and a great and glorious revival attended his labors, which resulted in numerous and permanent accessions to our beloved Zion. It was the same year which we traveled Knox circuit; and well do we recollect the cheering intelligence which came to our ears of the wonderful work of God in that town. During this revival John M'Lean, Esq., now one of the Chief Justices of the Supreme Court of the United States, and his brother, Colonel M'Lean, became the subjects of converting grace, and joined the Church, with many others, who became distinguished and influential members of the Church, some of whom still live as the fruits of his ministry. Great good was effected through his instrumentality, also, in the town of Xenia; and in Dayton, if he did not preach the first Methodist sermon, as in Cincinnati, he formed the first class, and organized a society, which long ago was divided into bands, there being two large and flourishing societies, occupying spacious brick churches in different parts of the city, besides an enterprising German Methodist Church. He obtained a lot of ground in the very heart of the city from Mr. Cooper, the proprietor of the town, and, with the assistance of the sainted George Housten and others, he built thereon a house of worship.

In the year 1812 he traveled the Mad River and Xenia circuit. Being a delegate to the General conference, on his way he passed through Fairfield circuit, where we then labored, and stopped over Sabbath at the house of brother Thomas J. Ijams. That was a memorable Sabbath, and the scenes and associations connected with it will never be erased from our recollection, as we hope to carry with us a remembrance of them, and many other happy scenes and seasons which we have witnessed, to the heavenly world. Such remembrances will, doubtless, augment the happiness of heaven. It was a day of spiritual "feasting, of fat things, full of marrow, of wines on the lees well refined." The congregation was large, and as the notice was extensively circulated, multitudes came from a distance to hear the wonderful preacher.

We don't know—perhaps it was the occasion and circumstances that made Methodist preachers great in those days; but one thing is certain, the arrival of Collins in a neighborhood would excite a hundred-fold greater interest then than the arrival of any of our presiding elders or great men, or even bishops, can produce at the present day. Upon the ears of that immense and deeply-interested congregation this flaming herald of the cross poured the full strains of the Gospel, and before he had finished his discourse, his voice, clear, shrill, and powerful as it was, was drowned, in the louder, clearer, shriller cries for mercy, which rent the heavens, mingled with the loftiest shouts of praise.

No man was ever more thoroughly stored with incident than was brother Collins. He possessed the faculty, in an eminent degree, of weaving into his discourses the every-day incidents of life, and of applying them with the most admirable judgment to his hearers. He was a profound student of human nature; and possessing the keenest perceptive faculties, united with his knowledge of the secret springs of the human heart, he was enabled to discriminate so nicely that every sinner felt under his preaching as David under the pointed personal reproof of the prophet Nathan.

Some time in the year 1833, when he was traveling

New Richmond circuit, in the bounds of which he lived, he attended a camp meeting near Batavia. It having fallen to our lot, on one occasion, to preach, and there being a large concourse on the ground, an incident occurred which we will relate, as it was quite singular, and we never heard of a similar one before nor since. The Lord assisted us, and we had great liberty in striving to preach Christ and offer his salvation to our dying fellow-men. We had progressed about two-thirds of the way through the discourse. It was a melting, moving time, a mighty troubling of the waters, and the excitement seemed to be increasing every moment. Right in the midst of our appeals father Collins arose in the stand behind us, and touching us on the shoulder, he said, "Now, brother, stop; keep the rest for another time, and throw out the Gospel net; it is now wet, and we shall have a good haul." We obeyed the directions, and sounded the invitation:

"Come all the world; come sinner, thou,
All things in Christ are ready now."

Every sinner on the ground was moved; the old and hardened trembled like aspen leaves stirred by the breeze; every eye was suffused with tears. Presently there was a move near the outskirts of the congregation. There came a mother leading a prodigal son, and falling in on each side of her way, by the hundreds, as she advanced to the altar, the multitude came. It was a time of unusual power, and the work of God, from that moment, went on gloriously.

Two years before he closed his effective labors in the itinerant field we had the pleasure of being his colleague in Cincinnati, and to us it was a season of great interest and profit. Here we lived and labored lovingly together, threading the streets and alleys of this great city in quest of the flock of Jesus, visiting the sick, attending the dying, burying the dead, and preaching Jesus and the resurrection. But he is gone. Father Collins is no more. The toils and hardships of an itinerant life are ended.

> "He sleeps his last sleep; he has fought his last battle,
> And no sound shall awake him to labor agaln."

CHAPTER XXIII.

NATHAN EMERY.

With all the efforts we are making to prevent it, how rapidly are the precious memories of our fathers passing away! Notwithstanding the numerous written memorials, much of what is known of the eventful times in which they lived and labored, dwells but in the recollections of a few revered survivors, and with them is fast perishing, unrecorded and irretrievable.

Nathan Emery was born in the town of Minot, Cumberland county, Maine, on the 5th of August, 1780. He was blessed with a pious mother, and, through her godly admonitions and holy example, lasting religious impressions were made upon his young and tender heart. In the year 1794, the region of country where he lived was visited by a Methodist preacher, and his father's house became a preaching-place, a bethel in the wilderness, where the man of God lifted up his voice in exhortation and prayer. How many will thank God in the day of eternity for that system of itinerancy which sent the feet of messengers of glad tidings over the mountains and through the vales, over the plains and along the rivers, to visit the destitute regions and offer the inhabitants the blessings of salvation! Under the ministrations of these Gospel heralds, young Emery became an early convert to Christ, and enrolled himself among the people of God. At the age of sixteen he was appointed leader of a class, and in this capacity he served the Church with all fidelity till he was called, in the providence of God, to a more extended field of labor and usefulness.

Early in the year 1799 he was licensed to preach the Gospel, and employed on a circuit by the presiding elder till the ensuing conference, when he was admitted on trial in the traveling connection, and stationed on Readfield circuit. Among the class of preachers admitted at the same time, we find the names of Joshua Soule and James Quinn, the latter of whom is gone to rest; but the former still lives and is the senior Bishop of the Methodist Episcopal Church South. His next field of labor was Needham. In the year 1801 he was appointed to Union circuit, in the Province of Maine district. In the following year he was stationed on the Norridgewock circuit; and in the year 1803, at the conference held in the city of Boston, he was ordained an elder and appointed to the Middletown circuit, where he remained two years, and formed an acquaintance with that estimable lady who afterward became his wife. The next year he was removed to the New London circuit. During this year he was married most happily to the woman of his choice, and never did wandering itinerant make a more judicious selection. Amiable, talented, and gentle as an angel of light, did this most estimable woman follow her husband from field to field of his labor; and united in work, as they were one in heart, did she, with gentle persuasion, assist her partner in leading souls to the fountain of a Redeemer's blood. She shunned no cross, despised no shame, for the sake of Jesus; but side by side with her husband did she toil to cultivate Immanuel's land. For a period of nearly forty years they journeyed on together over the rough and rugged path of itinerant life, strangers and pilgrims, seeking the city with foundations whose maker and builder is God. How many souls in the morn of eternity will bless God for the soft, persuasive eloquence of that mother in Israel, who, at the altar of mercy, taught them to look away to the

Lamb of God that taketh away the sin of the world! How many souls have been born into the kingdom while listening to her instructions, eternity alone can disclose. But a few years before the decease of father Emery, her sanctified spirit, released from earth, passed peacefully away to the land of the blest.

"But again we hope to meet her,
When the day of life is fled,
Then in heaven with joy to greet her,
Where no farewell tears are shed."

For a period of more than twenty years Nathan Emery labored with great acceptability and usefulness in the itinerant field, filling several of the more important stations in the New England conference. Excessive labors, however, broke down his constitution, and he became so much enfeebled that it was necessary for him to superannuate, which he did in the year 1821. Soon after he removed to Ohio, and purchased a small farm at Blendon. The next year, his health improving by the health-giving and invigorating exercise connected with a farmer's life, and being unwilling to be considered as a burden on the conference, he asked for and obtained a location. He remained in this relation to the Church for a period of six years, during which time his Sabbaths were occupied, as far as possible, in preaching at different points. In the year 1828 he was employed by the presiding elder of Lancaster district, Rev. David Young, to travel the Columbus circuit as a supply, Samuel Hamilton being his colleague. At the expiration of this year, finding that he would be able to do effective service again in the itinerant ranks, he was readmitted as a member of the Ohio conference, and stationed at Zanesville.

The appointment of father Emery, as he was familiarly called, to Zanesville, was at a time when a crisis had arrived in the history of the Church in that place which seemed for a season almost to threaten its destruction. That unhappy strife denominated the "Radical controversy" was then at its hight. Many had left the Church under the impression that the government was an oligarchy, and that the membership were oppressed with a tyranny from bishops, and elders, and preachers which they were not able to bear, and ought not if they could; through the overzealous labors of the new party, by means of sermons, papers, and tracts, scattered broadcast over the land, in which it was asserted that the clergy had taken away all the rights of the laity, and that they were "lording it over God's heritage." Among the number of those who left the Church in this excitement were several of the more prominent, wealthy, and influential members of the society; and when father Emery entered upon his labors, every thing pertaining to the Church wore a most gloomy aspect. He went, however, in the spirit of his Master, and entered upon his work. It was not the work of recrimination, however, in which he engaged. To all the thrusts and taunts of his opponents, he made no reply, except to turn his bland and open face, wreathed with smiles, which indicated the forgiveness of his benevolent heart. He well knew that fire could fight fire; but in the conflict all for which they contended would be consumed; and, hence, he went straightforward, preaching the blessed Gospel, and visiting from house to house and from shop to shop, in the streets and alleys, speaking a kind word to all he met on the subject of their soul's salvation. The people soon learned what manner of spirit he possessed, and were won by his kindness and concern for their souls to crowd to his ministry; and the little old frame church, which stood in the rear of the new brick, the foundations of which he laid, and over the elevation of the cap-stone of which he shouted, would literally be packed with anxious hearers. There, in that old-fashioned pulpit, in hearing of the murmuring waters of the Muskingum, rolling over their rocky bed, where a M'Kendree, an Ellis, a Burke, a Young, a Morris, a Durbin, a Bascom, and a Christie have stood and proclaimed the messages of mercy and salvation, the old man eloquent, with his face bathed in tears or covered with smiles, rocking from side to side, proclaimed the Gospel of salvation and peace "in strains as soft as angels use," or in thunder-tones uttered the dread language of Sinai. It was not long till the hearts of many were touched, and again the altar was crowded and souls converted, and the old temple of Zion was made to resound with shouts of praise. God turned the captivity of the Church, and harps that had been hanging unstrung on the willows were struck again to loftiest notes of praise. The Lord rendered to Zion more than double for all that she had suffered, in granting a most glorious revival, which swept over the town.

At that meeting strange things came to the ears of the inhabitants of Zanesville. It was rumored that two students from the Ohio University, one of whom was a son of the then Governor of Ohio, had arrived, and would preach in the Methodist Church. What was remarkable in that day was, that they were Methodist preachers. Who had heard, since the days of Wesley, of Methodist preachers coming out fresh from a college to preach the Gospel? But it was even so: brothers Trimble and Herr—for these were the young men—were found in that old-fashioned pulpit, and multitudes who had never darkened the threshold of the old church crowded to hear the students. God was with them, and many heard from their lips the first Methodist sermon. The revival spread with power, and hundreds were awakened and happily converted to God. Good "old David" himself, with his whitened locks and streaming eyes, as he would gaze upon the battle of the Lord from his seat in the altar, seemed to say, like old Simeon, "Now, Lord, lettest thou thy servant depart in peace; for mine eyes have seen thy salvation." It was a great and glorious day for Methodism in Zanesville. From that revival went out almost a half a score of young men to different and distant parts of the country, to preach Christ and him crucified.

But wonders did not stop here. It was rumored that the most eloquent divine that ever addressed a Zanesville audience had become a Methodist preacher, and was coming back from the east, whither he had gone on a visit, to identify himself with Methodism, in a place where before he had wondered at the audacity of a Methodist preacher in daring to ride along the main street. He came, and listening, wondering thousands hung upon his lips, if possible, with greater interest than they had done before. Under these circumstances, Methodism in Zanesville gained an influence and standing which it has not lost to this day. There are now, in that enterprising city, two large churches, both of which are in a prosperous condition.

We must now resume our narrative. After father Emery had finished his two years on the station, he was sent to Cincinnati, in company with ourself, E. W. Sehon, and S. A. Latta, where he labored with his accustomed zeal and success.

The next year he was continued in the station, with Thomas A. Morris, now Bishop, and William B. Christie. In 1833 he was sent to Marietta, with W. Young as his colleague, and the succeeding year to Chilicothe—in 1835 to Worthington, with W. Morrow. In the year 1836 he was, at the urgent solicitation of the Directors of the Ohio Penitentiary, appointed as chaplain to said institution. In this new field, all the sympathies of his benevolent nature were taxed to their utmost. He was untiring in imparting instruction, admonition, and comfort to those who, by violation of the laws of the land, had excluded themselves from society. His efforts to reform hardened criminals was not without its effect. Many an obdurate heart was made to feel the force of a kindness and sympathy to which for years they had been strangers, and many an eye, which had been as a sealed fountain, was made, like the smitten rock in the desert, to gush forth with penitential tears. All criminals incarcerated within the gloomy walls of a prison are not, as some would suppose, lost to hope and heaven. Many that we ourselves know have been truly converted, and have given evidence thereof in the fruits of righteousness, years after they have served out their time in the penitentiary. No man, with a cold, unsympathetic heart, should ever have any control in the instruction or government of a prison, as the discipline there is designed to be, under the regulation of our laws, of a reformatory character.

In the year 1837 he was appointed to Delaware circuit, at the close of which, from old age and feebleness, he was obliged to desist from labor, and take a superannuated relation, in which he continued till the day of his death. On all his fields of labor in the Ohio conference, he was in toils more abundant, ever active and zealous in his Master's service. No one ever knew father Emery either unemployed or triflingly employed. He was fully impressed with the idea that he had one great work to perform, and he was straitened till that work was accomplished. His whole study seemed to be to finish the work which had been assigned him, that in the end he might testify rejoicingly the grace of God.

The period at last came which was to terminate his labors in the kingdom and patience of Jesus. For some time before his death he had been in feeble and declining health, yet he still continued his labors both on the farm and in the pulpit up to the very close of life. On Sabbath, May 20, 1849, he preached, and gave out an appointment for the succeeding Sabbath; but it was his last sermon. The following Tuesday he was suddenly and violently attacked with inflammation of the bowels, from which he suffered most intensely; but he was enabled to "endure as seeing Him who is invisible." Sabbath at length came, the day on which he had announced to his congregation, Providence permitting, he would preach; but instead of going into the sanctuary below to warn sinners, and comfort mourners, and build up believers, just about the time he should have ascended the pulpit he entered the sanctuary above, the building of God, the house not made with hands, eternal in the heavens, to wave that palm, and sing that song, and wear that crown we have so often heard him glowingly describe in his happiest hours.

He was disposed always to look upon death with some degree of dread, and to speak of the last conflict with the "grim monster;" and as he saw the hour of dissolution approaching, he nerved himself for the dying strife. He sought earnestly for dying grace, and that grace in rich abundance was given. He realized that the God of Abraham, and Isaac, and Jacob was with him, and all was well. After taking leave of his friends, and especially his only daughter, Mary, to whom, in the most affectionate manner, he spoke many precious words of comfort and consolation, he calmly resigned himself to die. Visions of glory, however, were reserved for this dying herald of the cross, such as he had never witnessed before. As he neared the Jordan, and the land of Beulah spread out its bowers on either hand, like the dying Payson he was enabled to see the celestial city on the other shore, while he was fanned by its breezes, regaled by its odors, and enraptured by its transporting sounds. When his pilgrim feet touched the dark, cold waters, he exclaimed, "O, how gently my Savior leads me through!"

"Happy soul, thy days are ended—
All thy mourning days below;
Go, by angel guards attended,
To the sight of Jesus, go!"

CHAPTER XXIV.

THE CONVERSION OF A FAMILY.

WHEN we were traveling Knox circuit, at an appointment called Bowling-Green we were holding a quarterly meeting. After the love-feast exercises in the morning were ended, and many a soul had drank deeply from the fountain of redeeming love, the doors were opened for the admission of the congregation to preaching. As usual, on such occasions, the chapel was crowded to its utmost capacity. Many who never think of attending the ordinary appointments of circuit preaching will come out on such occasions, and it frequently happens that the truth takes effect in hearts that were before wholly careless and unconcerned in regard to their spiritual and eternal interests. It having fallen to our lot to preach the eleven o'clock sermon, we took occasion, in the course of our remarks, to address particularly parents, and, after pressing upon them with as much earnestness as we were able, the duties husbands owed to their wives, we presented, in as forcible a light as possible, the duties of parents to their children, but especially the duties of the husband as head of the family. We alluded to the fearful responsibility resting upon the husband and father, and the guilt involved in the neglect of such to look after the salvation of their families. In the presentation of motives to continued and unwearied exertion in behalf of the salvation of those God had committed to their care, we referred to the loss of such beloved ones to the society of heaven and the despair and ruin that awaited them should they die in their sins. We endeavored to carry our audience to the scenes of the judgment day, when wives will rise up against their husbands and children against their parents, and charge them with having been instrumental in banishing them from heaven, and shutting them up in the gloom of hell. While we preached, the Spirit applied the truth to many consciences. We noticed in the congregation one man in particular, a rich and influential citizen of the neighborhood, who grew pale and trembled as we endeavored to pour the thunders of Sinai upon the neglecters of salvation, and also labored to show the utter impossibility of an escape from the fearful doom of a violated law. This man had a large and respectable family, and he manifested no more concern for their salvation than to secure for them an inheritance and make them appear respectable in the world. No sum was considered too great to be expended in fitting out his sons and daughters for "genteel society," and his greatest happiness seemed to consist in seeing them figure highest on the list of the roll of fashion and folly. He seemed to have entertained the idea held by a certain gentleman in one of our western towns, who took his daughter to a fashionable boarding-school in the east, and who, on being asked by the principal what he wished his daughter taught, replied, "Teach her to shine." Alas! that so many, and even, we fear, professors of religion, appear to be governed by no higher views in the education of their daughters! This worldliness might do among the members of a certain Church we wot of, where, at a Bible class, when the question for the evening's investigation was introduced, "How shall we best teach our children reverence for God?" one of the gravest pillars thereof rose and said, "Reverence is politeness; and, therefore, if I wished to teach my children reverence for God I would send them to a dancing-school." But Methodists have not learned in such a school nor in that other "school of morals" denominated the theater, the principles of morality and the fear of God. We must be pardoned for dwelling a little here. As there are many professors who speak indulgently, if not encouragingly, of the opera, the theater, and the dancing saloon, it is time that a note of warning was sounded that would break like Heaven's loudest thunder on the ears of such.

"O, father," said a blooming girl of some eighteen summers, gentle and lovely as a rose of spring, "what harm can there be in going to the theater just once, to hear some of Shakspeare's best pieces rehearsed by star performers? Besides, haven't you got the works of that great author in your library?"

"I will answer your question, my dear," said the father, who was a minister, "by asking another. What harm would there be in letting this beautiful glass vase fall on the stone hearth just once?"

"Ah, but the case is not a parallel one," said the daughter.

"Why not? If it be true that, instead of being a 'school of morals,' it is a school of vice, and vice is contaminating to the soul, should it not be avoided? Can one take coals in his bosom and not be burned? Can one walk amidst a shower of soot, such as often falls in our city, and not have her garments soiled? Besides, who knows so well the nature and tendencies of such places as those who have been behind the scenes? And I tell you the most eminent tragedian of the country would never let his daughters enter the doors of a theater. You know Emma, who joined the Church a few Sabbaths since?"

"Yes, I recollect that young lady."

"Well, she is one of the daughters of that tragedian, and she never was inside of a theater. The very form in which you have put this question shows that you are convinced of the impropriety of visiting such places, because you speak of a single visit, and seem to think that no harm can come of a single visit. You well know by your education, and I pray God it may never become part of your experience, that

'Vice is a monster of such frightful mien,
That to be hated needs but to be seen;
Yet seen too oft, familiar with her face,
She's first endured, then pitied, then embraced.'"

Since the above conversation the father has heard no more from his daughter on the subject of going to the theater.

But where have we wandered? The gentleman above alluded to was seized with strong convictions. He felt that his whole life had been wrong, and all his sins and delinquencies rose up before him. What to do he knew not. On returning home he was met by his kind and affectionate family, and some of them, with a laughing sneer, asked about the shouting Methodists, whose preaching and religious exercises frequently constituted the theme of discourse. The father had but little to say. At length the dinner hour arrived, and the Sabbath with that family was a day of feasting; but the father, notwithstanding the many anxious entreaties, was too much oppressed and sick at heart to eat. While the family sat down he went into his parlor. We have already said it was an affectionate family, and the absence of the parent from the table seemed to have deprived the whole of an appetite. Dinner was, therefore, soon dispatched, and the wife and mother was not long in seeking the husband and father; for she was anxious to know what trouble filled his mind. That which he might keep from the children she knew he would communicate to her. Scarcely had she entered the parlor where he was sitting till his feelings, no longer to be repressed, overcame him, and he burst into tears, exclaiming, in sobs and broken accents, "O, Mary, I have sinned against God and myself, and you and our children, and I feel that I must change my course of life, or else we will all be lost together. You have been my faithful and devoted wife for twenty-five years, and I have never said one word to you in all that time about your soul, nor have I had any concern for the salvation of our children. Can you forgive me? I have determined this day to seek religion and lead a new life. Will you go with me in that path of life in which there is no death or sorrow?"

The wife was deeply affected, and, taking her husband by the hand, she said, "My dear William, I have been praying in my heart for years that you would take this course of life. You thought, perhaps, I was altogether careless and indifferent on the subject of religion. How often have I desired to talk with you on the subject, but my heart failed me! Yes, William, I give you my heart and my hand to journey with you to heaven. O, bless the Lord that I have lived to see this day!"

"But, Mary, we must take our children with us. The dear children that God has given to us must not be left behind."

"Yes, William, it would be a sad and melancholy thought to leave them in the broad road to destruction." So saying she called them into the parlor. Soon they were all in and seated—two sons, men grown, and three daughters, the youngest of which being about eight years of age.

The weeping, penitent father rose and addressed them: "My dear children, I have sinned against God in that, as a father, I have never said any thing to you about your salvation. You have never seen or heard me read a chapter in the Bible, nor have you ever heard a word of prayer from my lips. I have constantly set before you a bad example, and all my influence has been to lead you astray from the paths of religion. Now, God has smitten me with conviction for my sins, and I stand before him this day, and before your mother, and before you, a guilty, condemned sinner, and if God does not forgive me I must be eternally lost. O, my dear children, will you forgive your guilty father? Your mother and I have entered into a solemn covenant with each other, before God, that we will repent of our sins, and seek the Lord, that we may be saved, and we can not enter into the path of life without taking all our children with us that we may make an unbroken family in heaven."

By this time all the children, from the oldest to the youngest, were mingling their tears with those of their parents. While they were weeping the father said, "Now, if you will go along with us, come and give us your hands." At this the elder son arose and said, "My dear father and mother, if you go to heaven we will not stay behind." Walking forward he gave his hand to both, and was followed by the rest, who came weeping as if their hearts would break. The youngest, not being noticed in the midst of the excitement, which increased every moment, came up and said, "Father, may not I go too?" At this the parents burst out into a loud expression of joy and grief, and the father, taking his lovely child into his arms, thanked God that he had lived to see that day.

Such a Sabbath evening was never spent in that family before. The father and mother bowed with their children before God in supplications for mercy, was a sight which caused joy in heaven among the angels. Monday morning came, and when the hour arrived they all started for meeting. Many were the expressions of surprise to see Mr. ——— and his family all enter the little chapel, and take their seats in the congregation, which, on Monday morning, is mostly composed of members of the Church, and the immediate neighborhood. But how was their surprise hightened when, on invitation being given for persons to join the Church, the father, mother, and all the children went forward and gave their hands to the preacher! In the midst of the wave of feeling, which at this time had risen high, the father asked liberty to say a few words, which being granted he remarked, with streaming eyes, as follows: "My neighbors and friends, I have a word to say. I have not only sinned against God, my wife and children, but I have sinned against you. What influence I have had in this place has not been exerted for good, but for evil. I have been a man of the world, and sought only its pleasures, instead of being religious and setting a good example. For this I sincerely ask pardon of God and of you; and now, by the assistance of Divine grace, me and my house will serve the Lord. I ask you all to go with us, that we may save ourselves and our families." At the conclusion of this short speech the mourners were invited to the altar, and soon almost every sinner in the house was on his knees, pleading for pardon at the mercy-seat. From this moment a great and glorious revival ensued, and more than eighty persons were happily converted to God. Reader, if thou art a husband or a father, and living without God and without hope in the world, go and do likewise, and thou shalt save thyself and family from sin and hell. Part of the converted family has already passed over the "King's highway," and entered the celestial city, and the remainder, like Christiana and her children, are following hard after. O, the blessed ones that have entered heaven! No wonder good John Bunyan said, when in his dream, heaven opened its gates to let in Christian and Faithful, and the heavenly multitude greeted their arrival, "which when I saw, I wished myself among them."

"A few more days of sorrow,
And the Lord will call us home,
To walk the golden streets
Of the New Jerusalem."

CHAPTER XXV.

JOHN CRANE.

THE subject of our present narrative was born at ——— station, about two miles below Nashville, Tennessee, in the year 1787. Lewis Crane, his father, was among the very first settlers in Cumberland, and was one of those hardy pioneers who braved the dangers of the wilderness, constantly exposed, with his family, to savage depredations. At that early day there were but comparatively few means of grace enjoyed by the settlers. No sound of the church-going bell waked the echoes of the forests with its inviting tones; and it was only occasionally that a Methodist itinerant, in one of his long and weary circuits through the wilderness, following the emigrant population as they penetrated the western wilds, would lift up his voice in the log-cabins, or by the campfires of the almost homeless wanderers, and proclaim a full and free salvation in the name of Jesus. Though this class of ministers was often despised by black-gowned and white-cravated clergymen, with the lore of a theological seminary in their brains, and the powder and perfume of the toilet on their hair, and, by way of derision, called "circuit riders," or "swaddlers," yet, had it not been for their self-sacrificing devotion, Christianity would not have been kept alive in these western wilds. Often have these men traveled from block-house to block-house, from station to station, and from cabin to wigwam, bearing the messages of mercy to their fellow-men, without any means of support or any expectation of a pecuniary reward. But the history of one is, to a greater or less extent, the history of all those early pioneers of Christianity.

Lewis was not only the first among the adventurers to this western wilderness, but he was among the first that became religious and joined the Methodist Episcopal Church. Though Methodists at that time were few in number, yet they lived to love God and one another, and cheerfully bore the cross of Him who said, "If any man will come after me, let him deny himself, and take up his cross, and follow me." Hence, we may readily infer that young John, though born in a block-house, in the most troublous times of border warfare, was early taught the fear of God. At the early age of six he was brought under religious influence, and impressions were made upon his tender mind and heart that marked his character forever. And here we might remark, nothing is more important than giving the mind a proper training in the soft and flexible season of youth. The softest breath of summer may stir the stem of the delicate flower, while the rudest blasts of winter may not move the giant oak. In very early life the mind receives impressions that tell upon its future destiny.

> "A pebble in the streamlet scant
> Has turned the course of many a river;
> A dew-drop on the baby plant
> Has warped the giant oak forever."

The Prussian king, in urging reasons why the children of the realm should be religiously educated, said, "The youthful mind receives impressions with the flexibility of wax, and retains them with the durability of bronze." Said another individual, "Scratch the rind of the sapling, and the gnarled oak will tell of it for centuries."

Whatever these pioneer Christians learned, they learned the importance of giving their children a religious education. At the age of twelve John was made a subject of converting grace, during the great revival which prevailed in Cumberland and all over the west. He was regarded as one of the most remarkable children of his age; and during this early period of his life he frequently exhorted his friends and acquaintances to seek religion, with an effect that gave evidence of his wonderful eloquence and zeal, few being able to resist the wisdom and power manifested in the preacher-boy. Many of his young associates were brought under religious influence through his instrumentality; and had their parents possessed the belief that young children could love and serve God, and followed up the convictions received by proper religious training, many would have become, like John, burning and shining lights. We were well acquainted with a traveling preacher who had a lovely daughter, seven years of age, an only child, and she had been taught to pray from her infancy. Once at a quarterly meeting, after all the professors in the house had communed, this child, who was sitting by her mother weeping, looked up into her face with streaming eyes, and said, "Mother, may I go and remember my Savior at the sacrament?" The mother replied, "Go, ask your father, my child." The father was sitting in the altar, and the little girl approached him and said tremblingly, "Father, may a child take the sacrament?" "Yes, my dear," said the father, unable to restrain his feelings, "you may come; for Jesus said, 'Suffer little children to come unto me, for of such is the kingdom of heaven.'" She then went round on the outside of the railing, and kneeled down, sobbing as if her little heart would break. It was a moving scene, and the congregation was melted into tears, while some cried out aloud. The presiding elder, James Quinn, of blessed memory, in the full gush of his benevolent heart, when he saw the weeping penitent, immediately took the bread and broke it, administering to that lamb the body of Jesus. When he came with the wine and said, "The blood of our Lord Jesus Christ, hereby represented, preserve your soul and body unto everlasting life," his own feelings, as well as those of the audience, were intense and almost insupportable. He gave it to the child, and just as it touched her lips the Spirit was applied,

> "Which with the blood
> Doth wash and seal the sons of God,"

and heaven sprung up in the heart of that happy child. She was converted, and from that hour became a consistent and devoted disciple of Jesus. We knew her well, and after she had a large family of children; but she kept the faith, and brought them all up in the nurture and admonition of the Lord.

If it will not tire the reader, and be considered too great a digression from the subject, we will relate another incident illustrative of youthful piety, and tending to show the negligence of Christians in regard to children. At a camp meeting held on C. S. camp-ground, the venerable Bishop M'Kendree was present and preached to the children and young people. On this occasion the Bishop noticed a little boy who was much affected. Being intimately acquainted with the family, and knowing the child well, he invited him into his tent, and conversed and prayed with him, laying his hand upon his little head and commending him to God. That afternoon the doors of the Church were opened, and this boy went forward and presented himself as a probationer. He was received, and continued to attend regularly to his religious duties, never absenting himself from prayer meeting, or class meeting, or preaching when he could attend. He was but a mere child, and as he would sit in class, no one, either leader or preacher, would speak to him or pay him any attention. At this his young heart was much aggrieved, and he was sometimes tempted to go no more; but he concluded to hold on till his grandfather, who was a traveling preacher, would visit them, and he would speak to him on the subject. At length the grandfather came, and when he was sitting alone, one day, he came to him, and said,

"Grandfather, I want to ask you a question."

"Well, my child," said the old man, "what is your wish?"

"Well, it is this," said he; "do you think I am too young to serve God and belong to the Church?"

"No, not at all, my child," said the venerable saint, with emotion. "Your mother embraced religion when she was only seven years of age, and we have many examples in the Bible where children became religious in the dawn of life, such as Samuel, and Josiah, and Timothy; and the Scriptures say, 'Out of the mouths of babes and sucklings God has perfected praise.' But why did you ask this question?"

"At camp meeting," said the child, "when Bishop M'Kendree preached to us children, I resolved I would be a Christian, and when brother C. opened the doors of the Church, I went forward and joined. I have been to meeting every time since, and staid in class; but no person says a word to me about religion, and I thought they considered me too young to be noticed."

"Well," said the grandfather, "I will go with you to meeting next Sunday, and if the preacher does not speak to you when he meets the class, do you rise up and ask him the reason. Do you understand?"

"Yes, grandfather, I will."

The day came, and the grandfather and child were at meeting. When the congregation was dismissed, the preacher commenced leading his class, and all were spoken to as usual but the little boy. He made an effort to rise, but his heart failed him. The grandfather, seeing this, said, "Brother L., little J. has a question to ask you?" The child then rose, and, in a simple manner, gave his experience, not forgetting to allude to his not having been spoken to. At this the preacher blushed, and the class-leader wept, one after the other confessing their delinquency and promising to do better for the future. That child has grown to manhood, and has a family, and has been a useful and highly-acceptable member of the Church. God forbid that we should despise one of these little ones that believes in Jesus!

But we must resume our narrative. The astonishing progress made by young Crane in gifts, grace, and usefulness, was such as to indicate to the Church most clearly that he was called of God to preach the Gospel; and, accordingly, he was recommended as a suitable person to be received on trial in the traveling connection; His bones had not yet hardened into manhood, and his youthful appearance, and slender, delicate frame seemed to forbid the hope that he would be able to breast the storms and encounter the toils and hardships of an itinerant life. Nature and grace alike had fitted him for the work; and, though young, it was evidently the design of Providence that he should enter the field of his Lord and engage in gathering the harvest of souls. He was received at the Western conference, held at Nolichuckie, in Tennessee, in 1807, and sent to the Holston circuit, which he traveled six months with great acceptability and usefulness among the people. The remaining six months were spent on the French Broad circuit. His extreme youth as a preacher, his zeal and piety, together with his remarkable native eloquence, called large crowds to hear him wherever he went, and God owned his labors in bringing, through his instrumentality, many a wayward sinner, both old and young, from their wanderings to the knowledge of the truth and the salvation of God.

In 1808 he was removed from French Broad, and sent to the Deer Creek circuit, in Ohio, the colleague of that eminent man of God, Benjamin Lakin. On this circuit he had great influence, and the melting, moving strains of the youthful herald found way to thousands of hearts. Notwithstanding his great success, he had to encounter many fierce and fiery trials; but out of all the Lord delivered him and made him shine with greater brightness. At the ensuing conference at Liberty Hill, he was admitted into full connection and ordained to the office of a deacon. Having thus taken upon himself more fully the vows of God, and having consecrated himself more unreservedly to the service of his Master, he was ready for any field, however rugged, or any work, however toilsome. The wants of the great west were before him, and giving himself up into the hands of the appointing power, he was sent to the distant Mississippi. For a youth of his age, having just passed his minority, it must have been a bold and daring undertaking. It was a long and weary journey through a wilderness, and, when reached, the population was sparse, and that mostly Roman Catholic, whose first principles of indoctrination are to hate Protestants. Surely, nothing but an intense love for lost sinners and an unshaken confidence in the promise of the Savior, "Lo, I am with you alway, even to the end of the world," could have urged him on in this missionary work. He went; and the God of Jacob, who sustained and comforted him as he lay upon his rock pillow, was with this young soldier of the cross. He went as an evangelist, and was successful in the work of planting Churches in the wilderness, dedicated to a pure Christianity. Neither swamps, nor forests dense and drear, nor broad rivers, could shake him from his purpose or impede his way.

Onward, over craggy steeps, and through dells and dark morasses, he urged his course, and wherever he could track the foot of man he pursued, to bear to him the messages of mercy and salvation.

But his tour of hardship, which he had already borne as a good soldier, was not yet ended. He served so well and so bravely in this frontier field, on the outposts of civilization, that, at the conference in 1811, he was sent to Cold Water and Missouri united. In giving him this appointment, it seemed like putting him in charge of the whole far-western world. The circuit included both sides of the Missouri river, and often was he obliged to swim his horse across the great "father of waters." Nothing, however, stopped this bearer of heavenly dispatches. He was charged with a high trust from the court of heaven, and God had given him passports, which secured his right of way over the whole continent, and to every log-cabin and frontier wigwam he bore the messages of Heaven. Multitudes believed his report, and to them the arm of the Lord was revealed in mercy to save, and, doubtless, while we write, many of those redeemed through his instrumentality are rejoicing and praising God in the upper sanctuary.

In the year 1812 he was appointed to the Duck River circuit. While here, large numbers flocked from all parts of the country to hear the words of life. It was the year of the memorable earthquake, which shook so terribly the southern country. Thousands, by day and by night, flocked to hear the Gospel from the lips of this sainted youth; and such was his zeal and fervor, conjoined with the burning desire that

"All the world might taste and see
The riches of God's grace,"

he literally, like a lambent flame, burned out in the service of his Master. Wearied out with ceaseless labors by night and by day, and subjected to frequent exposures in traveling from one distant appointment to another, he was attacked with inflammation of the lungs. When his disease assumed such a form as to disqualify him from preaching, he was at the house of a Mr. Mitchell, where all the attention that could be shown him was paid by stranger hands. But all efforts were unavailing, and he rapidly declined, till it was evident to all that death was near, and he would never preach again. On one occasion his symptoms were of such a nature as to induce those who were present to believe that he was dying, and it seemed, after a short struggle, that his breath had ceased, and he was gone; but in a short time he revived again, and said to his friends, "What hath brought me back to earth again? I have been on the very suburbs of heaven and glory." It seemed as if his spirit had been trying its wings for the mystic but glorious flight, and had returned for some purpose. Shortly after this brief trance his father came, and, embracing him in his arms, he said, "O father, I love you; but I have a Father in heaven whom I love more, and I shall soon be with him in glory. My body will soon be consigned to the grave; but my soul will put on immortality and eternal life." His countenance, always winning and attractive, now beamed with an unearthly brightness, and, like the glories of the setting sun, throwing back, on its departure, the radiance of the better land on which it is rising, so his spirit seemed to reflect the radiance of heaven. His work was done for earth, his commission had expired, and death was waiting to sound his release. With a smile upon his lips, he bade his father and friends a last adieu, and soared to companionship with angels and God. Thus fell the youthful herald of the cross, at his post, in the distant wilds of Missouri.

CHAPTER XXVI.

WILLIAM YOUNG.

THE subject of our present narrative was the brother of the Rev. David Young, a short sketch of whose life the reader may find in the "Autobiography." William was a native of Virginia, born in Washington county, on the 16th day of May, 1786. In the year 1805, when he was in the nineteenth year of his age, he was awakened to a sense of his lost condition, convinced of the need of a Savior, and, through the instrumentality of Methodist preaching, he was happily converted to God. Two years after this he felt it his duty to exhort sinners to repentance, and entered upon that work with zeal and fidelity. Such were his gifts, grace, and usefulness in this vocation, that he was adjudged by the Church as called of God to the higher office of preaching the Gospel, and, accordingly, in 1808, he was licensed to preach. In due time he was recommended to the annual conference as a proper person to be received on trial into the traveling connection. He was received at the conference held at Liberty Hill, October 7th, and was appointed to travel Mad River circuit. In the year 1810 he was sent to the Tennessee Valley, where his labors were arduous and somewhat successful.

To show the wide extent of country over which the early preachers traveled—we do not allude to the first missionaries, such as Burke and Kobler, and others, but those who were regular circuit preachers—all that is necessary is to follow a sketch of their travels. The next year—1811—we find our brother sent back to Ohio, and appointed to the Cincinnati circuit. At that time this was a large circuit, and many of the appointments were difficult to reach. Presiding elders then had whole states in their districts; and at an earlier day several states and their contiguous territories were included in their field. There were then no public conveyances; but from month to month, and year to year, elders, bishops, and preachers pressed the saddle almost every day. Now one western state suffices to make two whole conferences and parts of three others, while a single circuit of olden time now makes several districts, and a presiding elder can reach nearly all his appointments in a railroad car, sitting on a velvet seat; and the idea of a bishop on horseback is as novel as it would have been to have seen one in a coach in the days of Asbury.

The person of brother Young was rather robust than otherwise, and he possessed a strong constitution; but so severely were his physical powers taxed in frequent, laborious, vehement pulpit exercises, that they at length gave way in some degree. He would preach till he was frequently exhausted, carried on by a zeal which knew no flagging. Every circuit that he traveled was blest with a revival of religion. His whole soul was enlisted to the utmost of its powers in laboring to save his fellow-men. In visiting from house to house, and pouring out his prayers and tears in personal effort for the conversion of all within reach of his ministrations, added to his regular circuit labors, he was a model of a hard-working preacher and pastor, worthy the imitation of some in the itinerant ranks at the present day. Though not a very pleasant speaker, or agreeable in his manners in the pulpit, he was, nevertheless, a burning and a shining light. He possessed a genial spirit; and such was his urbanity in conversation and the social circle, that all who knew him, whether saint or sinner, held him in the highest esteem, and courted rather than shunned his society.

In the month of December, on an extremely cold day, this devoted minister started out from Cincinnati to visit his appointment at North Bend. The wind blew from the river, in fierce and piercing blasts, directly in the face of the itinerant all the way. From this exposure he took a violent cold, which settled upon his previously-injured lungs, producing a hectic fever, which resulted in a settled consumption. He was now confined to his room, and no longer permitted to engage in his much-loved employ. While disease was consuming his system, his soul burned with the all-consuming fire of a zeal for God and his cause, which made it difficult for him to exercise patience enough to keep from going out and warning sinners to repent. Sometimes he would be greatly dejected in mind, and the adversary would assail him with temptations; but the trial of his faith, being more precious than gold, he was enabled to realize would work out for him, if faithful to the end, a far more exceeding and eternal weight of glory. He often expressed fears that he lacked that degree of patience and resignation to the will of God which it was his privilege to possess. He sometimes lamented the absence of that full, overpowering love of God which he had experienced when in full health and vigor; but he knew not that his weak, emaciated frame would have sunk under such a load of glory. Prayer was his constant exercise, and sometimes it would burst out in praise to God and the Lamb. So anxious was he to be in the field doing battle for the Lord, that on one occasion, in opposition to the advice of his physician and the entreaties of his friends, but three days before his death, he rode out to a camp-ground, where the people were adjusting their tents, and waited for the services to begin. He took his position in the preachers' stand, looked round upon the tents of Israel, and gazing upon the people, he burst into tears, saying, "O, my brethren, I am done with these things now. I shall be at camp meeting no more, but we'll meet in heaven." He returned home, and before that camp meeting closed he left the world in the triumphs of faith, and ascended to mansions on high. "For him to live was Christ, but to die was gain."

How often is the Church called to mourn the loss of the most useful and talented young ministers! A heathen poet has said, "Whom the gods love die early." The Bible tells us, "Precious in the sight of the Lord is the death of his saints;" and hence we infer it is more blessed to die than to live, if we are the beloved of the Lord. A Summerfield, a Cookman, a Blackman, and others, have been called away early, even before they reached life's prime; and as in nature the brightest flowers soonest fade, so in the Church the loveliest types of Christian character are soonest taken away to that world where flowers never wither, and where loved ones always stay. The providence may be mysterious which removes these lights from the Church below; but as with individuals, so with the Church—all things, we are assured, shall work together for her good; and though God removes the most useful and skillful laborers, yet the work goes on.

We had but a partial acquaintance with brother Young, yet his praise was in all the Churches where he labored, and he has left a name better than precious ointment, or all the fragrance of Yemen and Guhl.

CHAPTER XXVII.

THE CONVERSION OF AN INFIDEL.

When we were traveling the Cross Creek circuit, in the year 1814, one of the most wonderful manifestations of divine grace, in the awakening and conversion of an infidel, occurred that we were ever permitted to witness during our whole itinerant career. There lived in the bounds of the circuit, not far from Steubenville, an infidel of wealth and distinction. He belonged to the French school of infidelity, which, in the Reign of Terror in France, had, in consequence of its disgust at the crimes and corruptions, and mummeries of Romanism, renounced all religion, vetoing Christianity, deifying reason, and writing over the cemeteries, "Death an eternal sleep." He was a devoted student of Voltaire, and Rosseau, and D'Alembert, and being educated and talented but few were able or felt disposed to meet him in argument on the subject of religion. Indeed, he was a terror to all Christians in the neighborhood, and he never lost an opportunity to instill his infidel principles into the minds of all who would listen to his deceptive and dangerous philosophy—falsely so called. He was a man of great influence in the county, and all that influence was thrown into the scale of infidelity. His principles were not only destructive of the general morals of the community, but were insidiously working their way into the impressible minds of the young and rising generation, poisoning them with infidelity. When he met with one equally well skilled in argument, and capable of showing the sophistry of his reasoning, and of tearing off the vail from the hideous form of the monster infidelity, he never would fail to fly to that last resort of infidels as their test of truth, ridicule, well knowing how potent such a weapon is in skillful hands. Where few can reason all can laugh, and as the depraved human heart is always on the infidel's side, often has the multitude, which usually collected in those days around disputants, been excited to laughter at the sallies of wit and ridicule the infidel would bring to bear upon his antagonist.

Where the majority were irreligious it was easy to see how fearful would be the odds against the Christian, though armed with the panoply of truth. What men wish to be true they require but little evidence to convince them of its truth; and, on the other hand, what they do not wish to be true no amount of evidence is sufficient to convince them of its falsehood. The sinner would gladly believe, though there is a God, that the terrible denunciations which he has made against sin are the mere product of priestcraft, gotten up to frighten people into a belief of Christianity, and any denial of that fact, supported by the merest semblance of an argument, would be seized with the greatest avidity, even as a drowning man would catch at a straw. As an illustration of this, we once heard a public speaker, in a courthouse, haranguing a large crowd on the subject of religion. He had much to say about the priestcraft of orthodox preachers, and labored hard, and, as he thought, successfully, to prove that there was no hell; that it was all a mere bugbear to frighten the weak and credulous. One of his audience, a wealthy planter, on a visit from the far south, seemed to be in ecstasies at the preaching, and could scarcely restrain himself from shouting aloud his approbation. Good news from a far country, or cold water to a thirsty soul, could not have been more refreshing to the southerner than the glad tidings of this discourse. At length the speaker closed, and came down from the judge's bench, where he had been standing. The crowd gathered around him, but none were so eager to grasp his hand as the planter. "God bless your dear soul," said he, "I thank you a thousand times for that sermon. It's all true, every word of it, and commends itself to the reason of man." But, as he was turning to go away, a new thought seemed to strike him, and returning to the preacher, he said, "Your sermon is true—true, no doubt of it in the least, sir; but, by hell, I'll give you a hogshead of tobacco if you will insure it." There is the difficulty. Infidels *fear* that religion is true. With the best of them, in their brightest, happiest hours, there is "a fearful looking-for of judgment."

But we must resume our narrative. This infidel would not attend any religious meetings, and paid a total disregard to all the institutions of religion. Strange as it may seem, with all his avowed infidelity and unblushing opposition to religion, he was chosen to represent the county in the Legislature of the state. God save us when our liberties and rights are intrusted to the hands of those who neither fear God nor regard man; for, though we could not make religion a test of qualification nor require a profession thereof as indispensable to a legislator, we would, nevertheless, require in the candidate for public favor, a decent respect for the opinions and rights of others. If it may be argued that men of infidel sentiments have been good statesmen and patriots, and have served their country with fidelity, we reply, their statesmanship and patriotism were not the result of their infidelity, but they existed in spite of it.

The family of the subject of our narrative consisted of a wife and one child—a lovely daughter, beautiful and accomplished, having received what is termed a polite and fashionable education. The mother was alike infidel in sentiment with the father, and, of course, as it was with the father and mother, so it was with the daughter. Her youthful mind was made to take into its first impressions the blank and cheerless doctrines of infidelity. One has said, "Of all the melancholy sights that meet the gaze of mortals, nothing is half so drear and desolate as that of an infidel mother. For her there is no God and Savior; no bright and cheering hopes of immortality and eternal life beyond the grave. Home, with its endearments and angel faces, was designed to remind us constantly of the family of God in heaven; but where the cold night of infidelity reigns, and no voices of prayer and praise are heard, life is a dull, leaden dream, and death an eternal sleep." This lovely girl, notwithstanding the cold and dreary sphere in which she had taken her existence and moved, was, nevertheless, of an amiable disposition. She was the infidel's daughter, and the child of a prayerless mother; but yet she possessed a genial mind and a trusting heart. We have heard it said of some, "they are naturally religious," and if it were possible for any to have a native religious character such might be ascribed to her. But, like the young ruler whom Jesus loved for his amiability of disposition and morality of conduct, she lacked one thing, and that was the regenerating grace of God, without which all natural graces will prove unavailing as requisites for heaven.

Not a very great distance from her father's residence there was a preaching-place, where the Methodist itinerants held meeting regularly every two weeks. A special meeting had been appointed to continue several days, and as the father was absent at the Legislature, she went to the meeting without the knowledge of her mother. Dressed, as she was, in fashionable style, when she entered the rude cabin, and took her seat among the old-fashioned Methodists, she became an object of general attention, quite as much so as an old-fashioned Methodist now would be if she were to come into one of our fashionable congregations with her plain gown and Quaker bonnet. But she did not come out of mere idle curiosity; she was strangely drawn to the house of worship, and there was a power at work, in regard to the nature of which she was unconscious. She had, as we have already seen, been reared in utter ignorance of religion, and all that she was taught concerning it was, that it was a system of priestcraft; and though there might be some honest, deluded professors of religion, the most of them were arrant hypocrites. She never read the Bible; for her father considered it too immoral a book to put in his daughter's hands, preferring the writings of French infidels, and even the blasphemous scurrility of Paine himself, to that book. Beside this, she never heard a Gospel sermon, being prevented from attending all religious meetings. Of course to her every thing was new; and though she could appear with ease and grace in the drawing-room or gilded saloon, she felt embarrassed in the midst of a worshiping assembly. She composed herself, however, as well as she was able; and when the preacher rose, and with solemn voice announced the text, "God so loved the world that he gave his only-begotten Son, that whosoever believeth in him should not perish, but have everlasting life," her attention was absorbed. This was the first and all of the Gospel she had ever heard, and it sounded strangely in her ears. She had read Rosseau's opinion of Jesus Christ, and was disposed to look on him as an innocent, upright man, and she coincided with him in opposition to other infidel writers who had asserted that he was an impostor. When the preacher fully opened his theme, representing God's love in sending his Son into the world to die for us, and the love of Christ in coming and taking upon himself our load of guilt and shame, illustrated by scenes drawn from real life, and enforced and applied to the listening audience, the heart of the young girl was broken up, and she wept aloud. Every eye was suffused in tears, and many were the warm and ardent prayers that went up to heaven in behalf of that weeping one.

When the meeting was ended she returned home; but so deeply was she affected by what she had heard that it was impossible for her to conceal her feelings from her mother, who, in a stern voice, asked her where she had been, almost as soon as she entered the sitting-room. On being informed that she had been to meeting, she became very much excited, and said, in an angry tone, "If you go again those ignorant fanatics will ruin you forever; and if it comes to your father's ears that you have been to Methodist meeting, he will banish you from the house; besides, you ought to know better. The instructions you have received should guard you against all such improprieties, and I hope hereafter I shall never hear of your being at such a place."

Night came, and with it came the hour for meeting. Now commenced a conflict in the mind of the daughter. She had never disobeyed her mother, nor did she ever feel disposed to act contrary to her wishes in any respect; but her heart longed for the place of prayer, and she felt strongly drawn to it by a secret, invisible agency she could not resist. "Shall I," said she to herself, "disobey my mother, and incur the displeasure of my father, and perhaps banishment from home? But the preacher said that 'the Savior of the world declared that "whosoever loveth father or mother more than me is not worthy of me; and whosoever will not forsake father and mother for my sake and the Gospel's, shall not enter heaven."' I will forsake all for Christ." The crisis had come; the gate was passed; and her joyous destiny was sealed forever. She left her home and went to meeting. An inviting sermon was preached, at the close of which seekers of religion were invited to kneel at the mourner's bench, and pray for pardon. No sooner was the invitation given than she pressed her way through the crowd, and fell upon the bench, crying for mercy. Her full heart now poured forth its griefs in sobs and fervent prayers. The whole congregation was taken by surprise, and filled with utter astonishment at the scene, knowing, as the most of them did, the utter contempt in which her father and mother held religion and all religious exercises. Surely, thought they, this must be the special interposition of God, and every heart was lifted up in fervent prayer in her behalf. There, at that mourner's bench, she struggled in agonizing prayer for two hours. It was apparently the noon of night, and yet she was not converted. Never was mourner more deeply engaged. She had made the last resolve. One after another of the faithful had poured out their hearts at the mercy seat in her behalf; hymn after hymn was sung, as only those can sing who sing with the spirit; but still she came not through the dark valley. Faith began to flag, and some thought the penitent must disrobe herself of her hat, and plume, and flowers, and ruffles, ere the Lord could bless. But God looks at the heart, and he saw, down deep in its own recesses, a soul absorbed in grief, conscious of nothing but its guilt and sin. At length the last hymn was rolling up from swelling hearts and tuneful voices to heaven. The last stanza was reached,

"Yet save a trembling sinner, Lord,
Whose hopes, still hovering round thy word,
Would light on some sweet promise there,
Some sure support against despair;"

and as the last strain sounded in the ear of the penitent,

she gently threw back her head, and opened her calm blue eyes, yet sparkling with tears; but they were the tears that told of sins forgiven. She had emerged from the darkness, and the light of heaven was beaming upon her happy countenance, and an unearthly radiance gleamed like a glory on her brow. If before she was beautiful, now that she was adorned with heavenly grace one might think she could claim kindred with the skies. She arose, and embraced in her arms the sisters who had prayed with her, and pointed her to the Lamb of God, who taketh away the sin of the world. She had passed the noon of many a night in scenes of guilty mirth and revelry, where she was the foremost of the band, the fairest of the fair; but never did such joy and gladness come to her soul as she experienced on that occasion. She returned home, feeling now that she could gladly bear any thing for the sake of her Lord and Master. When she arrived she related to her mother what had occurred, and exclaimed, "O, how precious is the Savior!" She would have embraced her mother in her arms; but she repulsed her and reproached her, telling her that if she did not cease her nonsense she would drive her away from the house, and that she had disgraced the family and ruined herself forever. She retired to her room, and spent the remainder of the night in prayer and praise to God.

Soon it was noised abroad that the infidel's daughter was converted; and some of his friends, supposing, doubtless, that they would render him great service, wrote to him on the subject, giving him the most absurd and ridiculous accounts of her exercises while at the mourner's bench, and after she was converted. When Mr. P. received this intelligence he was greatly enraged, and swore that he would banish his daughter from his house, and she should be entirely disinherited and disowned. All this moved not the converted daughter; for she realized the truth of the Divine declaration, "When my father and mother forsake me, then the Lord will take me up." The day was at length fixed for his return home, and Eliza—for that was the daughter's name—placed herself at the window to watch his arrival. In the afternoon he was seen approaching on horseback, and Eliza hastened out to the gate to meet her father. When, with a pale, sweet countenance, she stepped up to her father to embrace and kiss him, he rudely seized her by the arm, and, with his horsewhip, whipped her out of the gate, telling her to begone, and, with many curses, forbidding her return. Sadly she went weeping down the lane; but she thought of what her Savior had suffered for her, and her heart was staid up under the mighty load which oppressed it. She realized then, to its fullest extent, what it was to love the Lord Jesus more than all else besides. Though she had lost natural friends she had found spiritual friends. That "manifold more in this life, and in the world to come life everlasting," is what only religion can give.

"Like snows that fall where waters glide,
Earth's pleasures fade away;
They rest in time's resistless tide,
And cold are while they stay.
But joys that from religion flow,
Like stars that gild the night,
Amid the deepest gloom of woe,
Shine forth with sweetest light."

Not far from her father's residence lived a pious Methodist—a poor widow—and she was apprised of the state of things at the house of Mr. P. When she saw Eliza coming to her house one evening, she was not at a loss to conjecture the cause. The poor widow gave her a cordial reception, and spoke to her words of kindness and comfort. Eliza asked permission to go into the little room, and be allowed to remain there undisturbed. No sooner was she alone than she fell upon her knees, and commenced pouring out her soul to God in prayer for her wicked father and mother.

But we must return to the father. As he gazed after Eliza, who went sobbing down the lane, it seemed as though a thousand fiends of darkness had taken possession of his soul. He went to the house, and met his wife; but she was equally wretched, having witnessed what was done. He sat down. They spoke not, except in monosyllables. The supper-hour arrived, but he refused to eat, though he had been riding all day. Now and then a groan would escape his lips. He went to his library, and turned over his books and papers; but it was in a hurried manner, and with a vacant look. At length he retired to his chamber, but not to rest. Sleep had forsaken his eyelids, and if he did close them, the sweet, angel face of his banished Eliza would send daggers to his soul. Thus he spent a sleepless night. Next day he wandered about over the farm, and through the woods, like one seeking, with the greatest anxiety, for something that was lost. It was evident to all that there was something resting upon his mind that greatly troubled him. The cause of that trouble his proud, infidel heart would not allow him to disclose, even if the human heart were disposed to lift the vail from the secret sanctuary of its bitterness. Unable to find rest he again sought his chamber; but, alas! his anguish increased, and he began to see the shallowness of his infidelity, and also its dark, horrid nature, in that it could prompt him to drive his lovely, and otherwise obedient daughter from his house, simply because she had become a Christian. From that moment he was a changed man—not that he was converted; but from a hard, impenitent sinner he was brought to relent and pray. There he prayed for hours; but not one ray of hope penetrated his darkness. His abused and banished Eliza would rise before him, and his convictions increased, till he raved like the demoniac among the tombs of Gadara. It seemed as if he would not be able much longer to support the mountain weight that was crushing him; for the sorrows of hell got hold upon him, and he anticipated the pain of the second death. Flying from his room, he called his servant-boy, and ordering him to saddle Eliza's horse and mount another, he directed him to go to every house in the neighborhood in quest of his daughter, and if he found her to bring her home. Seeing that his orders were immediately obeyed, he returned to his chamber; but the load that pressed upon his heart was removed, and the anguish that drank up his spirits was gone. He was comforted, but not converted. The raging deep was calmed, but the sun shone not upon its dark waters. He walked out into the garden, and there, beneath Eliza's favorite bower, he kneeled down, and again lifted up his heart and commended himself to God. Scarcely had his knees touched the ground till the Sun of righteousness arose, with healing in its beams, upon him, and pervading all the great deep of his mind, lighted it up with the peace and calm of heaven.

For twenty-four hours, without eating or sleeping, Eliza remained in that widow's room, engaged in earnest supplication for her father. The pious mother in Israel, in looking out of her window, as the day was drawing to a close, saw the servant coming with two horses, and she ran immediately into the little room, exclaiming, "Eliza, arise, your father has sent for you. I see John coming with your horse and saddle." The happy child arose, and burst out in rapturous exclamations of praise to God for his goodness and mercy in touching her father's heart. She was soon in her saddle, and the faithful charger bore her fleetly to her home as if proud of his burden. When in sight of home she saw her weeping father, standing at the same gate from whence, on the evening before, he had driven her a fugitive abroad. She sprang from her horse into his arms, and embracing his child with a love he never experienced before, he exclaimed, "My angel of mercy, I give you my heart and my hand to travel with you to the heavenly inheritance." It was a happy family; for the mother was soon converted, and joined with the father and daughter in the service of God, and they all continued faithful disciples of Christ till they were called from the Church militant to the Church triumphant in heaven.

CHAPTER XXVIII.

ALEXANDER CUMMINS.

Among that class of preachers, distinguished for zeal and talents, who entered the itinerancy in the great west in the beginning of the nineteenth century, was the Rev. Alexander Cummins, a short sketch of whose life and labors we propose to give. He was born in Albemarle county, Virginia, September 5, 1787. His parents sent him to school, and he received a liberal education for that day. In the twentieth year of his age, after having removed to Ohio and settled in the Scioto Valley, he was awakened to a sense of his lost condition as a sinner, and, after a severe struggle against sin and temptation, he at length was soundly converted, and entered the path of life. Being awakened and converted through the instrumentality of the Methodist pioneers, he connected himself with the Methodist Church as the one of his choice. It was not long till he became deeply and intensely exercised on the subject of calling sinners to repentance, and offering the cup of salvation, whose life-giving waters had so quickened and refreshed his own soul, to the souls of his fellow-men. He saw the world lying in wickedness, and guilty multitudes pressing on the way to death and hell, and his spirit was stirred within him to go out and warn them to flee the wrath to come. The same mercy which had been manifested in his own behalf, he was assured would be extended to others. His feelings could not be concealed. The Lord had called him, and the Church was not long in discovering that the concern of mind under which he labored, associated, as it was, with grace and gifts of no ordinary degree, united in constituting an indication of the will of God that he should enter the ministry. While the Church prayed "the Lord of the harvest that he would send forth laborers," she was ever watchful of the result, and waited for an answer, not by any miraculous interposition, but that God would, from their own number, raise up, call out, and qualify, by his Spirit, faithful messengers of salvation. Hence, the subject of this sketch was soon recognized as the called of the Lord, and license was given him as a local preacher.

At the conference held in Cincinnati in the year 1809, between two and three years after his conversion, he was admitted on trial in the traveling connection, and appointed to Brush Creek circuit. He went out in the spirit of his Master, and labored with a zeal and devotion which gave evidence that he felt the burden of souls as a mountain pressure resting upon him. If he could have had the time to turn aside from the rough and rugged toils of itinerant life and cultivate the flowers of literature, he had no disposition. He was "a man of one book" and one work, and, by night and by day, he exhorted sinners to flee the wrath to come. Filling out his appointed time on Brush Creek, he was next year sent to Pickaway circuit, where the same zeal and devotion characterized his labors. The ensuing years he traveled successively Delaware and Deer Creek circuits, on the latter of which he remained two years. During his labors he suffered many hardships and privations; and such was his burning, unconquerable zeal that his constitution gave way. The sword proved too sharp for the scabbard, or, in other words, his flaming spirit consumed the earthly tabernacle in which it was lodged. Rest was inevitable, as his overtaxed strength would not be able to stand another year of toil without it; and he must cease from toil or cease to live. Accordingly, he was induced to be left without an appointment for one year. But, alas! is there any rest for a Methodist preacher? Then they were poor and almost friendless, and when they were obliged, from want of health, to desist from preaching, it was absolutely necessary that they should work, or starvation would ensue. The Church then, and now, to a very great extent, virtually says to its preachers as a certain master once said to his servants on a holiday, "Boys, you may quit work and go to piling boards for the balance of the day, seeing it is Fourth of July." Teaching school in those days was a drudgery and toil that would not be likely to insure much rest to the body and quiet to the mind. In this employment Cummins engaged, and at the close of the year he became again effective, and entered the itinerant ranks. He was appointed to the Miami circuit, which, at that time, embraced an extensive and laborious field. The two following years he was stationed in Cincinnati, at the expiration of which term he was sent to preside over the Kentucky district. In that field he labored with his usual zeal and fidelity in the cause of his Master, and thousands in the day of eternity will thank God that they ever heard the voice of Alexander Cummins. Having filled his mission as the servant of the Church in Kentucky, he returned to Ohio, and was appointed presiding elder of the Miami district, where he labored two years, at the expiration of which time "he ceased at once to work and live." The following tribute of respect was paid to the memory of this sainted man by the Rev. Russel Bigelow, one of his cotemporaries, which we copy from the Methodist Magazine, Vol. VII, being an extract from the funeral sermon, delivered by that eloquent and powerful preacher:

"Alexander Cummins was a man of a sound mind and

good judgment, particularly in spiritual matters. He took considerable pains to improve his mind by reading and a close application to study. As a man and acquaintance, he was kind, and agreeable, and very much respected. As a husband, he was affectionate and provident. As a parent, he was tender, yet strict and particular. As a Christian, he was humble, pious, devout, sober, and cheerful. As a minister, he was regular, zealous, acceptable, and useful. His language was good; his sermons, in the general, pointed and weighty. His talents were not the most brilliant, but his greatness consisted in variety and goodness. And such was his zeal, variety, and usefulness, that few, if any, were more acceptable or popular. His success has been more than ordinary. I have been informed that many were converted during the first years of his ministry. The first information I ever received concerning him was just after he had left his third circuit. I formed an acquaintance in several neighborhoods in that circuit, in which his zeal and usefulness were much spoken of; and when I traveled that circuit nine years afterward, I found several of his spiritual children, who were still pressing through difficulties on their journey to the promised land. My acquaintance with him commenced in the latter end of the year 1815, at which time we were appointed to labor together on the Miami circuit. I was young and inexperienced, but in him I found a father, an instructor, and a firm friend. Long shall I remember the good advice and many instructions I received, and the pious examples set before me by the beloved minister whose funeral sermon I preach. He labored that year with diligence, zeal, and success. His zeal, piety, and usefulness, while stationed in Cincinnati the two following years, I need scarcely mention; you, my brethren, are his record; you call to recollection his piety, his devotion, his fervor, his diligence, his watchfulness, his anxiety, his pathetic sermons, his fervent prayers. You call to recollection the happy hours you enjoyed under his ministry; and many of you, I presume, consider him as the instrument of your conversion. You view him as your spiritual parent under God, and will have cause to praise God forever that you have had the privilege of sitting under his ministry. The three years he labored as a presiding elder in Kentucky, he was acceptable and useful, highly esteemed by preachers and people. His rides were long, and, in some parts, rough and mountainous, and his labors so abundant as to exhaust his debilitated system. The district he has traveled the two past years is also large and very laborious. He, however, performed his duties acceptably and usefully, but with great pain, often traveling and preaching when he ought to have had rest, particularly the last six months. I have already said considerable concerning our departed brother; but I can not forbear mentioning his wisdom and firmness as a governor in the Church. It was here he excelled; here his true greatness appeared. He was not one of those hasty, rash sort of men, but firm and fixed. His weakly constitution, which was severely racked with incessant labor, was often attacked with wasting disease; but he bore all with Christian patience. About six months before his death he was severely afflicted with the measles; but, by the Divine blessing, he partially recovered, and entered again upon his work. And I think it probable that his exertion, before he was fully restored to health, was one cause of bringing on the disease which terminated his earthly career. He visited the circuit of which I had charge but a short time before he was taken with his last sickness, and seemed equally diligent and fervent as formerly, though hardly able to be about. He left our camp meeting on Sabbath evening, and came home. On the following Friday, rode out to Mechanicsburg, about eighteen miles from this place, [Cincinnati,] to attend a quarterly meeting. On Saturday he preached his last sermon, with his usual zeal and pathos, on 'I am not ashamed of the Gospel of Christ, for it is the power of God unto salvation, to every one that believeth.' That night he was attacked with the disease which terminated in his death. He was brought home in a wagon, and laid on his bed, where he remained for eight weeks, a man of sufferings, racked with pain and scorched with fever; but he bore all without murmuring. He was grateful for every kindness shown him, and appeared calm, resigned, and patient. He said, indeed, but little about dying; nor did he praise God aloud as some have done. It was not his usual way when in health; but what he did say was satisfactory. To one friend he said that he had no anxiety about living, but should be willing to live till he could settle up his temporal business, if it was the will of the Lord, because he could do it better than others, and thereby prevent trouble after his death; but he was, nevertheless, willing to resign all into the hands of the Lord. I visited him one week before his death for the first time, and several times afterward. On one of my visits I talked to him respecting the state of his mind. He seemed composed and resigned, and said he felt that his peace was made with God. The brother who attended on him asked him, a few hours before his death, if he was sensible that he would soon go. He said, 'Yes, I shall soon be in eternity.' The brother asked him if he had any doubts or fears. He said, 'Not any; my way is clear.' His departure was on the 27th day of September, 1823, a little before seven o'clock in the evening. Thus lived and thus died our beloved brother Cummins, a pattern of piety, a waymark to heaven. We do not mean to say that he had no failings; but we say they were comparatively few. He now rests from his labors and his works follow him."

CHAPTER XXIX.

THE CONVERSION OF A CRUEL MASTER.

In the state of Virginia, in an early day in the history of Methodism in the western country, there lived a wealthy and influential planter, who owned a large number of slaves. He was a kind master, and treated his slaves with respect and affection, regarding them as members of his own household. As an evidence of this he procured for them every advantage of intellectual and moral culture within his power. When the neighborhood was visited by Methodist ministers, he invited them to preach on his plantation, and not only gave all his servants an opportunity to attend preaching, but was particular in urging them to go. It was not long till the Gospel, preached in simplicity and power, reached the hearts of the colored people, and they embraced religion. And not only were the servants brought to taste the joys of pardoning mercy, and made happy in a Savior's love, but the master and mistress were alike included in the happy number of the converted. If before the relation of master and servant was one of respect for the rights, and concern for the happiness of the latter, now that they had been baptized by the same Spirit, and made one in Christ Jesus, there was a bond of union far more powerful than could possibly grow out of any natural or social relations.

Among the number of the servants who had obtained religion and joined the Church, was one noted for his piety. This servant, whose name was "Cuff," was not particularly remarkable for any loud profession, though he was always ready, in the spirit of meekness, to be a witness for Jesus; but for unbending integrity and open, straightforward consistency of conduct, he had few superiors any where. For one who enjoyed no greater advantages, he possessed an order of intellect superior to most of his colored brethren. All having the most unwavering faith in his piety, he was unanimously selected by his brethren to lead in religious exercises at the meetings when no preacher was present. Every thing went on pleasantly and happily in this religious family for years. The religion of Jesus, which is adapted to all, and designed to bring the highest blessings to mankind in general, proves of especial benefit to the slaves; and that Church which is the most actively engaged in preaching the Gospel to this portion of our fellow-beings most certainly gives the strongest evidence of being the true Church of Him who said, "The poor have the Gospel preached to them." A Church having been established on this plantation, through the influence of Methodist preachers, meetings were kept up regularly, and when the intervening Sabbaths would come, at which time the preacher was absent at another appointment, the voice of praise and prayer would ascend from the humble chapel, and Cuff would pour out his full heart in exhortations, with an eloquence and power none could resist. Often have the hearts of proud and wicked masters, from adjoining plantations, who had been attracted out of mere curiosity to attend the meetings, been made to tremble, while the falling tear from proud and haughty mistresses, who would wonder at the audacity of the negro, would betray the emotions his eloquence had produced. Many a conscience had thus been smitten by burning words which had been proof against the Gospel in the fashionable Churches of the city.

The happy seasons enjoyed at the little plantation Church were fearfully broken in upon by a most melancholy event. The old master was called to pronounce upon his faithful servants his parting blessing, and then to pass away to that world where such relations are unknown. Death came to the aged patriarch, and he was followed by his weeping family and friends to his silent home. This event, as is often the case, broke up the family, and the servants were divided among the children. Cuff fell into the hands of one of the sons. This young man commenced the world as many do in similar circumstances, whose parents are affluent. Having formed no habits of industry, and wholly unfitted for business, improvident and careless, believing that to-morrow would be as to-day, and much more abundant of blessing, he was not long in squandering the estate left him by his father; and becoming hopelessly involved, an attachment was sued out by his creditors on all his property, and the servants, with the rest of the estate, were advertised at public sale. In that neighborhood there lived a young man, who had recently married, and was making preparations for keeping house. To complete these preparations it was necessary for him to purchase a good servant; and having knowledge of the sale, he accordingly attended. He was by profession an infidel, and carefully avoided going to any religious meetings, though his wife, previous to her marriage, had often attended, and had listened with unusual interest to the eloquent negro. Having gone round and inspected the slaves, as was customary among buyers, he was struck most favorably with the appearance of Cuff, and believing he would suit him, he began to question his master in regard to his good and bad qualities. The young master informed the infidel that Cuff was the most honest and upright negro he ever knew, and he could only think of one fault which he had that might make him objectionable to the purchaser, and that was, that "he would pray and go to meeting."

"Ah," said the infidel, "is that all you have against him? I can soon whip that out of him."

He made the purchase and took him home. Cuff, with a sad heart, left the old homestead, and his brethren, and the little chapel, where he had enjoyed so much religious comfort. When he had performed the duties of the day enjoined by his new master, he started out to seek a place for private prayer. Adjoining the garden was a nursery, and it being a secluded spot, he retired amid the thicket of young trees with which it was filled, and there alone he kneeled and poured out his burdened spirit to God. While engaged in his devotions his young mistress, who was walking in the garden, overheard him, and, drawing nigh to listen, she soon recognized the eloquent voice that had thrilled her at the Woodland Chapel. She was chained to the spot, as the low and melancholy tones of the supplicant were breathed into the ears of the Lord of Sabaoth; and when, with fervor, he prayed for the blessing of God to come down upon his new master and mistress, the unsealed fountain of her heart poured forth its tears.

On the ensuing Sabbath Cuff went to meeting, and also at night, but returned so as to be ready for duty early on Monday morning. He was not aware of the infidel character of his master, though, from what he had seen and heard during the short time he had been with him, he knew that he was a stranger to grace. Knowing, also, that there are many irreligious people, who, nevertheless, have a great respect for religion and its institutions, when Cuff was asked the next morning by his master where he had been, he said, "I have been to meetin; and, bless de Lord, it was a good time, massa."

"Cuff," said the master, in a gruff, angry voice, "you must quit praying; I will have none of it about the place."

"Massa, I do any thing you tell me dat I can do; but I can't quit praying. My Massa in heaven command me to pray."

"But you shall quit it, and promise to do so or I will whip you."

"I can not do one nor the other, massa."

"Follow me, then, you obstinate negro," said the master, greatly excited, "and we shall see whose authority is to be obeyed in this matter."

The slave was led out, and, after being stripped of the few tattered garments that covered his person, he was tied to a tree in the yard. With a rawhide the master inflicted twenty-five strokes upon his bare back. The master then said, "Now, Cuff, will you quit praying?"

"No, massa," was the reply, "I will pray to Jesus as long as I live."

He then gave the negro twenty-five more lashes, and the blood ran down to the ground. At the close of this horrid scene in the brutal tragedy, the master exclaimed, "You will quit now, won't you?"

Meekly as his divine Master bore the cruel scourge before him, he replied, "No, my massa, I will pray to my blessed God while I live."

This so enraged the infuriate fiend, that he flew at him with all the rage of a tiger thirsting for blood, and plying the bloody weapon with all his remaining strength, he stopped not till he was obliged to give over from sheer exhaustion.

"Will you stop your praying now, you infernal nigger, you?"

The same meek voice replied, "No, massa, you may kill me, but while I live I must pray."

"Then you shall be whipped this much every time you pray or go to meeting."

He was untied, ordered to put on his clothes, and go about his work. When out of sight and hearing of his master, he sang, in a low and plaintive tone,

> "My suffering time will soon be o'er,
> Then shall I sigh and weep no more;
> My ransomed soul shall soar away
> To sing God's praise in endless day."

While this cruel scene was transpiring, the young mistress was looking through the window weeping, and when S. M——— came into the house, she said, "My dear husband, why did you whip that poor negro so, just for praying? I am sure there can be no harm in that."

"Silence," shouted the enraged husband; "not another word on the subject, or I will give you as much as I gave him."

All that day S. M——— raved like a madman, cursing the negro and all his race, and cursing God for having created them. Night came. He retired to his chamber, and fell upon his couch to rest. In vain he courted sleep, if for nothing else than to shut out the horrid visions of his tempest-tossed mind. He turned from side to side with unutterable groanings. Just before day he exclaimed, "I feel that I shall be damned! O, God, have mercy on me!" He then said to his wife—the first word he had spoken to her since his threat—"Is there any one about the house that can or will pray for me?"

"None," said she, "that I know of but the poor negro you whipped yesterday."

"O, I am sure he will not, he can not pray for me!"

"Yes," said the weeping wife, "I think he will."

"Then, for God's sake, send some one to call him!"

A servant was soon dispatched; and when Cuff heard that his master wanted him, expecting a renewal of the scenes of yesterday—for he had been praying all night—he went from his low, dingy cabin into the chamber of his master. What was his astonishment, when he entered, to find his master prostrate on the floor, crying for mercy!

"O," said he, at sight of his injured slave, "will you, can you pray for me? I feel that I shall be damned before morning unless God have mercy upon me."

"Yes, massa, I bless God, I have been praying for you and mistress all the night."

He then fell upon his knees, beside his prostrate master and kneeling wife, and, with a fervor and a faith that opened heaven, he wrestled hard with God for the guilty man. Thus he continued in prayer and exhortation, pointing the guilty to the guiltless one, till morning light, when God, in mercy, stooped to answer prayer, and set the dark, sin-chained soul of the infidel at liberty, and wrote a pardon on his heart. Soon as the love of God was shed abroad in the master's soul, he embraced his servant in his arms, exclaiming, "Cuff, my dear brother in Christ, from this moment you are a free man."

Great was the joy and rejoicing in that house on that day. The wife had also found the pearl of great price, and now one in Christ, as they were before one in flesh, their souls were dissolved in the bliss of heaven. The slave was freed, and employed by his master as chaplain at a good salary, and Cuff went every-where among his scattered brethren preaching the word. The master himself became a zealous and successful minister of the Gospel, and lived many years to preach that Jesus whose name he had blasphemed, and whose disciple he had scourged.

CHAPTER XXX.

MARCUS LINDSEY.

THE subject of our narrative was born in Ireland, and brought to this country when quite a boy. His parents were Protestants, of which the "Emerald Isle" has produced some of the stanchest. Well was it for Ireland that the benevolent spirit of Methodism crossed the British Channel, and bore the messages of mercy to a spiritually-dead form of religion, on the one hand, and an equally-corrupt form on the other. Neither the Church of England nor the Church of Rome had done much for poor, unhappy Ireland, in rousing its poor, downtrodden masses from the sleep of death. The parents belonged to the Church of England, and, of course, young Marcus was trained up in the peculiarities of that faith. Being of a naturally-reflective turn of mind he was early impressed with religious thoughts, and convinced of the depravity of his young heart, as its waywardness manifested itself in disobedience to God and his parents. His convictions in regard to his sinful state were greatly increased in being permitted occasionally to hear Methodist preaching. The sermons that young Lindsey heard from Wesley's missionaries resulted in his awakening and conversion to God. It was not long after this event that he felt deeply impressed with the belief that it was his duty to exhort sinners to flee the wrath to come, and be saved from their sins. After exercising awhile in this relation, and his brethren being convinced, by the gifts and grace which he possessed, and the fruits which attended his labors, that he was called of God to devote himself exclusively to the work of calling sinners to repentance, he was recommended to the conference, and accordingly received into the traveling connection in 1810.

His first appointment was to the Hartford circuit, Kentucky, on which he labored with great zeal and devotion through the year, at the expiration of which time he was ordained a deacon for the missionary work, and appointed to Big Sandy river. This was a wild, mountainous, half-civilized region of country, and remains so to some considerable extent at the present day. The Big Sandy was a kind of neutral ground between Kentucky and Virginia, and its deep glens, and mountain gorges, and dense, unbroken forests, made it the home of a daring, reckless race of individuals, and the horse-thief, and gambler, and counterfeiter has often sought refuge in its dark defiles from the pursuit of justice. We could describe many scenes of terror and darkness that have transpired in that region, but we must proceed to our sketch. The youthful herald entered this field of labor, and braving every difficulty and danger, he penetrated its wilds, and proclaimed to its startled and scattered inhabitants, salvation in the name of Jesus. Many heard the joyful sound, and turned their feet from the ways of sin and wickedness to the ways of righteousness and peace. We may talk about the desolation that reigns in the jungles of India, and on the wild and gloomy mountains of Africa, or the solitudes of Oregon, but we have the heathen in the form of half-civilized man, in some of the wild places of the states of Ohio, Kentucky, and Virginia; ay, they may be found in some of the garrets and cellars of our dark alleys in the city full of Churches, where thousands are contributed yearly to convert the Hottentot, the Chinese, and the East Indian. We are not afraid, though we thus speak, that the charity that begins at home will end there; no, for those who care most for the destitute around them are sure to feel deeply and care largely for those who are abroad.

The next year he was appointed to Little Sandy, and here his labors were crowned with the most abundant success; and at the close of this year he was sent into Ohio, and stationed on the Union circuit. Here success attended his labors in the kingdom and patience of Jesus. We have not time, however, nor space, to enter into any detail in regard to the triumphs of the Gospel which he witnessed in this field. In 1815 he was removed to the Marietta circuit, where he was made the instrument of much good. While on this circuit he was instrumental, in the hands of God, in the conversion of John Stewart, the colored man, who went out as the first missionary among the Wyandott Indians. Stewart had been a very dissipated man, and, in one of his drunken fits of delirium tremens, he had started to the Ohio river to drown himself. On his way he had to pass by the place where Lindsey was holding meeting. Being attracted by the sound—for Methodist preachers generally cry aloud, and spare not—he drew up, and stood by the door, where he could distinctly hear all that was said. The preacher was describing the lost sinner's condition, his exposedness to death and hell; and then he presented the offers of mercy, showing that Jesus died for all, and the worst of sinners might repent and find pardon. It was a message of mercy to that poor, forlorn, and ruined soul. It turned his feet from the way of death to the path of life. He returned to his place, and falling upon his knees, he cried for mercy. God heard the poor Ethiopian's prayer. While piteously he pleaded for mercy, salvation came to his heart. At the next meeting he was found at the church, sitting in the back corner, but clothed in his right mind. When the invitation was given to persons to join the Church, he went forward, and the preacher received him and instructed him more perfectly in the way of the Lord. He had received some education, and was enabled to read and write. Like most of his brethren of the African race, he was an admirable singer, possessing a voice of unusual sweetness and power, and he took great delight in singing the hymns and spiritual songs of the Church. Some time after his conversion he became greatly exercised on the subject of preaching. So intense and all-absorbing became his thoughts on the subject that he could neither eat nor sleep. He was continually engaged in reading the Bible and in prayer for weeks. His long fasting and almost ceaseless vigils were broken by a vision which he told us came to him one night. Whether awake or asleep he could not say; but in the transition he heard a voice distinctly saying, "You must go in a north-westerly direction, to the Indian nation, and tell the savage tribes of Christ, your Savior." He had this vision for three successive nights.

It is said that dreams indicate the mind's anxieties, and it is highly probable that the things which engross the mind by day continue to occupy it by night—at least so far as to give a bent and coloring to the thoughts when the outward senses are locked up in sleep. This being the case, then, from the fact that Stewart was greatly exercised on the subject of preaching, we may be led to infer that his vision, or dream, was but a part of his call to preach the Gospel. The only thing wonderful and extraordinary in the dream, is the specific nature of the call, designating, as Paul's vision of the man of Macedonia, the very place to which he should go. Now that revelation is exhausted, and the Bible is to be regarded as a finality on all subjects pertaining to belief and duty, we have but little faith in dreams, or "spiritual communications," so called, as constituting any part of the rule of faith or practice. The sure "word of prophecy," which God has given us, will, if understood and followed, guide us into all the ways of truth and righteousness.

Stewart was poor, and destitute of friends, with the exception of the Methodists, who received and treated him as a brother; but, even among his brethren, who could he get, by any possibility, to believe that he was called to go on a mission to preach the Gospel to the Indians? Firmly impressed, however, with the belief that a dispensation of the Gospel had been committed to him, he made all the preparation his circumstances would allow, and, with his Bible and hymn-book, started out, not knowing whither he was going, save that the vision directed him to the north-west. Abraham, when called from the Ur of the Chaldees, had, doubtless, much greater faith when he entered upon his journey than this sable son of Ham; but there was not less uncertainty in regard to the unknown destination. Stewart continued his travels; and hearing of the Delaware Indians, on the Muskingum, he directed his course thitherward. When he arrived among them he commenced singing, and praying, and exhorting, but it was in an unknown tongue. The peaceful Indians gazed upon the dark stranger with silent wonder, but were not moved by his tears and entreaties. Being impressed that this was not the tribe to which he was called he hurried on. After a fatiguing journey, he arrived at Pipetown, on the Sandusky river, where he found a large concourse of Indians engaged in feasting and dancing. They were in the very midst of their wildest mirth and revelry when he appeared among them. Being a dark mulatto, he attracted their attention, and they gathered around him, and asked him to drink of their fire-water; but he too well knew the fatal effects of the deadly draught to allow it to pass his lips. At this refusal the Indians became angry, and were beginning to manifest signs of hostility; but he commenced, in a clear, melodious voice, singing one of the songs of Zion. Its strains rose above the din and uproar of the multitude. They were strangely enchanting, and, like the voice of Jesus on stormy Galilee, they calmed the tumult of passion which threatened his destruction. The war-dance and song ceased. The multitude gathered around him, and hung upon his lips in breathless silence, as if enchanted by the sound. When he ceased he fell upon his knees, and poured out his heart to God in prayer for their salvation. There stood by him an old chief, who understood his language, and as word after word escaped his lips he interpreted it to the listening hundreds. When his prayer was ended, he arose and exhorted them to turn away from their drunken revelry, and Indian ceremonies, to the worship of the true and living God, assuring them that if they continued in this course they would be forever lost. As the earnest entreaties of the colored preacher were communicated by the old chief, many were deeply impressed with the truths which he uttered, and the work of God might have then and there at once commenced, but for the interference of Captain Pipe, the head chief, who became violently enraged, and, brandishing his tomahawk, swore if he did not cease he would kill him on the spot. John ceased his exhortation, and turned, with a sorrowful heart, away. Being ordered to leave immediately, on pain of death, he again started out upon his journey, and, guided by an invisible hand, he went to Upper Sandusky. Here he found another band of Indians, and among them a black man named Jonathan Painter, who had been taken prisoner by them at the mouth of the

Big Kanawha, in Virginia, when a boy. He was a good interpreter. With this man he soon became intimate, and procuring his services, he went with him to attend a great Indian festival. When he arrived he begged permission to speak to the assembled multitude; but they paid little attention to his request. He still pleaded for the privilege; for his heart burned to tell the wandering savage of Jesus and his love. After much entreaty, through his interpreter, they agreed to let him speak to them the next day. The time and place of meeting were fixed, and when Stewart, with his interpreter, appeared, how was his heart chilled and discouraged only to find one old Indian, by the name of Big Tree, and an old Indian woman, called Mary! To these, however, he preached Christ and the resurrection. God attended his word; and though small and feeble was the beginning, yet the labors of Stewart were blessed. He continued to hold forth, as opportunity favored, the word of life to the Wyandotts, and as the product of so feeble an instrumentality, the mission to the Wyandotts was established by the Church, an account of which may be found in our History.

We now resume our sketch of brother Lindsey, through whose instrumentality this remarkable man, in some respects, was brought to God. After finishing his term on the Marietta circuit he was sent to the Salt River district, in Kentucky, where he continued for two years, laboring with his accustomed zeal and usefulness. From this district he was sent to the Green River district, which he traveled three years; thence to the Kentucky district, which he traveled four years. After this he was returned to the Salt River district, where he remained three years, and at the expiration thereof he came over to the Ohio district, which he traveled one year, when he was removed to the Cumberland district. Here he continued for three years in labors more abundant. His next appointment was Shelbyville, and the Brick Chapel. Thus we trace this indefatigable man from circuit to district, from district to district and station, laboring on with a tireless zeal in the service of his Master. Could a history of the fourteen years, in which he traveled over vast districts of country as presiding elder, be written out, how full would it be of stirring adventures and thrilling incidents; but the memory of them has perished with the departure of the man, and we can only give a rapid outline of the fields which he has successively and successfully cultivated.

We have already brought our readers down to the last appointment, and it only remains for us to say, that while actively engaged in this field of labor he was arrested by that fell disease, the cholera, which garnered such precious fruits for the tomb from among the ministry, and which, in July, 1833, terminated his career on earth, and ushered him to heaven. He was a man of stout, athletic frame, black hair, a keen, dark eye, overarched by heavy brows. He was much given to despondency, which would occasionally cast a gloom upon his countenance, that at times would make his appearance rather forbidding; but under all there was a large heart full of tender sympathies. When his mind was not overcast, and in heaviness through manifold temptations, his bright, happy spirit would make sunshine all around him. Some men can never be fully known in this life, however transparent their character. There is a deep, inner life that lies far down beyond the ken of mortals, which the tongue, if it could, will not reveal. That life can only be known hereafter. Till then we must wait for the solution of difficulties, inconsistencies, and mysteries, which here we shall never know. Lindsey was a powerful preacher, a faithful pastor, and a great terror to evil-doers. He abounded in zeal and good works, and thousands will bless God in the day of eternity, that to him was committed a dispensation of the Gospel.

CHAPTER XXXI.

THE DUTCHMAN'S EXPERIENCE.

WHEN we were traveling the Cross Creek circuit, in 1815, in a region of country which was mostly settled by German Lutherans, and not much regard paid to the Sabbath, or any kind of religion, there lived a German by the name of Gost. He was one of the principal men of the neighborhood, and had great influence among his German friends. At one of our love-feasts we heard him relate his experience, and though it was in very broken English, yet it was told with an unction and a power which melted all hearts, and which thrilled and interested us so much that we have not forgotten it to this day.

There is something peculiar in the German mind and character which shows itself, perhaps, more strikingly in regard to the subject of religion than any thing else. It seems that in whatever enterprise a German embarks, it engrosses his entire energies, and when once fully committed on any subject, he adheres to it with an energy, zeal, and perseverance worthy of all praise. Staid and sober as he may appear, he nevertheless has the excitability of a Frenchman without his mercurial nature. Luther was a noble type of the Teutonic mind, and exhibited the different characteristics of which we have spoken, when he said he would go to the Diet of Worms if there were as many devils in his way as there were tiles on the roofs of the houses; and when, in his excited imagination, he saw the devil before him in his study, and threw his inkstand at him; and, also, when on another occasion, he was arraigned before an ecclesiastical council for heresy, and threatened with punishment if he did not retract, he said, "Here I stand, God help!" One has said, "Get a German once converted, and there is little danger of his refusing to take up his cross, or turning back to the beggarly elements of the world." They seem to carry out more fully Mr. Wesley's idea of Methodism than even the English brethren themselves. When they sing, "they sing lustily;" when they pray, they pray with all their might; when they speak in class meeting or love-feast, they come right to the point of Christian experience without any circumlocution. Such was the case with our good German brother whose experience we are going to relate.

Shortly after the speaking exercises commenced, he arose and said, "Mine dear bruders, ven I comes to dis blace dare vas nobody here. Den after, mine freins dey comes too, and ve did comes along very goot, as ve dot. Ve did drink viskey, and frolic, and dance, and ve all dot it vas wery nice; but binebys der comes along into de neighborhoot a Metodis breacher by de name of Jo. Shackelford, and he breaches and breaches, and brays and brays, as you never see de like in all your lives. He says, 'You beeples all goes to hell unless you git conwerted, and be saved from your zins.' Now, vell den, de beeples begins to dink zeriously on dis matter, and dey say ve must do better, or, sure enough, de devil vill git us shust as he says. Den dey gits Christen, and begins to bray; and dey valls down, and brays, and croans, and hollers, and I says to my beeples, Dis is de devil; and it goes on till it comes to my neighbor Honnes. Vell, I does not go, and my vife and gals does not go, because I said it vas de devil. Vell, however, it gomes so near by mine house, I says I vill go and see vat is dis ting vat makes de beeples so crazy. So von night I goes to Honnes's to see de brayer meeting, and I sets down and sees de beeples come in, and dey all looks shust like dey used to do, and I dot it vas all vell; but dey soon begins to zing and bray, and I dot dis is all right. Den some pegins to croan, and valls down; and I says, 'Dis is de devil, and I vill shust go home;' but ven I vent to rise up I could not, vor I vas fast to de bench. Den I vas skeered, and I said, 'Dis is de devil sure enough.' I looked round, and I dot de door vas growed up, and I vas fast enough. Vell, vell, den I say, 'Mine Got, de devil vill git me now, by sure!' I looked more for de door, and bresently I sees him, and I makes von spring and out I goes headforemost. Den I gits up, and runs mit all my might till I comes to mine fence; and ven I goes to git over I comes down smack upon my pack, and now I says, 'De devil vill git me, py sure!' I lays dare for some time; den I gits up, and climes de fence, and goes to mine house, and dot I would shust go to bed mitout making any noise; but shust as I vas gittin in ped smack down I comes on mine pack upon de floor; and Madalana, mine vife, did shump out of de ped, and did schream; and Petts and Kate—dat ish my two gals—dey did shump up and schream and holler, and dare I lays, and I says, 'O, mine Got, tis ish te devil!' Madalana says, 'No matter for you; it shust serves you right; you vould go, and now you prings de devil home mit you to your own house.' Petts and Kate dey both cries, and mine vife she scolds, and de devil he shakes me over de hells, and all my sins shust comes up to mine eyes, and I says, 'O, mine Got, save me!' After a vile I goes to ped, but I not sleeps. I says, 'O mine Got, mine Got, vat vill become of me!' Shust at daylight I gits up and goes down to my parn, and gits under de hoss-trough, and smack I comes on mine pack again. Den I cries, mit all my might, 'O, mine Got, mine Got, have mercy upon me!' I dot I vas goin to de hells. Shust den someting say to me, 'Di sins pe all vorgifen.' Den someting comes down all over me at my head, shust like honey, and I opens mine mout shust so vide ash I can; but it filled so full it run over, and den O, I vas so happy as never I vas before in all my life! I did shump like a deer, and I hollered, 'Glory, glory to mine Got!' mit all my might. Mine hosses dey did veel round and shnorted, and I did veel round too, and hollered glory, and I did not know dem, and dey did not know me. Presently I saw my gray hoss, Pob, and I snatched him round de neck, and he did veel round, and I hollered, 'Glory, glory, and bless de Lort!' I love dish hoss unto dis day so petter than any. I now ish on mine vay to de himmels, and dare I vill bless Got for his pringing me down on mine pack, and for mine vife and mine gals; for dey now goes mit me to glory; so, mine bruders, ve vill all bineby meet in dat goot vorld, to braise de Lort forever and ever."

CHAPTER XXXII.

JOHN STRANGE.

THIS talented and useful preacher was a native of Virginia. He was born on the 15th day of November, 1789, and when quite a boy emigrated to the wilds of Ohio. Here, under the ministrations of the early pioneer fathers of Methodism, he embraced the religion of the Lord Jesus Christ, and united with the Methodist Episcopal Church. It was not long after his conversion that his talents and piety were exhibited to such a degree as to convince the Church, in connection with his own deep and powerful impressions, that he was called of God to enter the ministry. In the year 1810 he commenced his itinerant career under the venerable Quinn. His first circuit was Wills Creek, in the wilds of Muskingum, where he labored, with all the zeal and fire of youth, in proclaiming the Gospel to sinners. The next appointment which he received was Cincinnati, as the colleague of the venerable Burke. He traveled successively Whitewater, Oxford, Lawrenceburg, Whiteoak, Mad River, and Union circuits, and Charlestown and Indianapolis districts. His excessive labors, however, proved too much for his constitution, and during his whole ministerial life, with but slight intervals of rest, he was in abundant labors;

> "For Jesus day and night employed,
> His heritage he toiled to clear."

He was regarded, both in Ohio and Indiana—in the latter of which states he spent the close of his life—as a faithful, eloquent, and beloved minister of Jesus Christ. Numerous seals to his ministry, which will, doubtless, be stars in the crown of his rejoicing in the day of eternity, are to be found all over the west. On the second of December, 1834, in the forty-fifth year of his age, and the twenty-third of his ministry, he was called away by the gentle summons of his Master, to that world where labor is exchanged for rest, and prayer is lost in praise.

One who was entirely ignorant of the life of a preacher wrote the following: "How full of beauty, how desirable and picturesque, is the life of a preacher, especially in the country! Religion and poetry dwell with him like twin sisters, and his thoughts, when turned aside from heaven, rest on all that is most beautiful on earth." The truth is, the enjoyment of a faithful minister does not consist in his repose. When but a single glance upon the exhausting demands which are made upon his mind and body—demands under which many sink to an untimely grave; when we think of his exposure to wounds upon his feelings through all his every-day duties—wounds which he must bear in silence, or be liable to be charged with having a wrong spirit—his being cut off from the common resources of men, and made dependent for a support upon those for whom he labors, and thereby the selfishness of men is armed against him; add to all this that the sorrows of others lay a tax upon his sympathies, and compel him to bear a part; when all these are considered, this picture will be regarded as extremely fanciful. Whoever enters the ministry for the poetry of it will find the thorn with the rose. A thistle, when seen in the far-off distance, may contribute as much as the lily to beautify the landscape; but when it is approached and grasped its thorns are felt. So it is with the preacher's life to those who look at it from a distance. His position may be regarded as the abode of poetry and

Elysian sweets; but an experience of short duration will soon correct the error, and show how toilsome, and often unthankful, is his profession. To the Methodist preacher it is hard service and poor fare, so far as this world is concerned; and were it not for the comfortable reflection that the faithful shall be crowned with life, very few would enter the ranks of the itinerancy for the poetry connected with it.

A beautiful tribute from the pen of one of Indiana's most gifted daughters, with which we shall finish our sketch, will give the reader a better idea of the talents and character of the beloved Strange than any thing we could say:

"Among the heralds of salvation to a dying world, who have now sat down in our Father's kingdom, there is no name that comes up from the dim remembrance of the past, with a holier and more endearing thrill, than that of John Strange. In the morning of life he heeded not the siren voice that would have lured him to the flower-wreathed paths of pleasure, or pointed out to him the high seats of what men call honorable renown; but trampling on the bright hopes of earthly greatness, which are ever busy in the heart of youth, he took up and bore to the end of his course the cross of the meek and lowly Savior. He was one of those men whom the Lord saw fit, in his wisdom, to endow with every Christian grace, and set apart to carry the glad tidings of salvation to the humble homes of the western pioneers; and through many a night, in the dark and lonely wilderness, he pillowed his weary head on the green earth without a covering, save the blue canopy of heaven. There was no privation, discouragement, or danger that could induce him to forsake his Master's work; for he was truly a man that bore about with him, in his own body, the marks of the Lord Jesus.

34*

"When he came to Indiana it was comparatively a wilderness, and there were many parts where the story of the cross was but seldom told. His fervent piety, superior talents, and zeal for the souls of dying men, soon made him a home at every hearth, and the sound of his name brought a thrill to every heart that loved the cause of the Redeemer; and O, it is a glorious thought, that while his immortal part is worshiping with the blood-washed throng around the eternal throne, his name is treasured up

'Amid fond Memory's sacred things,'

in many hearts that will one day be stars in his crown of rejoicing.

'He, mixing with the brilliant hosts above,
Recounts the wonders of redeeming love;
While list'ning angels hear with sweet surprise,
And gusts of alleluiahs ring the skies.'

"Perhaps I can not better give an idea of his manner of preaching than by giving an instance. It was understood, in a remote part of Indiana, where the Gospel was but seldom heard, that on a certain day John Strange would preach. It was at once set down as an era among the people; and, on the day appointed, they, with almost one accord, assembled at the place, which was the temple of God's own building, the green, unbroken forest. Of the hundreds there collected, some had come to worship that God whom they had learned to love in the far-off land of their nativity, which they had exchanged for the wilderness, where the sound of the church-going bell might never salute them again; and some were there through mere curiosity, many of whom, perhaps, had never heard a sermon in their lives. Expectation was on tiptoe; and it was evident, from the restless movements and anxious whisperings of the groups collected apart from the crowd, that something out of the common order was about to take place. All eyes were turned in one direction for a moment—the whispered words, 'The preacher's come,' were heard, and all was silent as the day dawn of creation. He ascended the rude stand prepared for him, and sang a hymn, in a voice whose deep pathos went down into the heart, and seldom failed to cause some chord to vibrate there; then, as he kneeled beneath the bright blue sky, and poured his spirit out before the God that gave it, in behalf of those to whom he was sent with the words of everlasting life, the smothered sobs and flowing tears of the assembly, evinced the faith and fervor of that prayer. He then pointed out clearly the way of salvation through the blood of a crucified Redeemer, and besought those who had found the pearl of great price to hold fast their confidence, till they had conquered death, their last enemy, and meet Him all glorious within the light of eternity, where they should enter upon that inheritance prepared for them from the foundation of the world. 'But my friends,' said he, 'when the angel shall stand with one foot upon the sea and the other upon the land, and shall swear by Him that liveth forever and ever that time shall be no more; when the earth shall pass away and the heavens be rolled up as a scroll; when the thrones are set, and the dead, small and great, shall stand before the Lord, is there one here whose name shall not be found written in the Lamb's book of life? Forbid it, Lord! If there is one here who has never tasted of the joys of salvation, I warn him by the terrors of that day to flee the wrath to come, and to do it now; for now is the accepted time; behold! now is the day of salvation; choose ye this day whom ye will serve; and O, be careful to make a wise choice! Jesus has paid your debt, and now stands ready to receive you. Will you believe it, and enlist under the blood-stained banner of the cross, or will you put it off to a more convenient season? Will you spend a never-ending eternity in the dark caverns of irremediable woe, or be ushered into the New Jerusalem with songs and everlasting joy upon your heads, when the Lord shall come to make up his jewels?' His manner and shrill, soul-searching voice had raised with his feelings till they seemed to have reached their climax, and with his pale, upturned face and streaming eyes, he stood for a moment as if wrapped in the presence of the Lord; and then, as if the heavens were opened to his steadfast gaze, he exclaimed, with startling energy, 'Glory, glory, glory be to God, who giveth us the victory!' It seemed as if the enchained attention of the audience was broken up by an electric shock, and the Spirit of the Lord seemed to fasten on every heart like cloven tongues of fire, and glory, glory, glory was echoed back from every part of that worshiping assembly. Till the tale of time is told on the morning of eternity the effect of that sermon can never be known.

"I saw him shortly before he died, some ten years since, and never did I feel more sensibly the force of those beautiful lines of Dr. Young,

> 'The chamber where the good man meets his fate,
> Is privileged beyond the common walk
> Of virtuous life—quite on the verge of heaven.'

He was weak and very pale; but there was a serenity in his countenance that evinced to the beholder how easy it was for the Christian to die; and when he spoke of his departure hence, there was a gleam of glory upon his face that told there was a heaven in his heart. He had an interesting family, and when he spoke to them he remarked, 'I love my children, and would be glad to leave them in better circumstances; for I have made no provision for them; but that God into whose hands I resign them has promised to provide. I have not labored for earthly treasure; but I have an inheritance up yonder, and I expect to meet them all at God's right hand.' Soon after this he entered upon that rest prepared for those that love and serve the Lord. His remains were deposited in the graveyard at Indianapolis by hundreds of mourning friends, who had known him long and loved him well; and often are the bright flowers and green grass above that hallowed spot wet with the tears of those he was instrumental in bringing from nature's darkness to the marvelous light of God's dear children. There are few men who were more devoted, or spent their lives with an eye more single to the glory of God; few there certainly are who have done more good, were more revered, or will be longer remembered than John Strange."

CHAPTER XXXIII.

WILLIAM P. FINLEY.

WILLIAM P. was the third son of the Rev. Robert W. Finley. He was born in South Carolina, in the year 1785, and emigrated with his parents to Kentucky. From childhood he was remarkably inquisitive and talkative, possessing in a high degree those social qualities which rendered him companionable, as well as a nature full of wit and humor, which would gather around him all the young people of the neighborhood. He was rapid in thought and quick at repartee, yet full of benevolence and kindness. In addition to his genial nature and humorous disposition, he possessed a remarkable aptitude for learning. While at school studying Latin, Greek, Mathematics, and other branches of learning, he seemed to get his lessons almost by intuition. While others of his class would labor and grow weary over a hard sentence, or a difficult proposition, with him it seemed that it was only to look and receive. He always led his class, being perfect in all his recitations. What he received so readily he was disposed as lavishingly to bestow upon others; and hence, when other young men, during the winter seasons, would be out hunting and sporting, he would gather together a group of the neighbors' children in some lonesome log school-house, and there impart to them the rudiments of an education. Thus he spent his years till he arrived at manhood, when he married a most estimable woman, with whom he lived most happily till the day of his death.

Nothing very remarkable occurred in his history, till the year 1808, when, with his wife, on their way to a Christmas frolic, he stopped at the house of the writer of this sketch and heard a recital of his conversion, connected with an earnest exhortation and appeal, which awakened both to a sense of their lost condition; and instead of going to join in the scenes of mirth and revelry, they remained to weep and pray. They returned home and commenced seeking the Lord with penitential hearts, and God heard their prayer. One night, in the deep solitude of the forest, while William was prostrate on the ground crying for mercy, the blessing of pardon and salvation came to his soul with such power, that his soul was set at perfect liberty, and the peace of heaven flowed into his heart like a river.

His conversion wrought the most wonderful change, not only in his habits of life, but in his disposition. He seemed to have lost all that conviviality of mind and flow of spirits which so strongly characterized him, and became one of the most sedate and sober men we ever knew. Great trials awaited him. He was constantly impressed with the conviction that God had called him to preach the Gospel, and he was strongly impressed with the belief that if he did not yield to the call he must perish, notwithstanding all the Lord had done for his soul. Such were the deep, agonizing struggles of his soul, that his mind gave evidence to all of the storm within. Thus he continued almost distracted, till the Church of God, which is the best judge of Heaven's designs in this respect, saw that the burden of the Lord was upon him, and, accordingly, he was called out and duly authorized to preach the Gospel of salvation to perishing sinners.

How mysterious are the ways of Providence! The father of William, burning with a missionary zeal, left his home and friends for the then distant Carolinas and

Georgia, and the far-off cane-brakes of Kentucky; and when disposed to settle, having purchased a large tract of land, was turned out of house and home by land pirates, and driven out in the wilds of the North-western territory. Here he made another purchase of land, which was taken from him; and still another, but his plans were all frustrated, and he kept wandering. God at length converts his three sons, and sends them out into the waste places, to follow the fortunes of their father in calling sinners to repentance.

William having proved himself in the local ranks, entered the itinerancy at the conference held in Cincinnati, in 1814. His first appointment was Paint Creek circuit, which he was to travel alone. It was a four weeks' circuit, but he labored with zeal and fidelity; and at the expiration of the year he reported an accession of one hundred precious souls. His next appointment was Brush Creek circuit, where he labored with the same untiring zeal in proclaiming salvation to the lost. The succeeding years he traveled Miami, Scioto, and Paint Creek circuits. His last appointment was Strait Creek circuit, in the year 1820. He was obliged to take a location at the close of this year, from the following lamentable circumstances: On returning to his circuit from a visit to his family, his horse became frightened and threw him, his head striking violently against the bridge which he was crossing, fracturing his skull just above the left ear. This wound was of such a nature as to disqualify him from preaching. He suffered much from pain in the head, and was admonished that his work as an itinerant was done. Judging that he had not been sufficiently long in the itinerancy to entitle him to a superannuated relation, he chose to locate, and, with his wife and helpless children, trust to Providence. He bore his painful affliction for more than a year, and he continued to grow worse and worse, till at length his mind gave way, and he became at times a raving maniac. He was not disposed to do any harm. In his ravings he would pray, and sing, and preach, as if still in his beloved employ of winning souls to Christ; and many who heard the deep pathos of his soul, as it sent out its pathetic wail like the strings of a broken harp, were melted to tears. At other times his mania would assume a different form, and it was almost impossible to control him. After suffering thus for seventeen months, his physician finally concluded to trepan him as the only hope of giving him relief. When it was communicated to him, and the doctor told him he must consent to be bound, he firmly replied, "No; I can stand any thing," and laying himself down, without moving a limb or a muscle, he endured the operation. The moment the pressure was removed from the brain his mind at once resumed its healthy functions, and he commenced praising God for his deliverance. He lived in the full, bright, unclouded exercise of all his faculties for about three weeks after the operation was performed, and in the full, glorious triumphs of faith he went to that world where no derangement of human organization could obstruct the soul in its glorious exercise.

The pulpit exercises of William were of the tender and pathetic kind. None ever heard him preach that he did not, with his sympathetic Master, weep over his congregation, and beseech the sinner in tenderest strains to be reconciled to God, not ceasing till all were melted into tears. How often have we thought of the saying of the classic orator, in regard to the secret of producing feeling in the hearts of an audience:

"If you would have me weep, begin the strain;
Then I shall feel your sorrows, feel your pain!"

By many he was called Jeremiah, or the weeping prophet. He was not a Boanerges, but a son of consolation;

and though there was nothing very brilliant or showy in his talents as a preacher, yet he was enabled, through the Spirit, to find way to the hearts of saints and sinners. Christ and him crucified was the theme that melted his heart and flowed from his tongue. His devoted wife is still coasting the Jordan, waiting to cross over. The most of his children have already gone to join their sainted father in the better land. We stood by the dying bed of one of his lovely daughters, and never did saints or angels witness a more happy and triumphant death. In her last moments she said, "Dear mother, weep not for me. Angels are waiting to take me to Jesus and my home in heaven; there I shall see my dear father, and brothers, and sisters, and there I shall wait your arrival." Sweetest music filled our ears as she plumed her wings and flew from time's retiring shores to that bright world above. O, what a happy death! While we write it seems as if our precious kindred are hovering around. Our soul swells with glory as we contemplate the hour, not far distant, when we shall hail them on that sun-bright shore.

CHAPTER XXXIV.

RUSSEL BIGELOW.

AMONG the number of the gifted, devoted, and zealous preachers of his day stands the name of Russel Bigelow. He was received on trial in the Ohio conference in the year 1815, and appointed to the Hinkston circuit, in the bounds of the Kentucky district, the Rev. Samuel Parker being his presiding elder. He was at this time in the twenty-third year of his age. The history of his early life, and the circumstances connected with his conversion, are not known; and however interesting their detail might, and, doubtless, would be, we are sorry that our readers can not be gratified. So marked a character as was Bigelow's during his ministerial career, must have been distinguished in early life by some striking peculiarities.

In the year 1816 he was removed from Kentucky to Ohio, and stationed on the Miami circuit as the colleague of the Rev. Alexander Cummins. His early association with the master spirits of the Church doubtless had a happy effect upon his character, in developing those traits which distinguished him in the maturer periods of his ministry. The succeeding year he was sent to the adjoining circuit of Lawrenceburg, where he continued till the next conference, at which he was sent to Oxford, where he remained two years. In 1820 he traveled Mad River circuit, and the following two years Columbus. At the expiration of this period he went to Whitewater, and from thence he came to Cincinnati, which place he occupied with the Rev. Truman Bishop. Here he remained one year, and from hence went to Union circuit. The next two years he traveled the Scioto district, and at the expiration of this time was sent to the mission at Sandusky. Here he engaged in the work of preaching to the Wyandott Indians, superintending the farm and mission school. The tedious process, however, of preaching through an interpreter was wholly unsuited to his nature, and at the expiration of the year he retired from the work to seek a more congenial sphere. The four succeeding years he was sent to preside over the Portland district, and in the year 1833 he was stationed in Columbus, where he remained two years, giving full proof of his ministry, beloved and respected by all both in and out of the Church. Indeed, such was the esteem in which he was held that, during the next year, in which it was necessary for him, on account of his feeble health, to take a superannuated relation, he was appointed by the Board of Directors of the Ohio Penitentiary, as chaplain to that institution.

He entered upon his labors in the Penitentiary with a zeal and devotion characteristic of his truly-benevolent heart. He visited every cell, and conversed with every prisoner, and his prayers and exhortations were not lost upon the hearts of the convicts. Many an obdurate and sin-steeled conscience was touched by the eloquence of his tears and entreaties to win them from the ways of sin. The fruits of his labors in this field eternity can alone disclose. He might have avoided much labor, and incurred no charge on the ground of non-attendance of duty; but the worth of souls uncared for, as is usually the case with the inmates of a prison, pressed heavily upon his heart, and awakened all his sympathies. Under these labors he broke down, and before the year had expired it was necessary for him to resign his post.

About this time he visited our house on his way to Indiana. He had rigged up a jumper, there being snow on the ground, and in that backwoods conveyance he came into Ridgeville, the place where we resided. He seemed to be laboring under a melancholy, which had, for some time, been settling upon him, and his friends were somewhat apprehensive of the consequences. He was evidently passing through one of those severe trials with which God purifies his saints and fits them for heaven. There was a cause, however, for his despondency. He had given all to the Church—his time, his talents, and all—and while he was able to preach all was well. Bright faces and open hands greeted him in all his walks; but, alas! when disease preyed upon his system, and he was no longer able to preach the Gospel, faces were hidden and hands were turned away. A man must have had more faith than mortal can exercise under such circumstances, not to feel depressed. Before his enfeebled mind rose his helpless family—a wife and seven children—and they, in all probability, soon to be left without any to provide for their wants. His sad experience too thoroughly convinced him how cheerless would be their condition when he was gone; and to the Rev. J. C. Brooke he opened freely his mind upon the subject. Never did we feel more intensely for a poor itinerant than we then felt for Bigelow.

After remaining with us a week on his return, he made ready for his departure. The snow had melted, and there being no further need for a jumper, Mr. Brooke furnished him a saddle and fitted him up. He was loth to leave, and lingered about; and when with tears we bade him farewell, never to see him again in this world, Mr. Brooke gave him all the money he had. After riding off some distance on the road he returned, and taking his horse-collar and hames he threw them into the yard, all he had to leave as a memento, the remains of which we have on the farm to this day.

His work was done, and that devoted, self-sacrificing missionary went home to die. For more than twenty years he had toiled in the hard field of itinerant life, filling, with a zeal and fidelity characteristic of a faithful soldier of the cross, every post assigned him by the authorities of the Church. For a period of nineteen years it was said of him, that he had not missed a single appointment. Frequent exposures in traveling the hard circuits and districts of those days made heavy drafts upon his constitution, and ere he had scarcely reached "manhood's middle day" he was called from the field of his toil and conflict on earth to the scenes of his reward and triumph in heaven. In the midst of his sufferings he realized a perfect resignation to the will of God, and in the language of faith and joy he was enabled to shout the praises of his heavenly King. While a brother in the ministry was pouring out his heart in prayer to God in his behalf, the responses of the dying man illustrated the truth that

> "The chamber where he met his fate,
> Was privileged beyond the common walks
> Of life—quite on the verge of heaven."

Our sketch would be entirely too meager and unsatisfactory did it end here; and such, unfortunately, would have been the case, to a very great extent, had it not been for the very graphic and faithful pen of Dr. Thomson, who has given a most truthful and beautiful analysis of the sainted Bigelow's character. To this description we invite the attention of our readers.

"Russel Bigelow was an extraordinary man, and his merits were never fully appreciated even by the Church. Of his early history the writer has no knowledge, further than that he emigrated, at an early age, from New England to the west, and that, from his youth, being accustomed to read the Bible upon his knees, he soon became remarkable for piety. It is probable that he was favored with no more than a good common school education, before he entered the itinerancy, of which he was so conspicuous an ornament. I was a student in the beautiful village of W. when I first heard of him. Opposite our office was a coppersmith, a man of remarkable mind and character. He had been reared without any education, and had been unfortunate in his business relations; but having spent his leisure in reading and in conversation with persons of better attainments, he had acquired a stock of valuable knowledge, which his grappling intellect well knew how to use. He was an active politician. In times of excitement he gathered the multitude around him, and often arrested our studies by his stentorian voice, which could drown the clatter of his hammers and the confusion even of Bedlam. I think I may safely say that for many years he wielded the political destinies of his county. Never in office himself, his will determined who should be. This man had imbibed skeptical sentiments, which he often inculcated with terrific energy. He rarely went to the house of God, and when he did, I supposed he might as well stay at home; for I should have thought it as easy to melt a rock with a fagot, as to subdue his heart by the 'foolishness of preaching.'

"One Saturday evening he came into our office with a peculiar expression of countenance—the tear started from his eye as he said, 'I have been to meeting, and by the grace of God I will continue on as long as it lasts. Come, young gentlemen, come and hear Bigelow. He will show you the world, and the human heart, and the Bible, and the cross in such a light as you have never before seen them.' I trembled beneath the announcement; for if the preacher had prostrated a fainting multitude at his feet, he would not have given me as convincing a proof of his power as that which stood before me. This was the first account I ever heard of Bigelow; and from that time I avoided the Methodist church, till he left the village.

"One morning of the ensuing summer, my preceptor came in and said, 'T., come, mount old black, and go with me to camp meeting.'

"*T.* 'Excuse me, sir, I have no desire to go to such a nursery of vice and enthusiasm.'

"*P.* 'O, you are too bigoted. Presbyterian, as I am, I confess I like camp meetings. There man can forget the business of life, and listen to the truth without distraction, and then ponder on it, and pray over it, and feel it. Good impressions are made every Sabbath; but they rarely bring forth fruit; they are worn away by the business of the week. At camp meeting the heart can first be heated, and then, while yet warm, placed upon the anvil and beaten into shape.'

"*T.* 'I was once at camp meeting two hours, and that satisfied me. The heart may be warmed there, but I doubt the purity of the fire which heats it.'

"*P.* 'A truce to argument. I have a patient there I want you to see. You have no objection to go professionally.'

"*T.* 'No, sir, I will go any where to see a patient.'

"It was a lovely morning. The sun was shining from a cloudless sky, and the fresh breezes fanned us, as we rode by well-cultivated and fertile fields, waving with their rich and ripening harvests. After a short journey we came to the encampment. A broad beam of daylight showed things to advantage; and I could but think, as I gazed from an elevated point, and drank in the sweet songs that reverberated through the grove, of some of the scenes of Scripture. My rebel heart was constrained to cry within me, 'How goodly are thy tents, O Jacob, and thy tabernacles, O Israel! As the valleys are they spread forth: as gardens by the river's side.'

"Having visited the sick whom we had come to see, we were invited, with great kindness and cordiality, to partake of refreshments. The warmth of our reception excited my gratitude, and instead of starting home, when the horn blew for preaching, I sat down respectfully to hear the sermon. Bigelow was to preach. I dreaded the occasion; but had always been taught to venerate religion, and had never seen the day when I could ridicule or disturb even the Mohammedan at his prayers, or the pagan at his idol. In the pulpit were many clergymen, two of whom I knew and esteemed—the one a tall, majestic man, whose vigorous frame symbolized his noble mind and generous heart; the other a small, delicate, graceful gentleman, whom nature had fitted for a universal favorite. Had I been consulted, one of them should have occupied the pulpit at that time. All was stillness and attention when the presiding elder stepped forward. Never was I so disappointed in a man's personal appearance. He was below the middle stature, and clad in coarse, ill-made garments. His uncombed hair hung loosely over his forehead. His attitudes and motions were exceedingly ungraceful, and every feature of his countenance was unprepossessing. Upon minutely examining him, however, I became better pleased. The long hair that came down to his cheeks, concealed a broad and prominent forehead; the keen eye that peered from beneath his heavy and overjutting eyebrows beamed with deep and penetrating intelligence; the prominent cheek-bones, projecting chin, and large nose, indicated any thing but intellectual feebleness; while the wide mouth, depressed at its corners, the slightly-expanded nostril, and the *tout ensemble*, indicated sorrow and love, and well assorted with the message, 'Come unto me all ye that labor and are heavy laden, and I will give you rest.' As he commenced I determined to watch for his faults; but before he had closed his introduction I concluded that his words were pure and well chosen, his accents never misplaced, his sentences grammatical, artistically constructed, and well arranged, both for harmony and effect; and when he entered fully upon his subject, I was disposed to resign myself to the argument, and leave the speaker in the hands of more skillful critics. Having stated and illustrated his position clearly, he laid broad the foundation of his argument, and piled stone upon stone, hewed and polished, till he stood upon a majestic pyramid, with heaven's own light around him, pointing the astonished multitude to a brighter home beyond the sun, and bidding defiance to the enemy to move one fragment of the rock on which his feet were planted. His argument being completed, his peroration commenced. This was grand beyond description. The whole universe seemed animated by its Creator to aid him in persuading the sinners to return to God, and the angels commissioned to open heaven and come down to strengthen him. Now he opens the mouth of the pit, and takes us through its gloomy avenues, while the bolts retreat, and the doors of damnation burst open, and the wail of the lost enters our ears; and now he opens heaven, transports us to the flowery plains, stands us amid the armies of the blest, to sweep, with celestial fingers, angelic harps, and join the eternal chorus, 'Worthy, worthy is the Lamb!' As he closed his discourse, every energy of his body and mind were stretched to the utmost point of tension. His soul appeared to be too great for its tenement, and every moment ready to burst through and soar away as an eagle toward heaven. His lungs labored, his arms rose, the perspiration, mingled with tears, flowed in a steady stream upon the floor, and every thing about him seemed to say, 'O that my head were waters!' But the audience thought not of the struggling body, nor even of the giant mind within; for they were paralyzed beneath the avalanche of thought that descended upon them.

"I lost the man, but the subject was all in all. I returned from the ground dissatisfied with myself, saying within me, 'O, that I were a Christian!'

"It was two or three years after this that, being introduced into the Church, I became acquainted personally with this excellent man, of whose character I propose to record what I recollect.

"1. He was modest. To receive the plaudits of thousands, without forming a high estimate of one's talents, requires much grace. Hence, the orator is generally proud. Bigelow preached to audiences as large, and with results as astonishing, as we have ever witnessed. Though he could not have been insensible of his power, yet he appeared to set no high estimate on his superior qualifications or endowments; for he rarely alluded to them, or suffered any one else, unrebuked, to do so in his presence. He was a perfect gentleman in his deportment—to his inferiors kind—to his equals courteous—to those who had the rule over him submissive—toward those of elevated station independent, yet duly respectful—toward the civil magistrate *conscientiously* regardful, rendering unto 'Cæsar the things that are Cæsar's.' Though he scorned not the palace, he courted not its inmates; and while the circles of fashion delighted to honor him, he 'condescended to men of low estate.' Capable of standing, like the cedar on Lebanon, he loved the place

'Where purple violets lurk
With all the *lowly* children of the shade.'

"Though modest, he was not bashful. Without any

thing assuming in look, word, or action, he was a fine illustration of the truth, 'The righteous is bold as a lion.' He was as far from *diffidence* as presumption. Never pushing himself beyond his post, he was always ready to maintain it. His eye knew not to quail, nor his knee to tremble before mortal man. He asked no one to stand in his place in the hour of trial or of duty. Yet after the sharpest conflict, and most glorious mental conquest, he was ready to wash the feet of the humblest saint. The lark is his emblem, which, after pouring its heavenly strains upon the upper skies, descends to build its nest upon the ground. It may be matter of surprise to some that such a man should be so modest; but the explanation is at hand. He knew that he had nothing but what he had received. When his wondering audience seemed to say, 'He can do all things,' his spirit and manner breathed the addition, 'through Christ strengthening me.' Moreover, he seemed to have a method of hiding and diminishing his own excellences, while he sought out and magnified those of every one else. He was, however, far from every thing mean or low; indeed, there was an exquisite delicacy about all his thoughts, illustrations, and manners.

"2. He was humble. If any man could boast of graces he could. In him they all abounded—faith that works by love, and purifies the heart—hope, the anchor of the soul, sure and steadfast—love that burns with an even, intense flame, consuming all that 'opposeth or exalteth itself against the knowledge of God'—zeal, ardent and uncompromising, bringing body and soul to the altar; and yet he was

'Of boasting more than of a tomb afraid.'

He worked out his salvation '*with fear and trembling;*' he was meek and *lowly* in heart; he inserted the petition 'forgive us *our trespasses*' in all his prayers, and felt that his best actions needed the 'sprinkling of the blood of Jesus.'

"3. He was affable. His natural sweetness of temper, refined by the spirit of Christianity, gave him an unaffected politeness, which rendered every person perfectly easy in his presence. The young approached him as a father, the aged as a friend, and both felt encouraged, by his engaging air, to express their wants or inquiries without reserve. There are some whose affability invites familiarity, and leads to contempt; but he mingled with his urbanity a dignity which imposed respect, and a solemnity which banished levity. In his public addresses he would go before you as a pillar of fire, but in private he would suffer you to lead wherever you desired, taking care to follow you like the smitten rock which followed Israel, to pour blessings at your feet. His mind, like that of Christ, seemed filled with beautiful analogies, by which he could rise from the material to the spiritual, and make an easy path to heaven from any point of earth. He could charm even the worldly heart that would hold communion with him; for although he would direct it outward from its own defiled chambers, and upward to God, he would make the ascent so smooth and green, and would throw so much light and loveliness on all the paths of piety, that his retiring footsteps would call forth the assurance, 'At a more convenient season I will send for thee.'

"When he spent the night with a religious family, he was in the habit of conversing in a religious manner, without seeming to aim at it; and when his host lighted him to his chamber, he would take him by the hand when they were alone, and, alluding to the kindness bestowed upon him, would make his own gratitude an apology for inquiring into the highest welfare of his hospitable friend. He would speak of God's goodness, man's accountability, a parent's influence, a Savior's love, an approaching judgment; and when, with streaming eyes, he bowed down to plead with God for his friend, it would seem as though the heart of stone must melt. Wherever he went he was hailed as a messenger of God; and whenever he departed it seemed as though an angel was taking leave. His name still sheds fragrance from a thousand family altars. It is impossible to describe the estimate in which he is held by those with whom he was frequently called to hold communion in the discharge of official duty. He was the man whom his brethren in the ministry delighted to honor. At the conference, at the quarterly meeting, you might see them gathering around him to hear his counsel, receive his blessing, and present some token of their love. In such seasons he had no reason to envy the crowned or the mitered head. No incense offered to the conquerer of a hundred of earth's battle-fields like the incense offered to him at such periods; but he was not vain, and when he was the object of kind attention his heart was overwhelmed, and he wept as a father in the midst of his children. The stranger who witnessed such a scene could not refrain from saying in his heart, 'Behold how they love him!'

"4. He was cheerful, notwithstanding his habitual seriousness. Bearing in his bosom a load which might make an apostle cry out, 'I have great heaviness and a continual sorrow in my heart,' he, nevertheless, stood aloof from melancholy or despair. The shades of his brow were generally like the flying clouds of a serene day, which, chasing each other, 'now hide and now reveal the sun.' Meridian faith beamed from his countenance even in the storm, and threw the bow of promise over the darkest cloud. He illustrated the paradox, 'As sorrowful, yet always rejoicing.'

"5. He was frank. Perhaps this is the first characteristic which a stranger would notice on being introduced to him. He was far from every thing like reserve, hypocrisy, or concealment. His thoughts, words, and feelings were at ease, his natural language under no restraint, and his lips ready to utter the uppermost thoughts of his soul. Indeed, his countenance seemed so transparent, that you could see his heart as plainly as his features. At the same time, he had none of the impertinence of freedom, nor the indiscretion of openness. He was more ready to confess his own faults, than correct another's. If he opened his heart it was not from conceit, but from natural warmth; and when he poured forth its treasures, it was not that they might flow any where, but only over those fields which thirsted for refreshment. When he saw a friend in danger, he did not hesitate to proffer counsel; but this he did in such a manner as to inspire respect, if not to secure salvation. There was no superciliousness or display of superiority—no aggravation of the offender's faults—no tone of authority in his reproof; but he came upon you with such 'meekness of wisdom,' such a kind estimate of your virtues, such a voice of tenderness, that you could not but bless him, even though he probed you to the quick.

"There is a frank man who is not to be depended on. He will smile upon you, and promise you a favor, and the next moment, if he meet with your enemy, can promise him the same; not that he would be false; he is only changeable. But his inconsistencies often involve his honor, and place his ingenuity upon the rack to rescue it. Bigelow's promises were to be relied on. Of him we might say,

> 'His words are bonds—his oaths are oracles—
> His loves sincere.'

"There is a character that can not be understood—a

perfect mystery. The more you explore it, the more you are confounded. It is a Proteus; you know not whether to love or hate—whether to regard it as foe or friend, saint or devil. One moment you are allured by an excellence, and the next repelled by a blemish. But the greatest of all difficulties is, that it communicates with the world *entirely* by artificial language. You can not trace it; it seems to adopt its motives by stealth, and drag them to its heart as Cacus did the cattle of Hercules to his cave—by the tail instead of the horns; so that if you follow their tracks, you are sure to go the wrong way. It can hardly 'take tea without a stratagem;' and, like the ancient warrior, if it thought its coat could tell what it was about, it would burn it. Its whole business seemed to be to elude the world, which it draws, like a pack of gray-hounds, to its scent. Now, the very reverse of all this was Russel Bigelow.

"I shall never forget the childlike simplicity with which, on one occasion, in conversation about the comparative advantages of extempore and written sermons, he having dropped the remark, 'My happiest efforts,' added, 'O, pardon me for having used that term in speaking of any effort of mine.' A stranger having taken him aside, and presented him with a suit of clothes, which he much needed, he seized his hand, and looking up to him with tearful eyes, said, 'O, doctor, I will pray for you as long as I live!' If about to make a speech, he would tell you so, and perhaps explain to you the ground he was about to take, and the arguments he would employ; so that, if you chose, you might digest a reply before his effort was heard. Had he been in Joseph's place, he, too, would have told his dreams, and looked for his brethren in Shechem or in Dotham.

"6. He was benevolent and beneficent. Like his Master, he was touched with a feeling of human infirmities.

He had learned how to weep with them that weep, and rejoice with them that rejoice. One needed but to see him in the asylum, or the prison, or standing before an object of distress by the road-side, or uttering the sympathies of his broad heart at the pillow of the sick to be convinced, without argument, that there is such a thing as disinterested benevolence.

"His faith did not overlook the present world, in its concerns for the future; and while he struggled, and wept, and prayed for the sinful soul, he did not forget the suffering body. Nor was he content with knowing the sorrows of those who came in his way: 'The cause that he knew not he searched out.' He was emphatically the good Samaritan. His expansive benevolence embraced the whole human family; not that he cherished the wild speculation that all mankind should be regarded alike; but warming his charity at the fireside of his sweet home, he bade it. expand till it overleaped all national boundaries, and natural and artificial distinctions. He was not of those who content themselves with elevated views and warm sympathies, and who *say* to the shivering brother, 'Be thou warmed and clothed.' His beneficence knew no limits but his ability. As he received presents wherever he went—and his brethren, knowing his worth, would not suffer him to be deficient in his allowance—if he had husbanded what he received, he would have accumulated money. But his resources were expended as fast as they were received, and he died poor. Indeed, to those who walk by sight, he did not seem to have a proper regard for the wants of his family; and when he approached the borders of the grave, the sight of his helpless children, whom he was soon to leave fatherless, sometimes induced self-reproaches, connected with a gloomy despondency in view of the future, which, however, were instantly banished by the recollection of some sweet promise of Scripture, and a view of God's tender relation to the fatherless and the widow.

"7. He was liberal in his views. Never compromising or disguising the truth, warmly attached to his own Discipline, and firmly persuaded of his own doctrines, he was, nevertheless, as far from narrowness and bigotry as the east is from the west. He delighted to hail every Church that bore the banner of the Savior, under whatever uniform or name; and to the image of Christ his heart and hand turned as the needle to the pole. He looked with joy upon the prosperity of sister Churches; and notwithstanding he felt a deep interest in the welfare of his own department of Zion, he never could be accused of proselyting: his great aim was to bring honor to Christ, souls to heaven, and glory to God. But although he felt so little concern to attract converts into his Church, the people *would* follow him in flocks, as sheep follow a shepherd.

"8. His character was harmonious. We have heard of many a good man whose home was no paradise. Bigelow was to his family what he was to his congregation. Indeed, his spirit is said to have been, if possible, even more sweet and fragrant at the fireside than in the pulpit; and his prayers at the family altar were as fervent as those which were audible to the multitude. In short, his words and his works, his inner and his outer life, his public and his private character, were alike lovely and accordant.

"'Did you know Bigelow?' said the writer to Chief Justice L. 'Yes,' he replied; 'and it is one of the greatest regrets of my life that I did not know him better. Had I never known him, I should have loved him for the effects of his apostolic labors and holy example. We were a rude people when he was among us, and we never appreciated his worth.' That he had his faults and imperfections, we do not deny; but they were almost lost amid his excellences. Let the poet look out upon the plain or the mountain, the gorgeous sunset or the thundering cataract; but let *me* look upon a good man. The artist may mold matter into forms of enrapturing beauty, and make us feel their elevating and purifying influences; but what is the marble Moses of Michael Angelo, or the cold statue of his living Christ, compared with an embodiment of the Hebrew law and the spirit of Jesus in the sculpture of a holy life? Goethe said that he was not half himself who had never seen the Juno in the Rondanini palace at Rome. Well, then, may we say, that he knows not to what race he belongs who has never gazed upon such a man as Bigelow. If an angel were to move among us in celestial sheen, with what sublimity would he inspire us! But how much more is it to see moral majesty and beauty beaming from human clay!"

CHAPTER XXXV.

HENRY B. BASCOM.

BASCOM was emphatically a western man. Early taken to the head waters of the Alleghany, and reared amid the wild scenery of his forest home, his mind took its hue and coloring from those deep glens and craggy mountains; and the native bent which was given to his genius, from the sublime and picturesque scenes around him, grew with his growth and strengthened with his strength. But though reared in the west, and identified with its numerous interests, and its rapidly-expanding prosperity, he was not contracted in his views. His mind seemed to have been framed upon the same grand scale, in which the Creator had constructed the broad prairies, and mighty rivers, and towering mountains of the west. The whole country, from where Atlantic surges wash the rocky, sterile shores of New England, to where the Pacific's blue waters lave the golden sands of California, was his home, and he embraced the whole in his broad catholic sympathies. With him there was no north, no south, no east, no west; and in this respect his mind had a Websterian cast—massy, boundless in its sympathies and aims; or, like to that of the immortal Clay, whose friend he was during his whole life, he rose above all sectional views, soared beyond all sectional lines, and embraced his entire country in the arms of his benevolence.

As Webster, and Clay, and Calhoun were types of a race of statesmen, which have passed away from the political world, so may we say of a Fisk, Olin, and Bascom, they were types of a race of preachers, which, as the rare products of an age that is passing, may take a century to produce their like again. We would not be sectarian, though we thus confine our comparison to the Methodist Church; and yet, for solid learning, deep piety, and sublime eloquence in the pulpit and on the platform, we know not their superiors in any age that is past, as exhibited in any of the Churches of the land. They may not have excelled in Biblical learning, or devoted piety, or pulpit eloquence, according to the standards of the great master minds of some other Churches, but, according to our judgment, none excelled them in a union of all these.

However pleasant and perhaps profitable it might be to indulge in such a train of thought, and pursue it so as to resolve, as far as possible, the distinguished traits which characterized these great minds into their elements, and thereby form an analysis for the study of the youth of the present day—a model upon which future character might be constructed—we must forego that pleasure, and proceed at once to the subject of our chapter.

There was something very remarkable in the youth of Bascom. Very soon after his conversion, which occurred at a camp meeting on Oil creek, he gave evidence, in the relation of his religious experience and prayers, of a power and eloquence unusual to boys of his age. At one time he went from home to attend a quarterly meeting at Franklin. His singular appearance, with his fox-skin cap and rude backwoods dress, attracted the attention of every one present; but when, at love-feast, on Sabbath morning, he rose and spoke of his conversion and the love of a Savior, every heart was thrilled, and as the rough exterior sparkled with the light and fire of the soul within, the people wondered more at the boy than they had before been surprised at the rusticity of his appearance.

On Monday morning, Mr. William Connelley, who was a merchant in Franklin, took him to his store and gave him a new hat and some other articles to fit up his wardrobe. Mr. C. was subsequently, for several years, a member of the Pennsylvania Legislature, and from some cause or other lost his property and became poor. Traveling in the west, he stopped at Cincinnati, and being destitute of means, among strangers, he called upon Dr. Elliott, in Cincinnati, and asked for the loan of a few dollars to take him home. The Doctor promptly took out his wallet and handed him all he desired, saying, "Take that, brother, and welcome, for giving young Bascom a hat."

Soon after his father removed to the wilds of the west, and settled on the banks of the Ohio, nearly opposite to where the city of Maysville now stands, where he engaged with his family in farming pursuits. Many years afterward, while a professor of moral science at Augusta, he often visited the residence of his father, several miles above, on the Ohio side of the river. Here he has been seen with his coat off, and with mattock in hand, grubbing out the roots and briers of the soil. One season he prepared the soil and tended twelve acres of corn, at the same time attending to all his duties in College.

In the year 1812, at a quarterly conference, held on the Scioto, not far from Portsmouth, in a stone house still standing, he was recommended to the Western conference, to be received into the traveling connection. That recommendation, written and signed by the Rev. Robert W. Finley, is now in the possession of Dr. Elliott, together with numerous other documents of olden time, pertaining to Methodism in the west.

His peculiar talents as a preacher were early developed. He seemed at once to rise to eminence as a pulpit orator. The graces of oratory, which others gain, like Demosthenes, by a severe and tedious process, with him were gifts of nature, and not the product of education. We are strongly inclined to the opinion that the proverb "*poeta nascitur non fit*," applies with equal force to orators, though perhaps not to the same degree. Such was the case, we believe, with Bascom; he was born an orator, and to have cast his genius in any model would have destroyed his power. God makes but few such men. Towering up like Himalaya, or sublimely grand like Niagara, they stand out apart from their species to excite our wonder.

We were forcibly struck with the saying of a grave divine, who had been listening with intense and thrilling interest to Bascom in one of his loftiest moods, and who, on being asked, after the sermon, what he thought of the man, replied, "I did not think of the man at all. My mind was wholly absorbed in the contemplation of the character of the God who created him." Exhibitions of greatness and power in nature invariably send us up to nature's God. We wondered not at the saying of this grave and talented divine. Similar impressions have doubtless been elicited from others. Who that witnesses the tempest careering in majesty and leveling forests in its course, but has his thoughts transferred to the awful Being who "rides upon the whirlwind and directs the storm?" We once kneeled down on the verge of an overhanging cliff, and turned our ear to take in the full thunder of Niagara, as it rolled, a hundred feet below us, its everlasting bass, and such a sense of the majesty and power of God possessed us, as we were never conscious of before. We rose from our knees and shouted, "God!"

Father Taylor, of Boston, himself a child of nature, and boiling over with native eloquence and wit, was once listening to Bascom, as he was delivering one of his series of lectures on Infidelity, in Green-Street Church, New York. The old man eloquent stood by one of the pillars that support the gallery, and not far from the pulpit. As the lecturer proceeded, Father Taylor became more and more interested, and he was seen, unconsciously, to begin to raise his cane, elevating it gradually, as though he was indicating the orator's progress. There he stood, like a statue slightly inclined, drinking in every word till he heard the last, when, with his cane finally extended at arm's length above his head, he exclaimed, "Grand!"

Blessed with extraordinary powers, and a brilliant native genius, all that he needed was an appropriate direction, and a cultivation correspondent thereto; and we most firmly believe that, in the order of Providence, he was thrown into the very sphere of life where he was fitted to move, with as much adaptation, in regard to his nature, as the planets are adapted to their appointed spheres. Had his genius been cramped by the laws of the schools, which are often about as useful in making an orator as a note-book would be to a nightingale, or as the laws of motion and sound would be to the dash and roar of Niagara, the thunder of whose anthem is the voice of nature, we might have had, and doubtless would have had, a Bascom polished with all the arts of elocution; but, like the nicely-adjusted and exquisitely-wrought automaton, there would have been a stiffness in his movements; and although the precision which should mark them would indicate the wonderful power of art, still we should have had nothing but the mimic artificial man.

Nature is the fountain from whence the orator must draw his inspiration, and the field whereon he must develop his powers. As the eagle, who soars away from the homes and the haunts of man, to bathe his undazzled eye in the sunbeam, and pillow his breast upon the storm, so the child of genius must become familiar with Nature in all her aspects. One of the most eloquent divines, of the same school of theology to which Bascom belonged, discourses thus on this subject: "The orator must be much at home, that is, he must study himself; his own nature, and powers, and states of mind; and he must be much abroad, that is, he must go out and study Nature in all her moods." It is said of Cole, the great artist, that he studied Nature instead of the great masters, and the result was, that he excelled all the artists of his day, in transferring natural scenery to the canvas. His "Garden of Eden," and "Voyage of Life," two of the greatest productions of his pencil, were conceived from nature. As all the lines of Nature are lines of beauty, so are all her movements, and he who would be truly effective and graceful as an orator, must follow no other copy. Bascom has been heard to say, in reference to the composition of his sermons, that a room was so contracted it had an influence upon his thoughts, and he could only think freely and grandly when out in the midst of nature, beneath her boundless skies and extended landscapes. It is said that an Indian mound, in Kentucky, is pointed out to the traveler as the spot whereon he composed some of his greatest sermons.

It is seldom we see the blessings of poverty, and yet we believe that the very curse pronounced on man in Eden, has been attended with the greatest blessings, and has wrought out the most incalculable good to man. Bascom's father was poor, and in addition to this he had a large family to maintain by the sweat of his face. Had he been rich, the probability is that young Henry would have been sent to college, and then the idea of his being an itinerant preacher would have never been conceived. Having received but a limited education, at the early age of sixteen he entered the itinerancy as a freshman, in one of nature's colleges, in western Virginia.

The records of the Church show us, that he was

received into the ranks of the itinerancy in the year 1814, and went through his preparatory course in the wilds of Ohio, as the colleague of the Rev. Alexander Cummins; and after having completed his academical curriculum, he was sent out alone, the following year, to the wilder regions of western Virginia, to travel the Guyandotte circuit. We have already spoken of the grand and gloomy scenery embraced in this extensive circuit. Here he was subjected to all sorts of privation, toils, and hardship, but he endured all as a good soldier; and it was here, ascending the towering hights, or urging his way through the deep mountain gorges, or plunging into the rapid rivers and breasting their swelling tides, that his character as a preacher was developed. Frequently did he have to travel forty miles a day, through the unbroken solitudes of the wilderness, without rest, without food, and at night, in some lone cabin, would he pour out his full heart, in strains of Gospel eloquence, upon the rude and simple-hearted backwoods hunters, collected from different and distant points to hear him. On one of his solitary journeys he was followed for several miles by a large panther, which threatened at every moment to spring upon him, and from which he was only rescued by reaching, at nightfall, the cabin of a settler. Here, when he had a few hours for rest, would he retire to the woods as his study, and amid the rocks and grand old trees, all standing as nature made them, untouched by the hand of man, he would prepare his sermons. This he would do by walking back and forth, forming his plans, selecting his words, constructing his sentences, and uttering them; which being done, he would lay them up in the capacious storehouse of his memory, to be brought therefrom at his bidding, with all the rapidity of thought. We believe that this custom, adopted from necessity in the woods—for in a region infested with rattlesnakes and panthers, it would not be safe to sit or recline—he transferred to the parlor and the garden, in towns and cities.

At one time he ventured to recline, with his Bible, beneath the towering, outspreading branches of an oak, at one of his distant appointments, near the head waters of Elk river. He possessed, to a great degree, the power of abstraction, and it was not long till his soul was intently engaged in taking full draughts from the fountain of inspiration. In the midst of his spirit reverie he was aroused by the cry of a hunter, in tremulous tones, telling him, at the peril of his life, to lie still till he fired. Quickly glancing his eye in the direction from whence the voice came, he saw his friend, with his rifle elevated, and pointing toward the branches of the tree under which he was lying. Familiar as he was with backwoods life, Bascom saw that some terrible danger was hovering over him, and without the least perceptible motion of his body, he turned his gaze upward, when he saw on the branch of the tree, just over him, and not more than twenty feet distant, a huge panther, drawn up and just ready for a spring. It was a fearful, awful moment. The least motion on his part would have been the signal for a spring, and his fate would have been sealed forever. In that awful moment, when death seemed inevitable, with a self-control and a courage truly wonderful, he continued perfectly quiet, till the keen crack of the rifle was heard, and the ferocious beast, pierced by the unerring aim of the backwoods hunter, fell lifeless by his side.

At another time, while traveling this same circuit, he stopped, on his way to an appointment, at a log-cabin, recently erected by the road-side. Stopping for rest and refreshment, not long after dinner was ready, and he sat down with the family to dine. A lovely little child, about three years of age, which had attracted his attention by its innocent mirth and its gentleness, was playing before the door, while the family were engaged around the homely repast, when suddenly a heart-piercing cry was heard.

"My child! my child!" screamed the mother, and quick as thought all rushed to the door.

Father of mercies! what a sight was presented to that fond mother! A terrible panther had sprung upon that unconscious child, and was ascending a tree with it in his mouth.

"The gun! the gun! quick, for God's sake, the gun!" franticly exclaimed the father.

But Bascom had seized it from the rack, and was already in quick pursuit. He fired, and the ball pierced the panther, and brought him to the ground with its victim; but, alas! life had fled. Thus, amid such wild scenes and daring adventures, the first years of our young itinerant's life were passed.

When the fame of the eloquent young preacher first reached our ears, we were traveling on the West Wheeling circuit, in another part of the conference. Though rumor spoke, with glowing tongue, of his matchless and enchanting power in the pulpit, and we were prepared, as we often have been before, by such exaggerated descriptions, to be disappointed when we should have the opportunity of hearing him, yet, when that time came, which it did at conference, where he was literally surrounded with a battery of critics' eyes, in the persons of preachers, we were ready to say, after a long-drawn breath, when he had ended a most intensely-thrilling discourse, in the language of the Queen of Sheba, on her visit to Solomon, "The half had not been told us." Those who never heard him till after his soul had been caged in the cramped and narrow cell of scholastic study, and shorn of its freshness, strength, and power, by inhaling the atmosphere of a pent-up city life, can have but a faint conception of what he was, when he communed with nature and nature's God, and breathed the pure air of the mountain, in the bright and palmy days of his itinerant life. In the expressive language of one who was intimately acquainted with him, "Those who heard him then will never forget the feelings that he produced. The deep, thrilling tones of a voice then unimpaired by hardship and overexertion, now melting into the soft, melodious accents of love, and now bursting forth in thundering denunciations of the world's ungodliness, never failed to stamp upon the hearts of his hearers impressions lasting as life itself. At one moment his audience, moved by the charming pictures of his pencil, would be all radiant with smiles; at another, the pathetic, touching, and heart-moving scenes, which he would describe, would force tears of sympathy down the cheeks of the most obdurate; and then, in an instant, by the magic of his burning eloquence, he would make the whole congregation tremble, so wondrous, so real, so terrible was his Rembrandt-sketch of the doom of the impenitent. He controlled his audience at will. Perfectly familiar with all the motives of the human mind, and all the impulses of the heart, he could cause his hearers to smile with joy, or weep with penitence, or tremble with remorse, at pleasure. No man possessed a more fruitful imagination. His descriptions fairly glittered with poetic gems. Touched by his master hand, every picture of life assumed the charm and glow of beauty, or glared with the most hideous deformity, just as it suited his purpose. I well remember a discourse on the vanities of life, delivered by him some years ago; and never did all the charms and attractions of this world appear so little and so worthless to me as on that occasion. His description of the dalliances of the world, the siren whisperings of Ambition, and the luring charms of Pleasure, surpassed in beauty and power any thing I remember to have heard from the lips of man. His power as an orator was, no doubt, greatly aided by his fine person, his open, manly, honest expression of countenance, and his keen, piercing black eye. That eye none could describe. A venerable citizen, who knew him well, has often told me that, while Dr. Bascom was preaching, he could never 'unfix' his gaze from that earnest, soul-penetrating eye. 'Why,' said he, 'whenever he was denouncing any mean passion, or secret, ungodly propensity, his dark, keen eye seemed to look right through me, and say to my self-condemned spirit, '"Thou art the man."'"

He possessed that indescribable power, that magnetic charm, if we may so term it, with which all true orators are gifted, and which never fails to move the souls of men. What he described was real, and men saw it and felt it as a thing of life. A deep, earnest soul, and resolute and brave, was Henry B. Bascom. We will relate an incident as illustrative of his character, which occurred when he was connected with Augusta College. He had crossed the river to attend a meeting. During his discourse in the evening, he took occasion to come down with terrific, scathing denunciation upon the profane swearer. It is said that whatever citadel of vice or infidelity he attacked, so direct and powerful was his artillery, that he left nothing but the smoldering ruins. It being necessary for him to recross the river that night, it was agreed by a number of rough boatmen, who were writhing under his sermon, that they would ferry him over and retaliate upon him for his severity. Bascom entered the skiff, and they started from the shore. They had not proceeded far till they commenced a concert of oaths, horrid enough to make the cheek of darkness itself turn pale. There sat the preacher, wrapped up in his cloak, in the stern of the boat, apparently unconscious of what was transpiring. They became enraged at his stoicism, and raved and cursed like fiends from perdition, who had graduated in the dialect of the damned. When they were nearing the Kentucky shore, one of them asked him if he was not a preacher. To this he responded in the affirmative.

"Why, then," said he, "don't you reprove us for our swearing?"

"You may swear till you break your necks, for aught that I care," replied Bascom, fully conscious of their design to abuse and insult him.

One, who in later years heard Bascom, said of him as a preacher, "His delivery, naturally most eloquent, was injured, strangely as the assertion may sound, by being made to conform exactly to the matter delivered. It was his writing, in other words, that marred his delivery. Had he always spoken without writing, and formed the habit of easy, correct, extempore elocution, he would have been almost any thing that eloquence could have demanded." Had this friend known him in his early days, and been permitted to have heard him, he never would have spoken thus, because Bascom had formed the very "habit" of which he speaks, and had attained the high position for eloquence which such a habit secured. This criticism serves as an illustration of what we have already said; namely, that the systems of the schools, which, unfortunately, controlled him in after life, was what, to a great extent, destroyed his power as an orator. It was, in truth, "writing that marred his speaking;" but, notwithstanding all these disabilities, we aver that he had no superior in the world. Other speakers may have excelled in the beautiful, or the pathetic, or the fanciful, but for sublimity and grandeur, either as it regarded matter or manner, we confidently believe he was without a rival. We have heard him when it was painful to listen; when the souls of his vast auditory, wrought up to the highest intensity by his awfully-sublime descriptions, seemed ready to burst with emotion. Nor yet was he wanting in the beautiful. We have been borne away by his eloquence, as on beds of violets, to soft elysian bowers, and have almost breathed the air and heard the songs of heaven. But we have a word more in regard to the knowledge and eloquence which is to be derived from the study of nature. In this age, when books and colleges are flooding the land, it would be well for us to call ourselves back a little to the study of nature, where we find

"Books in the running brooks,
Sermons in stones."

An eloquent divine, at the head of one of our colleges, says, "How much better this unwritten knowledge than all written: it is unerring, adapted to each case. It was an experiment of modern times to restore a sick body by transfusing the blood of a healthy one into its veins; but it was unsuccessful, because the transfused current was not in a proper relation to the vessels which received it: it irritated and bloated the sinking system. Too much of our learning is of this kind—a transfusion of thought into channels unadapted to it, which only vitiates and puffs them up. The sick soul, like the sick body, must restore itself; its vital organs must be aroused to vigorous action before its streams can be enriched and purified.

"We in this land should be the *last* to complain of barrenness of mind; for the new world is around us. Alas! alas! we are thrashing over and over again the old world's dry straw instead of thrusting the sickle into the new world's green and waving harvest. These cloud-capt hills are strewn all over with legends ready to be bound into the bundles of Homeric odes and epics. These venerable woods stand thick with God's own thoughts; they leap by us in every deer that crosses our path, and fall upon us in every descending leaf. New forms of human love, and sympathy, and sin, and suffering, look out from those cabin windows and burning brush-heaps, from yonder cane-brakes and the far-off wigwams. We have book-teachers enough. O for more bookless ones!"

We have absolutely been sickened at the stereotype process by which preachers have been made in our colleges. They are the merest casts from some model teacher, and every thing about them is an imitation; their very tone of voice and manner of delivery, to the pointing of a finger, or the shake of the head, and even the alamode of their dress and walk are all the most servile imitation. Nature is smothered to death, and buried beyond the hope of a resurrection. And yet we would not eschew books nor colleges. God forbid! We want them all, but we want natural men, whose flash and thunder in the pulpit come from the Bible and the great battery of nature. Though Bascom, in later years, had lost, to some considerable extent, the power of

> "Sending his soul with every lance he threw,"

yet he never lost the power to charm, and he never preached to an audience but that

> " Their listening powers
> Were awed, and every thought in silence hung,
> In wondering expectation."

What Grattan said of the Irish orator, may with equal appropriateness be said of Bascom: "When young, his eloquence was ocean in a storm; when old, it was ocean in a calm; but whether calm or storm, the same great element, the sublimest and most magnificent phenomenon in creation."

But there were other traits of character, concerning which we must be permitted to allude in our sketch. Stern and sedate, as one might think, wrapped up in the solitude of his own thoughts and feelings, he possessed a heart filled with the kindliest sympathies. He was quite as ready to

"Feel another's woe,"

and to hide another's faults, as many who have considered him selfish and indifferent. It is not always those who have the most feeling that give evidence of it in their manner. Some hearts are like fountains on the surface, always seen—open to the gaze of all—others are like fountains hidden among the rocks, yet clear, transparent, full, and free. A frown may sometimes be on the brow, and the tearless eye indicate no feeling, when the heart is ready to break with tenderness; and then, again, we have seen smiles spread over the countenance, when stormy passions raged within. God looks at the heart, and we are to judge no man from appearance. Indeed, one of Bascom's faults, if it were a fault, was almost invariably to take the part of the oppressed, or to choose the weaker side of almost any question, without duly weighing the merits thereof. His error, however, in this respect, was pardonable. To pursue a man to "the bitter end," because of a difference of opinion, and, with bigotry and prejudice, question his motives and condemn his actions, was never the character of Bascom. He was above it, as far as the towering Alps, which bathes its pure summit in the light of heaven, is above the clouds and mists that creep along its sides and encircle its base, and we pity the man who could pursue so noble a spirit, or breathe an unworthy suspicion over his memory.

But he was independent; and we hesitate not to say, that, had it not been for his rare and commanding talents, he never would have been regarded, by the majority of the Church, as sufficiently safe to have been intrusted with any prominent ecclesiastical position. Never was man, from the very commencement of his ministerial career, through all its periods, down to the very close almost of his eventful life, more stoutly, bitterly, pertinaciously opposed, than was Bascom. Providence itself seemed to frown upon him, as he struggled with the hardest fortune all through life. But why was this? We have thought his mighty spirit required such severe discipline to school it for heaven. Like Schiller, he literally passed through storm, and tempest, and fire, to heaven, and yet, like Elijah and Daniel, he went unscathed. He rose, however, despite of all opposing obstacles, to the highest summit of human greatness, and to the occupancy of the most distinguished posts of honor and trust in the gift of that branch of the Church to which he belonged. From a President of Madison College, and Professor, in Augusta, he was promoted to the Presidency of Transylvania University. When the literary department of that institution ceased, he was elected editor of the Southern Quarterly Review, and finally a bishop of the Methodist Episcopal Church South, which distinguished office he held when he died.

Much might be said of this great man in Israel, who has been taken from our midst. We are sorry we could not do the subject more justice. Had it not been that our sketches of western preachers would have been incomplete without a notice of one who grew up in our midst, and filled the country with his fame, we would not have undertaken it. What we have written is almost entirely from personal recollection, not having a single scrap of material within our reach. We are aware that his life has been written and published, but, with all our efforts, we have not been able to procure a copy; and we had delayed writing this sketch till this late hour in the composition of our book, hoping to have some data from which to draw, to enable us to give a more satisfactory outline of the life and character of that wonderful man, but we have been disappointed. We hope our readers will regard it as a slight tribute to the memory of one whom we regarded as the greatest of American pulpit orators.

He is gone. Our Bascom is no more. The light that shone, kindled from God's altar, in that intellect, which was clear as an angel's, has not gone out; it has only ceased to shed its radiance and glory upon the earthly sphere. In yonder heaven, undimmed, it shines forever.

CHAPTER XXXVI.

SAMUEL HAMILTON.

In apostolic times there was among the ministers of Jesus a Paul, an Apollos, and a Cephas, all possessing striking characteristics, that in the wide range, under the diversities of gifts communicated, the Church might be supplied with a ministry adapted to all its peculiarities. This variety, in the order of Providence, has been kept up in the Church to the present day. The keen, logical mind of a Paul, the fervid eloquence of an Apollas, the intrepid boldness and zeal of a Peter, and the mild, persuasive, simple eloquence of a John, all have their representatives in ministers of the present day. Such a variety in mental constitution, physical temperament, disposition, and education is admirably adapted to the itinerant system of the Methodist Church, because the variety of talent is diffused over the Church, and there can be no monopoly of any peculiar gifts, grace, or usefulness, as exhibited in the ministry, by any one particular congregation. We have often thought there was as much difference in the mental as in the physical constitution and conformation of our race, and that every man possessed an individual character peculiar to himself, and as distinguishable from the rest of his species as his features differed from all others; and that it would be as impossible to find two minds exactly alike in every respect as it would be to find two faces exactly corresponding in features.

As it regarded the toils, and hardships, and privations

of the early preachers of the west, there was a wonderful identity. There was then no post of ease and honor tc be occupied by a Methodist preacher—no presidencies and professorships of colleges, no editorships or agencies, no splendid stations with large salaries, no easy circuits with only Sabbath appointments, to be reached on turnpikes and railroads—no, there were none of these things; and yet the ministers of those days went to their work, and continued in it as cheerfully as the ministers of the present day fill the various appointments assigned them. But while among the early preachers there was an identity in regard both to the kind and quantity of labor in which they were engaged, there was, nevertheless, as great a diversity of talent as is found among them at the present day. We will not particularize, lest we should be considered presumptuous, or, perhaps, invidious in our comparisons; but whoever reads our biographical sketches, will be able to discover diversities of temperament, talents, and character as great as ever characterized the ministers of the Gospel in any period of the Church's history.

Samuel Hamilton belonged to a class distinctly marked. His position among the itinerant ranks the reader will be able to fix after he shall have read our sketch. He was the youngest son of William Hamilton, who emigrated from Western Virginia, in 1806, and settled in the wilds of Muskingum. Having purchased his land, and made every preparation for settling upon it, he called all the members of his household together, and, like Abram in Mamre, erected an altar, and consecrated his family and possessions all to God. This patriarch, with his devoted and pious wife, having given themselves and children to God in an everlasting covenant, were encouraged, by God's promise, to expect that the children of their faith, and prayer, and godly example, would soon give evidence of the work of grace upon their hearts. At the removal of his father to Ohio, Samuel was in the fifteenth year of his age. His mind was early impressed with the importance of religion, and his tears and prayers gave evidence that the world and its pleasures could not fill the aching void in his aspiring soul. In the year 1812, when he was in the twenty-first year of his age, he attended a camp meeting, held on the lands of Joseph Thrap, in the bounds of Knox circuit, where he was powerfully awakened under the ministration of God's word. It was impossible for him to suppress the deep and overwhelming convictions of his soul, and in agony he cried aloud for mercy. For days and nights, in a distress bordering upon despair, he sought for pardon. We had witnessed his anguish, and the unavailing cries of his heart for mercy, and all the sympathies of our nature were deeply aroused in his behalf. We took him to the woods, and there, in the solitude and deep silence of the night, with the curtains of darkness around us, we fell prostrate before God in prayer. We arose upon our knees, and embraced him in our arms, while, with streaming eyes and faltering voice, he exclaimed, "O Lord, I do believe! Help thou mine unbelief!" Then, in a moment, quick as thought conveyed by lightning, the blessing of pardon came down, and heaven filled his soul. Instantly he sprang to his feet, and, like the man in the "beautiful porch," he "leaped, and shouted, and praised God" for the delivering grace he had obtained in that distressful hour.

At this time we were traveling the circuit on which his father lived, and we had the pleasure of aiding the young convert in taking up his cross. He was zealous, determined, and active, and the Church and world alike saw that God had a work for him to do. He exercised his gifts in exhortation, and sinners were awakened and converted through his instrumentality. In the year 1814, at the conference held in Cincinnati, he was admitted on trial as a traveling preacher. His first field of labor was the Kanawha circuit. The circuits in Western Virginia at that time were called the Colleges of the Methodist Church, where the young preachers were sent to get their theological education, or, in other words, take their theological course. Sometimes they were called "Brush Colleges;" at other times, the fields where the conference broke its young preachers. Some of the most prominent of our western preachers took their first lessons in the itinerancy upon this field. Here, amid the dense forests and flowing streams, the logical and metaphysical Shinn pored over his books, on horseback, as he traveled to distant appointments; and here, among the craggy mountains and deep glens, the eloquent Bascom caught his sublimest inspirations. In this wild region the preachers had to encounter much toil and hardship; and while they lived on the simple fare of the country, consisting of hominy, potatoes, and "mountain groceries," they were not afflicted with those fashionable complaints denominated dyspepsia and bronchitis. As a specimen of the trials of Methodist preachers, we will relate an incident that occured in the year 1836. One of the preachers of the Ohio conference, having reached his circuit, and finding no house for his family, built for himself a shanty out of slabs, on the bank of the Gaulley river. Having furnished his wife with provisions for a month—that being the time required to perform his round—consisting of some corn-meal and potatoes, he started out upon his circuit. To reach his appointments, which were sometimes thirty miles distant, it was necessary for him to take an early start. One morning, after he had progressed about half round his circuit, he started for an appointment which lay on the other side of one of the Gaulley mountains. It had rained through the night, and having frozen, the earth was covered with a sheet of ice. The travel was difficult even on level ground, so slippery was the surface; and unless it should thaw, the itinerant felt an apprehension that it would be difficult to ascend the steep sides of the mountain. Instead of thawing, however, the weather grew colder; but there was no retreat. His appointment was before him, and the mountain must be crossed. At length, after passing for some distance through a narrow valley, he came to the point where his narrow path led up the ascent. It was steep and difficult, and his horse would frequently slip as he urged him on. On the right the mountain towered far above, and on the left, far down, were deep and frightful precipices; a single misstep, and horse and rider would be dashed to pieces on the rocks below. After ascending about two-thirds of the elevation, he came to a place in his mountain path steeper than any he had passed over. Urging his tired but spirited steed, he sought to ascend; but the horse slipped. Seeing his danger, the preacher threw himself off on the upper side, and the noble animal went over the precipice, bounding from rock to rock, deep down into the chasm below. The preacher retraced his steps, and on coming round to the point where his horse had fallen, he found him dead. Taking off the saddle, bridle, and saddle-bags, he lashed them to his back, and resumed his journey, reaching his appointment in time to preach. The balance of the round was performed on foot, and at the expiration of four weeks from the time of starting, he joined his companion in her cabin, on the bank of the river, thankful for the providence which had returned him safely home.

Here young Hamilton studied theology and human nature, in both of which he became well versed. His preaching talents were peculiar, and often did he make his discourses sparkle with wit and eloquence. Sometimes he would indulge in a rich vein of humor, which, without letting down the dignity of the pulpit, would send a thrill of delight among his audience. No one enjoyed a little pleasantry more than himself; and having a peculiar horror for any thing like a sour godliness, he may, at times, have gone a little too far over to the other extreme. He had a quick perception of the ridiculous, and was not very well able to command himself even in the pulpit when any thing occurred to excite that sense in his mind. We recollect of his telling us of an occasion of this kind, which occurred at a meeting on the waters of the Little Kanawha. At a certain appointment there lived a Colonel ———, whose family were members of the Church, and who had a respect for religion, though he was too fond of the world to make a profession thereof. He was regular in his attendance, and on the occasion to which we have alluded, he was in his seat, attended by a neighbor of his, who was respectable enough, with the exception that at times he would lose his balance under the influence of intoxicating liquor. He had taken on this occasion just enough to make him loquacious without being boisterous. Hamilton, after singing and prayer, arose and gave out for his text the first Psalm, which reads as follows: "Blessed is the man that walketh not in the counsel of the ungodly, nor standeth in the way of sinners, nor sitteth in the seat of the scorner," etc. He entered upon the discussion of his subject by showing what was to be understood by walking in the counsel of the ungodly; and as he entered upon the description of the ungodly, and their various wicked ways and bad examples, he saw the friend of the Colonel punch him in the ribs with his elbow, and overheard him say, "Colonel, he means you." "Be still," said the Colonel, "you will disturb the congregation." It was as much as the preacher could do to control his risibles; but he progressed with his subject; and as he described another characteristic of the ungodly in standing in the way of sinners, the force of the application was too strong to be resisted, and the Colonel's friend, drawing up closely, elbowed him again, saying, "He certainly means you, Colonel." "Be quiet, the preacher will see you," whispered the annoyed man, while he removed as far from him as he could to the other end of the seat. The preacher had arrived at the third characteristic of the ungodly; and as he, in earnest strains, described the scorner's seat, the Colonel's friend turned and nodded his head at him most significantly, adding, in an under tone, "It's you, it's you, Colonel; you know it's you." By this time the most of the congregation were aware of what was going on, and cast significant smiles and glances at one another. Those who understood the features of the speaker could easily discover that he was moving along under a heavy press of feeling, and unless something should occur to break the excitement, he must yield to the impulses of his nature. Just at this crisis a little black dog ran up the aisle, and, stopping directly in front of the pulpit, looked up in the preacher's face, and commenced barking. The scene was ludicrous enough; but how was it hightened when the Colonel's friend rose from his seat, and deliberately marching up the aisle, he seized the dog by his neck and back, and began to shake him, exclaiming, "Tree the preacher, will you? tree the preacher, will you?" Thus he kept shaking and repeating what we have written, till he arrived at the door, when, amid the yells of the dog and the general tittering of the audience, he threw him as far as he could into the yard. This was too much for Hamilton, and he sat down in the pulpit, overcome with laughter. It would have been impossible for him to have resumed his subject, or even to have dismissed the congregation. Suffice it to say, that preaching was done for that day; and ever after, when the Colonel went to Church, he was careful that his friend was not by his side.

Samuel Hamilton was well instructed in the doctrines and discipline, and peculiarities of Methodism, and wherever he went his labors were appreciated, and souls were blest. His next field of labor was Barnesville circuit; and having completed his year of service on that field, he was sent successively to Steubenville and Marietta. While on the Marietta district, subsequent to this date, he furnished for the Methodist Magazine a sketch of Methodism in Washington county, which, while it will give the reader a specimen of his style as a writer, will also furnish a faithful history of the first settlement in Ohio, and the rise and progress of Methodism. In his preface to this sketch he says, "If such historical facts have not buoyancy enough to sustain them in this age, let them be joined to others more buoyant, and they will float down the stream of time, and be taken up by the historian of coming years as a valuable prize." That his facts possess buoyancy enough to float down the stream of time, we leave the reader to judge.

"The county of Washington was the first organized county in the North-Western territory. The town of Marietta, the seat of justice, is situated at the junction of the Muskingum and Ohio rivers, in latitude thirty-nine degrees, twenty-eight minutes, and forty-two seconds north, and in longitude four degrees, twenty minutes west of the city of Washington.

"In 1787 a company organized themselves in Boston, and took the name of 'The Ohio Company.' The principal part of this company were officers and soldiers in the Revolutionary war; men who had spent their time, strength, and property in giving birth to our nation, and who had but little at the end of that great national struggle, excepting the final settlement-notes given them by the Government, as a remuneration for their services. Those brave fathers of our nation, being unsupported by pensions, found it difficult to submit to the heavy hand of poverty in a country full of wealth; they, therefore, exchanged with the General Government their final settlement-notes for a million and a half acres of wild land in Ohio. One hundred thousand acres of this land were given to actual settlers—one hundred acres each. One thirty-sixth was given for the support of common schools, and as much more for the support of the Gospel. Two townships—or 46,080 acres—were given for the support of a state seminary. All this was done to invite emigrants, and for the good of posterity.

"On the 7th of April, 1788, forty-seven men landed on the spot where the town of Mariet a now stands. No traces of human beings were to be seen, excepting the marks of the ax-man who followed the surveyor, the recently-deserted wigwam of the modern Indian, and the mounds, covered ways, and fortifications of a people 'unknown to song.' Immured in an immense wilderness, this band of brothers were permitted to taste the sweets of solitude for a season; but the temperate climate, fertile soil, and flattering prospects of the country, soon induced others to follow them. Thus their number increased, and their prospects brightened, till 1790. It was then found that the country could muster four hundred and forty-seven men, one hundred and three of whom had families. But as their prosperous sun was rising to its meridian splendor, in a fatal hour it was obscured behind a dark and portentous cloud; nor did it again appear with its wonted brightness for four years.

"In 1791 the Indians became hostile, and their hostilities continued for four years. Considering the exposed situation of the whites, their means of defense, and the disparity of their numbers, it is utterly astonishing how they sustained the shock so long. Had it not been for the undaunted courage, unbending fortitude, and profound skill of those veterans, who had been educated in the school of danger, they must have fallen victims to the relentless fury of their savage enemy. It was their business to defend themselves. This they did so effectually that they lost but thirty in all—twenty-three killed, and seven taken prisoners. In 1795 they hailed with delight the return of peace, left their fortifications, and returned to their farms.

"The first settlers were principally *Predestinarians*, subdivided into Presbyterians, Congregationalists, and a few regular Baptists. Soon after the first company landed, a Church was organized in Marietta, and Doctor Story became the officiating minister in the congregation. From this time a form of godliness was kept up by them; how much of the power they possessed we are not prepared to say. The united testimony, however, of the people who lived in those days, and saw things as they were, leads us to conclude that vital piety was at a low ebb. Professors appear to have met the *world's people* on middle ground, offered up a peace-offering, and engaged with them in all the amusements and pastimes of the age. So great was the amalgamation of light and darkness, that an angel's eye might have failed to draw the line of demarkation between the man of the world and the member of the Church. In this condition Methodism found the great mass of the people in Washington county—in their own estimation rich, and increased with goods, and having need of nothing, and knowing not that they were wretched, and miserable, and poor, and blind, and naked.

"Reece Wolf—a local preacher—in a letter to me,

writes thus: 'In April, 1798, I settled on the little Kanawha, Wood county, Virginia. At that time Methodism was unknown in this country. As soon as I came I commenced preaching, and the next fall and winter a revival took place. I made up a class of twenty-one members, and soon found I had more work to do than I well could perform. I cried to the Lord for help; I wrote a letter to Bishop Asbury, and another to the Baltimore conference, to be held in Stone Chapel, near Baltimore, the next spring. In June following I had the best kind of evidence that God and the Church had heard my Macedonian cry. Brother Robert Manley was sent on to our help, and the little flock I had gathered submitted to the government of the Methodist Episcopal Church.'

"June 1st, 1799, Mr. Manley took charge of the infant Church in Wood county, Virginia. He appears to have spent nineteen days in that part of the country, where he found five or six preaching-places. These limits were quite too small for a man whose heart burned with zeal for the glory of God and the salvation of men, and who had received a commission from the great Head of the Church to preach the Gospel to every creature. He, therefore, cast an anxious eye across the Ohio river, where he saw a vast territory on which a Methodist preacher had never set his foot, and in which many families were *indeed* destitute of the bread of life. He beheld their souls in ruin, and hasted to give them relief, by setting before them the grace of our Lord Jesus Christ. On the 20th he crossed the Ohio, and came into Marietta; but found no rest for the sole of his foot—no Laban to say to the servant in pursuit of a spouse for his Master, 'Come in, thou blessed of the Lord;' for an itinerant Methodist preacher, Methodist doctrines, and Methodist economy, were to this people as strange and unlooked for as Columbus's ship and party were to the natives of our land. It was not his object to pull down others, but to feed the destitute with the bread of life; he, therefore, left the town, and directed his attention to the more destitute but less jealous people of the country, hoping to find some noble Bereans, who would test him and his doctrines by the infallible standard of truth. In his first tour he visited each settlement in the county—found a Presbyterian, a Congregational, and a Baptist minister; but many new and small, but growing neighborhoods, were totally destitute of all sanctuary opportunities. In the most of those settlements he found open doors for his reception. He also found Solomon Goss, and two members of his family, who had experienced the blessed effects of Methodism in their own hearts. This family, when on their way from the east to Ohio, stopped a season in West Liberty, where they were awakened and converted to God by the instrumentality of T. Fleming. If others opened their doors through vain curiosity, to hear what the babbler could say, this family opened theirs from the noblest and best feelings of their hearts. As their attachments to the Church were early in their beginning, so they have been deep and constant to the present time.

"This was an eventful year; for in it the public mind became deeply and correctly impressed with the beauty and importance of a plan perfectly adapted to the wants of a new and thinly-populated country. The way was opened, a number of small classes were formed, and a circuit was organized in Ohio; and much good seed was sown that ripened into maturity in after years. The next year Jesse Stoneman and James Quinn were sent on to take charge of these little flocks in the wilderness. Thus a regular succession of ministers has been kept up for thirty years, each watering in his turn the seed sown by the other; during which time the ranks of the wicked one have been greatly thinned, and the regions of glory peopled with many immortal souls.

"A number of years now passed with good success in the country. The classes which had been formed flourished in the principal part of the neighborhoods. Many had experienced 'the washing of regeneration, and the renewing of the Holy Ghost,' and loved the Church with great tenderness. But in town every effort appeared to be weak and unsuccessful. In 1804 the undaunted and deeply-pious George Askins made a bold push, and appointed a camp meeting in town, on a spot of public land. The members from the country erected a stand, fixed their seats, and pitched their tents; the people of the town attended, looked shy, and stood at a distance. And while the bending heavens broke in blessings on the former, there were no mighty works done among the latter, because of unbelief. The preachers broke up the meeting with mingled emotions, cast down and disappointed for the town, but grateful to God for what he had done for the country. All agreed to pray for the outpouring of the Spirit of God on Marietta. The next year Jacob Young and G. C. Light appointed a second meeting on the same ground. The congregation met as before. Great seriousness pervaded the whole assembly, and the sons of Levi were anointed afresh to explain to and enforce upon the people the nature and necessity of salvation. Many saw its importance, and felt that without it life is a maze of error and wickedness, death a gulf of horror and misery, and eternity a scene of indignation and wrath. The grace which accompanied the ministration of the word wrote the law of God upon many hearts, both in town and country. Of those in town, Jonas Johnson was the most prominent. This man had been a disciple of Thomas Paine. He was a most charming singer, and had a great redundance of wicked songs.

In this way he exerted an influence over, and led men who possessed intellects far superior to his own. When Johnson returned to the Shepherd and Bishop of his soul, he did it with all his heart, and in a short time came out in religion as bright as the noonday sun. In a few days he committed his infidel books and obscene songs to the flames; supplied their places with the Holy Bible and a Methodist Hymn-book; and, like Obed Edom opened his house to receive the ark of the Lord. *Hallowed house of grateful memory!* In a short time a lovely little class was raised up to worship God in spirit and in truth. For months and years together this class seldom ever met to worship without being assaulted by a lawless mob, who stoned the house, broke the windows, fired squibs, and covered the chimney, in order to annoy the worshipers with smoke, and drive them from the house of God. In this way a number of years passed. Some of the members let patience have its perfect work; but others were in danger of fainting. About this time God, in his merciful providence, raised up a few young men who knew their legal privileges, and who put down those heaven-daring mortals that had persecuted their fellow-men for no other crime than that of living godly in Christ Jesus, and enjoying their inalienable rights as free men. Those young men, by Divine providence, took Methodism in Marietta under their protection, and nurtured her as a mother would her first-born. Some of them have long since gone to their reward, while others have grown gray in the good work, and are this day pillars in the Church of God.

"From this time till 1809, the growth of the Church in town and country was like the well-set tree that takes deep root, and promises to stand the pelting storms of coming years. Then the Gospel net fell into the hands of a man who drew *good and bad* into the Church, but was not careful to separate the *precious* from the *vile*. This mismanagement led gainsayers to reproach the ministry with glorying more in quantity than quality; introduced lasting difficulties into the classes, loaded the succeeding pastor with many painful duties, and gave ample testimony that it is less difficult to get bad men into the Church than it is to prove their guilt and get them out again, when their good and the interest of the Church require it. This reproach being wiped away, by separating the wheat from the chaff, the chasm was filled up by men of the first standing, who gave a weight and influence to Methodism which it never had before in this place. A number of years now passed. The smiles of Heaven rested on the Church, and the mighty power that attended the word preached, and the living faith and unshaken confidence of the members in God, made her indeed like an army with banners; and had she kept the unity of the Spirit in the bond of peace, it is difficult to say to what extent she would by this time have spread her branches. But, alas! men do not know how to value the legacy given to them by Jesus Christ, when he said, 'My *peace* I give unto you.'

"In 1819 the spirit of *disaffection* entered in, and brought with it all its soul-destroying poison. The labors of many years wilted at its unhallowed touch, like herbage before the winter's frost. To see its desolating ravage was enough to break the heart of a good man. In 1825 the old men took an alarm, and gave the next conference a tender but faithful account of their situation; and petitioned the conference to send them some man who would regulate their Church matters. The Ohio conference had felt many fearful apprehensions for Marietta circuit. They took the subject into deep and prayerful consideration; and that indefatigable man, L. S——, was selected and sent to this circuit, with special orders to examine the state of the Church, and to attend to the Discipline. He felt the weight of his appointment, flew to God for help, and came in the fullness of the blessing of Christ. His divine Master was with him, and blessed him in all he did. The heathen story of the Phenix rising to splendor out of its own ashes, would no more than illustrate the change produced in the Church on that circuit, under the administration of this highly-honored servant of God.

"When alive to God, the Church has, at all points, and at all periods, met her share of opposition—not, indeed, directly or always from men of high standing, 'but from lewd fellows of the baser sort,' who are frequently the degrading instruments of others acting behind a screen. The spirit of opposition has frequently turned Methodist preachers out of meeting-houses belonging to other denominations, and shut public school-houses against them, with a manifest intention of putting them down. But, in about as many instances, this kind of opposition has had a contrary effect. Instead of putting them down in such places, it has led their friends to double their exertions to build houses of worship for themselves. In this way the Church has frequently gained permanency by the very means intended for her downfall. Under these circumstances, in different neighborhoods, two or three men of moderate property have been known, with their own funds, in a short time, to build houses of worship, to the utter astonishment and confusion of their enemies. If a jealous distance, scowling contempt, and gross misrepresentations, be calculated to inflict wounds, then Methodism has been lacerated often and severely, as well as he who said, 'Of the Jews five times received I forty stripes save one.'

"The system of doctrines held and propagated by the Methodists in Washington county, met a tide of opposi tion for many years. Its principal antagonists were Predestinarians. When Methodism was in its infancy, those men treated its doctrines with the most sovereign contempt; and in its more advanced state, it was scouted out of 'good company' and fine meeting-houses as a *dangerous heresy*. All this time the Methodist ministers were preaching in the flowing language of the Bible, with as much confidence in the correctness of their doctrines, and as great indifference to contempt, and scorn, and opposition, and persecution, as if they knew every being in the universe believed every word they were saying. In this way their sentiments elicited investigation, and gained ground daily, till many rallied around their standard. A great conflict of sentiments among the people was the natural consequence. In this state of public excitement, in 1808, the people of Belpre proposed a number of questions, touching those doctrinal points affirmed by Calvinists and denied by Methodists. They called two ministers to discuss those questions in public. Two days were spent in the discussion, and a great concourse of people attended. The Rev. Samuel P. Robins took the affirmative, and the Rev. Solomon Langdon the negative side. Each had his admirers, but no salutary effects were produced either way; for, it is feared, too many came out in the pride of their hearts to see the fight. If the people of Belpre saw the light, they still *loved darkness*, and, therefore, failed to make a clear distinction between the doctrines of *general redemption* and those of a *particular salvation*. They, in consequence, blundered into all the errors of modern Universalism. The subject then returned to the people of the county, who have not rendered a verdict in *form*, but have in *effect*. For if it be certain that the ingenious speculations of Descartes were overthrown by the more practical philosophers of the Baconian school, it is not less certain that high-toned Calvinism has suffered the like overthrow from Methodism in this county.

"The relative standing of the principal Christian denominations in the county at present is as follows: The Presbyterians have four ministers, two hundred and forty Church members, and five meeting-houses—two of them very good, the rest old, unoccupied, and in a decaying state. The Congregationalists employ a Presbyterian minister, have one hundred and eighty Church members, and one splendid meeting-house. The regular Baptists have one meeting-house, three small congregations, supplied by ministers from a distance, who visit them occasionally. The Methodists have two traveling and four local preachers, one thousand and twelve members, thirteen meeting-houses, and fourteen other stated preaching places, where the congregations meet in school-rooms and dwelling-houses. All have their Bible, missionary, tract, and Sunday school societies, doing about what they can to promote the good cause of Christ in the world. When we look over the history of our sister Churches, and see what they were once and what they are now, we are struck with the change that has taken place for the better, and can not help thinking that one member of this family has provoked the rest to love and to good works.

"Notwithstanding Methodism has been assailed by fierce and contrary winds, like the sea-tossed bark, she has possessed, and still possesses, some redeeming principles, which have at all times exerted a saving influence in Washington county. These are, First. *Her plan;* by which she meets the wants of the outskirts of human population, as well as the city full; that sends the Gospel to the poor as well as to the rich; and that distributes the various gifts of the ministry far and wide. Second. *Her doctrines;* which, if fairly explained, and properly understood, are calculated not to insult, but to carry conviction to the minds of all attentive and unprejudiced men. Third. *Her manner of preaching;* by which she instructs her ministers to stand at a proper distance, on the one hand, from senseless vociferations, as little calculated to correct the heart as to inform the judgment; and, on the other, from that criminally-cold indifference that makes truth look like fiction. Occupying this ground, she encourages them to grasp their subjects in all their extent, and to suffer themselves to be wrought up by a sense of their vast importance to the highest pitch of mental and devotional energy.

"We have seen Methodism in her infancy cast out and trodden under foot; and we have seen her, in her riper years, put on her beautiful garments, and walk abroad in the greatness of her strength. These things admonish us to 'rejoice with trembling.' If God has been with us, and made us a people who were not a people, we should rejoice greatly in the Lord, and incense of praise and gratitude should ascend to him from our feeling hearts, like smoke ascending from an ever-burning altar. But if myriads follow, and look up to us for the bread of life, we should tremble under a sense of our high responsibility, and the account we must render to our Judge."

In the year 1819 brother Hamilton was transferred to Missouri, and stationed on the Indiana district, which he traveled four consecutive years, and at the expiration of which time he was retransferred to the Ohio conference. His appointment was the Marietta district, which he traveled four years. From this district he was sent to the Kanawha district, which he traveled two years, and then successively the following circuits; namely, Asbury, Irville, Rehoboth, and Deavertown. In all his vast range of travel, and amid all the toils and conflicts of his itinerant life, he never for a moment faltered in his work. His friends were numerous wherever he went; and he understood that trait of the apostle Paul, to be all things to all men, so that by all means some might be saved. This he was enabled to be, in an eminent degree, without blowing hot and cold with the same breath. While he mingled, with ease and dignity, among the great, commanding their respect and esteem, he also condescended to men of low estate. His talents were, as we have already intimated, *sui generis.* He had a manner of illustration peculiarly his own, seeming to have taken no man for his model. Sometimes he would indulge in a vein of irony and sarcasm that was withering to the systems and principles he opposed. He was very plain in his dress, and any one, on meeting him, would be sure to guess he was a Methodist preacher. Indeed, he seemed to take delight, as he called it, in showing his colors. He was of the medium hight, thick set, with a bland, open countenance, indicative of great good feeling. His manner of preaching was somewhat peculiar. He would always divide his subject, with the greatest exactness, into a few simple heads, or propositions, after which, if there were any terms of importance, he would define them clearly, and then proceed, slowly and cautiously, in the discussion of his subject, illustrating the whole with the most appropriate figures, drawn from real life. Toward the close he invariably warmed up, and became vehement. In this respect he resembled the eloquent Christie, though he had not the same intense and fiery ardor. Though not exactly a memoriter preacher, that is, he did not write and commit his sermons, yet, like some few we have known, the very thoughts and words which he employed in the delivery of a sermon, would occur on its repetition even years after. He was evidently a master-workman, and none were more successful than he in the various fields in which he was called to labor, as the results have abundantly and clearly shown.

His last field, as we have already seen, was Deavertown circuit. While engaged in the performance of his ministerial duties on this circuit, he was attacked with a slight stroke of paralysis, which, for a short time, disqualified him from hard labor. Still, he continued in his loved employ, as his strength permitted, till a second attack, which totally prostrated him, and put an end to all his labors in the ministry. For two years he lingered in a helpless condition, yet he patiently and pleasantly awaited the will of his heavenly Father, full of faith and the Holy Spirit. No complaint ever escaped his lips; but keeping his eyes fixed upon the bright and joyous inheritance of the saints in light, when the messenger came, conscious of his dissolution, he said, in soft, sweet tones, to his spirit, "Arise, the Master is come, and calleth for thee." Then his worn-out and broken-down tabernacle went to the dust, and his happy soul, on wings of faith and love, entered the "building of God, the house not made with hands, eternal in the heavens."

CHAPTER XXXVII.

WILLIAM H. RAPER.

Among that class of preachers who entered the itinerancy, in the beginning of the present century, was the Rev. Wm. H. Raper. That he was born in troublous times, is evident from the fact that a block-house, belonging to one of the military stations in the wilds of western Pennsylvania, was the place of his birth, which event occurred in the year 1793.

His father was a surveyor under the Government, in the North-Western territory, which made it necessary for him to be much from home, in the discharge of the duties of his office. His mother was one of the matron pioneers of the west, and among the first class of Methodists in the North-Western territory. She was a woman of exemplary piety, of great faith and devotion. She was also a patriot mother of the Revolution, as her subsequent history, in relation to her sons, most abundantly shows.

When William was quite young his parents removed to Columbia, on the Ohio, a few miles above Cincinnati, where his early days were spent, in those sports and employments incident to frontier life. When he reached his nineteenth year his thoughts were turned to war. Having two brothers in the army of General Hull, whose base surrender has forever associated his name with an ignominy little less than that which attaches to Arnold, a call was made for volunteers, and the young American joined the company of Captain Stephen Smith, and went forth to try the rigors of the camp and field. Not long after entering the company, the sergeant being disqualified, by sickness, from filling his post, young Raper was chosen to the office. He felt an ambition to fill with honor and bravery the post assigned him, and labored with zeal and diligence to become master of all the arts of war.

A day or two before the battle of the Thames, his company was ordered to march up the Lake, some fifteen miles, to prevent the landing of the British. The engagement took place during their absence, and the battle was nearly closed before the company arrived on the ground. This circumstance rendered it necessary, as Captain Smith's company was now the strongest, that it should take charge of the prisoners of war, which had been taken by Commodore Perry and General William Henry Harrison, and bring them to the Newport station. All the officers who ranked above Raper in the company having taken sick, the command devolved upon him. It was a responsible undertaking, but, as the sequel will show, the young officer proved himself adequate to the emergency. The company consisted of one hundred soldiers, and the number of prisoners amounted to four hundred. Every arrangement being made, they commenced their march. On their route it was necessary for them to cross the Black Swamp, which, at that season of the year, was nearly covered with water, which extended for miles through a drear and desolate wilderness. In their march the company became bewildered and lost, and the commander was at his wits' ends to know what to do. For three days and nights they wandered about in the swamp, without food. The company had become scattered, and on the morning of the third day he found himself with a guard of only twelve men, and about one hundred prisoners. The prisoners, seeing the weakness of the guard, resolved on a mutiny, and refused to march, threatening to kill the few who had them in charge. No time was to be lost, and Raper, calling out his men, drew them up in line and commanded them to make ready for the emergency, which they did, by fixing their bayonets and cocking their guns. In this position both parties stood for some time. At length, finding that the prisoners refused all entreaties to march, the commander gave them five minutes to decide, and if, at the expiration of that time, they did not march, he would fire and charge upon them. At the end of each minute he announced the fact, but they would not move. When the last minute had expired the soldiers were commanded to present arms, take aim, and—but before the word fire had escaped his lips, a large Scotch soldier, fresh from the Highlands of his native country, cried, hold! and, stepping aside, asked the privilege of saying a word. The captain asked him if it was for peace. To which he replied in the affirmative. The privilege was granted, and, addressing his fellow-prisoners, he said, "We have been taken in a fair fight, and are prisoners, honorably so, and this conduct is disgraceful to our king's flag, and is not the conduct becoming true soldiers, but disgraceful to ourselves and country. Now," said he, "I have had no hand in raising this mutiny, and I propose that all who are in favor of behaving themselves as honorable prisoners of war, shall come to me, and we will take the others in hand ourselves, and the American guard shall stand by and see fair play." This speech had the desired effect, and the mutiny was brought to an end without bloodshed.

Raper continued in charge till he delivered them over at Newport, opposite Cincinnati. A few years ago we met with an old soldier, one of that company and guard, who told us that Mr. Raper was considered one of the best soldiers and bravest men in the army; that he had seen him under almost every position in which a soldier could be placed, and never saw him evince the least fear. They had among the prisoners two Indians, who, after very severe threatenings, and, indeed, at the point of Raper's sword, finally led them out of the swamp. That evening they reached a settlement, where they obtained provisions, and, notwithstanding the efforts of the officers, many of the men killed themselves by eating.

After his arrival at Newport with the prisoners, he was offered a commission in the regular army, which he consented to take, provided it was agreeable to the wishes of his mother. Such was his love for her, that he would take no important step without first consulting her. His mother's answer was characteristic of the noble mothers of that day: "My son, if my country was still engaged in war, and I had fifty sons, I would freely give them all to her service; but, as peace is now declared, and there is no such necessity, as a Christian mother, therefore, I can not consent, for I think something better awaits my son than the mere camp-life of a soldier in time of peace." We have often heard him speak with gratitude, in view of this advice of his mother, and that he felt it a far greater honor to be a humble minister of Jesus Christ, than to have been at the head of the American army. He, accordingly, declined the commission, and returned to his former occupation, which was that of a tanner.

In the spring of 1816 he joined the Church, under Rev. Russel Bigelow, at the house of Judge Ransom, at Newbury, Clermont county, Ohio, and after months of deep penitence, he was converted. Shortly after he assisted in holding meetings in his neighborhood, and the next year was employed by the presiding elder, on what was then called the Miami circuit.

In the year 1819 he was received on trial in the traveling connection, at the conference held at Cincinnati, and appointed to Madison circuit, with the Rev. Henry

40

Baker for a colleague. We will give some incidents connected with his early itinerancy. While traveling in Indiana, upon the first visit to one of his appointments, after the meeting was closed, a fine, large man approached him and called him brother, and said, "I knew you the moment I saw you, but I suppose you have forgotten me." Brother Raper told him he did not remember to have ever seen him. "Well, sir," said the man, "I am the Scotch soldier that made the speech to the prisoners, the morning of the mutiny in the Black Swamp." Their meeting, under such a change of circumstances, was remarked by brother Raper as being very delightful, when he added, "After we were exchanged as prisoners of war, my enlistment terminated. I had been brought to see the justice of the American cause, and the greatness of the country. I determined I would not return to the old country. I commenced working at such labor as I could find. I saved a little money, came to this state, rented some land, and opened a farm. I have joined the Methodist Church, and, praise God! the best of all is, I have obtained religion. And not among the least of my blessings in this new country, I have a fine wife and a noble child. So, come," said he, "dinner will be ready by the time we get home." All other claims from the members had to be set aside this time, and the two soldiers, now as friends and Christians, were permitted to renew their acquaintance. They were ever after fast friends.

At another time, having lost the direction on a strange road after night, he crossed at the mouth of a creek, which empties into the Ohio, where it was, perhaps, fifty feet deep, when the Ohio river was very high. The mouth of the creek being full of drift logs and brush, and it being dark, he mistook the drift for a bridge, and went upon it; he thought it was a very shackling kind of a bridge, but passed over, leading his horse, without injury, although, when upon it, he feared his horse would fall through, and knew no better till the next morning, when he was told of his danger by the family, to whose house he had been attracted late in the night, by seeing the light from their cabin window. But for that cabin he would have had to remain all night in the woods, as he had done several times before.

During that year he swam his horse thirty-two times, in order to reach his appointments. On one of these swimming excursions he met with a singular incident. His horse, by some means, became entangled while swimming, and sank, throwing him off. It was a cold morning, a little before sunrise; and being incumbered with a great-coat and leggins, he found it very difficult to swim; but, with great effort, he succeeded in catching hold of the limb of a tree, which was hanging over the stream, where he was enabled to rest and hold his head above the water. While thus suspended in the stream, the thought rushed upon him, "Mother is praying for me, and I shall be saved." After thus resting, for a moment or two, he made the effort and got ashore. His horse had also made a safe landing, having the saddle-bags on his back all safe. His clothes and books were wet, and himself very much chilled by the early bath. But while this was going on with himself in the stream, his mother, some eighty or a hundred miles distant, that morning awoke suddenly as from affright, when this thought rushed upon her, "William is in great danger;" when she sprang from her bed, and falling on her knees, prayed for some time in intense supplication for his safety, when she received a sweet assurance that all was well. When they met and related the facts, and compared the time and all, they precisely agreed.

As a man he was honorable and high-minded. In the language of the Committee on Memoirs, written by one who was a companion with him on the well-fought field of itinerant life:

"Brother Raper's ministerial qualifications, taken altogether, were far above the medium grade. Blessed with an extraordinary memory, he acquired a very large amount of historical and general information, and possessed the happy art of turning all to good account. Some ministers excel in some things pertaining to their office, and fall behind in others; but brother Raper succeeded well in almost every particular. He was a profound theologian, mighty in the sacred Scriptures, readily perceived the line separating truth and error, and evinced superior logical skill in advocating the one and opposing the other. Under his ministry thousands of souls have enlisted in the cause of Christ, many of whom went before to hail him welcome into everlasting habitations, while others yet follow him as he followed Christ. While this generation lives on earth, he and his labors will be remembered with delight by many both in and out of the Church. Spiritual gifts were conferred on him in great variety. He sang delightfully and usefully, and was highly gifted in prayer and exhortation. He was an eloquent preacher, an able expounder of the word of life, a very judicious administrator of Church discipline, and a faithful and affectionate pastor.

"Whether on a circuit, in a station, or over a district as presiding elder, he appeared to be alike at home, and every-where useful. His stated ministry was exercised chiefly in Ohio and Indiana; but his connection with several sessions of the General conference, and subsequently with the General Mission Committee, caused him to be well-known about the eastern cities, where he was highly esteemed. Indeed, his amiable social qualities, superior conversational powers, and rich fund of useful incidents, gathered from practical life, not only gained him access, but secured him warm personal friends wherever he went. But few men had more admirers, and none more devoted bosom friends, either lay or clerical, than had brother Raper. It must not be inferred, however, from any thing here stated, that brother Raper never had enemies.

"No one could expose sin as he did, plainly and fearlessly, without exciting opposition. On one or two occasions, in the earlier part of his ministry, some attempts were made to do violence to his person, if not to take away his life; but the Lord preserved him from harm, and the man who made the most daring attempt upon him was on the same day, by his faithful preaching, awakened, sought and found mercy, and became an acceptable member of the Church. Brother Raper was always disposed to put the best constructions upon the conduct of others, and ever ready to forgive an injury; and now he is where the wicked cease to trouble, and the weary are at rest.

"In the early part of February, 1852, he accompanied Bishop Morris to Aurora, Indiana, to attend a quarterly meeting and visit his old friends in that place. There he preached his last sermon, with peculiar clearness and effect. On Tuesday, the 10th of February, he started for home, in company with Bishop Morris, on the steamer Forest Queen. He was attacked some time in the night with spasms, and when his condition was discovered by the brother who was in the same room, consciousness was gone. The boat being in port, medical aid was immediately had, and all that human skill could do was done, but to no saving effect. He was carefully and tenderly borne to the bosom of his family, whose feelings we can not attempt to describe, where he expired about half-past six, P. M., surrounded by his affectionate and deeply-afflicted family and many sympathizing friends.

"That once beautiful and manly form, upon which we were wont to look, now lies in ruins in the charnel-house. But that is not brother Raper—it is only the earthly tabernacle in which he recently sojourned among men. Brother Raper is in heaven, free from all the shackles of mortality. He mingles with the glorified spirits of just men made perfect, enjoying the light and the smiles of the reconciled and pleased countenance of Him who loved him and gave himself for him.

"Let us not confine our thoughts of him to the cold and silent tomb, but let us contemplate him in heaven, in a world of peace and joy above, while his flesh rests in the promise of a glorious resurrection. 'Peace to his ashes!' May we imitate his virtues, and finally share his triumphs in Christ through eternity!"

He has gone from our midst, after being with us, as a preacher, for thirty-three years, and we shall no more hear his voice in our councils, nor be encouraged by his smiles. We recollect distinctly the last conference which he attended, and deeply impressed upon our mind is the last speech he made to his brethren. He had been afflicted for some time, and his disease was of such a nature as to render him liable, at any moment, to be called away. He addressed his brethren in a few words, in which he took occasion to allude to his sufferings; and, after referring to the many happy seasons spent with his brethren in the ministry, he told them he waited the will of his Master; and if, before another conference, he should be called away, he said, with uplifted eyes and tremulous tongue, "Look up on high and believe I am there."

At another time, and still more recently, when it was customary for him to tell his family that they need not be disappointed or alarmed, if he should die before morning, he said to a brother, "I feel like one at a way-station, on the platform, with my trunk packed, waiting for the cars." The chariot of the Lord at length came, and brother Wm. H. Raper ascended to mansions on high.

On a lovely spot, in the Wesleyan Cemetery, the hand of affection has reared a beautiful white marble obelisk, as a sacred memento, to tell the passer-by where sleeps the sainted dust of one of Ohio's best and bravest sons.

CHAPTER XXXVIII.

JOHN ULIN.

The subject of our sketch was born in Virginia, in the year 1792, and brought up to manhood in the wilds of Greenup county, Kentucky. Growing up, as he did, amid the scenes of border warfare, which, in his early life, prevailed between the whites and Indians, it might be expected that young Ulin would form a character corresponding to the times in which he lived, and the scenes by which he was surrounded. His father was a daring and adventurous backwoods hunter. A spot is pointed out to the traveler, as he passes along the banks of the Ohio, or floats over the surface of that majestic river, where a high, craggy rock rises up almost perpendicularly from the bank, on the Virginia side, called "Ulin's leap." It is a wild, romantic spot, even to this day. The summit of the rock is covered with scraggy trees and evergreens, and is wild and unbroken as nature made it. In olden time, the father of John, when hotly pursued by the Indians, with whom he was not able to compete, leaped over this frightful precipice into the depths below, and escaped unhurt from the savage foe. It was a deed of desperate daring, but it was better for him to make the fearful leap, than to fall into the hands of the merciless savages, whose revenge he had aroused.

Young Ulin shared the fortunes of his father, and entered, in early life, upon the stirring field of adventure. He became an expert hunter. The woods were his home, and in its deep solitudes he wandered in search of game.

There was a native buoyancy, if not wildness, in his composition, united, however, with great amiability, and a full flow of sociality, that made his society desirable among both old and young; and hence, in all backwoods sports and pastimes, in all scenes of mirth and gayety, or reckless daring, he occupied a place in the front rank of his associates.

But he was destined by Providence for another sphere. That brilliant mind and brave young heart was to be occupied in different pursuits from those which then absorbed them. A great observer of human destiny had said:

> "There is a Divinity that shapes our ends,
> Rough hew them as we will."

A book, however, older than that of the dramatic poet, and one from which he had drawn, uncredited, so largely, had uttered the sentiment in countless forms of expression long before; and we need only go to that old book of life to learn, that "it is not in man that walketh to direct his steps," and that "our ways are from the Lord."

We have already spoken of a pioneer preacher who had penetrated these wilds. On a certain occasion, gloomy and melancholy as the dark defiles and solitudes around him, he might have been seen urging his steed through the forest, in search of a new appointment in that wild region. At length he arrives, and surrounded by the old and young from far and near, he opens his message. One dark eye in that assembly scans the preacher, though the mind is intently fixed upon the sermon. Preaching gave the itinerant relief, as it afforded him an opportunity to unburden his heart in the description of another's. The shade passed from his countenance, the dark, lustrous eye was kindled with light and softened by tears, and the simple, truthful, loving eloquence which fell from his tongue found way to every heart. Young Ulin, for it was him among the rest of that backwoods assembly that we have alluded to, never was so strangely and powerfully touched before. He saw and felt, in the light of the Gospel of a free salvation, for the first time that he was a sinner, and that he must be converted or lost. He was among the first at the rude altar for prayer, as a seeker of salvation, and after an earnest struggle, with strong crying and tears, he found the pearl of great price, and was made happy in the love of God. His conversion was clear and powerful, and of such a nature as forever to shut up all avenues to doubt in regard to it. A glorious change had come over him, and he now withdrew from the sports of the wildwood, and directed his attention to the more staid and sober pursuits of life. Not long after his conversion, he felt moved by the Holy Spirit to engage in the work of calling sinners to repentance, and such were the gifts, grace, and usefulness that characterized his labors, that he was duly licensed to preach as a local preacher. He did not, however, continue long in this vocation. His ardent spirit longed for a wider field of usefulness, and he sighed to be given up exclusively to the work of saving souls. Though he had a family, and, in consequence of the great difficulty in that day of getting a support, few, if any, preachers with families were admitted into conference, yet, because of his extraordinary talents and burning zeal, he was admitted into the itinerant ranks at Hillsboro, October 4, 1826.

His first appointment was to Burlington circuit, on which he was continued one year, and where he labored with great success as a herald of the cross to perishing thousands. His next appointment was Charleston, Virginia, embracing a wild but beautiful country on the Kanawha and Elk rivers. Here he blew the soft and silvery tones of the Gospel trumpet, which waked the echoes of the mountains and vales of that picturesque land, and many were the hearts that were touched and melted at the sound. Reader, have you ever heard the Alpine horn, gliding in smooth cadences over the waters, floating through the vales, and echoing back in softer tones from the mountains, plaintive as the coo of a dove, and sweet as the lute of an angel? If you have, it will give you some conception of the clear, soft, far-reaching voice of John Ulin. We have heard the grand, sublime roar of the lion-like Bascom, as with the majestic sweep of a hurricane it leveled the forests of men at immense camp meetings, and we have heard the soft and eloquently-beautiful strains of the lamb-like Summerfield, as it won and melted all hearts in the crowded churches of our great cities; but we never heard a voice which, for sweetness, compass, and power, excelled that of John Ulin. He was emphatically a child of Nature, and grew up amid the sublime and beautiful scenes which God himself had formed, and the clumsy hand of man had not marred, and he gathered his inspiration from these scenes, together with the deep communings of his own heart with God.

From Virginia he was sent to Gallipolis, including that town and the country lying upon the waters of Raccoon, Chickamauga, Kiger, and Shade rivers. This was a large circuit, and it was laborious to travel, but the faithful herald sounded the clear notes of the Gospel in all its length and breadth. Methodism had made but little progress in Gallipolis. It was settled by the French, as its name imports, and they were mostly Roman Catholics, having brought their priest with them from Paris. From some cause or other, many years ago they were, we are informed, excommunicated *en masse*, and since then they have not felt disposed to unite with any Protestant denomination, though some of the descendants of the old settlers have laid aside their prejudices and become connected with different denominations. After laboring in this field for one year, Ulin was sent to Salt Creek circuit, embracing the towns of Piketon and Waverly and the surrounding country. Some parts of this circuit were settled by old Methodists from Virginia; and one neighborhood particularly, a few miles below Piketon, called now the Barnes neighborhood, was settled by an old brother Boydston and his family, who were stanch Methodists of the old school. Here brother Ulin found a welcome home, and was instrumental in the awakening and conversion of some of the children of the ancient families residing there. There was another settlement on the Big Bottom, called Foster's, which was a stronghold of Methodism, and there, also, our brother was made a blessing to the Church. Piketon was a wicked place, and there were but a few Methodists there in the days of Ulin, though the Church since has grown largely. His next and last field of labor was New Richmond, with the now sainted Collins. But his work was done. The cholera was doing its dreadful work. He and his beloved companion were engaged in ministering to the wants of the sick and dying. In the midst of her kind ministrations she was seized with the malady, and in a few hours death terminated her labors of love. The last sad office, of consigning the wife of his youth and the mother of his children to the grave, was scarcely performed ere the fell monster seized him, and there in his little hut, surrounded by eight lovely, helpless children, the father breathed his last. He had nothing to leave them but a father's blessing and a father's prayers. He gave up all for Christ, and when he died he gave his children to the Savior. After bidding them, one by one, an affectionate adieu, he told them to live for God, and meet their father and mother in heaven. In the midst of the tears and heart-breaking sobs of those children, he shouted victory over death, and went to join the sainted above. We were on another part of the district when the event occurred, but we hastened with rapid pace to look after the dear children. Before we arrived, however, father Collins and the stewards had them all provided with good homes, where they were brought up in the nurture and admonition of the Lord, and some of them, we know, this day are following in the footsteps of their parents to heaven.

Inscrutable as are the ways of Providence, we know that "He doeth all things well." And though unbelief might ask in such a time of trial, "where now is thy God?" yet the Providence which took the parents to heaven provided bountifully for the children, and he who is the Father of the fatherless will always "temper the wind to the shorn lamb."

CHAPTER XXXIX.

WILLIAM PHILLIPS.

THE subject of this narrative was born in Jessamine county, Kentucky, on the 7th of May, 1797. His parents were pious, and, as might be expected, William was brought up in the nurture and admonition of the Lord. We believe there are no children whose early training has been religious, but become, at a very early period in life, the subjects of the Spirit's awakening influences. "The promise is to us and to our children," and if we devote them to God, and labor to bring them up in his nurture and admonition, we may conclude, with certainty, that the germs of truth planted in their young hearts, and baptized by our prayers and tears, will receive the additional watering of the Holy Spirit, without whose genial and attractive influences all human agencies must prove unavailing. Thus educated, young Phillips soon became impressed with the importance and necessity of religion, and often was induced to turn his attention to the subject. After laboring hard all day—for the youth of that period were not brought up in idleness, whatever else might be said about them—he would spend the evening in writing prose and poetry, for both of which species of composition his mind took an early turn, and he seemed to take great delight in the exercise. Many of these lucubrations have been kindly submitted to our examination by his son, Mr. J. M. Phillips, chief clerk of the Book Concern. Some of his poetic effusions are highly creditable. Among his papers is a melodramatic performance, entitled, "*The Hypocrisy Unmasked*," the prologue to which is written in poetry, and which, for point and poetic merit, we think could not be excelled by any poetic wit of the present day.

It was customary for the farmers in the section of the country where young Phillips lived to raise their hogs in the woods; and there being an abundance of mast, they would grow fat without any other feeding. When the time for killing came, each farmer would sally forth and collect his hogs, which he was enabled to do from the fact that each owner had a private ear-mark, by which he could identify his stock, and distinguish it from those of his neighbors. It happened that there lived a family in the neighborhood, who, lacking that honesty which should have characterized all in those early times of privation and toil, did not scruple to appropriate their neighbors' hogs to their own use, without fear of discovery, as they cut off the ears of the hogs, thus obliterating all marks of ownership. Many efforts were made to detect them in their nefarious business; but as they carried on their depredations so secretly, usually taking the night season for their work of pillage, they eluded detection. The whole neighborhood seemed to be satisfied that they were guilty; but as it could not be proven, they continued to carry on their thieving with impunity. Young Phillips was aware of the state of things, and set himself to work to write a short poem descriptive of hog-stealing, and containing such an unmistakable description of the thieves, that all who read it would understand the application as certainly as though he had named the persons themselves. He knew the force of public opinion, if it could only be brought to bear upon the guilty; and, accordingly, keeping the matter a profound secret from every body, he waited till some public occasion would call out the neighborhood. It was not long till such an occasion presented itself. Taking his poem with him, which he had written in a disguised hand, and which none but himself could read, he went to the public gathering. While mingling with the crowd he purposely dropped it, knowing it would be picked up by some one. It was not long till it was rumored that a curious writing was found, and the ingenuity and learning of all was taxed to decipher its contents. Finally it was brought to Phillips, who, taking it, and looking at it for some time, said he thought he could make it out by hard spelling. When he had examined it sufficiently long, occasionally calling a knowing one to help him out with a hard word, he mounted a stump and began. At first he stammered considerably, which only increased the interest, making certain points more emphatic. As he progressed every eye was turned to the hog-stealers, whose persons and conduct were described to the life; and before he had finished they skulked away from the crowd, unable any longer to withstand the battery of eyes that was opened upon them, and the shouts and peals of laughter which rent the air. Suffice it to say, the hog-thieves left the neighborhood, and no complaint was ever after heard of such depredations.

But the most satirical thing in the English language we ever read, is his poem entitled, "*Alexander the Great; or, The Learned Camel.*" Many of our readers have, doubtless, seen this production, as it was once published and somewhat extensively circulated. It was designed as an expose of Campbellism, or the "Christians," as they are denominated; but more familiarly known as the Reformers, or Campbellite Baptists—a denomination quite numerous in Kentucky. It flashes throughout with the most keen and cutting satire, and gives evidence of high poetic talent, as well as a thorough knowledge of the system which it exposes.

We will give a few stanzas of the poem, which will enable the reader to form some judgment of its character. We would refer to the poem itself, but it has long been out of print. It begins thus:

"In times of old, as books relate,
Lived Alexander—called the Great;
Who conquered Greece, and Persia, too,
And did the universe subdue;
Made kings his slaves, and every nation
Filled with blood and desolation.
But Alexander, mounted on
Bucephalus, and clothed upon
With all the panoply of war,
Was more diminutive, by far,
Compared to modern Alexander,
Than is a goslin to a gander;
For, reader, know we have of late
A second Alexander great—
A man of more deserved renown
Than he who tumbled cities down:
More great, more bold, and learned, too,
Than e'er was Christian, Turk, or Jew;
And should you doubt his fame or glory,
Pray give attention to my story."

After this introduction there follows, in the same vein of cutting satire, a description of the tenets of the Rev. Alexander Campbell, in three hundred lines. At the close is an oration, supposed to have been delivered by Mr. Campbell, of which we give the first two stanzas, as follows:

"Ho, every mother's son and daughter!
Here's the Gospel in the water;
Here's the ancient Gospel way;
Here's the road to endless day;
To the kingdom of the Savior,
You must enter in the river.
Every mother's son and daughter,
Here's the Gospel in the water.

All ye sons of Adam's race,
Come and share this wat'ry grace!

Water is the healing lotion,
Vast as the Atlantic Ocean;
Water purifies the nation,
Water is regeneration:
Every mother's son and daughter,
Here's the Gospel in the water."

So much for the poetry of brother Phillips. His prose compositions we shall have occasion to refer to hereafter, and shall, therefore, resume our sketch.

When he arrived at mature age he entered the boisterous, stormy sea of political life. Leaving the quiet and beautiful vale of the muses, and the sacred walks of song, and embarking upon the stormy wave of popular excitement, he was well nigh being shipwrecked, at least so far as religious impressions and tendencies were concerned. To cut loose, if possible, from all religious thoughts and restraints—for his early religious training had a wonderful hold upon his conscience—he resorted to the reading of infidel books, and pursued their study till clouds and darkness, and doubt and uncertainty, gathered around his mind, shutting out the beautiful visions of his earlier days. His early training, however, in habits of virtue, proved a barrier too strong for the encroachments of infidelity; and though he had learned to doubt, he nevertheless retained a high regard for morality, and could not obliterate from his mind the truth of Christianity. He continued in this skeptical state, hovering, as it were, over the dark confines of infidelity, till he was settled in life, and had the charge of a rising family. The following account of his conviction for sin and his awakening to a sense of his lost condition, in which the blank and cheerless nature of infidelity was strongly contrasted with the satisfying portion religion imparts, was given by him, in a love-feast, soon after his conversion:

"One morning," said he, "I returned home in a mel-

except the time that elapsed between his appointment by the General conference and the termination of his conference year, which was still shortened by his unexpected death. He received deacon's and elder's orders at the regular periods in which these offices are usually conferred.

In the mean time he was appointed by the Book Committee assistant editor of the Western Christian Advocate; and after serving in this capacity one year, he was elected to that post by the General conference of 1836. Possessing talents of a high order as a writer, he contributed largely of the products of his pen to the columns of the Advocate. Among other of his numerous productions was a serial, entitled, "Campbellism Exposed; or, Strictures on the Peculiar Tenets of Alexander Campbell." This serial began with the January number of 1835, and closed in April, 1836, but a few months before his death. The articles, as they appeared in the Advocate, received a wide favor all over the country, and were read with interest and profit by thousands. The Ohio conference, which met about one month subsequent to his decease, passed a unanimous resolution, requesting the Agents to publish the Strictures in a book form, which was in due time accomplished, and the work placed upon the General Catalogue. This little volume has had an extensive sale; and we know of no work better calculated to expose the errors of the Campbellites than the Strictures. To those who have not read it, we take the liberty of calling attention to the able manner in which the subject is discussed. In the first chapter the author gives a clear statement of the Campbellite doctrine of baptism, and introduces the texts upon which the Campbellites rely in support of their doctrine. The clear and critical exegesis of the author on those texts shows that they are wrested from their obvious import by the advocates of Campbellism, and neither really nor apparently sustain their views. The next chapter discusses the true condition of regeneration as represented in the Bible, and as contradistinguished from water regeneration. Chapter third is devoted to an examination of the agency employed in the work of regeneration. The succeeding chapter examines the mode of baptism, and discusses the true import of the term *baptizo,* furnishing clear and cogent reasons for baptism by sprinkling, and against baptism by immersion. The fifth chapter is confined to the subject of Creeds, while the remaining chapters, in a most masterly manner, discuss the subject of Sects, Sectarianism, and the Call to the Ministry, concluding with a recapitulation containing a summary of what had been advanced in the foregoing pages.

From the way in which Mr. Campbell ranted and raved against the Methodists, about the time the Strictures appeared, and for a long time afterward, we are led to conclude that they told powerfully upon the strongholds of the system; for men generally lose their temper when they fail in argument. Among the papers of brother Phillips are many valuable manuscript sermons. The most interesting portion of his manuscripts were, however, unfortunately lost.

Elevated by his talents to the permanent post of assistant editor, a long and brilliant career of usefulness was before him. Associated with Dr. Elliott, whose extensive and varied learning eminently qualified him for the post of principal editor of the paper and books of the Church, he was, from his talents as a polemic and his acquaintance with polite and general literature, a most desirable acquisition; but, alas! how uncertain were all earthly hopes and prospects; for in the brief space of only three weeks and two days after his appointment, he was called away from the scenes of his toil on earth to the rest and blessedness of heaven. Short but brilliant was his career.

The ensuing annual conference filled the vacancy occasioned by his death, in the editorial department, with the gifted and eloquent Hamline, who, with Dr. Elliott, furnished the following brief memoir of the last hours, together with a tribute of respect to the memory of their fellow-laborer :

"On the 22d of June, 1836, he was confined to his bed by a violent attack of fever. For several days previous to this he felt manifest indications of an approaching assault of severe sickness. During his confinement of six weeks and two days, he suffered much pain of body, which was borne with great patience. When the fever was high he was affected with delirium; but when the fever abated he was in the full exercise of his mental faculties. Shortly after he was taken ill he gave instructions to his afflicted wife, respecting her concerns and future residence, intimating to her that the present disease would prove fatal. He also called his children to his bedside, and solemnly and without tears, yet deeply affected, gave them the *charge* and instructions of a parent on the verge of eternity. In his moments of self-possession, both when asked and unsolicited, he expressed himself strongly, yet very humbly, respecting his confidence in God and the enjoyments of religion, which he evidently possessed in a high degree. At one time, when it was thought he was dying, he was asked, 'If all was well?' he calmly replied, 'I feel for me to live is Christ, and to die is gain.' He then spoke of the goodness and mercy that had followed him all the days of his life. At another time, when he complained of a pain in his breast, it was said to him, 'When we get to heaven we shall then be done suffering. Pain and affliction will be over, and God shall wipe tears from every eye. Do you expect to get there?' He replied, 'Yes; my soul sometimes exults at the prospect;' and, with a faltering voice, he added, 'Yes, glory to God!' At another time he said to a friend, 'My mind is entirely at peace. It is doubtful whether I shall recover from this sickness; but to me death has no terror, the grave no gloom. If it were the Lord's will I would like to live, that I might make some better provision for the temporal and spiritual welfare of my family. But why do I talk thus? The Lord is sufficient. I now wish to leave this with you as my testimony, that my hope is in Christ, through whose blood I shall conquer. I now feel none but Jesus can do suffering sinners good.' Again he said, 'In retrospecting the past, contemplating the present, or looking forward to the future, I have nothing to fear.' There is no doubt in the minds of any of his friends concerning his triumphant entrance into the paradise of God. He departed this life on the night of the 4th of August, 1836, at half past twelve, in the city of Cincinnati. His remains were carried to Wesley Chapel, on Saturday, the 6th, at 10 o'clock, A. M., where an impressive sermon was delivered by the Rev. J. F. Wright, from Psalm xlvi, 10: 'Be still and know that I am God.' His body is deposited in the Methodist burying-ground till the resurrection of the just. In his death the editorial corps has lost a valuable member, and the Church has been deprived of the services of one of her most faithful and efficient sons.

"As *a Christian*, he is to be ranked among the excellent. Entire reliance on the mercy of God, and the vicarious atonement of Jesus Christ, was the strongest and most prominent exercise of his mind during his affliction; and, indeed, this was the settled disposition of his very soul from the time he first embraced religion; but which increased as he grew in grace, so as to form an abiding, firm exercise of his mind. His reliance on the Redeemer was such, that

> 'His blood and righteousness
> He made his only plea.'

"The expression, *Lord, have mercy*, which he repeated much during his sickness, indicated to those who heard him, that reliance on Jesus Christ was, with him, permanent and unwavering. In *patience* he possessed his soul to such a degree that the severest pains could not wrest a murmur from his lips.

"His *ministerial gifts and qualifications* were considered to be of the most useful kind. The following extract of a letter from an aged and experienced member of the Church, will place the ministerial character of brother Phillips in a very amiable light:

"'While we would cast in our mite in honor of his Christian character, and for the encouragement of others to follow his example, we being intimately acquainted with him for the two years he traveled Lexington circuit, Kentucky, our house being almost his constant home once in four weeks, as he traveled round his circuit, we, who have been acquainted with Methodist preachers for near fifty years, and some of us strict observers of men and things for more than forty years, are more than willing to give in our testimony to the Christian and evangelical or apostolical character of brother Phillips. And first, a more pious, studious, grave, cheerful, humble, loving, laborious, and effective preacher we have never known. In a word, he seemed all goodness, not only for a short time—as too many often are—but all the time alike good. In the pulpit, whether the congregations were large or small, he was like a lamp to light up their intellects—his doctrines so pure and evangelical, his reasoning so profound, his language so appropriate, that all acknowledged him much of a master workman. In company he was very social and friendly; in our family he was always instructive; unto the aged he was reverential; with the young he was familiar, and acted much of the philosopher; while all his language and deportment seemed seasoned with grace and warm affection. We recognize him this moment, fresh in our memories. His almost constant practice in the winter nights was to instruct our daughters and sons in the rudiments of singing, as also in the way of salvation, with several other branches of useful instruction. He often put us in mind of the old Methodist preacher that some of us knew nearly fifty years ago in old Virginia, that used to preach at my grandfather's. We were acquainted, also, with the circuit preachers that preached at my father's for several years in Kentucky, where the preachers made their home. Among those preachers were but few Phillipses to be found. For twenty years or more we have not known a more excellent and profitable man than brother William Phillips. But he is gone to glory. Is it possible that we are to hear from him no more this side of heaven?'

"To this unadorned and simple testimony other accounts precisely correspond.

"His attainments as a writer place him deservedly, if not among the foremost writers, at least in that respectable class which would raise him several degrees above mediocrity. But as he was called away at the early age of thirty-nine, and, therefore, before he had opportunity to come fairly before the public, it would be difficult to present him in his real character before the world. His writings in the Western Christian Advocate, over his proper signature, have evident marks of accurate research, sound judgment, and respectable attainments. Had he turned his attention to writing at an earlier period of his life, or had he been spared longer, he would probably have held a prominent place among the writers of this age.

"Brother Phillips was little above the ordinary hight, and rather spare. His personal appearance was not only agreeable, but might be considered dignified. His manners were courteous and pleasing, manifesting a disposition to be friendly to all; so that even the stranger was often prepossessed in his favor; but he was respected most by those who knew him best. He was truly a son of peace; and though he considered it his duty to contend earnestly for the faith once delivered to the saints, he delighted not in controversy. Yet into this he was willing to enter sooner than yield up any portion of truth."

CHAPTER XL.

THE INTREPID MISSIONARY.

THE Methodist Church has furnished missionaries, who for zeal and courage, in planting the standard of the cross on the battlements of heathendom, have not been excelled by any other denomination. Of this number was our young brother, Daniel Poe, a short sketch of whose life and labors we propose to give. He was born in Columbiana county, Ohio, on the 12th day of October, 1809, and was born again at a camp meeting, on Wayne circuit, five miles south of Wooster, Ohio, in August, 1825, in the sixteenth year of his age. He united with the Methodist Episcopal Church, at the house of Judge William Henry, near where the town of Massillon now stands, under the ministry of Rev. A. Goff. Though but a boy, he was remarkable for his exemplary piety, and was soon appointed a class-leader and licensed to exhort. In April, 1830, feeling a divine call to the ministry, and desiring to prepare himself by a better education, he went to Worthington, Ohio, and attended an academy through the summer. In the same autumn he went to Augusta College, Kentucky. During vacation, in 1832, he visited his brother, the Rev. Adam Poe, who was then residing in West Chester, and traveling Miami circuit. It was while he was there that we first formed an acquaintance with him, having attended with his brother the camp meeting which was held just before the session of the Ohio conference at Dayton. By our advice he was licensed to preach and recommended to travel. He was, accordingly, admitted on trial in the Ohio conference, and appointed to travel Letart Falls circuit, with the late Rev. A. B. Stroud as his colleague, and Rev. I. C. Hunter presiding elder. There he labored successfully and acceptably. The next year he was appointed to Eaton circuit, with Rev. W. Sutton, and we were his presiding elder, having succeeded Bishop Morris, who commenced his duties as editor of the Western Christian Advocate. The next year he was appointed to Hamilton circuit, with Rev. J. Hill, and in 1835 to Oxford circuit, with Rev. B. Westlake. In May, 1836, he was sent by Bishop Soule to the Oneida and Menominee mission, west of Green Bay, then under the supervision of Rev. John Clark, now of the Rock River conference. Here his labors were very arduous and responsible. He commenced a school among the Oneida Indians west, and extended his visits to Brothertown, and other fragments of tribes, scattered through the Wisconsin territory. On one occasion, in the month of February, 1837, after visiting an encampment of Indian hunters, between Green Bay and Lake Winnebago, he wished to go to Brothertown to meet an appointment; and as he made all these journeys in the wilderness on foot, finding that he could save some thirty miles in the distance by crossing the lake on the ice, he proposed to do so. An old Indian of the company, at his request, took him in a bark canoe on to the ice, which was at that point parted from the shore some thirty rods. After they reached the ice, the Indian drawing up his canoe, ran some distance forward, and stooping down placed his ear near the ice, then rising, he said,

"You can't cross, you must go back."

Daniel, however, replied, "I have an appointment, and I must go."

"Then," said the Indian, "you drown."

He, however, persisted in going forward. The Indian then bade him farewell with tears, saying, "I never see you more." As Daniel could see across the lake, he felt confident that he could run over safely, and started on a rapid trot. After passing quietly about five miles, he heard suddenly a report as of a cannon, and looking forward, saw the ice breaking and rolling up in waves toward him. Seeing his imminent danger, he ran with all his might in an opposite direction, to escape the opening made by the swell. Getting round it, he struck his course anew for the same point on the opposite shore at which he had before been aiming; but soon again he heard in advance a similar alarming report, and saw the ice again thrown up by the rolling waves. Again he was forced to run for life. In a word, this terrible race continued through the day. Still the resolute missionary kept his eye fixed on the distant shore, and ran forward as soon as he could avoid one opening, only to meet another, eating as he ran, when he became hungry, some parched corn, with which he had filled the capacious pockets of his coat. Just as night was closing upon him, he reached a place on the ice within some twenty or thirty rods of the shore, and springing into the water and swimming for the nearest point of land he reached it, but was so exhausted as to be unable to stand. He laid down upon the beach, a bluff of some forty or fifty feet being above him, which it was impossible for him to ascend. Here he thought his toils must end, and he gave himself up to die. After commending himself to God, he thought of the home and friends he should see no more; he thought how those dear to him would mourn him as lost, and never probably learn how he had died. At this the love of life sprung up in his heart as he had never felt it before, and with a powerful effort he rose upon his knees. Crawling along the beach some distance, he came to a small ravine, where the melting snow was running down into the lake. Up this he clambered on his hands and knees, taking hold of bushes and roots to help himself along, till he reached the top of the bank. Here he shouted glory! till the woods rang. The moon was shining beautifully, lighting up the snow-covered forest with its brightness, and, hence, there was sufficient light for him to find his way. He perceived that he had landed very near the point at which he had been aiming, and getting into an Indian trail, after resting awhile on his snowy bed, he started forward courageously toward his appointment, at Brothertown. After walking some distance along the path, he saw an owl light on a bush just before him. Being exceedingly hungry, and having a loaded pistol in his pocket, he thought he would shoot it and eat it raw. He approached near, with his pistol in his hand, and aiming it so as to make sure of his prey, he pulled the trigger; but, alas! his pistol only snapped. He then remembered he had been swimming with it in his pocket, and "I think," said he, "I never felt a disappointment more severely than to see that owl fly slowly away, leaving my hunger unsatisfied." After walking about five miles, he came to an Indian camp near the trail. He entered and found four or five Indians, who had been encamped there some time hunting. They were all fast asleep. At their fire he saw a pot, and without waking up the proprietors, to ask their leave, he helped himself heartily to its contents, which consisted of boiled venison and corn. Then lying down before the fire with a thankful heart, he fell asleep and rested sweetly till nearly ten o'clock the next morning, when finding his hosts all up and gone to their hunting, he again helped himself to the corn and venison, and pursued his journey to Brothertown, where he preached to nearly all the inhabitants who professed to be Christians. These Indians

suffering among them. She affectionately pointed them to the Lamb of God, who taketh away the sin of the world, and had seen some of them die happy. It was at her request that Daniel visited them and commenced his labors among them. At the first interview of these young missionaries, they found in each other congenial spirits, and mutually formed an attachment for each other, founded in Christian love. In the month of June, 1837, they were married. Jane then went with Daniel to the Oneida mission, and her place in the Brothertown school was supplied by brother Clark, the superintendent. At Oneida they felt the need of a house of worship. Jane had some three hundred dollars, which she had earned by school-teaching in Michigan; this she offered as capital to commence with. Daniel got most of the male members of the mission to go with him into the pine woods, on Fox river, and cutting saw-logs, they took them to a mill, ten miles distant, and prepared lumber for their house. He came out to the ensuing sessions of the Michigan and Ohio conferences, and obtained some funds, with which he returned, and soon they had a comfortable meeting-house. There has been a flourishing mission ever since at that place. Our young brother traveled on horseback through an almost solitary wilderness, from Green Bay to Alton, Illinois, in the autumn of 1838, to attend the Illinois conference. There Bishop Soule transferred him back to the Ohio conference. He could not get back to Ohio in time to get an appointment that year, but reached his father's house, in the neighborhood of Massillon, in December. He visited his brother, in Tiffin, who was presiding elder of that district, in January, 1839; and one of the preachers in the district having failed, he was employed on Mexico circuit, where he labored with zeal and usefulness, till the session of his conference, in September, 1839, when he was appointed to M'Arthurstown circuit. The next two years he was appointed to Tarlton. At the session of the Ohio conference, held at Hamilton, September, 1842, he, by the advice of Bishop Morris, took a transfer, with several others, to the Texas conference. He immediately started with his wife and three little children, the youngest but a few weeks old, to that then Republic of the Lone Star. His letter, published in the Western Christian Advocate, of May 19, 1843, gives an account of his journey there and the session of the Texas conference held that season at Bastrop.

During his first year in Texas, seeing the great want of schools and teachers throughout the country, after consultation with Rev. Littleton Fowler, his presiding elder, and with his consent and by his advice, he came to Ohio and obtained a corps of teachers, with whom he returned and commenced a number of schools at most of the prominent points in Eastern Texas. During his sojourn in Ohio, while he was gathering up his teachers, there occurred a great amount of sickness and suffering at Milam, where his family was located. While at the Ohio conference, we recollect distinctly the thrilling appeals of this intrepid young missionary. When some of his brethren expressed fears for his safety and that of his wife, whom he left in her shanty on the distant plains of Texas, coupled with what was a seeming intimation, that their courage would scarcely be adequate to breast the dangers and hardships of that border land, he replied, that "if he thought there was a drop of coward blood in his veins, he would let it out with his jack-knife, and as for his wife, there could be no fear on her account, as he found her among the Brothertown Indians alone, teaching the children in the wigwams of the distant west." It was an interesting season in the conference, and many of the brethren indulged in remarks relative to the missionaries of olden time. One brother related an interview he had suffering among them. She affectionately pointed them to the Lamb of God, who taketh away the sin of the world, and had seen some of them die happy. It was at her request that Daniel visited them and commenced his labors among them. At the first interview of these young missionaries, they found in each other congenial spirits, and mutually formed an attachment for each other, founded in Christian love. In the month of June, 1837, they were married. Jane then went with Daniel to the Oneida mission, and her place in the Brothertown school was supplied by brother Clark, the superintendent. At Oneida they felt the need of a house of worship. Jane had some three hundred dollars, which she had earned by school-teaching in Michigan; this she offered as capital to commence with. Daniel got most of the male members of the mission to go with him into the pine woods, on Fox river, and cutting saw-logs, they took them to a mill, ten miles distant, and prepared lumber for their house. He came out to the ensuing sessions of the Michigan and Ohio conferences, and obtained some funds, with which he returned, and soon they had a comfortable meeting-house. There has been a flourishing mission ever since at that place. Our young brother traveled on horseback through an almost solitary wilderness, from Green Bay to Alton, Illinois, in the autumn of 1838, to attend the Illinois conference. There Bishop Soule transferred him back to the Ohio conference. He could not get back to Ohio in time to get an appointment that year, but reached his father's house, in the neighborhood of Massillon, in December. He visited his brother, in Tiffin, who was presiding elder of that district, in January, 1839; and one of the preachers in the district having failed, he was employed on Mexico circuit, where he labored with zeal and usefulness, till the session of his conference, in September, 1839, when he was appointed to M'Arthurstown

While meeting was in progress on Saturday, the Doctor was at the tavern across the way, uttering bitter curses against the Methodists.

"The Sabbath came, and the congregation was unusually large. I was preaching on the doctrine of rewards and punishments, when my eye fell on the Doctor, who was seated in the very rear of the congregation. He seemed much excited; sometimes his face would redden, and then an almost deathly paleness would pass over it. He seemed very restless, too, and kept constantly turning on his seat. I knew not whether he was enraged or whether conscience was doing its office, awakened and enlightened by the Holy Spirit. I thought, however, that I would talk fearlessly and plainly, and leave the result with God. I spoke, in conclusion, of the fearful account that that man will have to render on the day of judgment who keeps his wife and children away from the house of God, and bids them follow him in the way to hell. An appointment was made for the afternoon, and the congregation dismissed.

"As I was returning to the afternoon service, I saw the Doctor standing at the corner of the court-house, where the meeting was held. When I was yet a few rods distant, he started out to meet me. I had heard that the Doctor possessed considerable personal courage, and that he had been through a number of bowie-knife and pistol fights. Whether he came in peace or came armed for a deadly encounter I knew not, nor was it my business to know; my business was to meet him. We met, when he gave his trembling hand, and said in accents broken with sighs and accompanied with tears, 'Mr. Poe, I wish you to open the door of the Church this afternoon for my wife to join.' I said, 'Thank you, Doctor, but what are you going to do? you are a sinner, and must have religion, or be lost eternally.' He answered, 'I feel as I never felt in all my life—is there, can there be mercy for such a wretched sinner as I have been?' I told them that there was mercy, free and full, and exhorted him to look to Jesus, as we walked together into the congregation. After an excellent sermon was preached by my colleague, I stated that I was requested to open the doors of the Church, and went on to give an invitation. The Doctor's wife immediately came forward, together with a number of others. I then invited all who desired to seek their soul's salvation, to come to the mourner's bench. The Doctor and many others came trembling and weeping, and kneeled in prayer.

"A glorious revival commenced that afternoon. God's people were heard shouting for joy, and sinners were heard weeping and crying aloud for mercy. The meeting lasted some two weeks, during which time many sinners were awakened and converted. The Doctor came forward at every invitation, and seemed powerfully awakened and deeply engaged, and yet he found no relief. I visited him often, and talked and prayed with the family. He did not attempt to conceal or extenuate, but acknowledged that he had been the greatest of sinners—that he had long hindered his wife from going to meeting and joining the Church—that he had set an awful example before his children. Mercy was his only plea. Sometimes he said, 'I am just entering the kingdom, when my sins rise up and shut me out.' He said he was determined to seek on, and if he went to hell he would go a praying penitent. I left him in this state of mind about the first of July last, well satisfied that if he persevered, his dungeon would yet shake, and his chains fall off, and his soul be set at liberty.

"I received a letter from my wife, saying that the Doctor was very sick and in great distress of mind—that he had sent for her very often to sing and pray for him. I have just received another letter from my wife, saying that the Doctor is no more.

"'I have just returned from the funeral of Doctor W——. He sent for me both by night and day, to sing and pray with him, and about two days before his death he found peace and died very happy. Just before he left the world, he called me to his bedside and said, "Tell brother Poe, of all the men I ever saw, I loved him the most; I would be glad to have him now about my dying bed, but that can not be. Tell him to go on and keep preaching Jesus, and I will meet him in heaven."'

"To be made the humble instrument in the hand of the blessed Savior, of plucking that brand from eternal burnings, more than compensates for all the sacrifices we have made, in leaving our native land and friends and all. But that is not all; the revival that commenced at that meeting, spread all around the circuit, and hundreds have been added to the Church."

After his return to Texas, he endeavored to commence an institution of learning at San Augustine. The ensuing conference adopted it and gave it their patronage. Daniel was appointed to the San Augustine circuit, and commenced his labors, having some three hundred miles to travel in filling his appointments every four weeks. After the first quarter, the teacher of mathematics, in their new college, resigned, and Daniel undertook to supply his place. While filling this post, he regularly rode into the country and preached on Friday night, twice on Saturday, and twice on Sabbath, and returned so as to attend to the recitations of his classes in the college, from Monday morning to the next Friday afternoon.

In June, 1844, his wife was attacked with congestive fever, but in a few days she seemed to be convalescent, and he went to an appointment six miles from San Augustine the first Saturday in July, to hold a two days' meeting. The congregation met in a grove, and he preached to them on Saturday, at 11 o'clock, from Lam. iii, 48. Dr. Greir, a member of our Church, told us that he wept profusely while he portrayed the desolations of sin, and exhorted the sinner to come to Christ for salvation. When he closed his sermon, he gave out the first two lines of a hymn, and stepping down from the stand, approaching the Doctor with his hand on his temple, he said, "Doctor, I feel as if my head was bursting." The Doctor perceiving that he had a violent fever, assisted him to his carriage, and took him to his house, and by prompt attention, through the afternoon and night, he thought him better next morning, and took him home. On Sabbath afternoon his wife was taken worse, and his two eldest children were violently attacked with the same fever. On Tuesday evening the Doctor told him his wife must die. About the same time Rev. L. Fowler, having returned from New York, where he had been attending General conference, brought him a letter from his brother, and spoke to him of the probable division of the Church. He read his letter, and laying it down exclaimed, "O, must Methodism be rent in twain!" He was unable to see his wife, as they were lying in separate rooms, and said to brother Fowler, "Tell Jane to commend her soul and her children to God. If I live I'll do the best I can for them, if I die I want Adam to come and get them." He grew rapidly worse, and on Wednesday morning he was told that he too must die. He immediately commenced giving some direction about his business, requested Rev. Lester Janes to write to his brother, and request him to come and settle his business, pay all his debts, and bring his children to Ohio. In the midst of these efforts, his mind wandered, and he complained of excruciating pains in his head and of choking. In this condition he remained till morning, when brother Fowler returned and found him dying. He took him by the hand and said, "Daniel, you are going!" He answered, in a whisper, "Yes!" Brother Fowler asked, "How do you feel?" He replied, "Happy, very, very happy!" and expired. His wife had conversed, after being informed that she must die, with brother Fowler on her spiritual prospects, and asked him to pray with her; and while he prayed she was powerfully blessed. She then had her children brought to her, and commending them to God in a few words of prayer, gave them her last kiss, and handed them to friends standing around her bed, saying, "Take care of them till their uncle Adam comes for them." She knew their father was dying too; and though she was one of the most affectionate mothers we ever knew, she seemed to give her children to her heavenly Father without a single distrustful fear; and then in bright and joyous vision of her home so near, she shouted glory! till her voice sunk to a whisper; and she breathed out her happy spirit into the arms of the Blessed, who waited to bear her to heaven. They died within forty minutes of each other, and were buried in one coffin, immediately in rear of the Methodist church in San Augustine. "Lovely and pleasant were they in their lives, and in their death they were not divided."

In December, 1844, his brother, Rev. Adam Poe, reached that place, and found all three of the children at different places, well taken care of by good friends, in pretty good health, having nearly recovered from their attacks of fever. After settling the business matters, according to Daniel's directions, and being ready to start home, he took the children, the youngest in his arms, and the others walking on each side of him, to the grave of the parents, to take a last look. As they stood by the grave, the oldest, a little girl five years of age, sobbing as if her heart would break, said, "O, uncle, can't you take up father and mother and take them with us to Ohio?" Her little brother, a year older, answered, "Susan, don't you know father and mother will be as near to us in heaven, after we get to Ohio, as they are now? They will not forget us; they love us still, I know they do." The little one in his arms lisped, "Yes, I know my pa and ma love me any where."

Thus died, and were buried in the red lands of Texas, as noble a couple as ever labored and suffered in the Methodist itinerancy, in the prime of life and the midst of their years. Both of these devoted missionaries were very highly esteemed, as far as they were known, in Texas, and Daniel was as widely known as any minister could be, in the length of time that he was there. Of his talents, as a minister, much might be said to his credit. He laid the foundation of a good education in his youth, under the direction of the late Dr. Ruter, who was his warm, personal friend. He was a diligent and enthusiastic student through life, and most conscientiously did he observe the rule of a minister, which we have frequently heard him quote with solemn emphasis, "Never be unemployed, never be triflingly employed."

He was in person almost gigantic, being six feet three and a half inches high, and weighing about two hundred and thirty pounds. He possessed uncommon athletic force and activity, and the whole energy of his powerful body and mind was devoted to his Master's work. His social qualities were such as to make him a favorite in every circle where he moved. In the wigwam of the Indian, and in the cabin of the Texan negro, as well as among the most refined in the higher walks of civilization, every-where he was beloved, and his ministry was crowned with many trophies, that no doubt will shine as stars with him in the kingdom of heaven forever.

Thus lived, and thus died one of the most zealous and indefatigable young preachers we ever knew. May God raise up many more such to carry the Gospel to regions beyond!

CHAPTER XLI.

THOMAS DRUMMOND.

THE subject of our sketch was born in Manchester, England, in the year 1806, and came to America with his father's family in 1811. His father sought a home in the west, the El Dorado of the emigrant, whose broad plains and rich soil invite the culture of the industrious yeoman. When quite a youth he devoted himself to the service of the Lord. He was not like many who think it quite sufficient for all the purposes of salvation to give the last sad remnants of their miserable lives to God.

> "A flower when offered in the bud,
> Is no vain sacrifice."

How precious are the memorials of that heart whose early affections have been given to God! Truly, as saith the inspired one, the ways of Religion "are ways of pleasantness, and all her paths are peace—she is a tree of life to them that lay hold upon her, and happy is every one that retaineth her." In the twenty-third year of his age—being called of God—he entered upon the work of the ministry, and began earnestly and eloquently to plead with sinners to be reconciled to God. After exercising his gifts as a local preacher for the space of a year, and giving full proof of his call by the fruits which attended his labors, he was recommended for admission into the traveling connection, and accordingly received by the Pittsburg conference in the year 1831.

His first appointment was to the Summerfield circuit, in the West Wheeling district, with the Rev. John W.

Minor. The next field of labor assigned him was the St. Clairsville circuit, where he continued one year; and at the expiration of his term he was sent to Pittsburg, with Dr. Martin Ruter for his colleague. The appointment of so young a preacher to a station of so much importance as Pittsburg, would necessarily lead one to infer that he not only had remarkable gifts, but that he had made astonishing progress in ministerial attainments, and such was the fact. Some preachers at first give but little promise, and develop slowly, yet in the end become learned, talented, and useful, even as stars in the right hand of Jesus, to shine upon the Church and the world. Others at once seem to flash over the horizon of life as the sun when he crosses the threshold of the ocean—first a circle of mellow light, and then a full burst of glory; but whether suns or stars, both have their appointed spheres, and roll on fulfilling their high and holy destiny. In the Church of the apostles there was a Paul, an Apollos, and a Cephas; and the diversity of talent was made to subserve the most important purposes in the erection of the spiritual building.

Drummond had rare and brilliant talents; and though but two years in the conference, and but three a preacher, he was regarded by the appointing power as adequate for so important a post. His next station was Morgantown, in Virginia, where he remained one year with great acceptability and usefulness. At the conference which was held in Washington, in July, 1834, his heart was touched with the wants of the west; and filled with a missionary zeal, he volunteered for Missouri, and was stationed in the city of St. Louis. At that post he labored hard, fulfilling all the duties of a preacher and pastor up to June, 1835, embracing a period little short of a year from the time of his transfer. On the Sabbath before his decease, though somewhat indisposed, he labored with more than ordinary fervor. The dead and the dying were around him; for that dread "pestilence which walketh in darkness and wasteth at noonday," was spreading death and desolation in the ill-fated city. To prepare his hearers for the scourge, and to converse and pray with those who were grappling with the dread monster, taxed all his energies to the utmost. Sabbath evening came; but, alas! the foe had seized the soldier of the cross himself—he was attacked with cholera, and all medical skill and attention were in vain. Monday closed the scene of conflict. The king of terrors aimed at length his fatal dart, and smote the saint; but he feared not the blow. The sting was extracted, and victory over death and hell was gained through faith in Jesus' blood. Just as his spirit was passing, he said to his weeping friends around him, "*All is well! Tell my brethren of the Pittsburg conference I died at my post.*"

When the brethren met at their holy convocation, which was shortly after, there were weeping eyes and sorrowful hearts; but the message which they had received from the dying soldier cheered them on in the battle of the Lord. One of their number—one of Zion's sweetest minstrels—touched his lyre, and it sent forth a dirge pleasant but mournful.

"Away from his home and the friends of his youth,
He hasted, the herald of mercy and truth;
For the love of his Lord, and to seek for the lost;
Soon, alas! was his fall—but he died at his post.

The stranger's eye wept, that, in life's brightest bloom,
One gifted so highly should sink to the tomb;
For in ardor he led in the van of the host,
And he fell like a soldier—he died at his post.

He wept not himself that his warfare was done—
The battle was fought, and the victory won;
But he whispered of those whom his heart clung to most,
'Tell my brethren, for me, that I died at my post.'

He asked not a stone to be sculptured with verse;
He asked not that fame should his merits rehearse;
But he asked as a boon, when he gave up the ghost,
That his brethren might know that he died at his post.

Victorious his fall—for he rose as he fell,
With Jesus, his Master, in glory to dwell;
He has passed o'er the stream and has reached the bright coast,
For he fell like a martyr—he died at his post.

And can we the words of his exit forget?
O! no, they are fresh in our memory yet;
An example so brilliant shall never be lost,
We will fall in the work—we will die at our post."

From this poet—the Rev. William Hunter, formerly editor of the Pittsburg Christian Advocate, and author of "Select Melodies"—we have received a sketch embracing some personal recollections of Drummond, which we subjoin:

"Yours of the 17th ult. is before me, asking for recollections of Rev. Thomas Drummond. I had no personal acquaintance with brother Drummond. He was my senior by two or three years in the Pittsburg conference, and left it for St. Louis at the close of my first year as a probationer. I never saw him but once; that was at the conference in Washington, Pennsylvania, in 1834. He came up to me before the conference door—having somehow associated my face and name together, as I had his—and said, in that free and peculiar manner which was characteristic of him, while he seized my hand, 'How are you, Hunter? *We* need no introduction." He passed into the church, and I am not certain that I ever saw his face again. I left the seat of the conference, perhaps, that day or the next; and he was transferred to Missouri, where he shortly afterward died. From that conference I was sent to Pittsburg, in company with T. M. Hudson and M. Simpson—now bishop. Thomas Drummond had been there with Doctor

Ruter, not the preceding year, but the one before that. I consequently heard much of him, and can testify to the universal esteem in which he was held. Some of the good old members could scarcely cease talking about him. I can not at this date call up particular incidents related to me concerning him, during his labors in Pittsburg. I can only state that the general impression made upon my mind by what I heard was, that he was quite a good preacher; studious in his habits, industrious in his pastoral work, and an exceedingly-agreeable companion in the social circle. He was a man of very kind feelings, although somewhat free and blunt in his manners. He was not one of those who continually wore a somber countenance, as if to smile was a sin, or a little pleasantry an iniquity to be punished by the judges. He was a cheerful, vigorous, energetic man, doing his duty with a good will, a light heart, and a radiant countenance; yet withal a man who entered deeply into the sorrows of others, visiting the sick and the needy, and ministering both to their temporal and spiritual wants. A poor woman, whom he had visited as a pastor, died happy in the Lord, leaving a little girl with no provision for her comfort. Brother Drummond adopted her as his own—I believe her father was dead also—and made arrangements for her rearing and education; though I think that from the pecuniary burden of this he was relieved by the liberality of the late Mrs. Dumars, of Pittsburg, in whose bosom beat the kindest heart of woman, and who took the little girl, bringing her up as her own. The little girl used to call herself Mary Ann Cooper Drummond Dumars. She became a member of the Church, and is now a married woman, with a family of her own, and living in comfortable circumstances. This incident will illustrate one trait in brother Drummond's character—his kindness and benevolence—the trait to which, perhaps, he fell a martyr in St. Louis during the cholera visitation there.

"Brother Drummond was the first stationed preacher in the station which I now occupy—Morgantown, Virginia. The parsonage in which I am now writing was built under his superintendence. The trees in the yard were planted by him, from which succeeding preachers, since that time, have eaten fruit. He frequently laid off his clerical coat, and went to work at the parsonage himself; and so well was the financial part of the business managed, that when the work was done there was a dollar over; though some of the credit of this is also due to the well-known liberality of the Church here.

"Here, as in Pittsburg, I have often heard brother Drummond spoken of in terms of kind remembrance. The families in which he boarded, especially, have a high appreciation of his worth. He was able in the pulpit, faithful in pastoral visitations, diligent in the instruction of the children, assembling them for catechetical exercises. He by no means confined his labors to the village; but had several appointments in the country round about, some of them as many as nine or ten miles out. There is a sweet little church a couple of miles out of town, now called Drummond Chapel, in memory of the fact that he was, perhaps, the first who established preaching in the neighborhood. The only week-day class that we have in the station is a female class, met by the preacher, composed generally of the older ladies of the Church. It was Drummond who formed this class, as he said, for his own especial benefit. There are some of the traces left by him in this, the last station which he occupied in the Pittsburg conference. I am not aware that there was any great revival in the place during his labors; but the Church was in a healthy and prosperous condition. I am told that he studied law, and passed an examination on it while here. I know not that he intended ever to practice. It is more probable that his object was to qualify himself better for the work of the ministry, by increasing his knowledge of legal science."

How many burning and shining lights have suddenly been quenched in the darkness of death! How melancholy the remembrance that the most talented and deeply-devoted in the ranks of the ministry are soonest called away from the walls of our Zion, while we are left to mourn their departure! May we imitate their virtues and aspire after their glorious immortality!

CHAPTER XLII.

INDIAN CAMP MEETING.

IN the year 1828, a short time after we left the Indian nation, we held a camp meeting at Messick's camp-ground, not far from Bellefontaine. To this meeting we invited the Indian brethren at the Wyandott mission. This invitation was generally acceded to, and the Indians came with their camping apparatus, to the number of one hundred and fifty. A place was assigned them for pitching their tents, so that they might all be as near together as possible. We have called this the "Indian camp meeting," because, as the sequel will show, the exercises were mostly confined to the Indian department of the camp, and the Lord seemed to have selected our red brethren as the instrumentality, through which all the glorious results that attended it were achieved.

The Indians being more expert in pitching tents than the whites, they, of course, were ready at an earlier hour to engage in religious exercises. It is characteristic of the Indian to devote exclusive attention, for the time being, to whatever pursuit or employment he may take in hand. If it be fishing, or hunting, or sugar making, or corn planting, nothing else is allowed to interfere in the time allotted to these things. So in regard to religion. The time devoted to God was the most sacred, and no people could unite with greater sincerity than they in singing those appropriate lines:

"Far from my thoughts vain world begone,
Let my religious hours alone."

Soon the Christian chiefs, and queens, and all, were formed into a circle, and the voice of praise and prayer made the forest arches ring. After singing one of their Christian songs, only as Indians can sing, they fell simultaneously upon their knees and lifted up their faces toward heaven, as if they expected to see the Great Spirit descend in blessings from the parted skies. One of their number would lead in prayer, and when the Indian words, "*tamentare*," and "*Homendezue*," would escape the suppliant's lips, a deep *amen* would be uttered in concert by all the circle.

The Indian has strong faith, and when he makes preparation for a sacrifice to the Great Spirit, he expects with the utmost confidence that it will be accepted. So was it in this instance; for while they were praying the Spirit came down upon them, and the power of God was manifested in the awakening and conversion of souls. As the shaking of the leaves in the tops of the mulberry trees was an indication to the prophet of the presence of God, so the excitement of the multitude engaged in prayer, as indicated by the tears, and groans, and shouts, was a sign that the Great Spirit was at work upon the hearts of these sons and daughters of the forest, and presently the tents of the whites were forsaken, and many might have been seen mingling with their red brethren and sisters in the exercises of the hour. From this hour, though so early in the meeting, the work of the Lord began, and the interest continued to increase and spread as the meeting progressed, till Saturday night, when the whole encampment was in a flame of religious excitement. There seemed to be no need of preaching or exhortation, the Lord having taken his own work into his own hands. All that the preachers and people had to do was to follow the leadings of the Spirit, and the hours passed away in singing and prayer, interrupted only—if, indeed, it may be called an interruption—by the loud cries for mercy, which rose from the burdened hearts of the kneeling penitents, or the louder shouts of praise to God for delivering grace, which rose up on the night air and re-echoed among the trees from the converted. The holy scenes and hallowed associations of that night of prayer among the Indians, will never be erased from our memory; and though many of our precious red brethren and sisters, who made that grove resound with their voices, have long since gone to join the innumerable company before the throne of God and the Lamb, yet we shall cherish the recollection of that hour till we too shall be summoned to the marriage feast above.

Sabbath morning came. It was one of those beautiful Sabbaths of an Indian summer, which, by its soft and balmy nature, reminds one of the rest and blessedness of heaven. Not many miles from the camp-ground there lived an ungodly man, whose wife, though not a professor of religion, having heard of the meeting, was desirous to attend. She had never been to a camp meeting before, and her desire to attend, like that which actuates too many others, was simply to gratify her curiosity. It was with some considerable difficulty that she could get her husband's consent, for even backwoods wives in that day were accustomed to look up to their husbands for advice. She finally succeeded, however, as women generally do when they take the right course, in overcoming her husband's opposition. He agreed to stay home and mind the children while she would be absent, but commanded her to come home by the middle of the afternoon, on pain of getting a whipping. The poor woman, with the brutal threat resting over her head, arrived upon the ground at an early hour. Scarcely had she got within the circle of tents and taken her seat in the congregation, till she began to feel sad at heart. A wonderful power had taken hold of her mind. Her thoughts were carried back to the days of her youth; her early religious thoughts were awakened; tears began to flow, as her children and husband passed rapidly but vividly before her; her sins rose up in frightful, hideous forms to her excited imagination and conscience; and tears and sobs gave place to groans and cries for mercy. She soon became an object of attention, and prayers from many a sympathizing heart went up to God in her behalf. She had already remained beyond the time allotted her by her husband, but her heart was too much burdened to think of returning. She could bear reproach, and scorn, and scourging, but a wounded conscience was insupportable. Through the entire day she continued to plead for mercy, and when the shades of night were gathering around, and forest and tent were lighted up with the watch-fires, and the voices of praise and prayer were swelling out in anthems and supplications to the God of heaven, she embraced the cross with all the fervor of her soul, and her burden, like that of Christian's in Bunyan's Pilgrim, rolled away from her and was lost in the tomb of forgetfulness. It was then that she passed from darkness to light, and from the bondage of Satan to the liberty of the children of God.

That night was spent in rejoicing, and when the morning came, with a glad heart and free, she started home to meet her enraged and cruel husband. She was always amiable, but she met him that morning with a smile and a sweetness that only grace can spread over the features. With meekness and humility she told him of the cause of her detention, and concluded by a simple narration of what God had done for her soul. This, however, as is usually the case, only enraged him the more, and taking his wagon whip he beat her most severely. This she could have borne without religion, for it was nothing when compared with the lashes of a guilty conscience; but now that her soul was full of the love of God, with a martyr spirit she could have borne the torture or the stake, in the name and for the sake of Jesus. From that hour the iron entered his soul only to be extracted by an omnipotent Hand. He raged like a maniac, and swore that he would take vengeance in firing the encampment that night.

Night came, and this inhuman fiend started out under its cover to execute his fearful threat. When he arrived upon the ground the Indian brethren were engaged in a most glorious work. The groans of the penitent, and the shouts of praise of the converted, were mingled together, and the sound of the many voices was like the roar of the distant sea. While this sound waked the songs of heaven, it was a "dreadful sound" to that ungodly man, and carried, like the sound in the Assyrian camp, terror to his heart. He drew near. There was terror in his face and wildness in his eye as the watch-fire gleamed upon him, but his heart had lost its courage, and his arm its nerve. As he gazed upon the scene, like Belshazzar, in the court of Babylon, in sight of the mysterious characters of fire, which blazed out upon him, his knees trembled, his heart quaked, and he fell prostrate upon the ground, crying for mercy. He was picked up by an athletic Indian, who fully understood the nature of his condition, and carried him into the circle. No sooner was the sturdy Saul prostrate before the Indians, than a volley of prayer went up in his behalf that almost rent the heavens. He was a prisoner, captured by one of the scouts of Immanuel's army, but he was wounded and dying. His captor bent down closely with his ear, to listen to his dying groans, and would say to him in Indian, "by and by."

There lay the prostrate sinner pleading for mercy.

The Indians stood by him, and sang and prayed till long past the noon of night. It was a desperate struggle, and seemed doubtful whether there was mercy for such a bold blasphemer and cruel persecutor. But just before day, when the stars began to fade in the light of the gray streaks of morning, God's mercy came, the long agony was over, and the blasphemer and persecutor was changed into a child of God; the heir of hell was made an heir of heaven. To the astonishment of all, after his first bursts of praise were over, he related his cruel conduct to his wife, and his intention, as a matter of revenge, of setting the encampment on fire. Some one present interpreted his confession and experience to the Indians. When he was through, the noble-hearted Mononcue stepped up to him, and taking him by the hand said, "Now, my white brother, God converted your wife, and you whipped her for it, and God has converted you. Go home and tell her what God has done for your soul, and let her take the same whip, if she desires so to do, and whip you in return. It is good that God has converted you both. Go in peace, and sin no more." This couple will never forget the Indian camp meeting.

But these are not all the incidents connected with this camp meeting; there were others still more interesting and thrilling, the relation of which, however, would occupy too much space for this chapter, and we shall reserve them for the next.

CHAPTER XLIII.

CONVERSION OF AN INSPECTOR-GENERAL.

At the Indian camp meeting, accompanied by her children, was a lady who claimed kindred with the natives of the forest, from the fact that, although her father and husband were white, yet her mother was a native of one of the Indian tribes. She was a most worthy, consistent, and zealous member of the Methodist Episcopal Church, and had pitched her tent at the commencement of the meeting. She possessed much of the true Indian character of integrity and perseverance, conjoined with a large share of gentleness and benevolence. Her fidelity and devotion as a wife and mother, beautifully assorted with the entire consecration of her heart to God. In all the religious exercises she took an active part, and her labors and example were particularly beneficial to her Indian sisters in the Lord.

Let us now call your attention to the husband of this devoted woman. Though wicked, unlike the case described in the foregoing chapter, he was not opposed to his wife on account of her religion; but rather assisted than prevented her in the discharge of her religious duties. He had been a major in the militia; but on account of his military skill was promoted to the office of an Inspector-General. We have already seen that he did not accompany his wife to camp meeting, the reason of which was, that at the time he was out on a tour of duty, inspecting the various regiments and companies. As a military man none was more popular; and his social, if not jovial disposition, led him to seek kindred society, and occasionally to partake of the festive cup, and enjoy a game of whist. These indulgences, however, as we have already hinted, were mere episodes in his otherwise temperate and sober life. Would that it were the case with all; but, alas! how few know where, or have the power to stop with only an occasional indulgence in drinking and gaming! He had a respect for religious institutions, and would regularly attend, with his wife, at the log church. When Saturday evening arrived the General directed his course toward the camp-ground, where he arrived dressed in full military costume.

But we will leave him for a while in the religious marquee, enjoying the society of his family, and call your attention to a short history of his wife's family connections. Her father, Ebenezer Zane, in an early day, was taken prisoner by the Indians, and from his home, near Wheeling, Virginia, was removed to the west, where he was adopted by the Wyandott tribe, and raised to follow all the pursuits of an Indian life. A dark-eyed, blooming Indian maid won his youthful affections—not by any of those arts of fashionable life, by which too many are decoyed in what are called the circles of refinement, but by a native gentleness, simplicity, and beauty, which needs not foreign adornment and art to captivate. Suffice it to say, the two young and unsophisticated hearts were united; and as the result of this union, and as pledges of its continued purity and genuineness, they were blessed with three sons and four daughters. We have not space to dwell upon their history, only to say that all their daughters, in process of time, married white men. Their names were Reed, M'Culloch, and Armstrong—the youngest, as we have already seen, was married to General Long. Two of the sons—Ebenezer, junior, and William—married Indian women, and the third—Isaac—married a white woman. This whole family were related to the Zanes at Wheeling, of whom there are some of the descendants still living. The Indian branch of this family were noted for sobriety, honesty, and respectability. They resided on Mad river, where a section of land was granted to them by the Government. The family of which Mrs. Long was a member were all religiously inclined. It was at the house of the younger Ebenezer Zane that the first quarterly meeting was held in the Wyandott nation. Isaac was converted, and joined the Methodist Episcopal Church, and continued till his death to exemplify, by his consistent deportment, the Christian profession. We have often heard him, in his broken Indian dialect, tell in love-feast and class meeting the wonders of redeeming grace and dying love. None could listen to the simple and touching recital of his conversion without being deeply affected, and realizing of a truth that he was a child of God.

M'Culloch, a brother-in-law, was a faithful and devoted Christian, and died in the triumphs of the Gospel. He left two sons, who followed in the footsteps of their parents. The elder son, Noah, yet lives to serve God and the Church. The younger became a reputable Baptist preacher. Sarah Zane married Robert Armstrong, who was taken prisoner by the Indians when a boy, and reared among the tribe. They had four children, two sons and two daughters, all of whom were sent to the mission school, at Upper Sandusky, when we had charge of the same. Hannah, one of the daughters, was converted while a member of the school. She was one of the most lovely and amiable children we ever knew; but, alas! death, who loves a shining mark, aimed his fatal javelin, and the idol of her parents and our school was smitten. She was just budding into womanhood when arrested by disease. Day after day we saw the bright and beauteous flower fade before us, and we knew she must die. Just before her death her weeping and disconsolate father bent over her couch, and, placing her arm around his neck, she said, "Dear father, do not weep for me, I am going to God and heaven. Angels are waiting to take me home. You and mother, and brother and sisters will soon come after me, and then we shall all be happy forever. Farewell, dear father and mother! My Savior smiles, and bids me come." Then, with the sound of glory on her tongue, her sainted spirit passed away to the land of the blest. That little Indian girl would not have died had beauty and gentleness been a security against the shafts of death. But, as the little prophet said, the father and mother, and the younger son, John M'Intire, have gone to join her in heaven.

But we must now return to the camp meeting. On Sabbath morning General Long was seen, in full military dress, in the congregation, and excited the attention of all, but more particularly his Indian friends. He was an attentive observer of all that transpired, and listened eagerly to all that was said. Those who knew him best saw, from his clouded brow, and his attempts to rally his spirits, that there was something pressing heavily upon his otherwise joyous and happy mind, and they were not much at a loss in conjecturing the cause. The Spirit of God was evidently at work in his heart. His affectionate wife and Indian friends were constant and earnest in pouring out their supplications in his behalf. His convictions increased, notwithstanding all his efforts to shake them off; and when Monday morning came, he was glad to avail himself of the opportunity his duties afforded in leaving for the muster-field, where companies awaited his inspection. He accordingly mounted his horse, and started; but his Christian friends did not give him up. They knew full well that God was at work upon his heart, and their anxieties were increased in the conviction that a crisis had arrived in his history which would, in all probability, decide his destiny forever. One has said,

> "There is a tide in the affairs of men,
> Which taken at the flood leads on to fortune."

Especially is this true in regard to religion. There is a period in the history of every man, when it may be said of him individually, as it was said by the Savior to the scribe, on a certain occasion, "Thou art not far from the kingdom of heaven." When the tide of Divine influence is up, and waves of mercy are gathering around, then the soul may start out upon that flood for heaven; but if this influence is resisted, the receding waves will bear away hope and happiness—it may be forever.

The General had not proceeded more than two miles on his journey till his feelings became almost insupportable. He was alone, and there being nothing to divert his mind, he was shut up to himself, and a horror of darkness came upon him. To go farther he felt it would be impossible. The cords of an irresistible influence seemed to be drawing him back, and having reached their utmost tension he must yield or break that influence forever. He turned his horse in the direction of the camp-ground, and rode rapidly back. When he arrived the congregation were assembled for the purpose of partaking of the holy communion. The elements of bread and wine had been consecrated by holy hands and prayer, and the pastor was inviting the flock to come forward to the rude altar, and participate in the eucharistic feast, which every want supplies. He stood and gazed upon the scene. He saw his beloved wife advance and kneel with the whites and Indians that crowded to their places; and as the minister said, "He that confesseth Jesus before men, shall be acknowledged by him in heaven; while he that denieth him shall also be denied at the judgment of the great day," he felt that he had neither part nor lot in the matter, and that he must forever be separated from his dear wife and the society of all the good, and the scene and associations so affected him that he wept aloud. After the sacrament was ended the presiding elder addressed the congregation, touchingly alluding to the scenes of Gethsemane and Calvary, which had been presented before them in the passion and death of the Son of God, and concluded by inviting all such as were desirous of fleeing the wrath to come, and of being saved from their sins, to come forward, and kneel at the altar and pray for pardon. Scarcely had he ceased till anxious souls in large numbers pressed to the mercy-seat. The General was standing, in full military costume, at rest, with one hand upon the stake that supported the altar-railing. His feelings were wrought up to the highest point of excitement, and unable any longer to restrain his emotion, which was raging with earthquake violence within his soul, he exclaimed, with a loud but tremulous voice, "Quarters! quarters! My God, quarters! I yield;" and then fell his whole length upon the ground. He was soon surrounded by the godly, and borne into the altar. The excitement produced by this demonstration, among the whites and Indians, was tremendous; and when they all fell upon their knees there went up such a storm of prayer as rent the very heavens. The General wept, and groaned, and prayed for the space of two hours, with a fervency that few ever prayed before. He was a shrewd, intelligent Yankee—a descendant of the Puritans—and many were astonished at the appropriateness of his language in supplicating mercy. But see! he ceases to pray, and quick as spark from smitten steel, the blessing descends! Hark! A shout, "Glory, glory!" in loud, full bursts, escapes from his lips. "Where am I?" said the converted man. "I never saw so beautiful a place in all my life before." In an instant his wife, who alone had been pouring out her heart to God in her husband's behalf, was at his side, praising God for redeeming grace. They embraced with an affection they never knew before; for they were now one in Jesus. His Indian and white friends turned their prayers into praises, and united with the angelic throng,

> "Whose hymns of joy proclaimed through heaven
> The triumphs of a soul forgiven."

He was greeted by the warm-hearted chief, Mononcue, who embraced him, and said, in broken English, "My brother, you must now fight for King Jesus." After his joy had somewhat subsided he found Judge —— lying in the altar, upon his face, weeping. Approaching him he said, "Judge, is this you? Get up and pray with all your might; you will never obtain the blessing of pardon lying there. Get up and pray with all your heart, and God will bless you."

The next day the General started for the muster-field. The officers had heard that he was converted, and had joined the Church. Many of them were not a little annoyed at the intelligence; and though they no doubt secretly felt that he had done right, and wished themselves in his condition, yet they resolved to put his religious fit, as they called it, to an end, at least to test the genuineness and strength of his profession. They had to this end prepared a fine dinner, with the accompaniments of wine, music, and cards. When the time for recess came he was ushered into a room decorated with national flags, evergreens, and flowers, where a sumptuous dinner was spread. Scarcely had he taken his seat before an officer—for whom the General had a great regard—

approached him with a flowing glass, which he presented, saying, "My dear General, you must be greatly fatigued with the arduous duties of the day; take a little wine, it will strengthen you." "No, my dear Colonel," said he, "not one drop shall pass my lips." By this time the eyes of all the officers were turned in that direction. It was the first trial, but nobly he met it. Raising his voice he said, "Fellow-officers and gentlemen, yesterday God, for Christ's sake, pardoned my sins, and I have sworn allegiance to the King of heaven. By this oath I will live, and by it I will die; and now let me say, in all kindness, unless you repent of your wickedness you must perish in your sins; and here I most cordially invite you all to go with me this evening to the camp meeting, that there you may seek religion." Then, espying a pack of cards on an adjoining table, he added, "Nor will I ever throw another card, by the grace of God, as long as I live." These announcements, though by some anticipated, yet to others were like claps of thunder in a clear sky.

That dinner was eaten in silence, and not a drop of wine was drank or a card shuffled, and the hour passed away in peace and quietness. The General lived many years a consistent and devoted member of the Church, adorning the doctrines of God, his Savior; and as a soldier of the cross, when he came to die, he was enabled to say, "I have fought a good fight, I have finished my course; henceforth there is laid up for me a crown of righteousness, which God, the righteous Judge, shall give me."

Many were the converts at that camp meeting, and the day of eternity will show, that of the whites and Indians who there embraced religion, the work was as genuine and lasting as that which characterized the conversion of General Long.

CHAPTER XLIV.

PIONEER WOMEN.

HISTORIANS may write of the brave and patriotic women of ancient times, of the mother of the Gracchi, and the mother of Napoleon, and Washington, and the more recent patriotic deeds of our Revolutionary mothers, who freely gave up their sons to fight the battles of liberty, and sacrificed every thing but their more than Roman virtue, in supporting our heroic fathers in the conflict for freedom; be it our pleasing task to record some of the achievements of our pioneer mothers in the west, whose zeal, and courage, and self-sacrificing devotion, afford specimens of a moral sublimity greater than was ever witnessed in the heroism of the patriot mothers of olden time.

When the Rev. Bennet Maxey traveled as a missionary in Georgia, about the close of the Revolutionary war, the following incident occurred, which he related to me with his own lips. It will be recollected that nearly all that country was a wilderness, inhabited by savage Indians. There were but few Methodist societies, and they were widely separated. The missionary, in his long and perilous journeys, could only reach them occasionally, and in doing so would have to encounter almost as much toil and hardship as the emigrant now does in crossing the plains to California. Even then, with all his zeal and perseverance, there were some settlements that could not be reached without a reinforcement of missionary laborers. In one of these settlements, six miles distant from each other, there lived two pious women, who had emigrated to the country from the state of Maryland, where they had been converted and joined the Methodist Church. They felt the loss of the ministrations of the Gospel. No Sabbath brought with it its holy scenes and sanctuary privileges. The time of the people seemed to be occupied, on Sabbaths, in the sports of the chase, or in idle and frivolous amusements. While, however, the neighbors were engaged in the desecration of the holy Sabbath, these two pious women agreed to meet half way between their respective cabins, and hold a prayer and class meeting by themselves. Sabbath after Sabbath these devoted females walked to their appointment in the woods, and there, in the depths of that southern forest, with no eye to see but God, they spoke to one another about their trials, and conflicts, and hopes, and "the Lord hearkened and heard, and a book of remembrances was written before him." The voice of praise and prayer echoed through the wildwood. They not only prayed for themselves and their neighbors, but they besought the Lord that he would send the Gospel into that wild and destitute region. One Sabbath, while thus engaged in religious exercises, they were overheard by a hunter, who came unconsciously upon their retreat; and there, in the language of the poet, in that

> "Scene where spirits blend,
> And friend holds fellowship with friend,"

around that common mercy-seat, they united their supplications. It was holy ground, and a sacred awe came over him, as from the covert of a tree he listened to their praises and their prayers. This hunter's cabin was not far distant from the place of meeting, and every Sabbath he would, at the appointed time, take his station and listen to the soul-thrilling eloquence of their prayers and songs. He had not, though a roving hunter, been reared altogether without the influences of religion. His pious mother, long since in heaven, had taught him the fear of the Lord, and her instructions and prayers would cross his memory in his wild, erratic course, and like the recurrence of a pleasant dream awaken hallowed memories. On a certain Sabbath he resolved to introduce himself to the strange, mysterious worshipers; and, accordingly, after they had concluded their meeting, and were taking leave of each other to return to their homes, he appeared before them, and in tones of kindness invited them to meet at his cabin on the next Sabbath, and he would collect his neighbors.

Here was a trial which they had not anticipated. But they regarded it as an interposition of divine Providence in their behalf; and though it would be a heavy cross, requiring the greatest amount of moral courage and endurance, to meet the rough and sturdy backwoodsmen, and hold meeting in their midst, they must not deny their Master in refusing to enter this open door. It was, accordingly, noised abroad that two women were going to hold meeting at the hunter's house; and as the thing was entirely new, the whole neighborhood went. The husbands of the two pious and devoted women, not knowing it was their wives, but being filled with curiosity at the singular announcement, were among the number of those who took their companions with them to the place of meeting. Their astonishment can better be imagined than described, when they saw them take their places in the cabin as the women that were to hold meeting on the occasion. One of them read a chapter in the Bible, which she did in a clear, strong voice, and then gave out a hymn, which was sung by the two and the congregation to some familiar tune; after which they kneeled down, and the one who had read the Bible offered up a most fervent and deeply-impressive prayer to God, in behalf of the congregation assembled. After prayer was over they united in singing one of those songs of Zion, with which they had made the woods ring at their Sabbath meetings previous. Many a heart was touched, as the divine strains rolled over the wondering assembly, and the tear stole down many a rough, sun-burnt face. When this was ended, the other rose tremblingly but firmly, as with the heart of a giant, and commenced telling the plain, simple story of her conversion. As she spoke, her voice assumed a majesty and a power truly wonderful. God sent down his Spirit and attended it with power to the hearts of the audience; and first the hunter, and then the two husbands, unable any longer to repress their feelings, broke out in loud cries for mercy. Several, while she was speaking, fell, as if smitten with lightning, to the floor, others fled from the house in the greatest consternation. These pious sisters in the Lord were not frightened by this exhibition of divine power; for although it was farthest from their anticipations, yet they had been familiar with such scenes in the days of their youth. They knew "it was the Lord's doings, and it was marvelous in their eyes," and they, therefore, commenced singing and praying with the slain of the Lord. It was not long till several were happily and powerfully converted to God, and this increased the power; and they were set immediately to work to pray for penitents and sinners. The work spread, mighty consternation fell upon all the people, and far and near, those who had not attended at the beginning flocked to the place of prayer. The hunter and his wife, and the two husbands were all converted, and the meeting continued with but little intermission, night and day, for two weeks. It was what might properly and most significantly be denominated a protracted meeting. The news of the wonderful work flew as on the wings of the wind, to the distance of forty or fifty miles, when it reached the ears of brother Maxey, who immediately started for the scene. When he arrived, he found the two faithful female heralds of the cross still on the ground, fighting most manfully the battle of the Lord. They had already received forty new recruits, all converted and happy in the love of God, and they were all living, speaking witnesses for Jesus—not a still-born child in all their ranks. Scarcely had the itinerant reached the scene of action, than, like the old soldier, at the sound of battle, the power of God came on him, and he entered the ranks of God's army with a shout of victory and triumph. They at once recognized his spirit, and hailed him as a fellow-soldier; but how great was their rejoicing when they found him to be one of Immanuel's officers, in the great army of God! To him the sisters cheerfully intrusted the leadership, and he led them forth valiantly to glorious war. With a voice like a trumpet, and a love for God and zeal for souls which was like fire in his bones, he went from neighborhood to neighborhood proclaiming salvation, and the work spread and prevailed, so that before the revival ceased, it had covered a sufficient extent of country to form a good large circuit, in the entire bounds of which there never had been preaching before.

And now, dear reader, what a field for reflection is here!—a wonderful manifestation of the power of God, through the agency of two pious, heroic, Christian women. How many would have said, could they have witnessed these two devoted females, commencing their religious exercises at that meeting, where were crowds of ungodly men, collected from all parts of the country, and impelled by mere curiosity at the novelty of the thing, "How improper! how unlike the decency and order which the apostle Paul enjoins should be observed in religious worship! And then, how shocking to delicacy, for women to speak in public, especially in such a mixed assembly!" But we see in this, as in other similar manifestations, that God's ways are not as our ways; and that He who has chosen the weak things of the world to confound the mighty, and things that are naught to bring to naught things that are, that no flesh might glory in his presence, the excellency of the power being of God and not of man, selected those two females as the chosen instruments of his Holy Spirit, to bear the messages of mercy and salvation to that dark and destitute region. We are obliged to concede this, or to admit what is abhorrent to every Christian; namely, that the Holy Spirit will sanction and set its seal to a work brought about by improper agencies.

Again: what Christian, who even believed that it was right and proper, and perfectly in accordance with that "decency and order" recommended by the apostle, for women to exercise their gifts in singing, and prayer, and Christian conversation or exhortation, would have had faith to believe that any good would have resulted from such a meeting? Yet these Christian females had faith, and according to that faith so it was to them. Besides, the circumstances were such as to justify such a procedure. In their neighborhood there were no ministers of the Gospel, and no Sabbath and sanctuary privileges; and impressed by the Spirit to pray the Lord of the harvest that he would send forth laborers, they went to prayer, and God heard and answered in a way that they had not anticipated, and that human reason could not have divined.

We will relate another incident of female devotion, which occurred in the bounds of the Ohio district. In the year 1817, while we were traveling with a fellow-itinerant, in passing along between the waters of Oil creek and Scrub Grass, which empties into the Alleghany river above Pittsburg, we came in sight of an old dilapidated log church. The sight of an old church gone into decay, never fails to awaken in our minds many reflections, and we never pass one without feeling an irrepressible desire to understand something of its history. My companion being somewhat acquainted with the history of this old church, related to me the following, in connection with the same: At an early day, in the settlement of that part of the country, which was then denominated the Holland purchase, a small Methodist society was organized by pioneer Methodist preachers. After some time the society built that log church, and flourished for several years. In progress of time, however, some of the old members died, and were buried in the graveyard close by the sanctuary, and others moved away, till it was dropped from the list of appointments as a preaching-place, and only one member of the class and society remained. She was a mother in Israel, and, like the prophet, she was left alone to sigh over the desolations of Zion. She loved the old sanctuary, and though deserted, she seemed to realize an increasing attachment as time wrought its inroads upon its doors and windows. Invariably on the Sabbath, when her health and the weather would permit, did she repair to this deserted temple and worship her God. There, in holy meditation, did she recall the scenes of her youth, the holy seasons, happy days she had spent with her brethren and sisters, some of whom were sleeping quietly in the adjoining church-yard, while others were far away. Here she would sit, and read, and sing, and pray, and talk to her invisible God and Savior. At length, it was noised abroad that she was a witch, that the old church was haunted with evil spirits, and that she met there to hold communion with the spirits of darkness, and thus increase her power of evil over the bodies and souls of those around her.

She was old and feeble, and heard of their surmises, but she remembered that her Master was charged of being possessed by the devil, and she heeded them not, but continued her Sabbath visits to the consecrated place. At length, two wicked young men of the neighborhood determined to watch her, and entering the church some time before she arrived, they climbed up and secreted themselves in the clapboard loft. After remaining there a short time, the old lady entered the church and took her seat by the rude altar. The young men, as they afterward related, experienced some sensations of fear, seeing, as they supposed, the old witch draw from her side-pocket an old leather-enveloped book, but their fears soon subsided when they heard her read, instead of an invocation to the spirits of darkness, the story of the widow of Sarepta. After she had finished, she drew from her other pocket an antiquated-looking hymn-book, from which she read that inimitable hymn,

"Jesus, I my cross have taken,
All to leave and follow thee;
Naked, poor, despised, forsaken,
All I am is lost in thee."

After having sung this beautiful hymn, which she did with a trembling, but sweet, melodious voice, she fell upon her knees and poured out her full heart to God in prayer and supplication. As friend holds fellowship with friend, so did she talk with her heavenly Father. She told the Lord all her complaints and grievances, and lamented the sad condition of the old and young of the neighborhood, who were alike on the road to perdition. She then alluded to the happy seasons she had enjoyed in that place, when Zion shed her holy light and converts crowded her gates. In piteous strains she lamented her desolations, and prayed that the Lord would build up her waste places, and again crowd her gates with living converts. She prayed especially for those who cast out her name as evil, that the Lord would change their hearts. She prayed, also, for the young and giddy multitude, who were forgetting God and living as if there were no hell to shun, no heaven to pursue. While she was praying God's Spirit was at work on the hearts of the young men on the loft, and they began to weep and cry for mercy. The old lady was not startled; she seemed to realize, while praying, an answer to her prayer; and as the Savior invited Zaccheus to come down from the tree, because on that day salvation had come to his house, so did she invite those young men to come down from their hiding-place. They obeyed her directions, and there at that altar, where, in other days, she had witnessed many conversions, before that Sabbath sun sank behind the western hills, they found pardon and salvation. From this hour the work of God commenced; the meetings were continued, and a flourishing Church was raised up, and the old dilapidated log meeting-house was again made to resound with the happy voices of the children of Zion.

CHAPTER XLV.

THE INDIAN CHIEF, RHON-YAN-NESS.

At the death of Rhon-yan-ness he was the oldest chief in the Wyandott nation. He was among the first that embraced the Gospel, and became a convert to the religion of Christ, among the Wyandotts. He was a great hunter, and first among the braves of his tribe, and was as much honored as a chief as any chief of any nation. Like Saul of Tarsus, who, as a brave and indefatigable opponent of Christianity, when converted, became equally courageous and persevering in the cause of Christ, so it was with this Christian Indian. There was no enterprise, however hazardous, that he would not undertake for the interests of his nation before conversion; nor was there any danger he would not brave, or sacrifice he would not make, for the sake of Christ and his cause, after he had been made partaker of the grace of life.

We will relate an incident which occurred in his life, that will serve to show, in some degree, his zeal and courage as an Indian, and will also illustrate several points in his character better, perhaps, than the most elaborate detail. Previous to the relation of this incident it will be necessary to refer the reader to a scrap of border warfare.

"About the middle of July, 1782, seven Wyandotts crossed the Ohio, a few miles above Wheeling, and committed great depredations upon the southern shore, killing an old man, whom they found alone in his cabin, and spreading terror throughout the neighborhood Within a few hours after their retreat, eight men assembled from different parts of the small settlement, and pursued the enemy with great expedition. Among the most active and efficient of the party were two brothers—Adam and Andrew Poe. Adam was particularly popular. In strength, action, and hardihood, he had no equal, being finely formed, and inured to all the perils of the woods. They had not followed the trail far before they became satisfied that the depredators were conducted by Big Foot, a renowned chief of the Wyandott tribe, who derived his name from the immense size of his feet, and his strength was represented as herculean. He had also five brothers, but little inferior to himself in size and courage; and as they generally went in company, they were the terror of the whole country. Adam Poe was overjoyed at the idea of measuring his strength with that of so celebrated a chief, and urged the pursuit with a keenness which quickly brought him into the vicinity of the enemy. For the last few miles the trail had led them up the southern bank of the Ohio, where the footprints in the sand were deep and obvious; but when within a few yards of the point at which the whites as well as the Indians were in the habit of crossing, it suddenly diverged from the stream, and stretched along a rocky ridge, forming an obtuse angle with its former direction. Here Adam halted for a moment, and directed his brother and the other young men to follow the trail with proper caution, while he himself still adhered to the river path, which led through clusters of willows directly to the point where he supposed the enemy to lie. Having examined the priming of his gun, he crept cautiously through the bushes, till he had a view of the point of embarkation. Here lay two canoes, empty and apparently deserted. Being satisfied, however, that the Indians were close at hand, he relaxed nothing of his vigilance, and quickly gained a jutting cliff, which hung immediately over the canoes. Hearing a low murmur below, he peered cautiously over, and beheld the object of his search. The gigantic Big Foot lay below him in the shade of a willow, and was talking, in a low, deep tone, to another warrior, who seemed a mere pigmy by his side. Adam cautiously drew back, and cocked his gun. The mark was fair; the distance did not exceed twenty feet, and his aim was unerring. Raising his rifle slowly and cautiously, he took a steady aim at Big Foot's breast, and drew the trigger. His gun flashed. Both Indians sprung to their feet with a deep interjection of surprise, and for a single second all three stared upon each other. This inactivity, however, was soon over. Adam was too much hampered by the bushes to retreat, and setting his life upon a cast of the die, he sprung over the bush which had sheltered him, and, summoning all his powers, leaped boldly down the precipice, and alighted upon the breast of Big Foot with a shock which bore him to the earth. At the moment of contact Adam had also thrown his right arm around the neck of the smaller Indian, so that all three came to the earth together. At that moment a sharp firing was heard among the bushes above, announcing that the other parties were engaged; but the trio below were too busy to attend to any thing but themselves. Big Foot was, for an instant, stunned by the violence of the shock, and Adam was enabled to keep them both down. But the exertion necessary for that purpose was so great, that he had no leisure to use his knife. Big Foot quickly recovered, and, without attempting to rise, wrapped his long arms around Adam's body, and pressed him to his breast with the crushing force of a boa-constrictor! Adam, as we have already remarked, was a powerful man, and had seldom encountered his equal; but never had he yet felt an embrace like that of Big Foot. He instantly relaxed his hold of the small Indian, who sprung to his feet. Big Foot then ordered him to run for his tomahawk, which lay within ten steps, and kill the white man while he held him in his arms. Adam, seeing his danger, struggled manfully to extricate himself from the folds of the giant, but in vain. The lesser Indian approached with his uplifted tomahawk; but Adam watched him closely, and as he was about to strike, gave him a kick so sudden and violent as to knock the tomahawk from his hand, and sent him staggering back into the water. Big Foot uttered an exclamation in a tone of deep contempt at the failure of his companion, and raising his voice to its highest pitch, thundered out several words in the Indian tongue, which Adam could not understand, but supposed to be a direction for a second attack. The lesser Indian now again approached, carefully shunning Adam's heels, and making many motions with his tomahawk, in order to deceive him as to the point where the blow would fall. This lasted for several seconds, till a thundering exclamation from Big Foot compelled his companion to strike. Such was Adam's dexterity and vigilance, however, that he managed to receive the tomahawk in a glancing direction upon his left wrist, wounding him deeply, but not disabling him. He now made a sudden and desperate effort to free himself from the arms of the giant, and succeeded. Instantly snatching up a rifle—for the Indian could not venture to shoot for fear of hurting his companion—he shot the lesser Indian through the body. But scarcely had he done so when Big Foot arose, and placing one hand upon his collar, and the other upon his hip, pitched him ten feet into the air, as he himself would have pitched a child. Adam fell upon his back at the edge of the water; but before his antagonist could spring upon him, he was again upon his feet, and stung with rage at the idea of being handled so easily, he attacked his gigantic antagonist with a fury which, for a time, compensated for inferiority of strength. It was now a fair fist fight between them; for in the hurry of the struggle neither had leisure to draw their knives. Adam's superior activity and experience as a pugilist gave him great advantage. The Indian struck awkwardly, and finding himself rapidly dropping to leeward, he closed with his antagonist, and again hurled him to the ground. They quickly rolled into the river, and the struggle continued with unabated fury, each attempting to drown the other. The Indian being unused to such violent exertion, and having been much injured by the first shock in his stomach, was unable to exert the same powers which had given him such a decided superiority at first; and Adam, seizing him by the scalp-lock, put his head under water, and held it there till the faint struggles of the Indian induced him to believe that he was drowned, when he relaxed his hold, and attempted to draw his knife. The Indian, however, to use Adam's own expression, 'had only been *possuming!*' He instantly regained his feet, and in his turn put his adversary under. In the struggle both were carried out into the current, beyond their depth, and each was compelled to relax his hold and swim for his life. There was still one loaded rifle upon the shore, and each swam hard in order to reach it; but the Indian proved the most expert swimmer, and Adam, seeing that he should be too late, turned and swam out into the stream, intending to dive, and thus frustrate his enemy's intention. At this instant Andrew, having heard that his brother was alone, in a struggle with two Indians, and in great danger, ran up hastily to the edge of the bank above, in order to assist him. Another white man followed him closely, and seeing Adam in the river, covered with blood, and swimming rapidly from shore, mistook him for an Indian, and fired upon him, wounding him dangerously in the shoulder. Adam turned, and seeing his brother, called loudly upon him to 'shoot the big Indian upon the shore.' Andrew's gun, however, was empty, having just been discharged. Fortunately Big Foot had also seized the gun with which Adam had shot the lesser Indian, so that both were on an equality. The contest now was who should load first. Big Foot poured in his powder first, and drawing his ramrod out of its sheath in too great a hurry, threw it in the river, and while he ran to recover it, Andrew gained an advantage. Still the Indian was but a second too late, for his gun was at his shoulder when Andrew's ball entered his breast. The gun dropped from his hands, and he fell forward on his face upon the very margin of the river. Andrew, now alarmed for his brother, who was scarcely able to swim, threw down his gun, and rushed into the river, in order to bring him ashore; but Adam, more intent upon securing the scalp of Big Foot as a trophy than upon his own safety, called loudly upon his brother to leave him alone and scalp the big Indian, who was now endeavoring to roll himself in the water, from a romantic desire peculiar to the Indian warrior, of securing his scalp from the enemy. Andrew, however, refused to obey, and insisted upon saving the living before attending to the dead. Big Foot, in the mean time, had succeeded in reaching the deep water before he expired, and his body was borne off by the waves, without being stripped of the ornament and pride of an Indian warrior.

"Not a man of the Indians had escaped. Five of Big Foot's brothers, the flower of the Wyandott nation, had accompanied him in the expedition, and all perished. It is said that the news of this calamity threw the whole tribe into mourning. Their remarkable size, their courage, and their superior intelligence, gave them immense influence, which, greatly to their credit, was generally exerted on the side of humanity. Their powerful interposition had saved many prisoners from the stake, and had given a milder character to the warfare of the Indians in that part of the country. A chief of the same name was alive in that part of the country so late as 1792; but whether a brother or son of Big Foot is not known. Adam Poe recovered of his wounds, and lived many years after his memorable conflict; but never forgot the tremendous 'hug' which he sustained in the arms of Big Foot." He was the grandfather of Adam Poe, present Assistant Agent of the Book Concern.

The great loss sustained by the Wyandott nation in the death of the Big Foot brothers, created an implacable hatred in every heart toward their destroyers. Many an Indian malediction had been poured out upon the head of Adam Poe, and many a prize had been offered for his scalp. His place of residence, which was on the west bank of the Ohio river, at the mouth of Yellow creek, was known to the Wyandotts. It seemed, however, that none of the nation possessed sufficient courage to encounter, single-handed, this foe of the redman, whose strength was considered equal to that of Big Foot himself. At length, having determined to wait no longer in seeking to be revenged of the death of their Goliah, the nation made choice of their bravest warrior, in the person of Rhon-yan-ness, one of their chiefs. Having made all the preparations necessary for the accomplishment of the fearful mission intrusted to him by his nation, he started out on foot for the residence of Poe. After passing through the then wilderness of Ohio, he at length reached the creek, which emptied into the Ohio, on the bank of which his intended victim lived. No sooner, however, had he placed his foot within the door of the brave backwoods hunter than he was received with the utmost cordiality and friendship, while every hospitality that the cabin afforded was, with true pioneer generosity, tendered to the Indian guest. When the time for retiring to rest had come, there being but one room and one bed, Poe made a comfortable pallet for the Indian on the floor by the fire, after which he and his wife retired to rest, without any suspicion whatever in regard to the designs of the Indian. It was now a time of peace, and the Indians, particularly the Wyandotts, were regarded as friendly. It was not long till they both fell asleep, when Rhon-yan-ness rose stealthily from his couch, and proceeded cautiously, with his tomahawk and scalping-knife, to the bedside of the unconscious sleepers. Scarcely had he arrived at the spot than the kindness of his host flashed upon his mind. "How," thought he, "can I perpetrate an act of so much cruelty upon one who has taken me into his wigwam, and treated me with so much friendship?" The better feelings of his nature overcame him, and finding it impossible to commit an act which, though it might bring honor to him from his nation as the avenger of the death of Big Foot, he could not nerve himself up to such a pitch of desperateness as to obliterate all the gratitude of his heart. Enemy as Poe had been to his nation, yet he could not think of imbruing his hands in his blood, and with these thoughts he crept back softly to his bed. He had not lain long till the question came up before him in a somewhat different aspect, and his thoughts took a turn something like the following: "Have you not been solemnly set apart by the nation to avenge the death of its bravest warrior? and will not the ghost of the departed haunt you in your chase in the wilderness, and in your midnight slumbers, till it is appeased by the death of Poe? Does not your religion require you to execute vengeance as the agent of the Great Spirit? and will he not frown upon you if you fail to do the work of death?" At this Rhon-yan-ness again seized his deadly instruments, and sprang to his feet. It was now past midnight, and all was still. No sound could be heard but the gloomy hoot of an owl, which had nestled in some tree in the surrounding forest. The light of the fire had gone out, and there were only a few burning coals left upon the hearth, from which was emitted a kind of twilight glare that enabled him to gaze upon the features of his victim. Summoning all his courage he raised the fearful tomahawk, and was about to bury it in the head of his host, when something whispered, "Shame on the Indian that can strike a friend. Mean and cowardly is the warrior who would kill even an enemy that has treated him kindly." His heart faltered, his hand trembled, and the tomahawk fell by his side. Without disturbing the family he returned to his pallet, and, dismissing all thoughts of revenge, he slept soundly till morning.

Poe rose early and made his fire, without disturbing his guest, who was in a heavy slumber. When it was fully day, and the bright fire blazed around, he had an opportunity of gazing upon the broad, open features of the manly Indian whose giant form was before him. There he lay, with his tomahawk and scalping-knife by his side. Poe understood enough of the Indian character to know that in the days of peace they were capable of the most sincere and lasting friendship; and though he had measured arms with them in the deadly strife, they were more sinned against than sinning, and whatever cruelties they may have committed, were excited by the depredations of the white man: hence he loved the Indian, and had often bewailed the unhappy fate of Big Foot and his brothers. Anxious to enjoy the society of his Indian guest he approached him, and gently touching him, said softly, "Wake, brother, wake; the morning has come." The Indian sprang to his feet instantly, and, seizing him by the hand, bestowed his Indian blessings. After again partaking of the humble but bounteous fare of the cabin, he made ready for departure. As he was leaving Poe furnished him with provisions for his journey, and, taking him by the hand, said, "Once we were at war, and were enemies; but now we are at peace, and are friends. We have buried the hatchet, and are brothers. Let us live in peace and brotherhood." Rhon-yan-ness was too much overwhelmed with a sense of gratitude for the goodness of his heart to make any reply; but the big tear which rolled down his bronze cheek told the sincerity of grateful emotion, and he left to join his nation on the distant plains of Sandusky.

He often told us that was a happy day in his life, and the more he thought and reasoned about the course he had pursued the more he was convinced that he had acted right. Not long after his return to his nation he became interested in the missionary labors among his people; and the wonderful story of the white man's God, as he came to earth and suffered and died for sinners, deeply affected his heart. Soon this bold, intrepid chief renounced his Indian religion and forms of worship, and embraced Christianity. He was soundly and happily converted to God, and became a burning and a shining light in the midst of a dark and perverse nation. Being now in Christ he was a new creature; old things had passed away, and all things had become new. He felt upspringing in his heart that love which worketh no ill to its neighbor, but makes its possessor kind, and gentle, and forgiving; and which teaches that "whomsoever hateth his brother is a murderer," in the eye of the holy law, as effectually as if he had plunged the fatal knife into his heart. He took a bold stand in religion, and as a class-leader and steward he rendered efficient service to the mission. Three years after his conversion he realized a maturity of Christian grace, which enabled him to rejoice in that perfect love which casts out all tormenting fear. His life was hid with Christ in God, and he walked as seeing Him who was invisible. His whole life was unblamable, and his character as a Christian irreproachable; and we never knew a Christian in any nation, or among any people, more innocent, guileless, and happy than Rhon-yan-ness. Rooted and grounded in love he was steadfast in his profession, and labored hard to elevate and improve his nation. His powerful influence as a chief was brought to bear upon the heartless trader, who would come among the Indians with his fire-water, and rob them of their brains and furs. The Indians have been cruelly treated, and it is high time the Government should interpose more effectually its authority in their behalf. How much we owe them as a nation none can tell; but it is high time that some move was made to repay the debt. We were deeply and intensely thrilled at the last anniversary of the Parent Society, which was held in this city, by the speech of Bishop Janes, who has charge of the Indian missions. It was so true, so appropriate, and so fearless that we would, had we space, hand it down to posterity as the testimony of the Church in behalf of our native red brethren.

After being a member of the Church militant for a period of sixteen years, Rhon-yan-ness was called to join the Church triumphant. He has attended a quarterly meeting at the mission on Sabbath, and while, as a steward, he was handing round the bread in love-feast, as emblematic of universal charity, he seemed to be unusually happy. When relating his Christian experience, in which he referred to his interview with Adam Poe, he thrilled every heart with the story of redeeming love.

Raising his streaming eyes toward heaven, he clapped his hands, and shouted in prospect of his long-sought home. Two days after this meeting he was called by the Master to enter his inheritance above, and full of faith and holy triumph he passed away to the spirit-land.

THE END.

www.ingramcontent.com/pod-product-compliance
Lightning Source LLC
LaVergne TN
LVHW021241110826
845150LV00002B/373

* 9 7 8 1 4 2 5 5 6 1 7 7 2 *